Film Moments

Film Moments

Criticism, History, Theory

Edited by
Tom Brown & James Walters

A BFI book published by Palgrave Macmillan

This book is dedicated to the memory of Robin Wood

First published in 2010 by
PALGRAVE MACMILLAN

on behalf of the

BRITISH FILM INSTITUTE
21 Stephen Street, London W1T 1LN
<www.bfi.org.uk>

There's more to discover about film and television through the BFI. Our world-renowned archive, cinemas,
festivals, films, publications and learning resources are here to inspire you.

Palgrave Macmillan in the UK is an imprint of Macmillan Publishers Limited, registered in England,
company number 785998, of Houndmills, Basingstoke, Hampshire RG21 6XS. Palgrave Macmillan in the
US is a division of St Martin's Press LLC, 175 Fifth Avenue, New York, NY 10010. Palgrave Macmillan is the
global academic imprint of the above companies and has companies and representatives throughout the
world. Palgrave® and Macmillan® are registered trademarks in the United States, the United Kingdom,
Europe and other countries.

Cover design: keenan
Cover images: *Bonnie and Clyde* (Arthur Penn, 1967), © Warner Bros.-Seven Arts; *8½* (Federico Fellini, 1963),
Cineriz di Angleo Rizzoli/Francinex; *Hotel Rwanda* (Terry George, 2004), Kigali Releasing Ltd; *Rear Window*
(Alfred Hitchcock, 1954), © Patron, Inc./Paramount Pictures
Designed by couch

Set by Cambrian Typesetters, Camberley, Surrey
Printed in China

This book is printed on paper suitable for recycling and made from fully managed and sustained forest
sources. Logging, pulping and manufacturing processes are expected to conform to the environmental
regulations of the country of origin.

British Library Cataloguing-in-Publication Data
A catalogue record for this book is available from the British Library
A catalog record for this book is available from the Library of Congress
10 9 8 7 6 5 4 3 2 1
19 18 17 16 15 14 13 12 11 10

ISBN 978–1–84457–335–6 (pbk)
ISBN 978–1–84457–336–3 (hbk)

Contents

PART ONE: Criticism

PART TWO: History

PART THREE: Theory

Notes on Contributors

MICHELE AARON lectures on film at the University of Birmingham. She is author of *Spectatorship: The Power of Looking On* and editor of *New Queer Cinema: A Critical Reader* and *The Body's Perilous Pleasures: Dangerous Desires and Contemporary Culture*. She has published widely on contemporary film culture, queer cinema and theory, and Jewishness and gender. She is currently completing a book entitled *Death and the Moving Image: Ideology, Iconography and I*.

RICK ALTMAN is Professor of Cinema and Comparative Literature at the University of Iowa. His main research areas are narrative theory (*A Theory of Narrative*), Hollywood genres (*Genre: The Musical*, *The American Film Musical*, *Film/Genre*) and film sound (*Cinema/Sound*, *Sound Theory/Sound Practice*, *The Sounds of Early Cinema*, *Silent Film Sound*). He is especially proud of his students' many publications on sound (Caryl Flinn, Jim Lastra, Charles O'Brien, Steve Wurtzler, Allison McCracken, Jay Beck, David Helvering, Jennifer Fleeger).

CHARLES BARR taught for many years at the University of East Anglia, and has since held Visiting Professor posts at Washington University in St Louis and University College Dublin. His publications include books on *Ealing Studios* and *English Hitchcock*.

JONATHAN BIGNELL is Professor of Television and Film at the University of Reading. His books include *Postmodern Media Culture*, *Big Brother: Reality TV in the Twenty-first Century* and *Popular Television Drama: Past, Present and Future*. His publications about film include the edited collection *Writing and Cinema* and articles on *Don't Look Back*, *Badlands*, *Excalibur* and various versions of *Dracula*. He serves on the editorial boards of the journals *New Review of Film and Television Studies*, *Symbolism: An International Annual of Critical Aesthetics* and the journal, *Science Fiction Film and Television*.

MARK BROUGHTON is Lecturer in Film Studies at the University of Reading. His publications include 'Nigel Kneale', in Mark Bould et al. (eds), *Fifty Key Figures in Science Fiction* and 'Landscape Gardens in *The Ruling Class*', in Paul Newland (ed.), *Don't Look Now: British Cinema in the 1970s*. He is currently writing books about *Brideshead Revisited* (for the 'BFI TV Classics' series) and Nigel Kneale.

TOM BROWN is Lecturer in Film at the University of Reading. His publications include *Film and Television after DVD* (edited with James Bennett), a forthcoming monograph on 'Direct Address' and he is currently developing a book on spectacle as a facet of film style in the 'classical' cinemas of France and the US.

STELLA BRUZZI is Professor of Film and Television Studies at the University of Warwick. Her most recent publications are a study of the seminal British television series *Seven Up*, for the 'BFI TV Classics' series and *Men's Cinema: Masculinity and Mise-en-Scène in Hollywood Movies* for Wallflower's *Close-Up* series. She is author of *Undressing Cinema: Clothing and Identity in the Movies*, *New Documentary*, *Bringing Up Daddy: Fatherhood and Masculinity in Postwar Hollywood* and co-editor of *Fashion Theory: Theories, Explorations and Analysis*.

ALISON BUTLER is a Lecturer in Film in the Department of Film, Theatre & Television at the University of Reading. She has published widely on women's film-making and alternative cinema, including the monograph *Women's Cinema: The Contested Screen*. Her current research is concerned with time and space in experimental and artists' films. She is a member of the Editorial Advisory Board of *Screen*.

ALEX CLAYTON is a Lecturer in Screen Studies at the University of Bristol and is the author of *The Body in Hollywood Slapstick*.

PAM COOK is Professor Emerita in Film at the University of Southampton. She is editor of *The Cinema Book* and author of *Screening the Past: Memory and Nostalgia in Cinema*. Her latest book is *Baz Luhrmann*.

ELIZABETH COWIE is Professor of Film Studies in the School of Drama, Film and Visual Arts at the University of Kent, Canterbury. Her publications include *Representing the Woman: Cinema and Psychoanalysis*, as well as essays on memory, trauma and video art. Her new book is *Representing Reality: Documentary and the Desire for the Real*.

RICHARD DYER teaches Film Studies at King's College London. His publications include *Stars*, *White* and *Pastiche*. He has just completed a book on Nino Rota.

R. J. ELLIS is Professor and Chair of the Department of American and Canadian Studies, University of Birmingham. His most recent books include *Liar, Liar: Jack Kerouac – Novelist* and *Harriet Wilson's 'Our Nig': A Cultural Biography*. He is currently one of the editors assembling the essay collection, *Visible Women*, and is working with Henry Louis Gates Jr on a new edition of *Our Nig*.

THOMAS ELSAESSER is Professor Emeritus in the Department of Media and Culture at the University of Amsterdam and since 2005 Visiting Professor at Yale University. His most recent publications are *European Cinema: Face to Face with Hollywood*, *Terror and Trauma* and *Film Theory – An Introduction through the Senses* (with Malte Hagener).

JONATHAN FROME is an Assistant Professor of Film and Digital Media at the University of Texas at Dallas. He received his PhD in Film Studies at the University of Wisconsin-Madison. Currently, he is researching how media generate emotions and why different media tend to generate different kinds of emotions. His other areas of interest include videogame studies, documentary film and aesthetics.

EDWARD GALLAFENT teaches Film Studies at the University of Warwick. He is the author of books on Fred Astaire and Ginger Rogers, Clint Eastwood and Quentin Tarantino.

JOHN GIBBS teaches Film at the University of Reading. He is the author of *Mise-en-scène: Film Style and Interpretation* and the co-editor (with Douglas Pye) of *Style and Meaning: Studies in the Detailed Analysis of Film* and of *Close-Up*, the annual publication devoted to the close analysis of film and television drama.

CLAUDIA GORBMAN is Professor of Film Studies in the Interdisciplinary Arts and Sciences Program at the University of Washington, Tacoma. She has written widely on film music, notably in *Unheard Melodies: Narrative Film Music*, and in a diverse range of journals and books since 1974. She has also translated four books by the French

scholar, critic and composer Michel Chion. She is currently co-editing *The Oxford Handbook of New Audiovisual Aesthetics*, and writing on Agnes Varda.

TOM GUNNING is the Edwin A. and Betty L. Bergman Distinguished Service Professor in the Department on Cinema and Media at the University of Chicago. He is the author of *D.W. Griffith and the Origins of American Narrative Film* and *The Films of Fritz Lang; Allegories of Vision and Modernity*, as well as over 100 articles on early cinema, film history and theory, avant-garde film, film genre, and cinema and modernism. In 2009 he was awarded an Andrew A. Mellon Distinguished Achievement Award, the first film scholar to receive one.

HELEN HANSON is Senior Lecturer in Film Studies in the Department of English at the University of Exeter. She is the author of *Hollywood Heroines: Women in Film Noir and the Female Gothic Film*, co-editor (with Catherine O'Rawe) of *The Femme Fatale: Images, Histories, Contexts* and co-editor (with Andrew Spicer) of *The Blackwell Companion to Film Noir*. Her current research investigates soundmen and their work in Hollywood's studio era; she has written on film sound in the journal *Music, Sound and the Moving Image*, and in *The Cambridge Companion to Film Music*.

BRUCE F. KAWIN is Professor of English and Film at the University of Colorado at Boulder. He has written three books of narrative theory (*Telling It Again and Again: Repetition in Literature and Film*; *Mindscreen: Bergman, Godard, and First-Person Film*; and *The Mind of the Novel: Reflexive Fiction and the Ineffable*), three books on Faulkner's screenplays (*Faulkner and Film*, *To Have and Have Not* and *Faulkner's MGM Screenplays*) and two textbooks: *How Movies Work* and a regularly updated revision of the late Gerald Mast's *A Short History of the Movies*. He is also a poet. He is currently writing a book on the horror film.

ANDREW KLEVAN is the University Lecturer in Film Studies at the University of Oxford and a Fellow of St Anne's College. His research interests are the close study of film style, film criticism and aesthetics. He is the author of two books on film: *Disclosure of the Everyday: Undramatic Achievement in Narrative Film* and *Film Performance: From Achievement to Appreciation*. He is currently editing a collection with Alex Clayton entitled *The Language and Style of Film Criticism*.

BARBARA KLINGER is a Professor of Film and Media Studies in the Department of Communication and Culture at Indiana University. Her books are *Beyond the Multiplex: Cinema, New Technologies, and the Home* and *Melodrama and Meaning: History, Culture, and the Films of Douglas Sirk*. She has published extensively in journals and anthologies on film exhibition, reception studies, and cinema and new media. She is currently working on a book on convergence before convergence culture in which she examines how classical Hollywood films were adapted across media and reissued through time.

JACOB LEIGH is a Lecturer in the Department of Media Arts, Royal Holloway. His publications include *The Cinema of Ken Loach* and *Reading Rohmer*, published in *Close-Up 02*. He is currently writing *The Cinema of Eric Rohmer*.

ADRIAN MARTIN is Associate Professor, Head of Film and Television Studies and Co-Director of the Research Unit in Film Culture and Theory at Monash University, Australia. He is the author of the books *What Is Modern Cinema?*, *Raúl Ruiz: Magnificent Obsessions*, *The Mad Max Movies*, *Once Upon a Time in America* and *Phantasms*; and co-editor of *Movie Mutations* and the Internet film journal *Rouge* (www.rouge.com.au).

LAURA MULVEY is Professor of Film and Media Studies at Birkbeck College, University of London. She is the author of *Visual and Other Pleasures*, *Fetishism and Curiosity*, *Citizen Kane* (in the 'BFI Classics' series) and *Death 24x a Second: Stillness and the Moving Image*. She has made six films in collaboration with Peter Wollen including *Riddles of the Sphinx* (1978) and *Frida Kahlo and Tina Modotti* (1980) and with Mark Lewis *Disgraced Monuments* (1994).

STEVE NEALE is Professor of Film Studies at the University of Exeter. He is the author of *Genre and Hollywood*, co-author of *Popular Film and Television Comedy* and *Epics, Spectacles and Blockbusters: A Hollywood History*, editor of *Genre and Contemporary Hollywood* and co-editor of *Contemporary Hollywood Cinema* and *'Un-American' Hollywood: Politics and Film in the Blacklist Era*.

STEVEN PEACOCK is a Senior Lecturer in Film at the University of Hertfordshire. He is the author of *Colour: Cinema Aesthetics* and editor/author of *Reading 24: TV against the Clock*. He is also co-editor of 'The Television Series' for MVP and is currently writing a monograph on Aaron Sorkin for the series.

LISA PURSE is a Lecturer in Film in the Department of Film, Theatre & Television at the University of Reading. Her research interests focus on the relationship between film style and the politics of representation in post-studio mainstream and independent US cinema, and she has published a number of essays on digital effects in film. She is the author of 'Reading the Digital' in John Gibbs and Douglas Pye (eds), *Close-Up 04*, and is currently writing a book on contemporary US action cinema.

DOUGLAS PYE is Visiting Fellow in the Department of Film, Theatre & Television at the University of Reading. He co-edited *The Movie Book of the Western* and *Style and Meaning: Studies in the Detailed Analysis of Film* and currently co-edits the annual *Close-Up* series published by Wallflower Press.

WILLIAM ROTHMAN received his PhD in Philosophy from Harvard University and is the author of several books, including *Hitchcock: The Murderous Gaze*, *The "I" of the Camera*, *Documentary Film Classics* and *A Philosophical Perspective on Film*. He is editor of the 'Studies in Film' series published by Cambridge University Press.

MARTIN SHINGLER is Senior Lecturer in Radio & Film Studies at the University of Sunderland. He is the co-author of two books, *On Air: Methods and Meanings of Radio*, with Cindy Wieringa and *Melodrama: Genre, Style & Sensibility*, with John Mercer. He has published a number of essays on the Hollywood film star Bette Davis, which appear in various books and journals. He is also the co-editor (with Susan Smith) of the *Film Stars* book series for Palgrave.

SUSAN SMITH is Senior Lecturer in Film Studies at the University of Sunderland. She is the author of *Voices in Film*, *The Musical: Race, Gender and Performance* and *Hitchcock: Suspense, Humour and Tone*. Other publications include 'Vocal Sincerity, Liminality and Bonding in *The Railway Children* (Lionel Jeffries, 1970)' in *Literature/Film Quarterly* and 'The Animated Film Musical', in Raymond Knapp, Mitchell Morris and Stacy Wolf (eds), *The Oxford Handbook of the American Musical*. She is currently writing a book on Elizabeth Taylor as part of a new *Film Stars* series that she is co-editing (with Martin Shingler) for Palgrave.

DEBORAH THOMAS is the author of *Beyond Genre: Melodrama, Comedy and Romance in Hollywood Films* and of *Reading Hollywood: Spaces and Meanings in American Film*, as well as of a monograph on *Buffy the Vampire Slayer* and numerous articles. Until her retirement in 2007, she was Professor of Film Studies at the University of Sunderland.

KRISTIN THOMPSON is an Honorary Fellow at the University of Wisconsin-Madison. Her many books include *Film Art: An Introduction* and *Film History: An Introduction* (both with David Bordwell), *Storytelling in the New Hollywood* and *The Frodo Franchise*.

GINETTE VINCENDEAU is Professor of Film Studies at King's College London. She is the author of, among others, *Stars and Stardom in French Cinema*, *Jean-Pierre Melville: An American in Paris* and *La Haine*. She co-edited, with Alastair Phillips, *Journey of Desire, European Actors in Hollywood* and, with Peter Graham, *The French New Wave: Critical Landmarks*. She is currently completing a book about the representation of Provence in film and television.

JAMES WALTERS is Lecturer in Film and Television Studies at the University of Birmingham. He is the author of *Alternative Worlds in Hollywood Cinema* and *Fantasy Film: A Critical Introduction*.

GEORGE M. WILSON is Professor of Philosophy and Cinematic Arts at the University of Southern California. He has also taught at Johns Hopkins and the University of California at Davis. He has written a book on film, *Narration in Light*, and a book on theory of action, *The Intentionality of Human Action*. He has published articles in the philosophy of language, theory of action, philosophy of mind, Wittgenstein, and the aesthetics of film and literature.

Preface

... the whole of beauty consists, in my opinion, in being able to get above singular forms, local customs, particularities, and details of every kind.

Sir Joshua Reynolds

Many dull movies are redeemed by unexpected, accidental bits of poetry. Many classics are nothing but those moments of poetry, connected by a narrative that has no other function than to make the necessary connections.

Neil Jordan

While neither of these quotations represent the aims of this book, they each provide ways into thinking about the status of the film moment in the study of cinema, and in the wider culture of which film is a part. The first quotation, which represents perhaps the opposite of the overarching contention of this book, appears in an investigation into the politics of the historical relationship between the part and the whole (of a work of art) in aesthetic analysis,[1] while the second features as part of a journalistic exercise whereby film or cinema history is broken down into its 'greatest moments'.[2] Of course, organising events and experiences into moments is a means of understanding and shaping much wider culture (important moments in history or sport, for example). But for film, the moment has special resonance. In its earliest form, the cinema *was* a moment: the projection of a few seconds recorded and exhibited for audiences. Film endures as a medium made of moments: the brief, temporary and transitory combining to create the whole.

The essays in this collection are divided into three categories: 'criticism', 'history' and 'theory'. The decision to organise the collection in this way is paradoxical. On the one hand, it aims to show the extent to which close analysis of the film moment is a valuable means of asking many different kinds of questions of film, films and film studies. At the same time, the central place of the film moment in the analysis of *all* the contributors to this collection questions the divisions that characterise the way modern film studies defines itself: the fact that many modern writers

on film are encouraged or even obligated to define themselves as *either* critics *or* historians *or* theorists. In this context, looking closely at the details of films and parts of films is sometimes suggested to be the preserve of a particular branch of scholars who 'do textual analysis'. However, whether it is to illustrate a wider aesthetic, conceptual or historical point, or whether it is for the purpose of uncovering the complex layers of meaning operating within an individual film, a concentration on the film moment is in fact central to many different traditions of investigation into film.

For this reason, it is appropriate to group the essays along the common divisions of criticism, history and theory. In practice, many of the essays blur and problematise these divisions; few can be pigeonholed in any straightforward way. However, it is useful to think of the distinctions in a simple way to begin with. We might provisionally suggest that film theory asks, 'what is 'film'?'; film history asks, 'what has 'film' been?'; and film criticism asks, 'what is this film and what is its relationship to others?' Inevitably, these become caricatures of these complex areas of investigation and the collection consequently reflects at greater length on the role of the moment in these fields in short introductions to each of the sections.

The theme of brevity inherent in the study of film moments is reflected in the relatively short length of the contributing essays in this collection. In one sense, this is intended to demonstrate the advantages and attributes of detailed, focused and concise analysis of films. To this end, the chapters provide not only contained and coherent discussions of the moments they centre on, but also offer a founding claim for the ways in which that film, other films or, indeed, *film* might be approached in future discussions. The length of the contributions in this collection also corresponds with the shorter-form essays students of film are often required to write in colleges and universities, especially at undergraduate level. The essays contained in this book are partly intended to provide a series of examples that demonstrate how a sustained appreciation of a film's overall characteristics, contexts and achievements can be conveyed in a format at least half the length of the scholarly articles and chapters which students might ordinarily be presented with. What can be achieved in such a concise exploration? This collection hopes to answer this question on every page.

The notion of a 'moment' in film is left deliberately ambiguous and contributors were invited to interpret that term with a degree of personal freedom. As a result, the essays presented in the following pages vary, focusing on a single shot, a whole sequence, an entire scene or even a number of these as they combine within a film's wider patterns and structures. It becomes clear, then, that for each contributing author the term 'moment' is not a fixed measurement. Maintaining this ambiguity places a weight of emphasis on the role of individual interpretation within the study of art, as opposed to an ostensibly scientific approach that might prove overly restrictive, by requiring the 'sample' of moments to be identical in length, for example. That task seems near impossible and, perhaps, even nonsensical. The moments described in this book *feel* like moments to those writing about them, and are judged to have significance in understanding a film, or *film*, in a wider sense. In a book striving for a variety of directions and approaches, this lack of uniformity is crucial.

Although the collection is divided into three interrelated parts, it is worth noting that one section, 'criticism', is larger. The imbalance here is designed to reflect the strong tradition of close 'textual' analysis and film criticism that has endured throughout the various trends and new directions that film study has followed. Generally speaking, it has been those concerned with the criticism of films who have argued for the validity and importance of focusing on moments in film. This is not to say, of course, that those interested in historical or theoretical directions have been blind to the merits of close sequence analysis or, indeed, have not contributed to the progression of that approach. But, as is suggested in the introductions to the second and third parts of this book, and by a number of the contributors themselves, the fields of film history and theory have not been defined by an emphasis on the moment in cinema. An attempt is made to redress this balance within this collection. But our understanding, which we take to be uncontroversial, is that criticism has led the analysis of the film moment, and so criticism leads the book itself.

NOTES

1. Quoted at the start of Naomi Schor, *Reading in Detail: Aesthetics and the Feminine* (New York: Routledge, 2007), p. 3.
2. From Jordan's introduction to *The Observer*'s '100 Most Memorable Film Moments', 6 February 2000: <film.guardian.co.uk/100filmmoments/> (accessed 18 February 2010). *The Observer*'s survey was part of the millennial mania for 'best-of' lists, but they are a regular 'filler' feature for all sorts of publications – see, for example, *Empire* magazine's '1001 Greatest Movie Moments' (no. 234, August 2009). Since the advent of video-sharing websites, the compilation of such lists has developed in more idiosyncratic directions: typing 'greatest film [or movie] moments' into www.youtube.com quickly demonstrates the range of ways film moments are defined and/or valued in contemporary culture.

BIBLIOGRAPHY

Schor, Naomi, *Reading in Detail: Aesthetics and the Feminine* (New York: Routledge, 2007).

Acknowledgments

We owe a debt of gratitude to the institutions in which we both studied: the Department of Film Studies at the University of Kent and the Department of Film and Television at the University of Warwick. This book is a product of the range and excellence of the teaching we were privileged to receive.

We wish to thank our respective universities, Reading and Birmingham, for providing the opportunity, culture and environment for research to grow and flourish. We also wish to thank Janice Brown for her tireless help with the manuscript.

This book would not have been possible without the love and support of our wives and families. Tom would like to thank Mel. James would like to thank Amy, Isaac, Ruben and Fergus.

PART ONE: Criticism

'What is this film?' The question at once seems a crude and inadequate summary of critical enquiry faced with the breadth of film moments, and the range of approaches to them found in the first part of this book. However, in comparison with the historical and theoretical approaches discussed in Parts Two and Three, which are more dependent (to varying degrees) on frameworks external to the film, the essays below are markedly more focused on the *internal* qualities of films and their moments. 'Qualities' can of course mean, fairly neutrally, observable characteristics: the arrangement of the *mise en scène*, the details of performance, systems of editing, the tone and timbre of a musical score, for example. However, 'qualities' can also imply judgments about value and, in particular, the value inherent in the film's ability to shape and control those observable characteristics. Essentially, then, the issue of value is crucial to the critical analysis of films.

This theme is picked up in a series of accounts founded upon a sustained attention on the film moment. When prefacing his persuasive account of one such key moment from Vincente Minnelli's *The Band Wagon* (1953), Stanley Cavell offers an explanation for his selection and its possible ramifications. He suggests that: 'The judgement I make in discussing the sequence here expresses my pleasure and sense of value in it and awaits your agreement upon this.'[1] This concentration upon and joining together of 'pleasure' and 'sense of value' strikes to the heart of film criticism, alluding potently to the ways in which personal feeling can form a strong foundation for film analysis. Cavell's honesty regarding the role personal engagement takes in his critical work is matched by the candour of Robin Wood in describing his own approach and attitude to film criticism:

> Here I am. *I am writing this* [italics in original]. I am not infallible. I am just a human being like yourself. What I have to say and the way in which I say it was determined by my own background, my own experience, my own understanding (or lack thereof). I make no pretence to Absolute Truth.[2]

The 'fallibility' that Wood describes is an underlying concern for any critic of the arts, connected as it is to the task of taking responsibility for personal interpretation and judgment. This sense of responsibility can understandably become a source of considerable anxiety for students encountering the study of film for the first time. Some, for example, may object to the film lecturer suggesting a particular reading. Here, more so than with the study of literature, in which interpretation and close reading have perhaps a more established cultural standing, it seems that the analysis of film is for some fraught with the worry of 'reading too much into it'. These concerns can in fact become effective catalysts in the course of analysis and debate conducted in the classroom, providing an impetus for critical conversation. No approach can be sacrosanct. In this same spirit, to suggest a single reading or interpretation is not to resist the possibility of others; but the admission of a multitude of possible meanings is not the same as saying all interpretations are of equal value. Interpretations require careful reasoning, argument and demonstration in close proximity to the observable detail of a film (and, indeed, a film's moments). As part of an arresting argument for the value of interpretation, John Gibbs and Douglas Pye suggest:

> … processes of argument and of persuasion are involved, rather than merely the demonstration of a position: that what I have found in the film is not simply my view but represents an understanding capable of being shared or challenged and, in the process, enhanced reworked or replaced … . A central advantage of rooting interpretation in the detail of the film … is that it provides a material and verifiable basis for discussion.[3]

As Gibbs and Pye make clear, the conclusions of one's analysis are always open to contention and challenge. This is, of course, a founding principle of critical debate. Nevertheless, there is a profound responsibility on the part of the critic to ensure that the evidence presented for such claims is precise, accurate and substantiated. How to select sufficient data from the film to support one's argument then becomes a key concern. How much is enough detail? How much is too much? The pressure, experienced to varying degrees by different critics, is to avoid an account that is too generalised to hold firm, its indistinctness risking irrelevance. The most reduced example of this might be found in a newspaper column rating films simply by means of a system of stars ranging from one to five. One would have to trust the individual compiling such a system with absolute confidence, given that no discernible evidence is provided for their judgments. Here, Cavell's earlier 'sense of value' would be articulated in only the shallowest terms, bereft of his stated impulse to discuss and invite agreement based on his judgments.

It is not only the brevity of a star-rating system that risks advancing broad or unsubstantiated judgments, however. Writing in 1962, Ian Cameron defines the journal *Movie*'s attitude towards contending with sequences from films in close detail by comparing that approach to the available alternatives:

> For talking about one small section of a film in great detail, whether in an interview or in an article, we have been accused of fascination with technical *trouvailles* [meaning roughly 'surprise discoveries'] at the expense of meaning. The alternative which we find elsewhere is a *gestalt* approach which tries to present an overall picture of the film without going into 'unnecessary' detail, and usually results in giving almost no impression of what the film was actually like for the spectator.[4]

Cameron's contentions place at stake the issue of how one arrives at an expression of meaning in film and, in doing so, he proposes that the value of a film as a whole might profitably be articulated through the concentration upon a small section. Here, we can return to Cavell's statement and speculate that, in laying out some of the achievements he believes to be found in a sequence from *The Band Wagon*, he is offering a judgment upon the value of the film as a whole, its ability to produce moments of excellence. In the context of this collection's aims, we might read Cameron's remarks as presenting a justification for centring evaluation upon moments from films as a means of measuring the work in exacting terms rather than giving only an 'impression' of its merits. The relating of this position to the film spectator is instructive. Cameron outlines *Movie*'s attempt at the time to return criticism of films to the immediacy inherent in the experience of watching: acknowledging the moment-by-moment process that forms patterns, structures and meanings in our minds. Thus, by staying with moments from films and discussing them in detail, the interpretative critic returns to the process by which we initially form an understanding of a film's significance and meaning: moment by moment.

Following on from these suggestions, it is also the case that a detailed critical concentration upon a moment can reveal the level of complexity at which a film is shaping its themes, patterns and dramatic relationships. We might recognise this strategy in V. F. Perkins's account of Alfred Hitchcock's *Psycho* (1960) from his 1972 book *Film as Film*.[5] Perkins's understanding of the film is dependent upon his judgment of Hitchcock as a great artist. Although there had been a number of attempts to 'take Hitchcock seriously' (the most sustained being Robin Wood's 1965 book on the director), at the time of *Film as Film*'s publication, the case for Hitchcock's greatness still had to be made with a degree of forcefulness and, certainly, with careful precision. Perkins's articulation of Hitchcock's achievement centres upon the director's ability to fluently, and seamlessly, establish profound stylistic resonances between moments within *Psycho* and, in doing so, create especially rich layers of meaning and significance. This understanding of the director's technique is a hallmark of what Perkins terms the 'synthetic' in movies. He explains (in a section of the book contesting the presiding assumptions of montage theory) that:

> Basic to the synthetic approach to movies which I believe most productive is the claim that significance, emotional or intellectual, arises rather from the creation of significant relationships than from the presentation of things significant in themselves ... the more dense the network of meanings contained within each moment of film, the more richly these moments will combine and interact.[6]

In the case of *Psycho*, Perkins takes as his central focus the scene of Marion Crane's (Janet Leigh) murder in the Bates' Motel room shower, offering an especially close appreciation of the success of Hitchcock's technique. But he then expands this precise critical description by relating the scene's crucial actions to moments found elsewhere in the film. The knife is shown to relate to the beaks of the stuffed birds in Norman Bates's (Anthony Perkins) office, its relentless downward motion echoing the sweep of Marion's windscreen wipers from an earlier scene. The rush of water in the shower – a notionally purifying element that becomes 'the means by which her life is "drained away"'[7] – is prefigured in the sudden, persistent rain that falls across Marion's windscreen in that earlier scene, the hiss of liquid meeting surface pre-echoing the noise of the water in the shower. The shot of Marion's still, dead eye at the shower scene's conclusion is related to Norman's numb stare as his personality is finally consumed by a fantasy of his dead mother. And the motif of descent, inherent in features such as the water falling, the knife plunging, Marion's blood draining and her finally falling to the ground, dead, is shown to encapsulate the film's overarching descent into 'an abyss of darkness, madness, futility and despair',[8] only to be reversed when Marion's car is hauled *up* and out of the swamp in the film's final image.

The depth and dexterity of Perkins's account cannot adequately be conveyed in such a brief description of the synthetic relationships he observes and articulates. However, it should go some way to conveying the extent to which his understanding of the film's complexity and richness is founded upon the matrix of significant relationships found within and across moments from Hitchcock's masterpiece. That such resonances between moments should occur without heavy assertion or an emphasis that would drag the film out of shape is an indication of the director's skill. As Perkins asserts:

> It is a measure of the greatness of *Psycho*, and of Hitchcock at his finest, that the achievement of precise and densely interrelated imagery should seem to involve so little effort. Revealing moments accumulate without subjecting the drama to any apparent strain. It is only by thinking oneself into Hitchcock's position after the experience that one realises what intensity of artistic effort must have been required.[9]

This final point is illuminating and leads us into a different area of interest regarding the study of moments in cinema. If Cameron earlier suggested that concentrating on small sections of a film can, in certain respects, help to bring the critic closer to the audience's experience, then it is also true that such an approach goes some way to aligning critical appreciation with the film-maker's experience of their craft. The director is charged with the task of composing an entire work from a whole array of fragmented moments that have been recorded, most often out of order, during the filming period. As with the case of Hitchcock, we can see how an accomplished director retains a firm sense of the film's overall structure and coherence. However, it remains the case that the film-maker is concerned with one sequence at a time, often one small moment at a time, as they progress through the making of a complete picture in pre-production, production and post-production. As John Gibbs explains:

> Making a film involves a myriad of choices. Every frame, every cut, every element of performance and every note on the soundtrack results from pursuing one option and refusing many others. When investigating a film, a valuable approach is to identify a decision, or a group of decisions, and ask 'What is gained by doing it this way?' Of all the thousands of ways of opening the film, say, what are the consequences of the particular approach employed? To think in such terms is to consider the crux of the artistic process: the relationship between decisions taken and a work's meaning.[10]

By exploring in detail the effects of those decisions taken – focusing on a small sequence or moment from a film for example – the critic moves closer to appreciating the level of detail at which the film-maker operates, as illustrated in Gibbs's account. This kind of careful attention rewards the director's equal show of care and attention, and a concentration upon 'technical *trouvailles*', to use Cameron's earlier term, goes some way to matching the film-maker's own handling of the technical requirements of their art. According to these terms, film criticism founded upon the appraisal of moments is fundamentally suited to an art form itself composed and constructed from moments.

Just as the interpretative critic might focus upon a specific moment, sequence or scene to convey in precise terms a film's achievement, so it could follow that moments could be selected from a film regarded as poor for the opposite intention: to illustrate in detail the extent to which its poorness operates. This is an endeavour that, for understandable reasons, has not been taken up by any of the contributors to this collection, but an interesting – and possibly illuminating – counter to the somewhat celebratory tone of the entries would be to subject a film regarded as 'bad' to the same level of rigour and scrutiny afforded in these pages. Such a contribution would perhaps need to engage with debates regarding the politics of taste and value (issues touched upon in the 'theory' section to this book), but it is nevertheless the case that a moment can serve to emphasise a film's shortcomings or at least undermine its aims and ambitions. Returning to Perkins's work, we can see an example of this latter point in his account of John Huston's *Moulin Rouge* (1952):

> In *Moulin Rouge* John Huston established (and exploited with, for the most part, enthralling results) a system of colour based on the palettes of the Impressionists and therefore owing nothing to naturalism. Yet he had not created a world whose reality could tolerate a room that changed colour in sympathy with its occupant's moods. When the director characterised his hero's jealousy by flooding the set with, in the film's own terms, inexplicable green light, he broke down the essential structure of his picture's relationships and thus destroyed the world within which his hero *existed*. A minor, momentary relationship between the hero's temper and a literary convention of colour ('green with envy') was surely not worth achieving – or, more strictly speaking, capable of being achieved – at the sacrifice of the fundamental pattern.[11]

The issues Perkins raises here are part of a much wider argument within *Film as Film* that is built upon the requirement for films to maintain their inner consistency and credibility at a fundamental level. In this instance, however, he uses this framework to evaluate Huston's skill in handling the elements assembled to create significance and meaning within his film. Even if we decide that such an aberration isn't substantial enough for us to reject entirely the director's work or, indeed, label the film an outright failure, Perkins's attention to the sequence described illustrates the pressure faced by the film-maker in organising every moment of their film in order to achieve the expressive significance they strive for but not at the expense of the style, tone and coherence they have equally sought to establish within the work as a whole. The momentary loss of control and discipline that Perkins identifies in *Moulin Rouge* threatens to unbalance the picture, compromising the extent to which we can talk about the film's effectiveness and Huston's accomplishment as a director. Every moment risks failure and, for a critic whose interest lies in focusing upon such moments in detail, an awareness of that danger becomes acute.

A short introduction to the relationship between criticism and film moments can never hope to be comprehensive and, by concentrating on a few examples, any number of omissions from the history of film criticism present themselves. Nonetheless, we can begin to appreciate, in these few short examples, the ways in which an understanding of film can be profoundly shaped by an understanding of the moment and, furthermore, the extent to which a critic may use their understanding of film as a moment-by-moment medium to structure their understanding of the ways that film can challenge, inspire and move us to thought. The essays in this book demonstrate this very clearly.

While the equivalent introductions to theory and history will be structured around the chapters contained in each part, this discussion has contrastingly elected to rely exclusively upon works not included in this collection in order to pursue the relationship between criticism and the moment. It is intended that this approach should present a strong foundation on which the following chapters are able to build. Finally, it is significant that, in outlining critical approaches to moments in film, this introduction has repeatedly returned to the work of V. F. Perkins. The bias is not without purpose. If film criticism is based upon fundamental claims for value and excellence, so it should follow that criteria of value and excellence should be placed upon works of film criticism. The work of V. F. Perkins is the best place to start for students, scholars and teachers wishing to know more about how to think about films closely and critically. It follows, therefore, that this meticulous body of work should provide a critical foundation for a collection claiming an interest in film moments.

NOTES

1. Stanley Cavell, *Philosophy the Day after Tomorrow* (Cambridge, MA and London: The Belknap Press of Harvard University Press, 2005), p. 21. Andrew Klevan discusses this moment and Cavell's engagement with it in an essay in this section.
2. Robin Wood, *Hitchcock's Films Revisited* (rev. edn) (Chichester, NY: Columbia University Press, 2002), p. xi.
3. John Gibbs and Douglas Pye (eds), *Style and Meaning: Studies in the Detailed Analysis of Film* (Manchester: Manchester University Press, 2005), p. 4.
4. Ian Cameron, 'Films, Directors and Critics', in *Movie Reader* (London: November Books, 1972), p. 12.
5. V. F. Perkins, *Film as Film: Understanding and Judging Movies* (New York: Da Capo Press, 1993), pp. 107–15.
6. Perkins, *Film as Film*, pp. 106–7.
7. Ibid., p. 112.
8. Ibid., p. 111.
9. Ibid., p. 113.
10. John Gibbs, 'Filmmakers' Choices', in John Gibbs and Douglas Pye (eds), *Close-Up 01* (London: Wallflower Press, 2006), p. 5.
11. Perkins, *Film as Film*, pp. 122–3.

BIBLIOGRAPHY

Cameron, Ian, 'Films, Directors and Critics', in *Movie Reader* (London: November Books, 1972).

Cavell, Stanley, *Philosophy the Day after Tomorrow* (Cambridge, MA and London: The Belknap Press of Harvard University Press, 2005).

Gibbs, John and Pye, Douglas (eds), *Style and Meaning: Studies in the Detailed Analysis of Film* (Manchester: Manchester University Press, 2005).

Gibbs, John and Pye, Douglas (eds), *Close-Up 01* (London: Wallflower Press, 2006).

Perkins, V. F., *Film as Film: Understanding and Judging Movies* (New York: Da Capo Press, 1993).

Wood, Robin, *Hitchcock's Films Revisited* (rev. edn) (Chichester, NY: Columbia University Press, 2002).

Shadow Play and Dripping Teat: *The Night of the Hunter* (1955)

TOM GUNNING

Movies are made up of moments, which both accumulate to an end and, in a sense, scatter across our memories. If we think of a movie as something which moves continuously, following the actions of characters and the trajectory of a story, then moments might seem to mark the points along the way. But if we dwell on the sense of *a moment* in its singularity, it seems less to evoke the momentum of a plot than something that falls outside the story and its pace.

A movie moment is generally a moment recalled, and seems to invoke the process of remembering a film as much as following it. In other words, we remember a story in its process of development and resolution, but a moment, although it remains embedded in a story and may well even supply a pivotal moment in the drama, also seems to stand out. Perhaps the tableau, the nineteenth-century stage practice which survives in a few of the earliest films (and is reflected, I think, in much of cinema), provides an emblem for such moments. In the stage tableau (or 'picture', as it was also called), when the action has reached a significant point, it freezes for a moment and the actors hold their positions to form a picture. Paradoxically, the device conveys the intensity of an action by stilling it, as if lifting it out of time. Roland Barthes has related the tableau to fetishism, cutting out a moment or element from a continuity and investing it with deep, erotic, emotional or even magical significance.[1] Thus a collection of moments of cinema would be perhaps the secret museum of the film fetishist.

Initially, I thought about writing about one of the most profound moments in American cinema, the moment towards the end of John Ford's *The Searchers* (1956) when Ethan (John Wayne) lifts up Debbie (Natalie Wood) and recalls her as a little child (rather than the victim of his racist fantasy), a moment which marks Ethan's pivotal conversion. But I decided instead to deal with images more lifted out from the narrative, more archetypal and even confessional, among the most obscene and most innocent film moments I have seen. The images come from one of the least typical films ever made in Hollywood, which nonetheless has become a film constantly referred to by contemporary directors and frequently revived, despite its initial financial failure: Charles Laughton's *The Night of the Hunter* from 1955, starring Robert Mitchum and Lillian Gish.

Laughton's film juxtaposes extreme differences in visual and acting styles: from tense suspense to outright farce, from location shooting to the most stylised sets ever seen in a mainstream film that is not a fantasy. Its sources are varied. The sharp highlights and shadows of cinematographer Stanley Cortez's lighting recall film noir and even German Expressionism; Laughton and scriptwriter James Agee intended Gish and the film's metaphorical editing to evoke the silent films of D. W. Griffith; and the abrupt breaking of realist conventions in favour of an overt theatricality certainly reflects the time Laughton spent with Bertolt Brecht translating and starring in a production of *Galileo* in Hollywood in 1947 (before the House Un-American Activities Committee drove Brecht out of the country).

In spite of its recurrent puncturing of illusion, *The Night of the Hunter* remains a terrifying film in which the Biblical (and peculiarly American) fantasy of children threatened by a vengeful father figure (recalling Nick Ray's *Bigger than Life* (1956) or Griffith's *Broken Blossoms* (1919) – or even *The Searchers*) is allowed to rise from our collective nightmares. However, the moment I want to dwell on not only contrasts with the film's suspenseful action, but pivots into another realm entirely.

In a terrifying sequence, Reverend Powell (Mitchum) chases the children John (Billy Chapin) and Pearl (Sally Jane Bruce) from the cellar where they have been hiding out into a dark Expressionist night. When John finds the adult world can offer him no aid, he turns and addresses the camera, more or less directly, saying, 'There's still the river.' Pursued by their vengeful stepfather through the riverside underbrush and mud, the children push off in a rowboat, as the film executes an amazing stylistic shift from dramatic pursuit to a dreamlike deliverance. Powell realises that the children's boat has been picked up by the current and moved just beyond his reach; he gives an almost comical moan of frustration, which the soundtrack picks up and echoes eerily. The next shot shows the boat from a high angle, emphasising the distance between the children and danger. John puts down the oar and settles as if to sleep and the tempo of the film transforms radically (the lassitude of John's gestures almost look like slow motion). As the boat seems cradled in the slow maternal pace of the river and moves through ever-more artificial and theatrical sets, Pearl begins to sing a haunting lullaby, and John sleeps. The boat slips through a series of highly stylised tableaux, encasing the voyage in images of nature (spiders' webs, bullfrogs, cat's tail reeds, and, later, a huge turtle, a pair of bunnies, an owl and a herd of sheep). Although these images have an uncanny quality, the overwhelming calm of the escape and the song marks them as protective totems rather than anything threatening.

The children's trip downriver apparently takes some days. After John sees sheep grazing, he declares to Pearl, 'We're going to spend the night on land.' As the boat edges into shore, a highly artificial set of farmhouse and barn appears against a diorama of fading sky. Another lullaby comes on the soundtrack, this time sung by a woman's voice, as John and Pearl climb from their boat. The farmhouse they approach seems little more than a backlit silhouette, a rooftop with chimneys and porch attached and a bright square of light indicating a window with the shade drawn. The camera cuts closer as John and Pearl stand before this light-filled aperture and listen to the motherly voice. A semicircular shadow fills the lower part of the window, while in the upper part the shadow of a bird in a cage projects onto the shade. The camera cuts even closer, showing the shadow bird hopping in her shadow cage as the voice sings, 'Birds will sing in yonder willow, hush, my little ones, hush.' In a reverse angle, Pearl asks John if they are going home. He shushes her and takes her hand, leading her to the barn.

Inside the barn, the lullaby continues at the same volume, making its diegetic or non-diegetic status ambiguous. In the earlier shots it seemed to be the voice of an unseen mother (the source of the circular shadow, perhaps) singing to her unseen baby, sheltered inside the home, in contrast to the dirty, tired and hungry children huddled outside the window. But heard over their entrance to the barn, the lullaby seems intended for them (can one steal a lullaby?). The framing of the dairy cows in the interior of the barn brings the theme of the protecting animals to a climax. The low-placed camera shoots from just above floor level, framing the children through the cows' legs. But unlike the earlier totem animals, only the lower parts of the cows are visible; framing and lighting juxtapose the children with the cows' hanging udders. The camera tracks in this low position (something only Ozu or Shimizu might do) past a succession of cow udders as the children move to the ladder to the hayloft. The tracking shot comes to rest as the children begin to climb up, and a drop of white milk falls from the udder. The lullaby intones: 'Rest, dearest one, rest, here on my breast.'

Maya Deren, the great avant-garde film-maker, presented a theory of poetry and film a couple of years before Laughton made *The Night of the Hunter*. She outlined different ways of organising a film, one in terms of drama and plot, which she called 'horizontal', and another, associated with poetry, which she called 'vertical'.[2] Although such a dichotomy could be reductive, I believe it clarifies the impact of moments such as this one. Deren suggests that certain films, such as her own *Meshes of the Afternoon* (1943), are primarily vertical, presenting images that explore the feeling of a moment rather than advancing action. However, there are also films that, like a Shakespeare play, move between modes and intersperse action and dialogue with poetic soliloquies. Clearly the sequence I am describing of John and Pearl going ashore to spend the night on land marks a sort of pause in the narrative of their escape and pursuit. Much of the trip down the river has a dreamlike, highly metaphorical quality, with the magnified animals and stylised river sets evoking childhood fantasy. This is not to claim that the narrative in which they are embedded carries no weight in these scenes. But the quality of the images is allowed to distract us from the suspense to create an alternative space of dreams and protection.

Laughton/Agee/Cortez create images that display the concrete materialism and the abstraction possible in the cinematic image. These overt, highly symbolic images embed the Oedipally driven narrative of the murderous father and John's ascension to being 'man of the household' into a more ancient infantile fantasy space composed of the river's flow, the lullaby's harmony, the totem animals and the nourishing breast. The shadow play which marks the mother's presence/absence nearly presents an image of nothing, at least nothing we can grasp. An embodied nursing mother might carry all the problems of literalism that Sergei Eisenstein objected to in the naked woman at the end of Dovzhenko's *Earth/Zemlya* (1930).[3] Laughton not only keeps the woman off screen, he embodies her only in her voice, creating an expansive maternal space that has nothing to do with naturalism. This shadow image enacts a drama of confinement: the window frames the screen as the cage contains the bird, and the shade itself marks the barrier between the inside as home and the outside as the place of cold and hunger. From this abstraction of two dimensions, the film moves to overt embodiment, as the nourishment that the voice promises the dearest one resting at her breast becomes almost obscenely (and yet, as I have said, innocently) visible in the dripping udder. Nature protects her children, and the image fulfils the fantasy.

And, as poignant as these images and sounds are, we are not allowed simply to lull in them. The reappearance of Preacher Powell as a distant silhouette framed in the barn window and singing a very different song offers the nightmare inversion of John and Pearl's private movie of love and protection projected on the window shade. This harbinger of murderous pursuit proves the impossibility of their idyll. If the animals seem like protective totems, they also have another potential. The spider's web evokes the stepfather's traps that they have just escaped. Nature is not shown to be entirely benevolent and the animal imagery introduced in this sequence will also be completed by the shot of the owl that seizes the rabbit later (illustrating Miss Cooper's (Lillian Gish) comment, 'It's a hard world for little things'). The fox in a tree that watches the next stage of their trip downriver threatens, rather than guards, their progress. And even this secure and gentle scene on the window shade is imaged not simply as a haven, but as exclusion. The baby within has a mother and protection; John and Pearl receive a hayloft and no real food; all the window view offers is shadow, not substance. Shadows are ambivalent in this film: Powell initially appeared to John as a shadow on his bedroom wall and is seen recurrently as a silhouette. The film evokes fantasies of childhood comfort against a very real political awareness of the realities of the Great Depression, when children run the roads without parents or protection.

Thinking of films in terms of moments, rather than a continuity composed of action, delays and resolution, highlights the transitions in mode and tone that occur even within a short sequence of shots. Laughton interbraids suspense and idyll and moves from shadow to overt embodiment, guiding us through a succession of contrasting moments and images, rather than simply careening towards a story's end.

NOTES

1. Roland Barthes, 'Diderot, Brecht, Eisenstein', in Stephen Heath (ed. and trans.), *Image Music Text* (New York: Hill and Wang, 1977), p. 71.
2. Maya Deren presented her theory of the horizontal and vertical axes at the 'Poetry and Film Symposium', transcribed in P. Adams Sitney (ed.), *Film Culture Reader* (New York: Praeger Press, 1970), pp. 174–5.
3. Eisenstein's criticism of Dovzhenko's 'naked woman' in *Earth* occurs in his essay 'Dickens, Griffith, and the Film Today', in Sergei Eisenstein, *Film Form: Essays in Film Theory* [ed. and trans. Jay Leyda] (New York: Harcourt Brace and Company, 1977), pp. 241–2.

BIBLIOGRAPHY

Adams Sitney, P. (ed.), *Film Culture Reader* (New York: Praeger Press, 1970).

Barthes, Roland, 'Diderot, Brecht, Eisenstein', in Stephen Heath (ed. and trans.), *Image Music Text* (New York: Hill and Wang, 1977).

Deren, Maya, 'Poetry and Film Symposium', in P. Adams Sitney (ed.), *Film Culture Reader* (New York: Praeger Press, 1970).

Eisenstein, Sergei, *Film Form: Essays in Film Theory* [ed. and trans. Jay Leyda] (New York: Harcourt Brace and Company, 1977).

Eisenstein, Sergei, 'Dickens, Griffith, and the Film Today', in Eisenstein, *Film Form*, pp. 241–2.

Heath, Stephen (ed. and trans.), *Image Music Text* (New York: Hill and Wang, 1977).

Between Melodrama and Realism: *Under the Skin of the City* (2001)

LAURA MULVEY

The moment that I have chosen to discuss takes place in a film that brings together two cinematic stylistic traditions, social realism and melodrama. In her film, *Under the Skin of the City/Zir-e poost-e shahr* (2001), Rakhshan Bani Etemad uses both to tell a story about crises rooted in class and gender inequality in contemporary Iran. This film encapsulates the way that realism and melodrama are, in different ways, stylistically important for dramas of social oppression and injustice. Realism records the state of things, without stylistic intrusion into a representation of the norms of everyday life and its fragile survival strategies. These are conditions that lack buffer zones or safety-valves; misfortune or error can quickly mutate into disaster leaving their victims struggling to comprehend, unable to articulate clearly their suffering or the strain that leaves relationships fissured. It is here that melodrama serves its purpose and the cinema takes on an expressive function that responds to both the intensity of the crisis and its protagonists' desperation. There is, of course, an implicit chronology in this dual style: in the order of the narrative, the melodrama takes over from realism's depiction of a day-to-day state of things. Bani Etemad's perspective is deeply political and it is this that gives the combined use of realism and of melodrama a 'social' perspective.

Under the Skin of the City is about a working-class family in Tehran, primarily revolving around the figure of the mother, Tuba (Golab Adineh), and her beloved eldest son, Abbas (Mohammed Reza Forutan). Their intense affection introduces another element intrinsic to the melodrama: a crisis affecting family life, particularly, the mother. Early on, the space of the family home is established: the small house with its courtyard surrounded by high walls evokes the topography of domesticity associated with the genre of melodrama, before the film comes to make use of a more marked melodramatic style. For Tuba, the house stands for her motherhood, her love for her children and their love for each other. The house next door, on the other hand, while identical in layout, is tyrranised by a brutal and conservative eldest son so that the high walls are more resonant of

a prison than of maternal comfort. In contrast to the enclosed space of the family home, Abbas moves around the city on his motor scooter, across wide shots of cityscape, motorways and surrounding urban development. For him, this should be a success story, an escape from the constraints imposed by class, lack of education and the destiny that seems to hold the family in poverty and impotence. He sees migration to Japan as the almost magical means to establish control over his own story, to rescue his mother from her debilitating job in a textiles factory, to ensure a university education for his younger brother, Ali (Ebrahin Sheibani), and sister, Mahboubeh (Baran Kosari). And on his successful return, he will marry the young woman he longs for from afar, now way beyond his social reach.

While melodramatic style tends to draw attention to itself, realism is associated rather with transparency. *Under the Skin of the City*, however, is 'book-ended' by two remarkable scenes of film-making, as a documentary crew interview Tuba and her fellow women workers about the coming parliamentary elections. These scenes not only draw attention to the constructed nature of the film-making process as such, but also reveal the lack of communication between the crew and the women. The presence of the cinema as process thus flows over, onto and into the first section of the film and its relatively transparent style. But various events precipitate a crisis that takes the film out of its early equilibrium. In his struggle to raise money for his visa, Abbas sells the family house to a developer. The story collapses around him and with it the fragile security of everyday life that Tuba struggles to maintain. The 'documentary' scenes are also a reminder that the family appeared briefly in Bani Etemad's 1998 film *The May Lady/Banoo-ye Ordibehesht*. The protagonist, Forough, is a middle-class documentary director who has been commissioned to make a film about motherhood during which she encounters Tuba, one of many working-class mothers whose tragic stories she tries to tell. By this time, Abbas is in jail and it is possible to piece together the terrible aftermath of the 2001 film (making *Under the Skin of the City* something like a 'pre-quel'). Increasingly aware of the gap between her film-making process and the reality of the women's lives, Forough finally abandons the commission.

It could be that Bani Etemad turned towards a more melodramatic style in order to attempt to express the gap between the medium and its aspiration to capture reality. As *Under the Skin of the City* shifts away from transparency, the narrative begins to fragment into emotionally charged tableaux, sounds (repeated and exaggerated) lose their nat-ural place in space and time, and the camera's angles and framings become tinged with strangeness, a dislocation that reflects the characters' disorientation and pain. This shift is quite slight rather than heavily marked, so that the film's use of a more melodramatic style demands attention and interpretation. As dramatic situations arise, as charac-ters are caught in impasses that cannot be transcended, the film summons up formal means of marking emotional crisis and the collapse of everyday normality. In this sense, the film is not following generic rules, but responding visu-ally to the characters' emotional distress, recognising the gap that Forough had encountered in *The May Lady*. Furthermore, the emotional crisis is caused by the discor-dant aspirations of mother and son, one centred on main-taining the family home, the other sacrificing it in the hope of escaping from its class-bound world, one represented visually by the domestic space, the other invested in nar-rative desire.

Tuba is an ordinary working-class woman, a mother of five children, whose husband cannot work. Her job in the textiles factory is undermining her health and, on all sides, life presents difficulties that she deals with as best she can. However, both Bani Etemad's direction and Golab Adineh's performance subtly bring out her resilience, her humanity and an implicit intelligence. The film constantly returns to and represents the physical and ideological oppression of women and their helplessness. The fact that Tuba has no legal rights over her own home is at the political heart of the story, while the crisis is precipitated as the neighbour's intolerance and brutality drives his young sister to run away from home. Mahboubeh, visiting her friend, now living destitute in a park, is caught up in a police raid and arrested. When Tuba fails to find the deeds needed to get her daughter out of jail, she realises that Abbas has finally sold the house. Her pain and bewilderment overwhelm the film, precipitating the scene that I have chosen to analyse.

The scene consists of a single static shot, but is pre-ceded by a shot of a black screen crossed by diagonal, inter-mittent, flashes of light. The flat, unreadable space of the screen seems to summon up, in the first instance, the cinema itself and the essential elements of light and dark out of which, potentially, recognisable forms and meanings may emerge. This (very short) initial moment creates a visual disorientation in the spectator that evokes, but is

not of course adequate to, the black hole of despair that has overwhelmed Tuba. The main shot then shows the inside of the (by-now-familiar) courtyard at night, taken from a high angle on the outside wall. The flashes of diag-onal light also mutate, out of abstraction, into streaks of pouring rain. In the courtyard, in long shot, Tuba is sitting on the ground in front of a small basin in which she is washing clothes with obsessive intensity. Her automatic actions are precisely in keeping with her lifetime of caring for her family, in which hard labour is inextricably bound with deep affection. This confusion is, of course, central to the mythologies of motherhood and, in these extreme cir-cumstances, Tuba resorts to a performance that poignantly reflects those underlying contradictions. Washing clothes literally gives her an occupation in a moment of crisis, but in the pouring rain and darkness, her habitual actions are obviously rendered grotesque and absurd. Overwhelmingly conscious of her inability to 'do anything', she does 'some-thing' that is symptomatic of the unconscious. As the camera maintains a distance from the scene of Tuba's clothes-washing, it draws into the shot all the constituent elements of the *mise en scène*: the space of the courtyard, the darkness and the rain. It also shows, without any sen-timentality, Tuba's crippled husband who briefly remon-strates with her ('This is no time for doing the laundry') and wraps his jacket around her shoulders before slowly and painfully retreating back into the house. His gesture is personal, affectionate and in character, but marks, at this

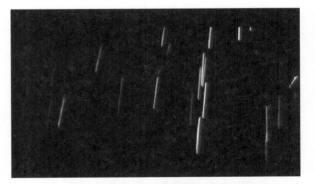

point, the inability of any individual to penetrate the mother's despair that this scene renders with a fusion of melodrama and restraint.

In this scene, the typical and homely is displaced into an empty gesture that caricatures the domestic, and its very irrationality becomes the sign of a core resistance to a dominant 'rationality'. From a dramatic perspective, there are two aspects to the scene. First, it vividly shows that, in the face of relentless ill fortune, Tuba is able to transform an action belonging to the everyday into a symptomatic action that evokes both her unconscious and a wider, collective unconscious of women unable to express, speak or articulate the pain and injustice they suffer daily. Second, Tuba's intense feelings are woven into the *mise en scène* and cinematic style, so that the spectator is forced to read the screen and move beyond any straightforward identification with character. Although the film has often shown the mother's face (lined by hard physical labour and unrelenting anxiety but enlivened by humour, affection and intelligence), there is no cut to close-up to break up the integrity of the shot. In this scene, the whole space evokes Tuba's emotions but also presents a topography that demands a further reading from the spectator. On one level, her irrational action is expressive of the way that her situation is beyond words. On another level, the film responds to that wordlessness and compensates for it cinematically. The scene does not ignore its participant's consciousness, but extends it formally with a cinematic consciousness that, while it might break with the unities of realism, is determined, and then stylistically overtaken, by the destiny or lot in which the characters find themselves. It is here that the film's style relates to melodrama. However, rather than consciously citing melodrama as a pre-existing or generic formula, known, for instance, from Hollywood or the popular Indian cinema, *Under the Skin of the City* suggests that *mise en scène* and the language of cinema must, and should, acknowledge silences rooted in oppression and repression. From this perspective, the film's move beyond language into the cinematic lends itself to this political form of expression and draws attention to particular conjunctures in which the political and the cinematic come together. To my mind, *Under the Skin of the City* is exemplary, due to the sparse beauty with which it juggles sympathy for its protagonists and a cinema that, while relating to them, transcends them. This is a film that resolutely maintained the clear vision of social realism, relevant to a working-class milieu, until that style could no longer adequately express the class- and gender-derived pressures suffered by particular characters. However, the recourse to a 'melodramatic' style inexorably returns to the social from another direction: the style is a response to oppression and the cinematic excess is a signifier leading back immediately to class, oppression and the crisis of gender in contemporary Iran. From this perspective, *Under the Skin of the City* shows that the style associated with melodrama works symptomatically and appears at moments that lead immediately back to reality, even though, on the face of it, the melodramatic style bypasses realism.

Finally, to my mind, that single shot of the courtyard, its melodramatic *mise en scène* and the intensity invested in Tuba's action within it, ultimately leads beyond the drama of *Under the Skin of the City* to the difficulty of representing the problems of motherhood. By and large, the mother is easily transformed into over-visible cliché or disappears into a miasma of ideological or psychic confusion. Rakhshan Bani Etemad, as a woman director, has confronted these contradictions: in *Under the Skin of the City* she refuses to idealise her main protagonist or extract her from the everyday into the heroic. In this film, it becomes possible to understand the way a woman director can register the contradiction between the image and the reality of motherhood. At the very end, the film suddenly mutates and something beyond either melodrama or social realism takes over the screen. The film's final scene returns to the documentary film crew recording ordinary people's responses to the coming election. As Tuba makes an impassioned statement to camera, the technicians ask her to repeat what she has just said on the grounds that there is a technical fault. She looks at the (diegetic) camera and says: 'Why can't you film what's in my heart?' Then, looking straight past the camera, she addresses the audience, saying, 'Who sees these films anyway?' Tuba's statement directly challenges the adequacy of realistic representation; that is, her heart can't be shown and the camera crew can't hear her words. However, the courtyard scene (analysed above) not only poignantly represents the suffering and contradictions of an individual, but materialises, on film and with film, a complex interweaving of signification, reaching into the unconscious and out into the intractable reality of the everyday.

Internalising the Musical: *The Band Wagon* (1953)

ANDREW KLEVAN

In his collection of essays examining the intersection of philosophy and criticism, *Philosophy the Day after Tomorrow*, Stanley Cavell analyses the opening musical number of *The Band Wagon* (Minnelli, 1953), entitled 'By Myself'. Tony Hunter, played by Fred Astaire, is a song-and-dance man whose star has faded in Hollywood, and who is returning apprehensively to New York to make a comeback on Broadway. The short number consists of him walking down a train platform and into the main concourse of the station. According to Cavell, this is as 'uneventful as a photographed song can be' and he finds it therefore to have significance that may be 'missable'.[1] He writes that the dramatisation of the sequence and the form of the song establish a sense of 'emotional hovering, not so much a feeling of suspense as one of being in suspension'.[2] He then discusses the matter of Astaire walking:

> Recall to begin with its jauntiness, the slight but distinct exaggeration of his body swinging from side to side as he paces along the platform. Narratively, he is hoping to cheer himself, letting his body, as William James once suggested, tell him what his emotion is … it is the walk of a man who is known to move into dance exactly like no other man. It is a walk from which, at any step, this man may break into dance … . Now if his walking does turn into dancing, then isn't what we see of his delivery revealed to have been already dancing, a sort of limiting case, or proto-state, of dancing?[3]

Later in the *The Band Wagon*, Tony and Gabrielle Gerard, played by Cyd Charisse, travel by horse and carriage to a park in the evening to ascertain whether, despite their different professional backgrounds, they are able to dance together, hence whether they are able to make love together. Before they dance there is a prelude. As they enter the frame (our first sight of the park), they are not simply walking but stepping in unison with a slight sway. Their walk is deliberate yet restrained, measured, and their position in the middle ground of the shot – their

entry at first masked and then somewhat overshadowed by the carriage driver and the horse's head drinking from the deep blue-water pool in the foreground – also reduces the appearance of embellishment. Music is playing, but it is soft, leisurely, meandering, not quite properly accompanying them. Their entry to the park is exquisite and poised but it is disguised as merely establishing and preparatory.

Before they dance with each other properly, there is a period of suspension where they appear to be in a slow, hesitant, exploratory dance with the camera. Couple and camera tentatively move towards and away from each other, trying to stay in touch, and this gives the sequence a subliminal harmony, fragile and faint, and contributes to a supernatural undercurrent. As they turn the corner, their steps drop out of time, and the camera drops down too (from a high position up by the park lamp). There appears to be no special place to consummate their partnership as a crowd of dancing couples halts them and they sidle around the periphery; the camera, reflecting their situation, backs off, a retreat that enables the dancing couples to fill the frame and further emphasises their exclusion. They drift lackadaisically among the crowd *and* seem gently drawn towards the patiently waiting camera. They pass close to the little orchestra, a wistful irony, so near to the music, and yet so far … and yet … as they walk on, leaving the band and the dancing couples behind them, they subtly begin to move in time with each other *and* the music *and* the slow, retreating camera. They come round the corner (on a cut), the melody has disappeared, and the soundtrack is tremulous. Has the camera guided them courteously towards a better place? They continue to walk, and it is still pulling back, serenely, but a touch quicker than they, so a space emerges in front of them. Perhaps this clearing for their dance, quiet and empty, was fatefully waiting, but it appears to grow at this moment, for this moment, out of an empathetic relationship, an unspoken understanding, between the camera and the performers. Recognising the moment, Gabrielle throws a leaf, lifts her leg and spins.

The deferment of the dance creates an aura of erotic hesitation, partly because the preamble resembles an indeterminate and apprehensive wander by soon-to-be lovers. The sequence is straightforward and misleading: clearly arranged to be a prelude to a dance *and* subdued enough not to be clearly anything. As well as reflecting the state of the characters' relationship, it is also a meta-musical moment in that it lays bare the anticipation, and sense of suspension, that is a common feeling while viewing musicals. Just when, exactly, will the talk become song and the walk become dance?

Unlike the 'Dancing in the Dark' sequence, 'By Myself' does not proceed to unequivocal dancing. Cavell notes that we do not see Astaire's feet, a point particularly worth noting given how rarely his body is fragmented during his dance sequences: head, torso, arms, legs, feet, environment, partner, décor and objects are shown together within the frame. The disappearance of his feet is further emphasised, according to Cavell, when he drops a cigarette and we do not see his foot snuff it out. When he finally appears in the station we also

> hear him repeating or continuing the tune he has just sung to himself, not precisely by humming it but with the kind of syllabification, or proto-speech, that musicians sometimes use to remind themselves of the exact materialisation of a passage of sound, but which can occur, as here, as an unguarded expression of a state of consciousness, in its distraction, disorientation, dispossession: Da: da, da da; da, da da.[4]

Cavell understands Astaire's song and proto-dance as a 'psychic hovering, of dissociation from the body, within a state of ordinary invisibility' (the song is partly stimulated by his feelings of isolation as the press photographers ignore him and instead gravitate towards Ava Gardner, appearing in a cameo).[5] The first part of the film, at least, will be about him finding his way back to dancing, finding his feet again. This sense of hovering is present in the prelude to the 'Dancing in the Dark' sequence too, where the couple, as they move through the crowd, are invisible, their emotional state unknown (to each other and the crowd). In fact, although Cavell does not mention it, Tony's 'da da'ing starts a few moments earlier on the train and is *resumed* later on the platform, further suggesting something trying to emerge, but then submerged, stuttering, broken, unable to find a clear and continuous articulation, or musical elaboration.

There is another sequence in *The Band Wagon*, at the after-party, after the failure of the show, which illustrates that a quality of film, perhaps an under-appreciated quality, may be found in moments that are preparatory (or succeeding), passing or apparently unrealised. This might be especially worth pointing out in a genre where the major song-and-dance sequences, extraordinarily striking and

declamatory in their skilfulness (and so eagerly awaited), steal the spotlight. Endeavouring to cheer themselves up, Tony and the crew sing a song about beer and someone called Louisa (entitled 'I Love Louisa'). The song ends exuberantly, with arms aloft and joyous laughter. Then they droop, realising the sad predicament of the failed show. The camera pans over their pensive faces. What do they do now? If the prelude to the 'Dancing in the Dark' sequence plays on anticipation regarding when a musical sequence will begin, the explicit loss at the end of this song nods towards feelings of withdrawal and depletion at the end of numbers. Songs crescendo, joyously, and then they stop, jarringly, and suddenly a void, silence (the absent presence of applause), and then the return to mundane ordinary speech.

Indeed, if a musical is to succeed as an achieved film rather than a more or less interesting framework for song-and-dance numbers, it must solve the problem of how to strengthen its non-musical periods (without necessarily contradicting their status as interludes). Quite often second-hand plot mechanisms and generic conventions, for example those from farcical comedy and sentimental romance, anxiously kick in to take up the slack and assert intensity. This only further foregrounds the genre's structural difficulties regarding balance and integration. As one might expect, the anticlimax after the song about Louisa becomes the spur to ambitions for a reformulated show, quickly injecting momentum into the plot, but more importantly rhythm and choreography permeate the drama and this provides body and shape. Musical forms appear as a trace so the scene avoids becoming merely a watered-down musical number, or an arch mirror of one.

Tony moves through the crew to the phone and they move round to watch him, packing together and settling on and around the bed. Ostensibly, they gather because they are eager to know the purpose of his call and the consequences of it, but they assemble as if they were awaiting a performance from him. This assembled audience is itself a performance (of viewing); they have taken their positions and are in an artful pose (and their casual clothes now appear as colourful costumes). On the phone, Tony tells Jeff (the producer of the show, played by Jack Buchanan) about how the show should go on but it must undergo radical change and free itself of pretension. He *stresses* the matter in his own particular way and then, having announced that it 'will be *our* show', he really *swings* it:

> We're going **on**/
> we're going to keep it on the **road**/
> and we're going to **redo** it from **top** to **bottom**./
> It won't be a modern version of **Faust**/
> Pilgrim's Progress/
> Or the Book of **Job** in **Swing**time/
> It will be **our** show/ *(pause)*
> [faster] the-**show**-we-**star**ted-**out**-to-**do**/

the-**book**-the-**Mar**tins-**wrote**/
with-the-**songs**-**you**-threw-**out**/

When he finally asks for a response, a foreign voice answers: 'Hello, ze's nobody here'; and the film now cuts to show Jeff's hotel room with a chambermaid listening on the end of the phone. The gag is easy, but it has the effect of focusing Tony's phone call as a monologue in blank verse, a little routine of its own, a spoken song, and, like so much of Astaire, self-contained and self-possessed – somewhat sealed off. Astaire's talking here is close to singing, but then Astaire's singing is always close to talking. The gag relies on setting up the expectation of Jeff's response, everyone waiting to see if he will accept the new arrangement, but his absence confirms that it is Tony's delivery that matters, not the narrative outcome.

Jeff is in fact in the same room as Tony, sitting secretly in an armchair behind the crowd. He accepts the new plan, but is worried about finances. In response, Tony starts pacing back and forth, closely surrounded by the crew, and, in a series of apparently unconscious movements, his arms and hands jangle and twitch uncontrollably this way and that, up and down around his body, refusing to stay on hips or in pockets. His escaping arms and hands appear like fragments of a dance, secretions, any full manifestation inhibited by the unsure situation and claustrophobic space.

In this transitional scene following the breakdown of the show, and including her break-up, Gabrielle also moves insecurely as if guided by uncertain memories of a dance. Forming a two-shot with her boyfriend, played by James Mitchell, she pushes onto him with both her hands. He is stiff and closed; he does not know how to move with her (ironically, he is her choreographer in the movie, but he turns out, unsurprisingly, to be the wrong type). She falls away from him but carefully, softly sitting down upon the bed (her calm retreat poignantly absorbing the melodrama of the break-up). Her torso is upright, pointing towards him; she looks up to him, remnants of affection (and adulation). She is hoping that he might stay, but she is also tightening,

reining herself in, after all she is hoping that he won't. She turns slowly, as if yearning to be part of the group, but he snaps her out of it with 'I don't want you to do it.' A few moments later, she turns again, but towards him as he departs. On both occasions, she moves her arms from her lap to by her side and this enables her upper body securely to rotate, and reach out. It also keeps her steady, holds her to the bed, and expresses her desire to stay put. This is the sketch of a dance, reaching out and holding back, playing with release and restraint, her body opening and closing, but with the music removed, and the gestures minimal, undemonstrative and discrete, and in prosaic register.

The performers infuse their gestures with the spirit of *the musical* without lapsing into affected or accentuated mannerisms that would upset the 'realism' of the dramatic continuity. However, as so often when judging the credibility or integrity of incident or behaviour in artworks, this is not simply a matter of measuring against a fixed body of conventions. The film (including the performers) is partly responsible for establishing the possibilities and parameters of its 'realism', and determining whether an aspect will integrate or protrude. Just after Gabrielle gets up from the bed and turns towards the crew (who are eagerly hanging on Tony's every word and laughing) is a moment that straddles the musical and nonmusical worlds, spotlighted and discreet. As she gets nearer the group, she turns her body once again to face the door, and then, still facing out, she drops down beside Tony. Looking away from the group nevertheless positions her ideally to (go) back into it.

Her legs, hidden behind the long white dress, need to manoeuvre her carefully into this seating position: she must remain composed, keeping her posture, upper body and head, upright as she slips in, and cause no disturbance. Here, for once, Charisse's celebrated legs are withheld; they are not part of a spectacle, flaunted and gleaming, or visibly hard at work. We may appreciate her skill in using them free from the satisfactions and distractions of viewing them.

And as she is turning and dropping, Tony places his arm around her shoulder, increasing the sense of her nestling in, and presses her gently into position (as if she was the last to enter into a group photo, her place ready and waiting for her). There is an automatic quality to Tony's gesture that suggests inevitability and obliviousness to the emotional upheaval that has just taken place. Indeed, this rather eventful moment, one that cements Gabrielle's new relationship with Tony as the old boyfriend leaves, is free of dramatic elaboration. Extended attention would be unworthy and disingenuous, and her succinct and graceful movement allows the film to hurry through the predictable narrative and generic adjustment while avoiding the callousness that is a danger of necessary elision. It faithfully condenses different emotions so that the abbreviation is tactful and reflective. Her body neatly completes the composition, expressing willing acceptance *and* inescapable absorption, but the outward force of her gaze strains its harmony. While Tony talks about the future, giving his roll-call of cities to perform in, she settles back into (t)his vision *and* looks out towards her past. Feelings of fitting in are in balance with those of dropping down (and the quiet deflation of her dress).

The shot remains for some time after she comes to rest, like the final pose of a dance routine, the ensemble all gathered and stilled in tableau, waiting for applause, the incongruous silence interrupting continuity. It ruefully mocks that customary plea by gesturing towards the lack of (live) acknowledgment that is the condition of the filmed musical (and poignantly frames Gabrielle's insufficiently recognised moment). Charisse's movement encapsulates the possibilities for containment: the internalisation of musical forms in a genre more commonly celebrated for its outward, exuberant show of song and dance.

NOTES

1. Stanley Cavell, *Philosophy the Day after Tomorrow* (Cambridge and London: The Belknap Press of Harvard University Press, 2005), p. 22.
2. Ibid., p. 22.
3. Ibid., p. 23.
4. Ibid., p. 25.
5. Ibid., p. 26.

BIBLIOGRAPHY

Cavell, Stanley, *Philosophy the Day after Tomorrow* (Cambridge, MA and London: The Belknap Press of Harvard University Press, 2005).

The Visitor's Discarded Clothes in *Theorem* (1968)

STELLA BRUZZI

Pasolini's *Theorem* (*Teorema*), made in 1968, is notorious for many things, but not often noted for its costumes, despite the fact that it exhibits many of the traits of the 'clothes movie'. The 1960s Italian couturier Roberto Capucci (in what proved to be his one foray into cinema) provided the clothes for Silvana Mangano as the mother Lucia,[1] while Marcella de Marchis – Roberto Rossellini's former wife, confidante and collaborator – designed the remainder of the costumes for Terence Stamp (as the stranger) and others. *Theorem* centres on the arrival of an unnamed visitor to a wealthy house in Milan's affluent San Siro suburb who, when he arrives, proceeds to have sex with all five members of the household in turn (Emilia the maid [Laura Betti], Pietro the son [Andrés José Cruz Soublette], Lucia the mother, Paolo the father [Massimo Girotti] and Odetta the daughter [Anna Wiazemsky]). The effect of these sexual encounters on the family members is traumatic: Emilia, for example, returns home, refuses to eat and is found levitating by her neighbours, Odetta becomes catatonic, while Lucia, hitherto an impeccable bourgeois housewife, goes cruising. The controversy surrounding *Theorem* is the result of the similarities between the Visitor and Christ: that the name of the postman who brings news of his arrival and departure is Angelino (Ninetto Davoli), that the effects of the sexual encounters themselves are extraordinary and catastrophic, and that inserted into most of the seduction scenes are sporadic images of the bleak slopes of Mount Etna, which for most critics recall the Biblical wilderness into which prophets and others went for spiritual contemplation.

Within this elliptical framework, clothes feature prominently, used at various times to convey and not merely reflect meaning. In a film so lacking in the conventional narrative traits of character development, dialogue, logical exposition and cogent plot development, additional signifiers such as costume are granted elevated importance. For example, being a study of sexual and spiritual awakening, undressing features prominently in *Theorem*: the Visitor and Pietro, compelled to share a bedroom when other visitors descend, undress awkwardly in front of each other; in the scene I am about to discuss, Lucia undresses while waiting for the Visitor to return from running with the dog; and, most notably, right at the end, the father Paolo divests himself of all his clothes (his conventionality, his heterosexuality, perhaps even his 'mortal coil') on the concourse at Milan station before running naked and screaming into the wilderness, an image with which *Theorem* concludes. Lacking certain conventionalised modes of exposition, piecing together meaning in *Theorem* is much like compiling a patchwork – moments and gestures in isolation appear opaque and even irrelevant, but make sense viewed in tandem with each other. The undressing scenes are three such moments. The first two function relatively straightforwardly as preludes to sex with the Visitor, and although the third does not literally lead to a sexual encounter, if the Visitor is likened to Christ, then the naked and screaming Paolo's flight into the wilderness – in conjunction with the cumulative connotations of undressing – could be read as an empathetic flight towards both spiritual and sexual enlightenment.[2] There are several such clothes moments to choose from, but I will, in a moment, focus on one scene in which the specific conjunction between desire, sexuality and Terence Stamp's quintessential cool 60s look is made central. Coolness is indeed key to *Theorem* because, despite the prominence afforded sex and desire in its plot, the sexual act remains repressed, mimicked by the repressive implications of many of the costumes. Stamp dons the 1960s capsule wardrobe for the casually dressed young man of slacks, shirts and pullovers in subtle and unremarkable shades. His unremarkable appearance, however, is ironic considering the remarkable effect he has on the household; it also complements his character: he is promiscuous and bisexual but also emotionally detached. As if reconfirming this, *Theorem* dwells on the build-up to and the traumatic effects of desire rather than on the sexual encounters themselves. And within the film's mannered, precise but ultimately cold style, the coolly unsensuous costumes start not to reflect the characters but rather to create barriers to them.

My moment is an extended prelude to the Visitor's seduction of Lucia, when Lucia comes across a set of clothes the Visitor, out running with a dog, has left on one of the sofas in a summer/holiday house in the Po Valley. The sequence (about eighteen minutes into *Theorem*) opens with a static wide shot of the exterior of a luxurious, contemporary house whose modernity is at odds with the unkempt, woody landscape in which it sits. A sombre, regular church bell tolls and continues to do so for over a minute. The Visitor's presence in the house is signalled by a close-up of his copy of Rimbaud's *Complete Works* left on the floor. In his first full scene, immediately following the party to welcome him, the Visitor sits in the garden of the Milan villa reading first a law textbook and then this same edition of Rimbaud's *Complete Works*. The casual but repeated interest in Arthur Rimbaud, the restless, peripatetic lover of fellow poet Paul Verlaine, suggests the Visitor's own promiscuous bisexuality. Mangano picks up the book and places it on a footstool before looking across the room towards a sofa, on which lie the Visitor's casually discarded clothes. The parallels between the dynamics of this earlier encounter with Rimbaud and the scene in the Po Valley are significant, for on both occasions the Visitor's inferred interest in homosexuality is witnessed by a woman (in the first instance Emilia, in the second Lucia) who then finds herself irresistibly and obsessively drawn to him. The sequence in the garden culminates in the Visitor's sexual encounter with Emilia, just as the Po Valley scene will conclude with the Visitor's seduction of Lucia, a seduction that marks the mid-point of the Visitor's cycle of sexual conquests.

The men's clothes on the sofa are laid out with not entirely dishevelled abandon and Lucia feels compelled to go over to them, just as Emilia felt compelled in the garden scene to rush over and brush away the cigarette ash that had fallen from the Visitor's cigarette onto his thigh as he sat reading Rimbaud. Here, Lucia is similarly drawn to the Visitor's clothes but, unlike Emilia, walks towards them in a measured way. Rimbaud, it is again proposed, is a rival for the Visitor's affections and, as if signalling this threat, Lucia's control recedes as she gets to the sofa. As she moves towards the clothes, a rougher handheld camera

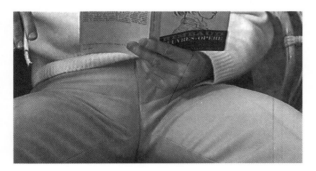

style takes over from the slow low-angle pan that had followed her across the room. The agitation implied by the rougher visual style conveys – within a film so pointedly reluctant to use dialogue for this purpose – the urgency and encroaching passion of Lucia's thoughts as she surveys the shirt, trousers, jumper and underpants strewn before her.

The first item of clothing is a pristine white shirt which, lit from the left, acquires the quality of coldly sensuous alabaster (an apt substitute for the Visitor) as its folds, collar and buttonholes are picked out and accentuated by the directional light, their sculptural whiteness luminously pale against the muddy green of the sofa behind. The second is a salmon-pink pair of trousers, the third a flecked pink and white pullover with a white vest nestling in its folds and the last a pair of decidedly grubby briefs.

Particular emphasis is placed on Terence Stamp's vacated trousers, garments which feature prominently in several of *Theorem*'s seductions. The opening shot of the garden scene when we first see the Visitor reading Rimbaud (and the first time we see the Visitor in close-up) is a low-angle view of Stamp's crotch as he sits back in a low chair.[3] Stamp is fond of recalling how Pasolini's minimal direction included the command (conveyed in English through Pasolini's close friend Laura Betti who played Emilia) to keep his legs open and get an erection.[4] Although the actor failed to oblige, the eroticism generated by the juxtaposition here between the disconcertingly bland beige light wool slacks and the sexual promise they cocoon is an adequately tumescent substitute. The irony is that all this promise of arousal is never matched by the perfunctory and cold sexual gestures that ensue. The garden sequence, for example, concludes with a close-up of Stamp's buttocks, sheathed in the unerotic banality of his trousers, shifting mechanically around on top of Emilia, a familiar motion heralding an act of perfunctory lovemaking. The slight sheen of the trouser fabric, their taut 60s cut revealing the lines of underwear lurking beneath, their neat little pocket, the freshly ironed crease inching down the back of Stamp's thigh all serve to kill the eroticism of the moment, the final deadly flourish being the post-dubbed sound of mixed fibres brushing up against each other. This earlier indication of the complex erotic importance of Terence Stamp's trousers is the veiled force that informs the later scene.

What sets the Visitor's clothes apart in the Po Valley scene is that they do not adorn a body; they have become objects rather than adornments, spectacular in their own right, but also sculptural and inert. Roland Barthes articulated the eeriness of clothes detached from the body thus: 'It is not possible to conceive a garment without the body … the empty garment, without head or limbs (a schizophrenic fantasy), is death, not the body's neutral absence, but the body decapitated, mutilated.'[5]

Barthes's nihilistic notion of unattached clothes as death is just one theorisation of the detachment between clothes and the body. There is also the idea, grounded in Freud, of unattached clothes as fetishistic sexual substitutes for the veiled genitalia or sexual object. Both of these arguments find their way into the moment when Lucia contemplates the Visitor's abandoned clothes, which come to function as eroticised substitutes for the absent body but also as signals that such a dislocation between body and clothes will prove traumatic.

Stamp never regards his seduced victims warmly; instead, he looks through or away from them even as he gets close, and the actor has referred in interview to his mannered performance style emanating from his intention to remain 'not in the moment' but divorced from it.[6] This detachment is also signalled through the distancing of costume and body. In the most often cited scene in Paul Schrader's 1980 film *American Gigolo* (in which, like *Theorem,* the prioritisation of the male protagonist's costume signals both his desirability and his ability to remain emotionally detached from those whom he attracts), Richard Gere, the eponymous gigolo, chooses his clothes for a date by laying a selection of Giorgio Armani ensembles on his bed. The gesture of looking at the clothes, scrutinising them, indicates that he is about to assume a role. These are costumes, not extensions of the self. Likewise, in *Theorem*, the Visitor's clothes, so frequently set apart from his body, are not part of him. The clothes wear the man.

This disassociation is brought sharply into focus by what we see of the Visitor before he returns to the villa. In one of *Theorem*'s rare energetic and spontaneous asides, we understand that Stamp has abandoned his clothes to frolic in the woods with a dog, dressed only in trainers and a pair of grubby grey shorts. This juxtaposition is heavily ironic. First, there is the fact that this dog, the one partner with whom he does not have sex, is also the one partner with whom the Visitor appears to have fun; second, his carefree running reminds us that the prim but provocative clothes lying on the sofa should not be mistaken for him but are rather impoverished, empty and even fraudulent fetish objects.

Lucia's contemplation of her guest's clothes is thereby infused with lack: lack of passion, lack of corporeality, lack of fulfilling consummation. The object of her desire is not merely 'not in the moment' but away enjoying himself, his body unshackled from his clothes. This absence is most keenly felt when Lucia alights on his trousers. Beige-salmon in colour, they offer a classic example of late 1960s styling with their flat-fronted fit, visible stitching around the hems and small front pockets. Lucia finds them unzipped at the fly with one side bent back to reveal a distinctly more sensuous blue silk lining, a metonymic representation perhaps of the Visitor's repressed passion, the vivacity he is capable of expressing when with the dog. The trousers have been (as always) neatly pressed, with a visible pleat down the front of the leg and one would not automatically mistake these slacks for the garment of a sexual predator. The trousers' shade, though unusual, is anonymous, in keeping as it is with the soft browns and pinks that permeate the scene, from Lucia's striped dress to the décor. The pink is also an androgynous mix of femininity and homosexuality, in conflict with the aggression of the opened fly. It is also fleshy and so recalls what is absent here but was present the first time we saw the Visitor's crotch close up: his penis. The pornographic juxtaposition of the heavy, fleshy penis emerging from a three-piece-suit in Robert Mapplethorpe's photograph *Man in Polyester Suit* (1979) is also missing here, but alluded to via the intercutting of Lucia's observation of the clothes with the Visitor cavorting in the woods. That the Visitor's pinkish slacks are the site of trauma comes to the fore specifically as Lucia picks them up. The bell that has been tolling mournfully until this moment finally ceases and on Mangano's face we see that desire has given way to panic. In this instant *Theorem*'s tense elusiveness, its intellectualisation of desire, its detachment and its persistent repression of feeling become focused in one moment that conveys to us more or less definitively that the members of this household are not attracted to the Visitor *per se* but to what their longing for him unleashes in themselves.

The provocatively opened trousers serve paradoxically to figuratively re-emphasise the Visitor's body, but his actual absence makes it possible for the essentially passive Lucia to access her own hitherto repressed carnality, the expression of which is the moment when she discards *her* clothes and sits naked on the terrace of the house waiting for the Visitor to return. The erotic potential of clothes to function as substitutes for the body is evident throughout *Theorem*: eroticism is there even if the erotic object is jogging through the rustic woods. *Theorem*'s final, triumphant perversity is that, while it remains Pier Paolo Pasolini's most explicitly homosexual film, it also remains resolutely inexplicit and coldly, intellectually dispassionate. Its costumes are similarly ambivalent: precise and inherently unsensuous, yet overloaded with erotic promise.

NOTES

1. Capucci was an ardent admirer of Mangano, referring to her as a woman 'of such refinement, beauty and elegance … she wasn't an ordinary woman, an ordinary actress' ('Di una raffinatezza, di una bellezza, di un'eleganza … . Non faceva parte delle donne normali, delle attrici del cinema'). Capucci quoted in <www.modaemodi.org/rivista>.

2. Just prior to undressing, Paolo had made eye contact with a younger man at Milan Station whom he seemed to be going to follow into the gents' lavatories. Instead, he undresses himself and runs off, arguably preparing himself for the Visitor, in whom are combined the twin attractions of religion and homosexuality.

3. This moment is used on the BFI's DVD of *Theorem* (2007) as the backdrop for the menu, so it appears on a continuous loop until you press 'Play'.

4. In the interview on the DVD of *Theorem*, Terence Stamp recalls how Betti came up to him just before shooting and said: 'He just wants you to keep your legs open. Keep your legs open … . He wants you to get erection in this take. Can you get erection? He wants you to have erection …'. Stamp says: 'So I dreaded Laura Betti coming towards me.'

5. Roland Barthes, 'Erté, or À la lettre', *The Responsibility of Forms: Essays on Music, Art and Representation* [trans. Richard Howard] (Oxford: Blackwell, 1984), p. 107.

6. See interview on DVD of *Theorem*.

BIBILIOGRAPHY

Barthes, Roland, 'Erté, or À la lettre', *The Responsibility of Forms: Essays on Music, Art and Representation* [trans. Richard Howard] (Oxford: Blackwell, 1984).

British Film Institute (BFI), *Theorem*, DVD, 2007.

<www.modaemodi.org/rivista>: 'Una finestra id dialogo con un Maestro: Roberto Capucci', *Imore: Rivista Online di Moda e Cultura*.

Style and Sincerity in Quentin Tarantino's *Kill Bill Vol. 2* (2004)

JAMES WALTERS

BORROWING STYLES

In a collection pursuing the relationship between the moment and the wider patterns of a film, how are we to account for Quentin Tarantino's *Kill Bill* movies (2003, 2004), which present a succession of sequences whose divergent styles might render them thematically distinct from one another? M. Keith Booker's description of the films as 'largely lessons in how to borrow styles gracefully' offers one potential direction.[1] In one sense, Booker provides a judgment of value: his use of the word 'gracefully' proposes that there might be ways of borrowing styles that are less than graceful, or even disgraceful. This favourable account of the films is compromised, however, by the words 'largely lessons', as Booker here raises the notion that the films are *best* understood as works that borrow styles gracefully: that this is perhaps their key attribute or attraction. This view of the films has pertinence, to an extent, in that they might well prove in some fashion instructional to film audiences or film-makers on the merits and possibilities available in drawing upon existing movie styles and tropes. Furthermore, it would be difficult to dispute that an immediate pleasure of the *Kill Bill* films is their aptitude for amalgamating styles of film-making from various periods and national cinemas.

However, one danger of placing the weight of emphasis too heavily on such 'lessons in borrowing' is that we risk characterising each movie as *only* an exercise in pastiche or self-conscious reference and assess their merits primarily against those criteria. Although there is fun in recognising such references, as a way of understanding the films' shape and significance, this represents a limited enterprise. Booker's assessment sounds persuasive at a surface level, but his initial emphasis on 'lessons' suggests an almost clinical detachment that the films themselves don't consistently exhibit. His second emphasis on the borrowing of styles courts the misleading notion that the films do not possess a discernible style of their own, and instead comprise a patchwork of other styles adopted, albeit carefully, from elsewhere. In this appraisal of the

films, sincerity is a compromised notion, and the implication is that the films are in some way 'hollow'.

We might address these two points together by suggesting that Tarantino understands and makes use of the ways in which style can bring us close to human beings in cinema, promoting an intimate engagement with the facets of their characters and the facts of the fictional world they inhabit. This position is distinct from an understanding of the films as mainly exercises in stylistic pastiche or parody. Instead, my contention is that the *Kill Bill* films mark a sincere stylistic investment in their fictional world as a reality, replete with emotionally and intellectually complex characters experiencing that world as a tangible reality. A danger of seeing the films as only exercises or lessons is that we might take characters to be only representations of people manoeuvred from set piece to set piece in order to facilitate new instances of cinematic self-reference. In departing from this position, I focus on a moment that places a weight of emphasis upon characters within their fictional world.

'REVENGE IS NEVER A STRAIGHT LINE'

It is certainly the case that unique challenges exist in evaluating fully the nature and form of the fictional world in the *Kill Bill* films. Some of these challenges derive from choices made by Tarantino regarding the ordering and portrayal of the events that take place there. Time and vision are made unstable in the films as events are reordered and a range of audiovisual styles are used, such as ostentatious lighting and editing, split-screen and switches from black and white to colour. These breaks in form and progression are in fact alluded to by a character, the sword-maker Hattori Hanzô (Sonny Chiba), towards the end of *Vol. 1* when, in voiceover, he describes the nature of revenge: 'Revenge is never a straight line. It's a forest. And like a forest it's easy to lose your way … to get lost … to forget where you came in.' By the time this voiceover occurs, we may be sharing at least a sense of this disconcertion as the film's storyworld has, indeed, come to resemble something like a dense forest. Tarantino has effectively disrupted the 'linear' progression of the film's events up to that point, a feature that Edward Gallafent analyses fully in his account of the *Kill Bill* series.[2] Likewise, the director has moved through a range of representational strategies in his account of the fictional world, thus creating further potential rupture.

Hanzô's words take on extra resonance, therefore, as they describe not only his interpretation of the processes of revenge that take place in his fictional world, but also some of the ways in which that fictional world may appear to us in Tarantino's account of it. We are reminded that a series of representational choices have been made by a director willing to adopt attitudes towards and perspectives on events and characters, profoundly affecting the manner in which they are shown to us. So, for example, when he drains the screen of colour, or places events out of sequence, it graphically reinforces our awareness that this world is being displayed for us, by Tarantino, rather than its events simply being relayed to us without choice or prejudice.

Hanzô's words are of further interest, however, in that he establishes a strong relationship between revenge and disorientation. In the film, this relates potently to the character of Beatrix Kiddo (Uma Thurman). As Hanzô delivers his line on revenge, we see Beatrix preparing for her revenge mission on a plane back from visiting him and receiving a sword. She writes and numbers the names of five people whom she intends to kill in acts of revenge, with Bill at number five. In the context of Hanzô's voiceover, we understand her writing to be a strategy for retaining some sense of order amid the passion of the revenge impulse. And yet, as Hanzô's words draw connections between Beatrix's desire for revenge and the films' collage style of representation, we come to appreciate – or at least to speculate – that the films' dramatic order has been shaped to resemble precisely the fragmentation associated with the emotional drive of revenge, as described to us by Hattori Hanzô. In this way, the films' style is aligned with the psychological perspective of its central character, Beatrix, as she carries out her mission of revenge against each member of the Deadly Viper Assassination Squad – the five names contained in her list.

Tarantino connects the films' style of representation with Beatrix's impulses, structuring the manner of their progression in harmony with her revenge drive. Tarantino's style therefore brings us close to a character's emotional perspective, to share in her despair, joy and rage through a series of representational choices that might otherwise be seen as an interesting but essentially hollow patchwork of incongruous aesthetic vignettes. The potential coldness of such a strategy is avoided, a fact mirrored in Beatrix's own experience of revenge and its demands. A famous quotation is displayed at the beginning of *Vol. 1*, which reads:

'Revenge is a dish best served cold'; and this line is defined for us as 'an old Klingon proverb'. The joke reference to the second *Star Trek* film, *The Wrath of Khan* (Meyer, 1982), might prompt us to consider further how sincerely we should read this quotation in the context of the acts of revenge performed by Beatrix in the *Kill Bill* films. Indeed, if we follow this line of enquiry, it becomes striking that revenge for Beatrix is *not* a cold act, and in fact involves an intense emotional and physical engagement consistently throughout the films. In these films, revenge brings with it an emotional burden brought about by a close and intense engagement between adversaries. Thurman's performance of Beatrix conveys this fact with clarity as, throughout the film, she allows a series of tensions and strains to contort her features while in combat. She furthermore punctuates movement with an array of sighs, screams, bellows and cries that contribute to her portrait of a human experiencing immediate and forceful emotions within the act of revenge.

THE FIVE-POINT PALM EXPLODING-HEART TECHNIQUE

The close linking of style to Beatrix's emotional perspective continues and culminates with her final act of revenge: the killing of Bill (David Carradine) through her use of the five-point palm exploding-heart technique. Beatrix's reason for revenge is that Bill arranged on the day of her wedding rehearsal to have her bridegroom and everyone in attendance killed, courtesy of the Deadly Viper Assassination Squad. Bill himself put the apparently fatal bullet through Beatrix's skull, but she survived. Until the climax of *Vol. 2*, Beatrix had also understood that her unborn child was also killed that day, an assumption that turns out to be false.

It is evident that the sequence in which Beatrix finally kills Bill involves reference to major existing genres: the music and impossible physical choreography of martial arts cinema as the two engage in brief swordplay while seated at a table, and the music and iconography of the Western as Bill walks to his death. Here, styles are borrowed from two genres simultaneously but it is also the case that this moment between these characters is defined by a contemplative tone, and is especially settled in the context of this highly kinetic film (the moment of seated combat a matter of mere seconds). It is as though the characters are able to exist temporarily apart from the world of violent motion that they have been immersed in up to this point; they are uniquely allowed the time and space to meditate upon events that have passed between them.

Once Beatrix has delivered her decisive strike, the soundtrack shifts to a pared-down, acoustic arrangement and the editing rhythm settles into a steady sequence of reverse close-ups. Within this aesthetic arrangement, Beatrix and Bill's conversation is guided by an impulse for honest exchange, removed from the self-conscious, smart and witty show of language that has almost defined communication in the films. In this sense, Beatrix's fatal blow returns the effect of the serum dart that Bill shot into her in a preceding scene, injecting fresh honesty into their exchange. They are themselves. Once death is a certainty for Bill, the need for performance and posturing is perhaps ended. The couple look unflinchingly into each other's eyes now, in calm acceptance rather than hostile intimidation. They are wilfully exposed. On his asking why she never told him that Pai Mei (Gordon Liu), their shared martial arts mentor, taught her the five-point exploding-heart technique, Beatrix replies simply, 'I don't know.' While in another context this might be read as self-consciously evasive, in this moment we come to understand it as her admission that her decisions and instincts can be mysterious to her as well: that she can be guided by them almost against her conscious will. Her subsequent description of herself as a 'bad person' is countered by Bill's tenderly worded reassurance: 'You're not a bad person. You're a terrific person. You're my favourite person.' The words bring tears to Beatrix's eyes and she closes them momentarily, moved by his sentiment and sensitivity.

He goes on to make a joke about her being a 'real cunt' once in a while, confirming that humour can also still exist between them, and crucially that they can still *share* a sense of humour. The choice of the word 'cunt' is striking in that it is still a jarring term (not part of anyone else's vocabulary in either films) and given further impact here as the final word of Bill's sentence. The minor shock of its use recalls something of the violence that has existed between these characters, now diminished and reduced only to a verbal jolt in an otherwise gentle moment of humorous teasing. It is as though that world of violence,

revenge and brutality is diminished: its traits can no longer impose themselves on these characters.

Then it is Beatrix's turn for reassurance as Bill wipes the blood from his mouth and face and asks her, 'How do I look?' She pauses, apparently on the verge of breaking down, touches his hand and replies softly, 'You look ready.' This can be read in terms of generic reference, of Bill being ready to enact a climax befitting a Western movie, but it also brings to mind an exchange that might occur in a domestic conversation between partners, lending an air of everyday security to this event that takes the sting out of one person telling another that they are ready to die. The effect is furthered as Bill fastens one button and straightens his jacket before walking purposefully away from Beatrix, his actions resembling the routine of a husband preparing to leave the marital home.

The domesticity inherent in the moment reinforces the familial unity that exists briefly between these characters now, at the end: the extent to which they know and trust one another absolutely for only these few moments before death. A reversal occurs, then, as the quest for revenge ends not in one character finding decisive satisfaction in killing the other, but in them both finding comfort in one another, albeit an impossible mutuality that cannot be sustained. Where we might have anticipated a defining culmination of four years' worth of hate, we instead find that these two killers modestly express their profound affection for one another.

We might conclude that this moment is out of step with the tone and mood of the rest of the *Kill Bill* series, to the extent that it becomes an unconvincing climax to what has, in any case, been a somewhat unevenly structured narrative. This is not dissimilar to the view adopted by a number of critics, with Philip French, for example, seeing it

as an incongruously sentimental ending to a 'hollow' pair of films.[3] From there it is no leap to start thinking about the films as exercises or lessons in borrowing styles. But, in avoiding that assessment, I want to suggest that the film complements sincerely the emotional perspective of its heroine in this moment, just as much as the earlier more energetically styled sequences in the films corresponded with her frantic search for revenge. As the film apparently suspends the world for this moment of intimacy between the two characters, so an alignment is created with Beatrix's profound need for pause and reflection. If we take this as a surprising, or a surprisingly sentimental, occurrence, it is also the case that Beatrix herself is caught out by the strong sentimentality she feels towards Bill when the moment of her revenge is exacted. This is certainly the effect Thurman creates in her acting of the scene, as she struggles to reconcile herself with the reticence and reflection inherent in their moment together. Throughout the films, the style of representation has kept pace with its central character's emotions, creating a fragmented aesthetic that altered with her changes in perspective and intensity. In this climactic moment, then, the film rewards Beatrix's contrasting desire for quietness, stillness and resignation. Crucially, this shifting of style and tone succeeds in bringing us *closer* to the fact of this character as a human being within a discernible fictional world. As she sits, Beatrix too reflects upon the conditions of the world she inhabits, the nature of the decisions she has taken within it and her ultimate relationship to the man who has shaped her identity within that world. Here the film reminds us of the reality of its fictional world, and avoids portraying Beatrix as a representation or pastiche of a type borrowed from cinematic codes found elsewhere. She is a woman facing the consequences of a world alone.

The moment might offer a kind of happiness, but we shouldn't be too quick to assume that the characters have been shuffled awkwardly towards a happy conclusion. Likewise, we might resist suggestions that the individuals have been slotted into scenarios whose chief effect is the replication of certain genres and styles of film-making. In raising the notion that synthesis exists between character and style in the *Kill Bill* films, and that this represents an achievement, I am suggesting that understanding a film's fiction relies upon understanding the manner in which a fictional world is presented to us. The film-maker stands between their audience and the world they wish to portray, with any number of potentials available to them. Tarantino proves himself to be an agile compiler of genres and styles in his films, composing collage works of shifting tones and moods. His skill in the moment described lies in his ability to suspend those techniques to create a contrasting mood of stillness and calm, complementing fundamentally the emotional perspective of Beatrix Kiddo.

NOTES

1. M. Keith Booker, *Postmodern Hollywood: What's New in Film and Why It Makes Us Feel So Strange* (London: Praeger, 2007), p. 93.
2. Edward Gallafent, *Quentin Tarantino* (Harlow: Pearson, 2006), pp. 99–120.
3. Philip French, 'Mother of All Battles', *Observer*, April 2004.

BIBLIOGRAPHY

Booker, M. Keith, *Postmodern Hollywood: What's New in Film and Why It Makes Us Feel So Strange* (London: Praeger, 2007).
French, Philip, 'Mother of All Battles', *Observer*, April 2004.
Gallafent, Edward, *Quentin Tarantino* (Harlow: Pearson, 2006).

The Moves: *Blood* (1989)

ADRIAN MARTIN

A life is ethical not when it simply submits to moral laws but when it accepts putting itself into play in its gestures, irrevocably and without reserve – even at the risk that its happiness or its disgrace will be decided once and for all.

Giorgio Agamben[1]

Looking back at *Tout va bien* (1972), the film he co-directed with Jean-Luc Godard, Jean-Pierre Gorin remarked in 1987: 'It's not a great movie, but it does have *moves* – and you can't say that about every film.'[2] A film that makes moves: what could this mean? In my view, the concept does not refer to the literal, physical movements of either the performers or the camera (although it can include these elements). It does not necessarily involve powerfully dramatic (or comic) large-scale alterations in plot. It does not have to entail any grand-slam subversion of social, ideological or cultural conventions. But something, in a filmic move, will indeed have to shift, perhaps gently, but tellingly so.

A cinematic move is something like the category of the *gesture* in the philosophy of Giorgio Agamben. He gives a splendid example from Dostoevsky's 1869 novel *The Idiot*, when Nastasya, in the midst of a tense domestic power game, impulsively decides to hurl a bag of 100,000 rubles into the fire. The character, according to Agamben, is not guided by 'anything like a rational decision or a moral principle', by anything that is predetermined by will or reflection, but rather appears to be 'gripped by a delirium'.[3] This moment of decisive but blind action, fantastic and unexpected, henceforth changes everything in the lives of the characters, as well as in Dostoevsky's narrative itself. We could also think of this gesture as a moment of *turbulence*, arising mysteriously but with absolute rightness amid the flow of fictional life. Screenwriter-theorist Yvette Bíró uses these terms – a moment prompted by the interplay of complex subterranean forces, and immediately compelling radical change or transformation.[4] Shigehiko Hasumi makes a similar point in relation to the surprisingly crucial role played by seemingly banal, endlessly repeated observations about the sunny weather in Yasujiro Ozu's films:

Such references are not at all theatrical; they bring about a narrative transformation, play a role similar to a punctuation mark by shifting an episode to the next scene ... . We might say that, with these exchanges as opportunities, the film *moves*.[5]

To make a move: it means (in cinema as in life) to scramble the bases, rearrange the given elements of a scene or situation. For a film, it especially means imaginatively exploiting, from moment to moment, all the resources of *surprise* – from sly wit to outright shock – on all available levels of cinematic form and content (characterisation, performance, narrative, *mise en scène*, rhythm, montage, sound, plastic treatment of the image). There are those film-makers who prepare their comparatively few moves very slowly and gradually (Ozu, Erice, Dreyer), and there are those who merrily multiply the surprising, table-turning strategies (Lubitsch, Godard, Boris Barnet). Making a move implies, on its creator's part, a willingness (so rare in cinema) to consider any fragment as not fixed or given in advance (in the scenario, say, or in the iron-clad logic of the fiction's world) – but open, at every second, to potential revision, to a redrawing. The challenge for us, as viewers, is to grasp the stirring of moves in the smallest, most material levels of cinema – not simply in the sudden, extravagant gesture of a character or a carefully prepared narrative turning point.

A rich example of micro-moves, one atop the other, is provided by the Portuguese director Pedro Costa in his low-budget, black-and-white, début feature, *Blood/O Sangue* (1989). This is a highly charged but enigmatic film about family life, and the fraught rite of passage for children once they are freed from the 'symbolic order' of their home. The passage on which I will concentrate comprises a mere eight shots, running less than a minute in total. It occurs twenty-one minutes into the film (coinciding with the beginning of chapter 4 on the Second Run DVD edition); the pieces of narrative leading up to it have been deliberately elliptical, wandering and mysterious. The centre of the plot, to this point, would appear to be the difficult relationship between a father (Canto e Castro) and his two sons, Vicente (Pedro Hestnes) and Nino (Nuno Ferreira); just before the scene under discussion, the father has passed away, a fact that Vicente is determined to hide from public knowledge. According to Yvette Bíró, a key way that a film finds and reaches its deepest thread is by appearing to meander, to lose itself in detours. *Blood* proceeds in exactly this way. By the time we reach the scene in question, the film has already deftly lost what appeared to be its main thread by following the lure of diversions: the scene of a teacher, Clara (Inês de Medeiros), with the small children in her care; a search for two runaway kids near a river. Stealthily – as we shall see – the ground is being prepared for a major moment of intensity, a turning point that is dramatic but beyond any strict (or even loose) cause-and-effect logic of linear narrative connections.

What now takes place is a true anthology piece, a condensed moment of pure cinema – executed with modest, minimal production resources (two main actors, a few kids and props, a real street, a passing cyclist). It resonates deeply in its context, but works almost as well upon members of an audience who experience it detached, suspended outside its wider narrative frame. In Costa's loose, treatment-like script, the action might have read like this, simply and briefly. A man (Vicente) follows, at a distance, a woman (Clara) along the street. Some time passes. Finally, he catches up with her and poses a grave question. One could imagine many ways of staging and filming this scene – some rather banal, or merely functional. One can also imagine the action being covered in either very few shots (perhaps only one, with a dissolve to mark the necessary temporal ellipse), or analytically dissected into many shots in a Hitchcockian style.

Something odd and intense about this scene should be noted at the outset. Clara and Vicente are not strangers to each other; we have already seen them search together for the runaway children. And yet Vicente's action casts him (generically speaking) in the role of a stalker, spying and trailing Clara from a distance. However, *Blood* is not a mystery-thriller. Clearly, Vicente is holding back, preparing himself and building up the courage to pose his proposition (whose content we do not know until he utters it – and even then only elliptically) to Clara. Such moments of waiting, in which something unsaid or not yet said is stirring and brewing, are crucial in the form of international, contemplative cinema in which Costa has come to be a figurehead in the years since *Blood*.

In the first shot of this passage we see Clara accompanying three small children who gather about her – kids from the kindergarten where she works. Sparse natural sound from the street occupies the soundtrack; there is no music. Costa's camera tracks this action from behind, keeping the figures in the centre of the frame. This distance (neither a conventional close shot nor a conventional long shot) maintains a good deal of space, and registers much detail of the street, in the image. Planned or not, a small bit of business dynamises this opening shot: while the camera, Clara and two children keep moving, a boy in the company has to stop for a moment, fix his shoelace, and then catch up with his companions.

The change to shot 2 marks the first move. The camera is tracking in front of Vicente, as he intently watches and briskly paces. It is a mid-shot, with a more focused concentration on the human figure – location detail (such as a background bridge) occupies only the bottom quarter of the frame, while Vicente's head looms in the sky's whiteness. This shot change carries a slight shock effect which is akin to Martin Scorsese's frequent surprise tactics: suddenly we read, retroactively, the preceding shot not as Costa's camera following or recording the action, but as Vicente's subjective point of view; the distance between camera and figures is instantly recoded as the distance between Vicente and Clara.

This would be a common enough device in any decent thriller. But the switch to shot 3 takes us from Hitchcock territory to the Bressonian legacy which is so powerful in Costa's work. A disquieting ellipse occurs. It is another shot of Vicente, but the light on him has changed, he is now slightly off centre in the frame, he is completely surrounded by the walls of dwellings, and his pace has slowed; only his gaze on the 'target' remains fixed as before. This superb cut is simultaneously concrete and abstract in its effect: it signifies (as in a screenplay indication) 'later', but the exact interval (minutes? hours?) is indeterminate. Note, here, the strict, lean economy of stylistic means: where so many other film-makers would have been tempted to continue the alternation between the mobile set-ups in shots 1 and 2 – to 'double-cut', in the

astute terminology of John Cassavetes[6] – Costa pares away such (to him) redundant repetitions.

So far: three shots, two moves. Now the tempo quickens, the action becomes 'thicker', and many micro-moves enter this intimist fray. (It is frequently useful to gauge the modulation and articulation of elements in any well-realised film scene in terms of a thickening and thinning.) We see Clara again, much closer in now, entering the frame from its left side. She is walking at a different, brisker pace than we saw previously, and the children have departed, disappeared. Something in the order of an event then occurs in this fourth shot: a boy on a bicycle blocks Clara's path, its bell providing the first really distinct, individual sound effect of the scene, above the murmur of the street and the audible trace of footsteps. Clara stops, but the camera does not cease its quick movement towards her (the energy of this motion again recalls Scorsese, or Samuel Fuller). She turns her head and smiles at the presence off screen whom she recognises.

But then – with the camera still travelling in – there is another surprise move, both in the literal and figurative senses: Vicente's arm shoots into frame from the right, as he places his hand on Clara's arm. This move would not be out of place in a Brian De Palma or P. T. Anderson film: what at first appears to be a subjective POV shot is transformed into an objective view, when the 'looker' enters what seems to be the field of his own gaze. On top of all this, in the chain reaction of these few brief seconds, Vicente's gesture causes a small but notable catastrophe: Clara drops her books. The camera has halted at her head as she tilts it to look down at the ground, and now it whips down with her (a reframing in the unostentatious, Fritz Lang mode), holding the close-up.

After this very packed shot, a fast flurry. Shot 5, a low angle on Vicente, is brief, and creates an instant rhyming of

body movements: where she went down, he at first rises slightly (as if in hesitation, or fear) and then lowers himself. And yet this short shot has a particular emotional tenor: it creates a split-second pause on Vicente and a soulful complicity with him, as he readies (as we will soon discover) to at last speak his (presumably long-imagined or rehearsed) entreaty. Shot 6, then, marks a key moment of their interaction: in a very Bressonian play of bodily extremities (framed against the spilt books on the ground), she grasps his bandaged hand (which he has wounded in a previous scene) and turns it over, revealing the blood seeping from his palm. Shot 7 returns to the same set-up as shot 5, but – in this transformation of repetition into difference that is constitutive of Costa's style – instantly introduces the first spoken words of the scene: 'Salva-me … . Só confio em ti' (English subtitles: 'Save me! You're the only one I trust'). This sublimely grave, even melodramatic, utterance itself constitutes a move: here indeed, as per Agamben, in this verbal gesture, a life 'puts itself into play'.

The end of the scene (shot 8) has already arrived. The angle on Clara is very similar to where we left her at the end of shot 4. It could be the same set-up or a different take of it, but variation is provided by the fact that the camera is now even closer to her face. At first – again, as if hesitating, as Vicente did only moments ago – she keeps her head down, but then lifts it up, staring off screen into his eyes. Wind blows hair across her face and the lighting is noticeably different from all previous shots: an effect of overexposure, of bleached-out saturation that is familiar from cinematographer Martin Schäfer's work with Wim Wenders on *Kings of the Road* (1976). Clara returns Vicente's gaze and appears set to respond to the force of his life-or-death question; but no spoken answer comes.

Instead, Costa stretches out the open moment of her contemplation. Music intrudes for the first time in the scene: sampled notes from an orchestral piece by Stravinsky, suspended phrases separated by dramatic silences. Then the light on Clara's face softens as an overlapping dissolve begins: the beginning of the following scene, Vicente driving his motorbike in the dark veil of night that is punctuated by a string of bright city lights. Costa deliberately holds the overlay of both images – Clara's face and the darkness – for longer than might be expected. Plus something truly miraculous, and not a little nostalgic, happens within the materiality of the image work: as in an old Hollywood film, this 'special effect' of the dissolve comes with added slow motion. After blinking several times in this slowed-down pose, Clara tilts her head back to the ground, and there is a fast fade-out. The music continues, and the transition to the next scene is now complete.

Let us note the principle – no doubt derived by Costa from several 'minimalist' masters – of strategic stylistic withholding for maximal cinematic effect: one by one, during the fifty or so seconds I have considered, we are present at the 'birth' of sound effects, of dialogue, of music, of inventive and expressive camera framings or movements ... . Even more centrally, where this scene began is, forcibly, not where it ends: it started with Vicente's subjective point of view (albeit with the signalling of this delayed for ten seconds), and it concludes with Clara's inner experience, conveyed not in a POV gaze but on other, multiple levels: framing, editing decision, musical 'sting', slow motion, dissolve. A remarkable journey, and a complete switch-around, in under a minute: these are the moves. Something has truly *happened* in this scene, and we feel it – even if, at this point of the unfolding of *Blood*, we cannot yet fully say what it is.

And for us, as viewers, it is not so much a matter of 'reading' these moves – of interpreting them – as of simply but carefully and sensitively *following* them: staying alert to the shocks, surprises, fluctuations, tremblings, intensities. Moves are on, and of, the cinematic surface; they are the palpable, visible, audible articulations of the filmic material. Depth happens elsewhere: at the level of what I have called the 'inner life' of a film by Costa, its dense web or lattice-work of patterned interrelations between moves, its overall atomic cell of particles ceaselessly rearranging themselves.[7] 'All the rest is psychology,' comments Agamben, 'and nowhere in psychology do we encounter anything like an ethical subject, a form of life.'[8]

NOTES

1. Giorgio Agamben, 'The Author as Gesture', in *Profanations* [trans. Jeff Fort] (New York: Zone Books, 2007), p. 69.
2. Spoken on the stage of the Melbourne International Film Festival, Australia 1987.
3. Agamben, 'The Author as Gesture', p. 69.
4. See Yvette Bíró, *Turbulence and Flow in Film: The Rhythmic Design* (Bloomington and Indianapolis: Indiana University Press, 2008).

5. Shigehiko Hasumi, 'Sunny Skies', in David Desser (ed.), *Ozu's Tokyo Story* (Cambridge: Cambridge University Press, 1997), pp. 125–6.
6. Interview with Cassavetes, in Joseph Gelmis, *The Film Director as Superstar* (London: Penguin, 1970), p. 125.
7. See my 'A vida interior de um filme'/'The Inner Life of a Film', in Ricardo Matos Cabo, *Cem mil cigarros – os filmes de Pedro Costa* (Lisbon: Orfeu Negro, 2009), pp. 91–8; an extract from the English-language original appears in the booklet accompanying the Second Run DVD of *Blood*. See also Raymond Durgnat, '... And in Theory: Towards a Superficial Structuralism', *Monthly Film Bulletin* no. 609 (October 1984), pp. 313–15.
8. Agamben, 'The Author as Gesture', p. 72.

BIBILIOGRAPHY

Agamben, Giorgio, *Profanations* [trans. Jeff Fort] (New York: Zone Books, 2007).

Bíró, Yvette, *Turbulence and Flow in Film: The Rhythmic Design* (Bloomington and Indianapolis: Indiana University Press, 2008).

Cabo, Ricardo Matos (ed.), *Cem mil cigarros – os filmes de Pedro Costa* (Lisbon: Orfeu Negro, 2009).

Cassavetes, John, 'Interview with John Cassavetes', in Joseph Gelmis, *The Film Director as Superstar* (London: Penguin, 1970).

Desser, David (ed.), *Ozu's Tokyo Story* (Cambridge: Cambridge University Press, 1997).

Durgnat, Raymond, '... And in Theory: Towards a Superficial Structuralism', *Monthly Film Bulletin* no. 609, October 1984.

Gelmis, Joseph, *The Film Director as Superstar* (London: Penguin, 1970).

Hasumi, Shigehiko, 'Sunny Skies', in David Desser (ed.), *Ozu's Tokyo Story* (Cambridge: Cambridge University Press, 1997).

Martin, Adrian, 'A vida interior de um filme', in Ricardo Matos Cabo (ed.), *Cem mil cigarros – os filmes de Pedro Costa* (Lisbon: Orfeu Negro, 2009).

The Properties of Images: *Lust for Life* (1956)

STEVE NEALE

Lust for Life is a biopic about the Dutch-born artist, Vincent Van Gogh. It was produced by John Houseman, scripted by Norman Corwin from Irving Stone's novel, and directed by Vincente Minnelli for MGM. Starring Kirk Douglas as Vincent Van Gogh and Anthony Quinn as Gauguin, it also featured James Donald as Vincent's brother Theo, Pamela Brown as Christine, and Jeanette Sterke as Vincent's cousin Kay. The film was photographed in CinemaScope and Metrocolor (the MGM brand name for Ansco Color) by Russell Harlan at the MGM Studios in Los Angeles and by F. A. (Freddie) Young on location in Belgium, Holland and France. It premièred in the USA on 17 September 1956. By this time, the aspect ratio for CinemaScope films had become standardised at 2.35:1. (The ratio had been 2.66:1 for Scope films released in 1953 and 2.55:1 for Scope films released in 1954 and 1955.) It remains unclear as to whether the version of Ansco Color used in the filming of *Lust for Life* was a new or an old one.[1] Either way, along with properties of the moving image, the capacity of the camera to frame and reframe still and moving images, and the ability of filmmakers to select and edit in sequence a number of different views of any setting, staging or subject, the properties of Ansco Color, and the proportions of CinemaScope in particular, played key roles in *Lust for Life*'s aesthetic concerns.

Lust for Life begins in Belgium. Having been interviewed, appointed, then dismissed as a Christian minister, Vincent returns home to his family in Holland. He spends a lot of time drawing. He also falls in love with Kay. Kay rejects his offer of marriage and Vincent is in despair. However, he meets Christine and moves in with her and her baby. He is happy and productive. The apartment they live in is strewn with his maquettes and pictures. Vincent is shown drawing a picture of Christine and the baby. A little later on, he is shown attempting to paint a full-length portrait of Christine on a nearby beach. This scene is the focus of this essay, though reference will be made to other shots, scenes and moments too.

The scene on the beach consists of three shots. The first begins with a dissolve from a view through the window of Christine and Vincent's apartment (with Vincent and the baby playing on the left on Vincent's desk) to a view of the wind-tossed sea. The camera tracks back to reveal fishermen gathering nets on a boat on the beach. The second shows Vincent from behind in three-quarter profile. He is just in front of the portrait, which is now nearly finished but still incomplete, and which is fully visible in the centre of the widescreen frame. Christine herself is slightly further away from the camera, posing on the left. Her clothes are blowing in the wind. Behind her, stretching across the width of the frame, are the sea, the shoreline and, on the right-hand side, two boats and a number of fishermen.

The fishermen, five in all, become fully visible when Vincent bends down to replenish his brush. He is struggling to complete the picture and Christine is getting tired. She tells him that she is going to feed the baby and walks away into the foreground.

A 180-degree, reverse-angle cut precedes the third and final shot. Christine is now shown from behind on the right-hand side of the frame as she continues to walk away. Vincent and his canvas are on the left, and the reverse-angle view means that the image on the canvas is no longer visible.

(As in the second shot, the extent to which visibility is dependent on viewpoint as well as on the nature and proportion of frames is here brought to the fore.) Trying to persuade her to stay, Vincent crosses the frame from left to right towards the figure of Christine. As he does so, a gust of wind blows the canvas off its easel and out of frame left. He begins to follow the canvas, turns back to plead further with Christine, then runs out of frame left in pursuit of the picture as Christine walks away from the camera and into the middle distance on the right. The scene ends at this point, with a dissolve to an interior view through the window of the apartment some time later. Christine pulls a curtain across the window, thus blocking out the view through the window's frame. The camera tracks back to frame Christine and Vincent in medium long shot as the next scene continues.

The scene on the beach is one of a number of scenes in which Vincent is shown as struggling, and often failing, to realise his aims, to control his life and his environment, and to engage successfully with those he loves, admires or depends on. The subsequent scene in the apartment, in which he and Christine argue about money, is another. So, too, is an earlier scene in which he tries to persuade Kay to marry him; the later scene in which he fails to persuade Gauguin to remain with him in Provence; and the scenes in which, as in the beach scene, he tries but fails to represent the world around him in his paintings and drawings. (A later example is the scene in which he and Gauguin attempt to paint the landscape in Provence in the midst of a mistral.) There are several forms of failure in the beach scene itself. Vincent fails to finish the portrait because his canvas is blown away, because he fails to control the physical conditions in which he is working. He also fails because he fails to persuade Christine to stay, because he is so impractical, so demanding and so single-minded that he alienates the person on whose love and co-operation he here depends. These failures in turn mean that he does not succeed in painting Christine's portrait as he set out to do.

These failures all entail, or are marked by, movement and time. Christine walks away. The canvas is blown away by the wind. Both events involve motion and duration, and both occur before Vincent has had time to finish his portrait. A finished portrait consists of a definitive configuration of visual ingredients. The configuration of ingredients in a portrait-in-process may be altered prior to completion or else left incomplete. But in all Vincent's failures the ingredients themselves are always immobile. Thus, while there is always an element of contrast between a finished and an unfinished picture, an element of contrast dependent on time, there is also an element of similarity, an element marked by the absence of motion. The other elements of contrast in the beach scene are those between the immobile image on Vincent's canvas and the mobility of the canvas itself, those between the immobile figure in

Vincent's painting and the wind-blown figure who walks away, and those between the immobile configurations in any kind of painting or drawing and the ever-changing ones that mark both the world we see around us and the world as represented in a time-based, moving-image medium such as film.

Contrasts of this kind occur throughout *Lust for Life*. They are apparent in nearly every scene in which Vincent is shown engaged in drawing or painting. But they are apparent in other kinds of scenes as well. At one point *Lust for Life* reconstructs the 1889 painting, 'Vincent's Bedroom in Arles', which we have been shown in the previous shot. Initially the reconstruction is still, just like the painting. But after a few moments, Vincent's coat flies across the frame and the room from right to left, followed by the figure of Vincent himself. Vincent's movements, those of the coat and those of a towel on a peg on the wall on the left-hand side, which is blown gently by a breeze coming through the window, all alter the previously fixed configuration of the shot, thus marking its temporal dimensions and drawing attention to one of the major differences between a filmed and a painted image. Earlier on, in the sequence in Paris, Vincent is shown engaged in discussion while standing in front of 'A Sunday Afternoon on the Island of La Grande Jatte', one of Seurat's paintings. At one point, he pauses in profile. Looking just like one of the statuesque figures in 'La Grande Jatte', he momentarily becomes part of a still composition that includes both himself and Seurat's painting. But he is soon shown in motion again in a manner that not only contrasts with the figures in the painting but that paintings themselves cannot depict.

Sometimes contrasts such as these depend on the respective proportional properties of the CinemaScope frame and Vincent's paintings and drawings. In these instances, the width of the frame is often used to display the views Vincent depicts alongside the depictions themselves. Thus, in shot two of the beach scene, we are shown Christine on the left-hand side of the frame and Vincent's portrait-in-progress in the centre. In addition, we are shown a number of things that are not in Vincent's portrait, notably the fishing boats and fishermen on the right-hand side of the frame (who, as already noted, can only be seen when Vincent bends down, when his movement changes the configuration of the image and what is visible within it from the camera's position). In shot 1, we can see the sea in close-up, but only one of the boats and three of the fishermen. In shot 3 we are unable to see any of these things. But we *are* able to see a number of things we have been unable to see before: the back of Vincent's canvas, the sand dunes in the rear and the small wooden hut on the right.

In all these ways, the sequential as well as the simultaneous juxtapositions of still and moving images in the beach scene are used to highlight the ways in which fram- ings, mobile or fixed, narrow or wide, close or distant or somewhere in between, determine not only what we see, but also what we do not see, not only what framings include, but also what they exclude. A particularly marked example can be found later in the scene in which Vincent visits Theo and his family prior to moving on to Auvers.

This scene consists of a single three-minute take. It begins with Theo's wife, Johanna (Toni Gerry), framed by the living-room window in medium long shot. She waves at Vincent and Theo on their way to the apartment, who she can see in the street through the window but who we are unable to see from the camera's viewpoint. The camera tracks with her as she crosses the room from right to left to greet them, pausing to check her hair in an oval mirror. The camera resumes its movement as she continues to cross the room, then pauses once again as she walks through an open inner doorway toward the outer door. Framed through the inner doorway, Johanna opens the outer door. Vincent and Theo enter the camera's field of vision as they rush up the stairs to greet her. As they all enter the room through the inner doorway, the camera resumes its move- ments, tracking and panning from left to right. It pauses again as they themselves pause and Vincent asks to see his new baby nephew. At this point they are all standing in front of the mirror but, with the exception of a brief glimpse of Theo as he rushes out of frame, their reflections cannot be seen. This changes, though, when Johanna and Vincent follow Theo out of frame right as they all cross the room to see the baby. Instead of panning or tracking with them, the camera tracks forward towards the mirror. As it

does so, the moving reflections of all three characters (though not that of the baby) appear in its frame.

This scene continues for another two minutes. During this time Vincent draws attention to the number of his paintings that are mounted on the apartment wall behind him. But by then it is already clear that one of the purposes of the scene and the way it is shot is to investigate the respective properties and possibilities not just of framings and frames (including those formed by doorways and win- dows), nor just of still and moving pictures, nor just of drawn or painted or filmed or mirrored images, but of images as such. These are modernist concerns. But *Lust for Life* is not a modernist film. It does not flaunt the nature of its aesthetic interests in the manner of an avant-garde or art film. Indeed, its interests are so subtly integrated into the telling of its story that they appear not to have been noticed before.

NOTE

1. In his commentary on the *Lust for Life* DVD (Warner Home Video, 2006), Drew Casper claims that the version used was new. In his autobiography, *I Remember It Well* (London: Angus & Robertson, 1975), p. 289, Minnelli himself claimed that he used the last remaining batch of an old one. Minnelli's account is probably correct, as Ansco ceased production of its colour stock for professional productions shortly thereafter.

BIBLIOGRAPHY

Minnelli, Vincente, *I Remember It Well* (London: Angus & Robertson, 1975).

Two Views over Water: Action and Absorption in Ingmar Bergman's *Wild Strawberries* (1957)

EDWARD GALLAFENT

The moment that I wish to reflect on occurs during the last two minutes of *Wild Strawberries/Smultronstället* (1957). It is an image seen from the point of view of the film's protagonist, an old, much-honoured professor (Isak Borg, played by Victor Sjöström). He is looking across a calm sound or inlet to a spit of land on the other side. Near the centre of the image is Isak's father, his fishing rod making a long diagonal which is continued downwards in the line made by the edge of the reflections of trees in the water, so that the line bisects the figure of the father and his reflection. A few feet away sits Isak's mother, and just to her left is a parasol, canted at an angle parallel to the line of the fishing rod.

Two insights have been offered by several of Bergman's critics regarding this image. The first is that it resembles a tableau or a painting.[1] The elements of the composition are clearly intended to confront us with the presence of careful design, to make the resemblance unavoidable. But why?

Less attention has been given to the meaning of this acknowledgment, or invocation, of the painterly. If this is like a painting, what kind of canvas are we thinking of?

The second critical point is that the image represents a reconciliation between Isak and his parents, and this is a moment of great positive value.[2] But again this is a little puzzling. Isak's mother has been treated at length earlier in the film – it is not self-evident that she needs to recur at its close – and his father has been out of the way for all of the narrative up to this moment. Is the meaning of introducing them here so obvious?

My argument is that, while the nature of the image has been broadly correctly identified, its significance has perhaps been too briskly assumed, taken to serve as part of a positive conclusion to the film, but not read for the significance of its local context and the specific kind of painterly image that is invoked.

To pursue this train of thought we will need to retrace our steps a little. I want to go back, to rewind the film about five minutes in time, so to speak. I take it that *Wild Strawberries* is too well known to need its plot summarising; we have arrived at the point at which Isak, having accepted the jubilee doctorate conferred by his old university in Lund, has returned to his son's house, where he will retire to bed while the younger generations engage in their amusements of the evening.

We see a trio of encounters that are also departures, as if characters are leaving a stage. The first of these is Isak's long-standing housekeeper, Miss Agda (Jullan Kindahl), appropriately enough in that this relation was one of the strands which began the film. Bergman cuts directly from the degree ceremony to the bedroom in which Isak will sleep. The scene introduces the idea of old age as invoking, or recovering, a kind of childhood: Isak is already in pyjamas and dressing gown while Miss Agda still wears her handsome dress. Isak must retire to bed some time before the surrounding adults, even before this grandmotherly figure: shortly she will ask him if he has cleaned his teeth. The encounter begins with some sparring, as Isak apologises for his behaviour earlier in the day, and is treated sharply – 'Are you ill, professor?'[3] – as if apology must be a kind of malady in such a man. He goes on to suggest that now, as the two of them have known each other 'for a lifetime', they might drop the formal titles in addressing each other. I take this to be not so much a genuine question as a kind of gift, a presentation of an opportunity. Miss Agda will of course refuse and thus offer Isak the opening to feed her a line, one about her doing what is right, and give her the satisfaction of replying 'almost always', a nice moment of pride and reservation. The sequence ends on a note of the nurture that she provides: a listening ear in the watches of the night.

The next to depart is Sara, the girl who, accompanied by a couple of young men, has hitched a lift with Isak to Lund. She is also (by virtue of having the same name and being played by the same actress, Bibi Andersson) a kind of a ghost, that of the cousin Isak might have, or could have, or should have, married: a figure who has appeared earlier in the film. Here the trio have been marking their farewell by serenading Isak. Sara's final call to Isak – 'Know that it's you that I love, today, tomorrow and forever' – allows for a happy coincidence, between the exuberance of a young girl who is conscious of being the object of ideas, or hopes, of love and what Isak might now feel about his memory of his cousin Sara, that she represented the eternal stirring of those feelings rather than their finding any mooring in the literal world. It is as if by some fabulous piece of luck the words strike exactly the right chord, and she departs, forever lost to Isak and forever preserved by him.

The final scene addresses the present reality of relations in the Borg family, between Isak and Evald (Gunnar Björnstrand) and Marianne (Ingrid Thulin), his son and daughter-in-law. Isak is now in bed, and the note that he is allowing himself to occupy the place of a child in this household is strongly sounded, as the adults return briefly to the house. This is the result of a trivial accident – Marianne has to change her shoes – and she peeks in on Isak: 'I think he's asleep.' Isak now calls out to Evald. The subject of their conversation is the state of Evald's marriage, but the dialogue plays much as if an anxious child is reassuring himself about his parents' situation, rather than working only, or primarily, on the level of a father enquiring about his son's marital position. The final confirmation of this scenario is the appearance of Marianne, unmistakably in the role of the glamorous mother figure, who arrives to show off her dancing shoes to this child for a moment, to exchange endearments and to bestow a night-time kiss.[4] It is part of the force of this moment that we know Marianne to be pregnant; we might say that it is a shadow of another night that may come to pass if this marriage survives, and, being such a portent, perhaps implies that it

might do so. Marianne and Evald depart, leaving Isak to his slumbers.

All is happily, almost idealistically, concluded. We could say the passage that will follow it is unnecessary in terms of the preceding narrative. The body of the film has mainly addressed Isak's relations to a number of women and one man (Evald), and, as we have seen, Bergman has employed the sequences leading up to this point to bring those relations to a series of conclusions. With a few words in voiceover, the mode in which it opened, the film could now end as Isak drifts into sleep. But Bergman wants to show us something else.

Lying in bed, Isak makes a declaration to us: 'If I have been feeling worried or sad during the day I have a habit of recalling scenes from childhood to calm me.' What follows is not exactly a recollection but something we take to be a scene created out of the materials of childhood. I will sketch some elements of it:

1   We dissolve to a familiar image, a shot of the family summer-house which featured in earlier parts of the film. It is still evidently the same long-ago summer, but now the wind is blowing, and there are 'no more wild strawberries'. Isak appears: as earlier, his body is that of the old man of the film's present time.

2   From a distance, Isak watches his family at a quay-side boarding a small yacht. One of the older children is pushed into the choppy water; a lifebelt is thrown to accompanying shouts and laughter.

3   Isak and his companion (the Sara of that past time) exchange smiles and leave this group to their fun. Announcing that she will help him find his father and mother, Sara takes his hand and leads him through wood and field. They arrive at a vantage point, and she gestures with her free hand.

4   The shot that follows is from their point of view, and is the image with which I began this discussion (p. 30). The couple respond to Isak and Sara's presence; the mother waves and the father briefly looks in their direction.

5   We cut to a medium shot of Isak watching, scarcely aware that Sara is departing. Bergman sustains the shot until the last trace of her disappears, leaving Isak alone.

6   We cut back to the parents; the framing is exactly the same as in (4). They have resumed their occupations and pay no further attention to the observing figure.

7   We cut to Isak and the camera moves in slowly on his smiling face as he contemplates his parents' image.

8   There is a dissolve to Isak in bed, and the film ends.

To read this sequence we need first to observe that a shift has taken place in Isak's relation to the figures in his past. In his earliest visions he was invisible to that world, unable to do more than watch and listen as it unfolded. Later he was present to these figures, say in his nightmare of the medical examination or the scene in which Sara showed him his aged face in a mirror, but their relation to him was partly or wholly negative. Here for the first time he is both present (to Sara) and welcomed by her. This is to say, for the first time, his experience is not a matter of the isolation of an elderly man in a world dominated by the young.

The key to the sequence lies in the contrast between two worlds, that of the family on the quayside and the father and mother on the spit. The former (2) refers back to what was established much earlier (in the sequence of a birthday meal), the haphazard energy and brio of a large family. It is a world of action, one in which there is little or no time or inclination for contemplation, where each act is an urgent call on the attention of others: incessantly and inevitably social.

The latter (4) and (6) is an invocation of a type of painting of which the main feature is what Michael Fried has called the quality of absorption.[5] In such works, figures are typically depicted reading, or thinking, or playing a game, or in a state of reverie induced by single-minded attention. Here, fishing (the father) and sewing (the mother) exactly fit this model. The couple are absorbed in their activities, detach themselves sufficiently to acknowledge the spectators on the other shore, and immediately return to their former state.

The importance of this quality of absorption is the relationship that it imposes between the world viewed and the viewer. The world containing the parents' image is one that does not require Isak's presence. The function of the water is precisely to make the space impassable. He can contemplate the scene but he cannot insert himself into it,

any more than he could insert himself into a painting or an image on a cinema screen. It also seems to be a world without sound; we see Sara speaking but no sound reaches us.

Yet this is not a negative quality. We would expect the recovered child that is Isak to desire to bring to his sleep the best version of finding father and mother that his recalling will allow. Separating the parents from himself, making them figures in this kind of painting, is what he most desires of them, or possibly what he can most happily bear of them. Looking at Isak's face in (7), we see that this affects him not as a form of estrangement but as an ideal relation. Creating the image, he also creates the relation to it, one of ecstatic contemplation.

The contrast between the world of the extended but non-parental family (1)–(3) and that of the mother and father (4) and (6) is reproduced in the two images that I have taken from the film. In the second image, the wooden jetty ascends vertically in the frame until cut off by the boat and its half-furled sail, to be continued in the mast which completes the vertical bisection of the image. These elements of the composition take the eye forward directly to the knot of activity at the centre, causing us to feel its depth: the movement, also emphasised by the density of the group of figures, between foreground and background. In the first image the diagonal lines of shores and rod lead the eye across the frame. The openness of the view has the effect of flattening the composition, as does the positioning of the two figures so that they appear in the same plane, neither one significantly nearer to the viewer. It is a world of balance, exemplified by the cloudy sky and the calm water beneath that reflects it.

We see in Isak's extended family a world both of friendship and of eros, of compliments accepted and turned off, and of gestures that can be both a gift and a form of touch, like a kiss. Above all it is an existence lived in the company of other men and women. It is characterised by physical contact – a shove into the water, a hand held – and by awareness of the age of one's body, that is to say, of mortality. One of the most poignant details here is an assertion of age and youth; as Isak and Sara walk hand in hand across the field to the vantage point, he almost stumbles, and her hand prevents this.

The invoked world of the parents is characterised by none of these things, but by a different relation between spectator and image. The only form of contact possible is that of seeing, but this is experienced, at least for a brief moment, as ideal.

Wild Strawberries has commonly been discussed in terms of loneliness.[6] In addition to thinking of it as a subject diffused throughout the film, we can detect here a more specific project, to do with what Isak needs to learn, or to understand. Once the social business with those other physical bodies – Agda, Sara, Evald, Marianne – is happily concluded, we are taken to a world in which you can be content to be solitary, in the presence of a vision which satisfies you. In these last moments Bergman finds a way of expressing the thought that Isak has learned to accept being alone.

NOTES

1. The general resemblance to painting has been widely observed by writers on the film. For example, Philip and Kersti French use the term 'tableau', Philip Mosley calls it a 'painterly scene' and Robin Wood's description is 'a stylised group as in a painting'. See Philip and Kersti French, *Wild Strawberries* (London: BFI, 1995), p. 37; Philip Mosley, *Ingmar Bergman: The Cinema as Mistress* (London: Marion Boyars, 1981), p. 79; Robin Wood, *Ingmar Bergman* (London: Studio Vista, 1969), p. 80.

2. A surprising (to me) number of writers on the film take this moment to be one of relatively unambiguous reconciliation between Isak and his parents. For example, see A. Richard and S. J. Blake in Stuart Kaminsky (ed.), *Ingmar Bergman: Essays in Criticism* (New York: Oxford University Press, 1975), p. 165; Seldon Bach, in Kaminsky, *Ingmar Bergman*, p. 200; Jesse Kalin, *The Films of Ingmar Bergman* (Cambridge: Cambridge University Press, 2003), p. 72. The helpful and scholarly account given by Laura Hubner places the moment in the context of Bergman's 'visionary endings' and reminds us of the connection between this ending and that of Strindberg's *The Ghost Sonata* (1908). There the final vision is literally one of a canvas, albeit an intriguing and gloomy one, Arnold Böcklin's painting 'Island of the Dead'. See Laura Hubner, *The Films of Ingmar Bergman: Illusions of Light and Darkness* (Basingstoke: Palgrave Macmillan, 2007), pp. 52, 151.

3. The dialogue used in the film differs in some respects from that in the published screenplay. I have taken my English words from the subtitles on a widely circulated DVD version (Tartan Video, 2002).

4. The positioning of Isak as a child is reinforced by the fact that this scene is so familiar from other films. Lisa kissing her infant son goodnight in *Letter from an Unknown Woman* (Ophuls, 1949) is one of many examples of it.

5. My understanding of this term is heavily indebted to Michael Fried's comprehensive establishment of it in his *Absorption and Theatricality: Painting and Beholder in the Age of Diderot* (Chicago, IL: University of Chicago Press, 1980).

6. Jörn Donner's argument, that the 'central theme of *Wild Strawberries* is loneliness', in one of the first books on Bergman in English, may have initiated this. See his *The Personal Vision of Ingmar Bergman* (New York: Arno Press, 1972), p. 167, first published in English by Indiana University Press in 1964.

BIBLIOGRAPHY

Donner, Jörn, *The Personal Vision of Ingmar Bergman* (New York: Arno Press, 1972).

French, Philip and French, Kersti, *Wild Strawberries* (London: BFI, 1995).

Fried, Michael, *Absorption and Theatricality: Painting and Beholder in the Age of Diderot* (Chicago, IL: University of Chicago Press, 1980).

Hubner, Laura, *The Films of Ingmar Bergman: Illusions of Light and Darkness* (Basingstoke: Palgrave Macmillan, 2007).

Kalin, Jesse, *The Films of Ingmar Bergman* (Cambridge: Cambridge University Press, 2003).

Kaminsky, Stuart (ed.), *Ingmar Bergman: Essays in Criticism* (New York: Oxford University Press, 1975).

Mosley, Philip, *Ingmar Bergman: The Cinema as Mistress* (London: Marion Boyars, 1981).

Wood, Robin, *Ingmar Bergman* (London: Studio Vista, 1969).

Making an Entrance: Bette Davis's First Appearance in *Jezebel* (1938)

MARTIN SHINGLER

Bette Davis storms into her 1938 film *Jezebel* on a wild colt, sporting a riding outfit of leather boots, tailored jacket and a cavalier-style hat. Having leapt from the horse, she hooks up her long skirt with a riding crop to maximise her freedom of movement. Davis's Julie Marsden, a young woman of independent means, proceeds to shock her assembled guests by striding into their midst attired in her 'horse clothes', ignoring the etiquette of 1852 as observed by the New Orleans social elite. Sipping sherry, the older ladies look upon her with astonishment and disapproval as Julie further flouts convention by drinking the whisky toddies reserved for the gentlemen, making a toast to a financial institution. Thus Davis's difference is established. Davis is different because she is the star of the film and the 'Jezebel' of its title but also because she is more masculine than the other women. This is highlighted in the images of her taming the horse, horse-breaking being more typically the preserve of men in her world. As she proceeds, entering the party unsuitably attired and drinking whisky, Julie's unconventional character is confirmed. However, Davis's first appearance in *Jezebel* does more than simply establish her as masculine. The fact that she rides her horse side-saddle, that her hat is adorned by a large decorative feather and that the tightness of her waist reveals her curvaceous figure emphasises her femininity. Thus, she presents an ambiguous and androgynous persona. It was partly this kind of persona that fascinated audiences in the late 1930s and early 40s, particularly wartime female audiences, making Bette Davis the most profitable adult female star in America from 1939 to 1941.[1]

For Thomas Schatz, '*Jezebel* marked a watershed in Davis's career.'[2] After six years as a contract player at Warner Bros., appearing in twenty-eight of their films, she was given a star vehicle commensurate with her talent as an actor. Davis had previously caught the attention of film critics with sensational performances in *Of Human Bondage* (1934) and *Dangerous* (1935), gaining an Oscar for the latter. In 1937, *Variety* declared that Bette Davis was 'among the Hollywood few who can submerge themselves in a role to the point where they become the character they are playing'.[3] This, along with her Oscar for Best Actress of 1935, gave her some distinction among her peers, persuading Jack Warner to reward her with a lavish prestige picture.[4]

Jezebel was an expensive historical costume drama, adapted from a Broadway play by Owen Davis Sr. Director William Wyler was commissioned to showcase and refine Davis's acting talents, while Irving Rapper was appointed dialogue director to help her rehearse her lines and develop her characterisation. Moreover, Wyler and his assistant, John Huston, refashioned Clements Ripley and Abem Finkel's screenplay to exploit her persona more fully. Consequently, as Schatz writes, 'the studio finally had a fix on Davis's screen persona and began tailoring projects to suit her'.[5]

Bette Davis's first scene in *Jezebel* reveals some of the ways in which Wyler's direction showcased the star to best advantage. Her character enters from the right on horseback in an establishing shot outside the gates of her home. On reaching the centre of the shot, the horse executes a full anti-clockwise spin before exiting to the left, the camera panning left to reveal the gateway. Matching on action, there follows a cut to a high-angled long shot, taken from the top of the steps outside the front door of the house. A black boy in livery is waiting to receive the horse in the lower centre of the frame. Played up to this point by a stunt-woman, Julie keeps her head turned down towards her left shoulder so that her face is disguised by her hat. The first image of Bette Davis now appears in a medium shot as she dismounts from the horse. While Davis and the horse occupy the left side of the frame, a black manservant enters from the lower right, raising his hat in a greeting to 'Miss Julie'. She turns towards him smiling, holding out her arms as a signal that she's about to leap from the horse. The servant reaches out towards her and she falls into his arms. He takes her weight as she descends and she thanks him just as her feet (below the lower edge of the frame) reach the ground, instantly turning away as he respectfully doffs his hat. Directing her riding crop at the boy at the left edge of the screen, Julie instructs him to take the horse round to the back of the house. She then exits to the left, breaking into a run, the camera panning to the right to reveal the horse dragging the boy towards the gate.

Davis's first shot establishes some crucial aspects of her characterisation. When first seen, she occupies the upper left side of the frame, sitting on the horse, her lofty position suggesting her status as an heiress of wealth and property who commands respect. However, the descent from the horse is emblematic of her fall from grace, which results from her defiance of the custom of unmarried ladies wearing virginal white to the Olympus Ball in favour of a shocking red gown. Thereafter, Julie is ostracised by polite society and rejected by her fiancé. It is, therefore, not insignificant that Bette Davis's first action in the film is to fall. However, something more is established here, namely Julie's empathy for her black slaves. Davis shows no hesitation when throwing herself into the arms of her manservant, nor does she register any sign of restraint when he takes her in his arms and pulls her closely towards his body. This establishes her liberal attitude, which she maintains throughout the film. Although proud among her white peers, Julie is most at ease with her black slaves.

A series of reverse shots follows, cutting between Julie on the front steps and her point of view of the boy being dragged by the horse. This begins with a medium shot of Julie's back as she reaches her house, tapping lightly on the door with her riding crop while twisting round to look at the boy behind her. An eyeline match motivates the cut to Julie's first point-of-view shot, followed quickly by a reverse shot of Julie in front of the door, facing the camera. Here she flares up, directing her whip at the camera as she instructs the boy (off screen) to be more commanding with the horse, delivering her first significant line of dialogue: 'Now Ti Bat, don't stand there with your eyes bulging', laying the stress on the word *bulging*, 'he knows you're scared.'[6] A reverse shot reveals the boy (Matthew 'Stymie' Beard) continuing to struggle with the horse as it drags him beyond the gates, the boy replying that he's afraid of the horse because he bites. Returning to a long shot of Julie, she tells him to 'just plain bite him back' and laughs. This shot provides a good look at Julie as she stands centre stage, enabling the audience to take in the various details of her outfit: the bandanna at her neck, the large white gloves, the long skirt with a train and the tightly corseted waist accentuating her slender physique. Without pausing, Davis shakes the whip at the boy and the horse (both being off screen) and then uses it in a complicated and beautifully choreographed gesture to hook up the train of her skirt, lifting it over her shoulder and raising the hemline to reveal her boots.[7] By this time, the door behind her has opened and she makes an elaborate turn, the train of the skirt swinging over her shoulder and across her back like a cloak. In this way, as Julie marches off through the doorway, briefly glancing back over her left shoulder, she looks more like a cavalier (i.e. a gallant and swaggering seventeenth-century knight) than a nineteenth-century southern belle.[8]

This series of reverse shots reveals several things about Davis as an actress and Julie as a character. For instance, her first notable line of dialogue is not only an instruction to the young black slave to be more masterful but also contains the key word 'bulging', which she stresses by increasing the volume, extending it over several beats and widening her large eyes. In this way, Julie's first major line highlights Davis's most idiosyncratic physical feature – her big eyes – one she shares with many people of African descent and one of their most impersonated features by blackface minstrels. At one level, therefore, Julie appears to ridicule the boy's racial features but, at another, she seems to identify herself with him. Meanwhile, the film establishes a link between Julie and the wild colt. In the party scene that follows, Julie apologies for being late, saying, 'So sorry! But you know when a colt gets high-headed, it's teach him his manners right now or ruin him.' Ironically, it turns out to be Julie's high-headedness that leads to her downfall, along with the fact that no one is able to make her behave as a demure debutante or rein in her wild spirit. Davis's first scene, which culminates in her swaggering gesture as she deftly swings the skirt of her riding habit over her shoulder, evokes the pride that will precede her fall. Here she lacks any trace of modesty, suggesting that her character's unrestrained behaviour will be her undoing.[9] Having been given too much free rein, Julie will be forced to learn some painful lessons in how to deport herself and how to exercise self-control.

Throughout *Jezebel*, Wyler's direction remains sensitive, intelligent and nuanced. Often his scenes are highly mobile with elaborate pans and tracking shots, in and out of which Davis moves, the camera inevitably rediscovering her moments after she has eluded its frame. Wyler, as much a choreographer as a director, often makes Davis and the camera execute an elaborate dance, moving around each other, synchronised to each other's movements. Each shot is as carefully framed as Davis's performance is finely crafted, the two being intricately linked to capture the most telling images so that audiences can perceive the motivations of Julie's actions. These images provide glimpses of the forces that drive her, impulses propelling her towards her downfall. Though Julie may be imperious and impulsive, Bette Davis remains under control, her tendency to fidget held in check, without ever impeding her constant motion.[10] Her gestures are smaller, more intricate and purposeful than in her earlier films, her energy more modulated and contained, so that Ernest Haller's camera can register these in fine detail. Indeed, *Jezebel* is so meticulous – both in the way it is shot and performed – that it is best appreciated with close and careful scrutiny. This is a film that rewards detailed examination. For what seems a sprawling melodrama comprises tightly wrought sequences designed to hone and harness the extraordinary power of Bette Davis in her ascendancy as a star and performer. To borrow the film's own analogy, it presents a wild colt being reined in. Wyler's direction, which consisted of many retakes without telling his actors what he wanted from them, gave his star a certain amount of free rein by enabling her to determine her own performance, assisted by dialogue director Irving Rapper. At the same time, however, it subjected her to the discipline of carefully choreographed long takes, shot repeatedly until her director was fully satisfied. The result of his painstaking direction of Davis was to take her raw and largely untutored talent, along with her ferocious drive and energy, and transform them into something more polished. Wyler's tutelage on this film and their subsequent collaboration on *The Letter* (1940) and *The Little Foxes* (1941) enabled Bette Davis to produce an impressive body of work that established her claim to being one of Hollywood's greatest actors as well as one of its most unconventional stars.

NOTES

1. After 1941, Davis was superseded as the top box-office female in the USA by Betty Grable and Greer Garson. See Jeanine Basinger, *A Woman's View: How Hollywood Spoke to Women 1930–1960* (Hanover, NH: Wesleyan University Press, 1993), p. 509.
2. Thomas Schatz, '"A Triumph of Bitchery": Warner Bros., Bette Davis and *Jezebel*', *Wide Angle* vol. 10 no. 1, 1988, p. 27.
3. *Variety*, 'Review of *Marked Woman*', 14 April 1937, p. 12.
4. Jack Warner intended *Jezebel* to steal a march on David O. Selznick's epic *Gone with the Wind* (1939), which was in production at MGM in 1938.
5. Schatz, '"A Triumph of Bitchery"', p. 27.
6. In the script this speech is slightly different: 'Now Ti Bat, you can't handle horses with your eyes bulging out like that (bulging her eyes). He knows you're scared.' Instead, Davis says, 'Now Ti Bat, don't stand there with your eyes bulging.' However, the important thing to note here is the instruction for her to bulge her eyes at this moment (Clements Ripley and Abem Finkel, Screenplay of *Jezebel*, 25 October 1937, p. 14; copy held at the Howard Gotlieb Archival Research Center, Boston University, Boston, MA).
7. Following Ti Bat's line about the horse biting, the script states that 'Julie hooks up the train of her habit with her crop and throws it over her shoulder' before announcing: 'Then you just plainly bite him back.' Not only does Davis change the word 'plainly' to 'plain' but, more important, she delays the action with the train until after she has spoken this line, preceding it with the action of shaking her whip at the camera (which is not called for by the script). See Ripley and Finkel, Screenplay of *Jezebel*.
8. Ed Sikov has noted that this shot took forty-eight takes before Wyler was satisfied with Davis's performance: Ed Sikov, *Dark Victory: The Life of Bette Davis* (New York: Henry Holt & Co., 2007), p. 118.
9. The script describes Julie as 'imperious'. It states: 'Julie is about twenty. Beautiful, imperious.' See Ripley and Finkel, Screenplay of *Jezebel*, p. 14.
10. Ed Sikov claims that Wyler forced Davis to subdue many of her mannerisms, recognising that many of them were 'itchily nervous and beyond her control, expressions not of a character's psychology but of her own' (Sikov, *Dark Victory*, p. 118).

BIBLIOGRAPHY

Balio, Tino (ed.), *The American Film Industry* (rev. edn) (Madison: University of Wisconsin Press, 1985).
Basinger, Jeanine, *A Woman's View: How Hollywood Spoke to Women 1930–1960* (Hanover, NH: Wesleyan University Press, 1993).
Davis, Bette, *The Lonely Life* (New York: G. P. Putnam's Sons, 1962).
Higham, Charles, *Bette: The Life of Bette Davis* (London: New English Library, 1981).

Klaprat, Cathy, 'The Star as Market Strategy: Bette Davis in Another Light', in Balio, *The American Film Industry*, pp. 351–76.

Ripley, Clements and Finkel, Abem, Screenplay of *Jezebel* (adapted from the play by Owen Davis Sr), 25 October 1937.

Schatz, Thomas, '"A Triumph of Bitchery": Warner Bros., Bette Davis and *Jezebel*', *Wide Angle* vol. 10 no. 1, 1988, pp. 16–29.

Sikov, Ed, *Dark Victory: The Life of Bette Davis* (New York: Henry Holt & Co., 2007).

Variety, 'Review of *Marked Woman*', 14 April 1937.

A Narrative Parenthesis in *Life Is Beautiful* (1997)

DEBORAH THOMAS

Life Is Beautiful/La vita è bella (Benigni, 1997) openly presents itself as a fable – and not a reconstruction of the Holocaust meant to be taken literally – right from the introductory words of its off-screen narrator, Giosué, spoken many years after the events the film depicts: 'This is a simple story, but not an easy one to tell. Like a fable, there is sorrow, and, like a fable, it is full of wonder and happiness.' Alternative ways of reading the world – and ambiguities among them – are thus self-consciously in play throughout, with representations of actual historic events openly transformed through processes of subjective and figurative reconstruction. For example, the present moment of remembrance by the narrator further reworks a past in which experiences were already filtered both through his childhood perspective and through the stories his father Guido (Roberto Benigni) recounted to him at the time. Thus, the adult Giosué who narrates the film is trying to recapture a past he never quite experienced first-hand (and never experienced at all, in the case of the parts before his birth). For the audience too, past events are mediated, in our case by the film's insistence on its fictional devices and by our access to hindsight, offering the film's viewers a very different understanding from that of the characters immersed in the narrative world and the historical past alike.[1]

An early instance of the co-presence of different dimensions of meaning – and the film's frank acknowledgment of this – is provided by the opening sequence when Guido and his friend Ferruccio (Sergio Bini Bustric) are driving towards Arezzo and the brakes fail. Guido tries to clear a path for the runaway car by frantically waving his extended arm from side to side to get the expectant crowds awaiting the arrival of the king to disperse. Mistaking Guido for the royal visitor, the crowds enthusiastically return what they take to be a fascist salute. The culmination of the joke is that the king himself, when his car pulls up, is completely ignored, as well as being visually overshadowed by his much larger wife. This is the first of many instances where the dignity of those in authority

(especially where they are explicitly coded as fascist) is punctured. There is a further doubling, not only of the symbolic and the mundanely functional (the same gesture capable of being read in either way), but also of the comedic and the more melodramatic. The danger of one being in a car speeding out of control is here outweighed by the 'Keystone Kops' feel to the runaway car, which reassures us that Guido and Ferruccio will survive intact.

This illusion of a safe world successfully submerging a potentially more dangerous one will be more and more difficult to sustain as the film progresses. Indeed, the story Guido tells Giosué (Giorgio Cantarini) in an attempt to allay his son's fears on the way to the camp and subsequently – by convincing him that they are willing participants in a competition to win a tank – is so flimsy that even Giosué will have recurring moments of doubt about their safety and the accuracy of Guido's cover story.

In this first example, Guido himself is unaware of, and then bewildered by, the crowd's mistake (being too preoccupied by the speeding car, at first, to notice, and then not hanging around for the 'punchline' of the joke), and his gesture involves no intention on his part to deceive. Elsewhere, in his stories to Giosué, his evident intention that events be reconstrued by his son is completely self-conscious, but his own construal of events – the extent of his knowledge about what's really going on – is nonetheless uncertain. Guido's ignorance of what is happening in the camps is revealed with most devastating irony when he unsuccessfully tries to persuade Giosué to take a shower with the other children, as the boy has been instructed, rather than to hide, as Giosué has chosen to do. One could say that Guido himself is too quick to believe in stories: here, the Nazi story that a shower is just a shower and nothing more.

So there are many differences between the early and later stages of the film. Most important, in the early stages, it is still just about possible for the film's viewers (and Guido) to read a dangerous world as a safe one, despite a steady accumulation of ominous portents. Furthermore,

Guido is in on the behind-the-scenes mechanics that make possible his 'magical' courtship of Dora (Nicoletta Braschi), understanding the workings of the world and making use of them for his own benefit. For example, he calls to the Virgin Mary to throw down from heaven the key to Dora's acquiescence (having earlier observed a husband, at the very spot where Guido and Dora now find themselves, shouting to his wife Maria to throw down a key from an upstairs window), and it falls from the sky on cue, to Dora's amazement. Though Guido, despite his confident courtship, will consistently struggle to understand what goes on in the camp, the film doesn't split easily into two halves. The changes in the film's tone and in Guido's knowledge of the nature of the world – that is, the parallel disillusionments of both Guido and the audience, disillusionments with the benevolent nature of the world and the comedic nature of the film respectively – are more gradual and intermixed.

The moment I have chosen to look at in detail is when Guido follows Dora into a sort of greenhouse, only to have their son Giosué emerge to his waiting parents several years later, though apparently within the same shot. It is the most dreamlike and cinematically magical transition in the film, preceded by Guido helping Dora down off the back of the horse upon which they've made their escape from Dora's engagement party. The horse is covered in garish green paint which fascist thugs splashed on it earlier, including a painted skull and crossbones outlined in black against the green.

However, as we cut to Guido and Dora walking around a corner of the house and approaching the door, the animal is left behind and it remains outside the frame from this point onward. Relegated off screen, the horse's unwholesome shade of neon green no longer clashes with the pale pink of Dora's gown and the natural greens of the plants, nor is its painted body visible as an insistent reminder of a harsh and poisonous world besmirching its innocent victims – both animal and human – outside the present enchanted space. Yet the enchantment will necessarily be short-lived. Much later, amid the greys and browns of the concentration camp, Guido will speak of a dream he had of Dora, addressing her over a loudspeaker he finds in an unguarded office: 'You were wearing that pink suit that I really like. You're all I think about …'. The pale pink of the suit he remembers, a colour which is also visible in Dora's dress throughout the first part of the greenhouse scene, is, by the time of the later scene, a colour at three removes: a mere memory of a dream of a memory.

As Guido now tries to force open the door of his uncle's house, not having remembered to get the key from Ferruccio (and no longer able to call it down from heaven), Dora wanders into a room in the adjacent building while Guido fumbles at the door of the house with a piece of wire. She pauses to look back at him, and her stillness is in contrast to his busyness and inattentive chatter.

I used to make toys out of wire when I was a kid.

Turning away, Dora enters what appears to be a greenhouse or conservatory filled with plants. We then cut to Guido as he kicks open the door and realises that Dora has wandered off. This is followed by another cut to him in close-up, now silent and becalmed, looking after her retreating figure.

Finally, we cut to Guido from behind as he too steps into the greenhouse in search of her, the music intensifying and becoming louder throughout. Without a further cut, their young son Giosué comes running out, the camera pulling back before him to his parents outside, no longer in the formal clothes they were wearing earlier in the shot.[2]

There is something tentative and extremely affecting in the inquisitive tilt of Guido's head as he enters the greenhouse, seen only from behind, and peers around the plants while moving slowly forward. Despite his ill-fitting clothes, he is suddenly less of a genial clown and more a man in full possession of himself. That Dora has asked him to rescue her for himself – that his deepest wish is also hers – makes all the more moving and delicately erotic the moment of his hesitation on the brink of entering the bewitching world before him. Now Dora is the agent of his captivation as he, earlier, had 'magically' masterminded their courtship for her benefit. The effect of Giosué's subsequent emergence from the same space in the same shot is as if the threats of imminent catastrophe for Italian Jews like Guido and his uncle, which ran rampant throughout the engagement party scene, have been held in suspension by Guido and Dora's marriage and Giosué's birth and early childhood. The unseen depths of the greenhouse present a

space and time apart: they form a sort of narrative parenthesis – a shelter – which temporarily prises Guido, Dora
and Giosué away from the realities of wartime Italy and
offers them a private alternative reality from which viewers are discreetly held back.

In the single shot that contains the intervening years
of the marriage, unseen, within its depths, but with their
richness suggested by the abundant plants and blaze of
colour that can be glimpsed inside, somehow the inner
spaces of the room are transformed into a temporal plenitude as well, despite the short duration of the shot in cinematic terms. The moment answers Guido's earlier
evocation (in the courtship scene when Guido had stolen
Dora from her fiancé after the opera) of a future from
whose vantage point their courtship would be remembered as a spellbinding night in the past. In that earlier
scene, in answer to Dora's question about where they are,
when their car breaks down in the rain, he tells her they've
been there before. 'Don't you remember?' he says. 'The
night it was raining …'. And he goes on to describe events
that are only just happening as if they were already located
in the past.[3] The poignancy of his playfully imagining those
presently occurring moments as memories inheres in the
way the scene juxtaposes Guido's wish that they grow old
together and that they look back on their courtship fondly
across a vista of many happy years with our own chilly pre-
monition, as viewers armed with hindsight, that such a
prospect is already doomed. Now, in the greenhouse scene,
Guido has once again rescued Dora from her fascist fiancé
Rodolfo (Amerigo Fontani), this time for good, but the early
years of their marriage – virtually all of the marriage, as it
turns out, since they will be separated forever the next day
– are reduced to a mere instant off screen. As the war and
its consequences increasingly come to permeate the narrative world, an uncontaminated realm of personal desire
and fulfilment can no longer be convincingly represented
but can only be momentarily and obliquely implied as both
provisional and veiled.

In its harmony and abundance, the image of the greenhouse answers and reverses the presentation of a topsy-
turvy world in the immediately preceding scene of the
engagement dinner when Guido, working as a waiter, discovers that Dora is set to marry someone else. Guido, a
master of improvisation in the earlier scene where he
hijacks Dora after the opera, is suddenly at a loss. At
Rodolfo's words, announcing his engagement to Dora in
front of the assembled guests (to her evident displeasure),
and with the sudden prospect of Dora being yanked out of
his world, Guido loses his earlier grace and skills of
enchantment as he trips over a chair and stands up in a
daze. He lifts his tray aloft, oblivious to the poodle perched
on top, where it had been deposited by Ferruccio when he
came to Guido's aid. The poodle on a tray presents a gently
humorous image of a world gone wrong, and the whole
scene functions as a preliminary version of his much more
brutal and definitive separation from Dora in the camp
when the repressive Nazi environment will be so much
more rigid and resistant to his efforts to reconfigure it for
the sake of his son. By that stage, the defining image of a
world out of joint is a mountain of bodies piled on bodies
rather than a misplaced poodle held aloft.

In all these ways, the greenhouse moment may be seen
as the structural centre of the film, the pivot on which it
turns. It marks the point when Giosué comes into existence
and, thus, when the basis of his framing narration moves
from hearsay alone to first-hand experience. It also offers
us the narrative 'parenthesis' mentioned earlier when the
anti-Semitic world outside the frame can be momentarily
suspended, allowing for a rich burst of colour before the
greyness of the camp. The poetic delicacy of the scene is
intimately linked to the way the early happy years of the
marriage are already shown as being out of reach (by being
kept off screen, in the depths of the greenhouse, and lasting
for mere seconds of cinematic time) even as they unfold.

NOTES

1. However, Giosué as narrator partly escapes these particular limitations, even if Giosué as child does not.
2. At least, there is no cut that I can spot, though the lighting
   on the plants perceptibly brightens to mark the change
   from early evening to day.
3. Nevertheless, he mischievously adds: 'When I stopped in
   front of you, you kissed me', an outcome which Dora, in
   fact, withholds.

The End of Summer: *Conte d'été* (1996)

JACOB LEIGH

In Eric Rohmer's *Conte d'été*/*A Summer's Tale* (1996), the boundary between friendship and love is marked by four kisses between Gaspard (Melvil Poupaud) and Margot (Amanda Langlet), with each character initiating two of them.[1] When Gaspard and Margot first kiss, her preliminary joshing of him, teasing him with the grass to get his attention, gives way to her apparent surprise that he kisses her. Part of her welcomes him; nevertheless, she pulls away from him, rejecting his opportunistic advances. Their second kiss is the first of those begun by Margot and it occurs on the beach, after they fight. This time Gaspard is surprised and confused. Rohmer shows their third kiss during their last outing together. It is one of the director's most beautiful scenes, with performers, camera, setting, dialogue and costumes connecting in a densely expressive style.

For their last walk together, they drive to a romantic spot on the coast, where lush green trees overlook wide bays and cliffs. It is a gloriously sunny day. Weather is always part of Rohmer's palette and in *Conte d'été* he uses Brittany's changeable summer weather to provide meaningful background. This sunny Friday, which Gaspard spends with Margot, contrasts with the cloudy following day, when he meets Solène (Gwenaëlle Simon) at the statue, the different summer weather accentuating the contrast between the warmth and eroticism of Gaspard's walk with Margot and the cool mistiness of his confused conversation with Solène. Both the weather and the season in *Conte d'été* function metaphorically, for the film's setting of a summer holiday relates to the time of life experienced by Gaspard and Margot.

Summer holidays sometimes provoke feelings of purposelessness. Gaspard's passivity derives in part from his being on holiday; with no work to do while waiting for Léna (Aurelia Nolin), he responds to whatever comes along. In addition, though, Gaspard feels that he is on holiday from adult life, a life that need not begin, as he remarks, until he is thirty; like many men of his age, Gaspard defines himself by his independence from person or place. Both Margot and Gaspard have finished postgraduate studies – Poupaud was twenty-three in 1995 when the film was made, Langlet

was twenty-eight – and this may be their last free summer before committing to relationships and careers. For Rohmer, Gaspard is 'in a period "before choice"'.[2] The end of summer heralds the end of this period 'before choice'; until that point, Gaspard postpones commitments and indulges his liberty, unwilling to say goodbye to youthful freedom.

Their final walk begins with a shot of them walking together downhill, away from the camera; this brief shot enables us to see their costumes and the rhythm of their movements. As usual, Gaspard wears black jeans and a black T-shirt; Margot wears a red dress. The colour of the costumes helps contrast the three women in Gaspard's life: just as they each have their own location (Gaspard's girl in every port), so they each have their own colour. Red is important to Amanda Langlet's Margot, who at different times wears a red bikini, a red T-shirt, a red vest, a red sleeveless T-shirt and two red dresses. Red matches her skin tone, which is reddy brown, and the same is true of the olive-green bikini worn by the dark-haired and tanned Solène and the blue bikini worn by the pale-skinned, blue-eyed Léna. In contrast to the red, green and blue worn by the three women, Gaspard's wardrobe is monochrome and he wears black clothes for almost the entire film. When he first arrives in Dinard, his black attire singles him out from the holiday-makers dressed in pastel-coloured shorts and T-shirts; in the middle of summer, Gaspard wears a black corduroy jacket, black jumper, black jeans and black shoes, varying this only occasionally with a grey sweatshirt and shirt or white T-shirt and jeans.

The symbolism of black as a colour for clothing is long-lasting. As Anne Hollander writes, when worn by men, from the period of literary Romanticism onwards, black is associated with 'spiritual unrest and personal solitude'. Besides black having the 'visual property of sharp contrast to other colours, or the anti-fashion function of distinguishing an individual, or the ritual quality continually associated with mourning, in the nineteenth century', Hollander notes, 'it *represents* sartorial drama, in an essentially literary spirit'.[3] She describes the man in black as a wanderer, somehow in league possibly with the devil but certainly with a kind of dark power that exempted him from the responsibilities of common feeling and experience. He was unhappy; black was his natural colour … . It [black] emphasised an austere male detachment from female emotive and procreative life (expressed in colour and change).[4]

The red, green and blue worn by Margot, Solène and Léna connect them to the world, whereas Gaspard's black clothes typify his negative passivity: his outfits absorb light as he absorbs the attentions of the three women. Through his black attire, Gaspard expresses his unrest, solitude and youthful rebellion; he is refusing responsibility and routine, preserving his detachment from society. Gaspard's precursors are Beau Brummell and Lord Byron, although, as Hollander argues, the black worn by young men now ('Student Black' and 'Modern Bohemian Black') is 'deliberately scruffy rather than romantically sombre'.[5] Gaspard's black clothes distinguish him from Léna's bourgeois friends (who work 'in plastics') and signal his independence as a young musician, free to sail away whenever he chooses.

Margot, in contrast to Gaspard, wears a close-fitting red print dress for their last excursion. The finale of her red costumes, her dress is tight above the waist, loose in the skirt and cut above the knee; as she walks along the coastal path, the pleats of her skirt brush around her legs. Immaculate white pumps provide a faultless finish. When they stop to admire the view, they stand with their backs to us, facing out to sea, but not next to each other, as Margot stays behind Gaspard. The green foliage, the distant coastline and the patches of sky and sea focus attention on Gaspard's black outfit and Margot's red dress, the greenness of the surrounding trees providing an attractive foil to

the dress. The cutaway back of her dress plunges to a wide v-shape, from the edges of her shoulders to the base of her spine, revealing the glowing ruddiness of her skin, which the design and colour of the dress, red with white flowers, heighten. This scene features intense backlighting and dense saturated colours; when Margot sits down, a close-up of her shows her backlit by the low sun, the light glorifying her beauty and highlighting her youthful vitality; close in, the colour of the dress and background trees increase the appeal of her dark brown hair and eyes. Margot looks as wonderful as she has ever looked in this moment of concentrated visual harmony, produced by the combination of her skin colour, her brown eyes and hair, her red and white dress, and the natural splendour of Brittany's Emerald Coast.

In these conditions, it is unsurprising that when they discuss his trip to Ouessant with either Léna or Solène, Gaspard insists, 'If I go, it will be with you.' She thinks that Léna might not mind because she, Margot, 'doesn't count', though she agrees that maybe Ouessant is not a good place for a 'romantic escapade'. Initially, he sits on his own, separated from her by a tree and its shadow; Rohmer offers us a shot/reverse-shot sequence of close-ups of Margot and Gaspard as they talk. Showing self-awareness, he says, 'I'm only myself with you.' The shot/reverse-shot sequence ends when he crawls towards her on all fours, a sleek panther prowling towards its prey. Placing his arm around her, he invites her to Ouessant: 'I'd give them all up for you.' Margot's response is important:

I'd like to take a few days off, get some fresh air, get away from the restaurant, spend a few days with you, even if it's risky. But I'd just be a stopgap. And I don't want to be. We'll go later, when you've failed. Winter is the best season.

As she says this, Margot strokes his arms, leaning her face against his shoulder, her arm drawn across his.

She resists him verbally, yet approaches him physically, a contradiction that makes evident her indecision.[6] While she talks to him, Gaspard either looks at her stroking fingers or glazes over, as if thinking about her actions not her words. As she is telling him that she does not want to be a stopgap, she leans her chin on his arm. Poupaud's performance ensures that we notice him perceive the pressure of her head on one arm and her light caressing of his other arm. She extends herself around him, almost wrapping him towards her. He hears her refusal of his invitation to Ouessant and he feels her body close to him; he responds by turning to kiss her. He moves first, but she lifts her lips to meet his – without surprise or displeasure. Her fingertips remain on his arm; her arm remains outstretched, holding his forearm as he turns to put his arm round her back. They kiss, but her smiling causes their lips

to separate. She looks away, hiding her eyes, as if crying. Gaspard asks: 'What's wrong? Are you crying?' We cannot see if she has tears in her eyes. Maintaining her distance from Gaspard, she tells him that she is laughing: 'Your predicament makes me laugh. You're like a tramp who wakes up a millionaire. Aren't three girls at a time too many?'

Margot's knowledge of his activities prevents her engagement with him: his frankness with her, a result of their relaxed relationship, draws them together, but his divulgences to Margot about Léna and Solène prompt her caution. She spends time with him because she finds him attractive; she flirts with him, but she holds herself back from him, using quips to disentangle herself from his embraces. Caressing his arm encourages him to approach her; they then kiss ardently, but she uses humour to interrupt the passion, rational thought causing physical disengagement. She is indecisive about him, yet her indecision is a reaction to his indecision. In the two scenes when Gaspard kisses her, Langlet's performance makes this visible.

Their fourth and final embrace takes place on the jetty as she sees him off. Gaspard's last weekend in Dinard is an escalation of his entanglements with Léna and Solène, both of whom declare their willingness to visit Ouessant with him. The friend who phones to invite Gaspard to La Rochelle to buy an eight-track tape-recorder helps Gaspard sail away from romantic complications, just as Henri (Féodor Atkine) does in Rohmer's *Pauline à la plage* (1983).[7] Like the first four of Rohmer's *Comédies et proverbes* (1981–7), *Conte d'été* ends as it began, on the jetty. Gaspard recognises that Margot 'counted' all along, for he says, 'Now you and I can go to Ouessant whenever we want.' But the moment has passed; her boyfriend has written to say that he is returning in September.

She will go to the fabled island of Ouessant with him. They stand facing each other on the jetty and she says that she is in Rennes now and then. They can meet. She kisses him lightly on the cheek and he says, 'I won't forget our walks.' 'Me neither,' she replies. She then reaches up and, with her hand on the back of his neck, pulls him towards her to kiss him passionately. She releases him and he turns to board his boat. Rohmer matches the two diminishing figures: Margot walks away from the camera and away from us; then the boat departs. The penultimate shot is of Margot turning and walking up the jetty; the last shot is of the ferry taking Gaspard away from Dinard.

Conte d'été can appear so light and insubstantial and yet it concludes movingly with an opportunity not taken, an emotion not expressed. Margot's relationship with Gaspard has been a holiday romance that did not happen, the opposite of Marion (Arielle Dombasle) and Henri's in *Pauline à la plage*. The haunting conclusion ends a film that has felt almost featherweight, drifting along as Gaspard does. His pointless milling around, indulging in reverie, preferring chimerical figures to Margot, lead to an ending touched with despair. He acts selfishly and stupidly, dishonest with himself and others; a young man in his twenties keeps his options open, until it is too late. We all daydream of a life elsewhere, particularly when we are young; with verve and originality, Rohmer's fertile art shows how a young man's fatalistic preference for vaporous daydream and his lack of effort in the face of difficulties end in a disturbing crisis. Confident in his youth, refusing commitment and believing that he cannot escape his fate or destiny, Gaspard envisages an unavoidable future in which, to recall de la Fontaine from Rohmer's second *Comédies et proverbes*, *Le beau mariage* (1982), 'The world's riches and honours seem/Ours then, and all its lovely women at our feet.'[8] Rohmer shows that Gaspard's vagaries and his daydreaming of the future are ruinous. Sabine (Beatrice Romand) and Edmond (André Dussollier) in *Le Beau mariage* have no opportunity to miss; she builds castles in the air. Gaspard's fabrications are more serious because they blind him to the present. Margot's disappointment hangs over the tragedy of their final parting and embrace. For three weeks, Margot refuses to be a substitute; although they kiss near the beginning, she pushes him away because she senses that he is seizing an opportunity not expressing genuine feeling. When she kisses him at the end of the film, she does so with the confidence that they may not meet again. At the end of *Conte d'été*, there is an unexpected shock that misunderstandings and meanderings have led to a chance of happiness getting lost.

'Youth', says Rohmer, 'it is the epoch of hopes but also of empty waiting.'[9] Rohmer is not the only person to tell stories about the emptiness and waiting of youth; it has attracted dramatists, novelists and artists because so many major changes can happen during that period of life. But in *Conte d'été* Rohmer turns his deepest concern for the ambiguity, complexity and contradictoriness of our interior lives into a profound study of human relationships. He analyses male behaviour in a film that is as insightful and intense on this subject as *Vertigo* (1958), its moral value resembling that of the Hitchcock film in that it scrutinises the way men think and behave and, like *Vertigo*, offers a warning.[10]

NOTES

1. The major theme of *Conte d'été*, youth and its passing, is elaborated with motifs and metaphors that derive from music, sailing, summer and holidays, all things associated with the film's location, Dinard in Brittany. In this essay, I refer to summer and holidays. In *The Cinema of Eric Rohmer* (Wallflower Press, forthcoming), I write about music, sailing, travelling shots and the choreography of walking and talking that dominates the film's action.

2. Cedric Anger, Emmanuel Burdeau and Serge Toubiana, 'Entretien avec Eric Rohmer', *Cahiers du cinéma* no. 503, June 1996, p. 46.

3. Anne Hollander, *Seeing through Clothes* (Berkeley, Los Angeles, London: University of California Press, 1993; first published 1975), pp. 374–5.

4. Ibid., pp. 375–6.

5. Ibid., p. 386.

6. With an overriding interest in the relation between imagination or desire and reality, it is no surprise to find that Rohmer has often filmed the discrepancies between what people say and do, concentrating on pauses and silences, moments where people may be listening to someone or thinking of something else. I have written about these discrepancies and contradictions; see Leigh (2006 and 2007) in the following Bibliography.

7. Michel Serceau also notes the way that *Conte d'été* reprises the telephone call as a *deus ex machina* that features at the end of *Pauline à la plage*: Michel Serceau, *Éric Rohmer: Les jeux de l'amour, du hasard et du discours* (Paris: Les Éditions du Cerf, 2000), p. 83.

8. Jean de la Fontaine, *Selected Fables* [trans. James Michie] (London: Penguin, 1982; first published by Penguin, 1979), p. 88.

9. Anger, Burdeau and Toubiana, 'Entretien avec Eric Rohmer', p. 46.

10. I have not quoted it in the main text, but I am indebted to Adrian Martin's review of the film. He emphasises that *Conte d'été* 'does accrue, by the end, a haunting, caustic, and rather devastating emotional quality'. I agree with his conclusion that 'the character-portrait of Gaspard is one which most thoughtful, urbane guys will find genuinely unnerving. Seeing this chap on screen is like seeing some dark secret shared among men, leaked out for the whole world to see': Adrian Martin, 'Some Kind of Liar: A *Summer's Tale*', *Senses of Cinema* no. 5, 2000. Available at <www.sensesofcinema.com/contents/00/5/summer.html> (accessed 5 September 2002).

BIBLIOGRAPHY

Anger, Cédric, Burdeau, Emmanuel and Toubiana, Serge, 'Entretien avec Eric Rohmer', *Cahiers du cinéma* no. 503, June 1996, pp. 45–9.

de la Fontaine, Jean, *Selected Fables* [trans. James Michie] (London: Penguin, 1982; first published by Penguin, 1979).

Hollander, Anne, *Seeing through Clothes* (Berkeley, Los Angeles, London: University of California Press, 1993; first published 1975).

Leigh, Jacob, 'The Caprices of Rosine or the Follies of a Fortnight: Parallel Intrigues in Eric Rohmer's *Conte d'Automne*', *Undercurrent*, July 2006. Available at <www.fipresci.org/undercurrent/> (accessed 1 July 2006).

Leigh, Jacob, *Reading Rohmer, Close-Up 02* (London: Wallflower Press, 2007).

Leigh, Jacob, *The Cinema of Eric Rohmer* (London: Wallflower Press, forthcoming).

Martin, Adrian, 'Some Kind of Liar: A *Summer's Tale*', *Senses of Cinema* no. 5, 2000. Available at <www.sensesofcinema.com/contents/00/5/summer.html> (accessed 5 September 2002).

Serceau, Michel, *Éric Rohmer: Les jeux de l'amour, du hasard et du discours* (Paris: Les Éditions du Cerf, 2000).

Enter Lisa: *Rear Window* (1954)

DOUGLAS PYE

Fade in on a partial view of the courtyard at night, the apartments to the right of Jeff's window catching the orange glow of the night sky, the rest of the space almost dark. Camera movement from right to left catches glimpses of people in their rooms; a few lights are on in the apartments (one comes on as we pass). The camera movement ends on Jeff (James Stewart), asleep in his wheelchair, his body parallel to the window, his face turned in towards the apartment. The dominant sound is of a soprano practising scales, accompanied by a piano, the sound unlocated but evidently nearby, the first chord on the piano timed to the opening of the shot and followed by three scales, then a longer final scale which ends as a shadow – cast from frame left, inside the apartment – rises over Jeff's body and onto his face. Until the dialogue begins there is now only the faintest of ambient sound. Cut to a low angle close-up of Lisa (Grace Kelly), dimly lit, lips slightly parted, looking directly into the camera and growing larger in the frame as she moves towards us. Cut back to Jeff, still asleep, the shadow moving up to cover his face. His eyes open, he looks up and faintly smiles. Cut back to Lisa in even tighter close-up, again looking into the camera (now that Jeff is awake the shot seems to be POV) and moving down to fill the frame. Cut to a profile two-shot, very close to the faces, Jeff on the right looking diagonally up and Lisa to the left looking down and moving into a kiss, her movement apparently step-printed to produce a fractionally staggered effect. She kisses him.

Her tone is affectionate and gently teasing.

LISA: How's your leg?
JEFF: Hurts a little.
LISA: And your stomach?
JEFF: Empty as a football.
[Lisa kisses Jeff again.]
LISA: And your love life?
[She smiles and looks into his eyes.]
JEFF: Not too active.
LISA: Anything else bothering you?
[Jeff nods slightly.]
JEFF: Uh huh. Who are you?

Lisa smiles and draws back, leaving the frame. The camera pulls away slightly and moves to the left so that we see Jeff almost full-face, looking out of frame towards Lisa.

The handling of Lisa's first appearance, at the beginning of *Rear Window*'s third movement, some fifteen minutes into the film, is strikingly different from the style adopted in the rest of the film. Through most of *Rear Window* the rhetoric of the image is subordinated to action, the elaborate artifice deployed to create a sense of plausible incident in a workaday world. These few shots (lasting just over a minute) present Lisa's entrance in a mode of heightened imagery and stylised action that briefly but significantly shifts the balance between what we might call the literal and poetic dimensions of the film and in doing so disturbs the predominantly light-hearted tone of the early scenes. I want to ask what might be at stake in this complex of decisions.

The significance of the lovers' first meeting in the film has been carefully trailed, most overtly in Jeff's complaint to his insurance nurse Stella (Thelma Ritter) in the previous scene that Lisa's pressure towards marriage is going to cause 'trouble' and his perverse claim that she is 'too perfect'. Their encounter is relaxed and playful, though it hints at underlying tensions. Lisa's approach is loving and tender; Jeff smiles and accepts her kisses but makes no move to embrace her. Is it this that shapes Lisa's dialogue and tone, as though play is her way of negotiating Jeff's sexual reserve? Her lines are gently suggestive ('How's your leg? 'And your stomach?' 'And your love life?'); her look and actions invite a demonstrative response that isn't forthcoming. Jeff's 'Who are you?' in reply to Lisa's 'Anything else bothering you?' is a teasing continuation of her playfulness, but it simultaneously rebuffs the sexual invitation. Lisa smiles and pulls back, gracefully acknowledging that she is in effect being pushed away, and then engages in another playful performance, designed to make Jeff focus on her in a different way, by moving around the room, switching on lights as she announces her names ('Lisa … Carol … Freemont') and finally posing briefly for Jeff's gaze. The interaction between them is played as comedy but beautifully dramatises the conditions that define their

relationship and the games that sustain but limit their intimacy. Jeff will repeatedly puncture the romantic situations
Lisa attempts to create.

It is possible to imagine many ways of organising this
action for the camera that would maintain the performance emphases and what is implied about the relationship;
nothing here seems to presuppose a particular way of
shooting or editing. For the third time in the film, the
camera scans the courtyard before pulling back to the
sleeping Jeff, reinforcing its independence from Jeff's viewpoint as well as extending what is becoming a strange
motif – the protagonist asleep.

The first two such shots occur during the film's opening with its lively music, full daylight and flow of early-
morning activity. Here, however, the atmosphere
generated by the combination of the livid remaining light
in the gathering dark of the courtyard and the singer's
scales, precisely timed to the camera movement, is distinctly eerie. While the action is anchored within the terms
of the created world, the way in which it is presented
denies the everyday. Lisa's sudden presence – her entrance
neither seen nor heard – borders on the uncanny. Her

shadow precedes her, yet when we see Lisa's face the
space behind her is dark and there is only a hint of backlit halo in her hair: available light, such as it is, comes
from outside the apartment. The condition of the
shadow's visibility, its presence to us, is its impossibility
within the world of the film. In a parallel decision, the
optical manipulation of the kiss momentarily breaks with
the normal flow of time. The stylistic register here evokes
the gothic.

The cluster of imagery is at its densest in these twelve
seconds or so from the introduction of the shadow, bringing into sharp association two images of Lisa – her shadow
and the stunning beauty of Grace Kelly's face in close-up –
with her direct looks into the camera and the step-printing
that creates a brief tremor, akin to slow motion, making
the movement into the kiss slightly, almost intangibly,
strange. The suppression of ambient sound after the
soprano ends her scales further abstracts the whole passage of action and intensifies its poetic charge. Although
the tonal disturbance that these images produce is short-
lived, with the bantering dialogue quickly restoring the
predominantly comedic mode of the film so far, the shift is
marked and the moment has a connotative power that
reverberates backwards and forwards through the film.

What should we make of these decisions? Some writers understandably evoke ideas of dream or fantasy. Jeanne
Allen suggests, 'The camera offers [Lisa] not as a mortal
entering the two-room apartment, but suddenly appearing
before the sleeping Jeff – a waking dream.'[1] John Belton
writes of a 'materialization of male erotic fantasy, appearing ... out of the dream of the still sleeping Jeff'.[2] Certainly
the passage possesses the rich associations as well as the
puzzling and paradoxical nature of dreams. It is *Sleeping
Beauty* in reverse, the Prince awoken by Beauty's kiss, the
gender roles of the tale inverted. The shadow enveloping
the sleeping Jeff evokes a familiar visual lexicon of threat,
yet it emanates from the gorgeous Lisa. Nowhere else in
the film are the connotations of dream and/or fantasy so
difficult to avoid; in fact Hitchcock's treatment, involving a
shift of register and densely evocative imagery, seems positively to encourage them.

Backwards, the paradoxical images connect with Jeff's
anxieties about Lisa and marriage: she is both 'perfect' and
yet threatening because he does not want to marry. At no
other point does the film offer us such overtly opposed
images of Lisa – the apotheosis of female beauty and desirability but simultaneously an archetype of menace, almost
vampire-like in her silent approach to the unconscious Jeff.
Hence, as Allen argues, this is 'the point in the film where
the simultaneity of lure and trap is most explicit';[3] or, in
Tania Modleski's words, 'These two shots – shadow and
vibrant image – suggest the underlying threat posed by the
desirable woman and recall the negative and positive
images of the woman on the cover of *Life*.'[4] The 'underlying

threat' is to 'the male fear of impotence and lack' that is intensified by Jeff's 'helplessness, passivity, and invalidism',[5] an idea that resonates both with the dual image of Lisa and the gender role-reversal (passive male/active female). In these powerful arguments the moment expresses, in its paradoxical imagery, what lies beneath Jeff's bewildering objections to Lisa.

Yet the implications of such ideas are not straightforward. The fantasy or waking dream invoked by Belton and Allen are Jeff's, yet this is not a 'dream sequence'. If the imagery is dreamlike it is equally significant that the action retains its place within the flow of events in the film's world and that although our view is strongly linked to Jeff's (we experience Lisa's erotic power before Jeff by occupying his position in space, and then share his look), the film's point of view is not identified with his. It is the treatment of the action – the *mise en scène* – that, without embracing Jeff's subjectivity, momentarily images the unconscious dread that underlies Jeff's attitudes to Lisa.

Essential to thinking about these decisions – and to an overall interpretation of *Rear Window* – is that through most of the film the relationship between its literal and poetic dimensions is not flaunted. Unlike the overt rhetoric which introduces the doubling of Guy (Farley Granger) and Bruno (Robert Walker) in *Strangers on a Train* (1951) and of Uncle Charlie (Joseph Cotten) and young Charlie (Teresa Wright) in *Shadow of a Doubt* (1942), what will turn out to be the vital doubling of Jeff and Thorwald (Raymond Burr) is initiated as a low-key moment, the chance entrance of Thorwald onto the scene as Jeff talks to his editor on the phone. It is only in retrospect that we are likely to see how significantly the moment is managed, via Jeff's vision of marriage as entrapment.

Other parallels between characters, that have been central to readings of the film since Robin Wood's perception in his seminal chapter on the film in his 1965 book that 'Each apartment … can be taken as representing possibilities before Jefferies and Lisa',[6] are also discreetly managed. For instance, during the film's opening, there is a cut from a close-up of James Stewart, asleep and perspiring, his hair slightly grey, to a thermometer on the wall, followed by a pan to Jeff's paunchy neighbour shaving in the studio nextdoor, then angrily switching off the radio ad that blares out 'Men, are you over forty? When you wake up in the morning do you feel tired and run down?' before the camera moves on. The link between the two men in terms of the insecurities of middle-aged masculinity remains implicit; together with the forms of looking that will come to define the film's structures of point of view, the parallels between characters are carefully woven into the unfolding introduction of the film's world.

The processes of response and modes of understanding invited by these films are quite different. In *Shadow of a Doubt* and *Strangers on a Train* it is clear that Hitchcock wants the spectator to be alert to the pattern of doubling and to be able to reflect on its significance from the outset. *Rear Window*, by contrast, embeds its poetic dimensions in less eye-catching forms of narration. This has important consequences for how we think about the role of Lisa's entrance in Hitchcock's unfolding design.

To return to the critical literature, some writers make dream a pervasive concept in their readings, connecting it to the unusual number of times we see the film's protagonist sleeping (the beginning and end of the film, Lisa's entrance and four occasions during the night of the murder) and the several sweeping shots of the courtyard that end on close-ups of Jeff asleep. For John Fawell, who usefully summarises some of the critical arguments involved, the contrast in scale between 'huge close-ups of Stewart's face and distant shots of miniature people across the way communicates an idea of the neighbours as various thoughts or as Jeff's dreams – visualised, cartoon-like compartments of his brain'.[7]

Once such compelling ideas have been implanted they can seem inescapable, changing forever how we see the film. But in applying the retrospective clarity such insights afford we need to be cautious not to distort the film. When Fawell writes that the contrast in scale of shot between close-ups of Stewart and the other inhabitants of the courtyard '*communicates an idea* of the neighbours as various thoughts or as Jeff's dreams' (my italics) or Robert Stam and Roberta Pearson suggest that '[t]he first time we see Jefferies, significantly, he is asleep, as if everything we are about to see were in some sense his dream',[8] they alert us to interpretive frameworks that illuminate the way the film works but they imply processes of making meaning that feel too immediate and overt to be true to Hitchcock's methods.

My argument is that the methods of the film imply not direct signalling of doubling or dream but the opposite, patterns of action and image that are gradually revealed and that take on significance through evocation and association. What is at stake, then, in the treatment of Lisa's entrance is precisely its unique status within the film's implied dynamic of response and interpretation. Lisa's visit is a literal event in the film's world, yet the condensed, overtly dreamlike imagery in which it is presented evokes Jeff's neurotic anxieties as inseparable from the event itself. Because this is not a dream sequence and our view is not identified with Jeff's, the effect is of his subjectivity suffusing action and place. His vision of Lisa becomes the heart of an elaborate network of relationships that connect Jeff to the world beyond the apartment. The threatening shadow links back, via the conversation with Stella, to the Thorwalds' first appearance as the embodiment of Jeff's view of married life, and forward to the elaborate doubling of the two couples. If, for Jeff, Lisa at first most obviously parallels the 'nagging' Mrs Thorwald (Irene Winston), it is startling to recognise in retrospect that, in a telling rhyme across the film, Lisa's look into the camera and at Jeff is echoed when Thorwald's more obviously threatening gaze moves from Lisa's gesture with the wedding ring, up and across the courtyard, to meet Jeff's eyes as he (and we) look through the telephoto lens.

The change of register at this moment bares the poetic dimension of *Rear Window* – it offers us a glimpse of the pervasive relationship between Jeff's subjectivity and the fictional world that is at the heart of the film but that elsewhere is subsumed in its predominant style. Lisa's entrance offers us what George M. Wilson calls 'a rhetorical figure of narrational instruction';[9] it is a moment in which Hitchcock (briefly) reveals his hand.

NOTES

1. Jeanne Allen, 'Looking through *Rear Window*: Hitchcock's Traps and Lures of Heterosexual Romance', in Deirdre E. Pribram (ed.), *Female Spectators: Looking at Film and Television* (London and New York: Verso, 1988), p. 38.

2. John Belton (ed.), *Alfred Hitchcock's 'Rear Window'* (Cambridge: Cambridge University Press, 2000), p. 78.

3. Allen, 'Looking through *Rear Window*', p. 38.

4. Tania Modleski, *The Women Who Knew Too Much: Hitchcock and Feminist Theory* (London: Methuen, 1988), p. 76.

5. Modleski, *The Women Who Knew Too Much*, p. 79.

6. Robin Wood, *Hitchcock's Films* (London: Zwemmer Ltd, 1965), p. 64.

7. John Wesley Fawell, *Hitchcock's 'Rear Window': The Well-made Film* (Carbondale: Southern Illinois University Press, 2004), p. 76.

8. Robert Stam and Roberta Pearson, 'Hitchcock's *Rear Window*: Reflexivity and the Critique of Voyeurism', in Marshall Deutelbaum and Leland Poague (eds), *A Hitchcock Reader* (2nd edn) (Chichester: Wiley-Blackwell, 2009), p. 202.

9. George M. Wilson, *Narration in Light: Studies in Cinematic Point of View* (Baltimore, MD: Johns Hopkins University Press, 1986), p. 91.

BIBLIOGRAPHY

Allen, Jeanne, 'Looking through *Rear Window*: Hitchcock's Traps and Lures of Heterosexual Romance', in Deirdre E. Pribram (ed.), *Female Spectators: Looking at Film and Television* (London and New York: Verso, 1988).

Belton, John (ed.), *Alfred Hitchcock's 'Rear Window'* (Cambridge: Cambridge University Press, 2000).

Deutelbaum, Marshall and Poague, Leland (eds), *A Hitchcock Reader* (2nd edn) (Chichester: Wiley-Blackwell, 2009).

Fawell, John Wesley, *Hitchcock's 'Rear Window': The Well-made Film* (Carbondale: Southern Illinois University Press, 2004).

MacDowell, James, 'What We Don't See, and What We Think It Means: Ellipsis and Occlusion in *Rear Window*', in Richard Allen and Sydney Gottlieb (eds), *The Hitchcock Annual Anthology*, Vol. 16 (London: Wallflower Press, forthcoming).

Modleski, Tania, *The Women Who Knew Too Much: Hitchcock and Feminist Theory* (London: Methuen, 1988).

Pribram, Deirdre E. (ed.), *Female Spectators: Looking at Film and Television* (London and New York: Verso, 1988).

Stam, Robert and Pearson, Roberta, 'Hitchcock's *Rear Window*: Reflexivity and the Critique of Voyeurism', in Marshall Deutelbaum and Leland Poague (eds), *A Hitchcock Reader* (2nd edn) (Chichester: Wiley-Blackwell, 2009).

Walker, Michael, *Hitchcock's Motifs* (Amsterdam: Amsterdam University Press, 2005).

Wilson, George M., *Narration in Light: Studies in Cinematic Point of View* (Baltimore, MD: Johns Hopkins University Press, 1986).

Wood, Robin, *Hitchcock's Films* (London: Zwemmer Ltd, 1965).

Wood, Robin, *Hitchcock's Films Revisited* (New York: Columbia University Press, 1989).

Opening up *The Secret Garden* (1993)

SUSAN SMITH

Frances Hodgson Burnett's *The Secret Garden* (1911) has been admired by feminist critics on account of its ability to give expression to the psychological and imaginative needs of childhood, and girlhood in particular. The story's ending, though, has been viewed with some disappointment as entailing a relinquishment of the power and individual creativity that the garden – in its secret state – offered the children. Their return to the adult-governed world is seen to involve a reassertion of the social structures and hierarchies of power inherent therein, as Colin's recovery and reunion with his father (and the continuation of the male aristocratic line at Misselthwaite Manor that this signifies) is privileged at the expense of the increasing marginalisation of female protagonist Mary and Yorkshire working-class boy Dickon.[1]

With such a reading of the book in mind, this essay sets out to explore the very different meanings and effects arising from Agnieszka Holland's reinterpretation of the ending in her 1993 film adaptation of Burnett's story. In doing so, it will take as its focus of analysis the poetic epilogue (entirely new to this version) that closes the film, especially the moment of transition between the two brief shots making up this sequence. In analysing the rich interplay that occurs between voice, image and music, the chapter will consider how this epilogue offers an imaginative response to the implied dilemma facing the story at the end: namely, what happens when the children's secret garden is no longer secret.

After the emotional drama of Colin's (Heydon Prowse) reunion with his father and the excitement of the children's joyful walk back to the house with Lord Craven (John Lynch), the epilogue begins, serenely, with a close-up of a water-lily pond. In the pond, a slender female hand, its wrist edged with a white lace cuff, slowly trails through the water while on the soundtrack can be heard a lyrical reprise of one of the film's main musical motifs together with the haunting diegetic cry of a curlew overhead. In effecting this shift, the director immediately resists the ideological implications of the father and son's walk back to the manor at the end of Burnett's story, restoring us instead to a tranquil, private

space within the secret garden that is unmistakably feminine in nature.

But whose hand is this? At first, we might be forgiven for thinking it belongs to Mary (Kate Maberly), whose voiceover we are soon to hear, but on closer inspection the mature, slender reach of its fingers and the sensuous manner in which it feels its way through the vegetation of the pond point to a more adult female presence. Another possibility that might arise on a first viewing is that perhaps this is an image of Mary, now grown up and still enjoying the delights of this special space, but the childlike status of her voiceover once it begins undermines such a reading by grounding the epilogue in the film's present tense. Given the garden's all-important associations with Colin's dead mother and the film's extension of such a link to Mary's dead mother (transformed from distant sister-in-law to twin sister of Colin's mother in this adaptation), and the more specific echoes in the long, white lace sleeve here of the dresses worn by these two women during Mary's and Lord Craven's dreams respectively, we are left to wonder whether the person relaxing by the pond is in fact none other than one of these ghostly maternal figures.

As the hand touches a water-lily flower and tenderly caresses it, Mary declares: 'The spell was broken. My uncle learnt to laugh and I learnt to cry.' The intimation subtly imparted by this image – namely, that Colin's dead mother is still (perhaps now along with her twin sister?) the ongoing

presiding spirit *within* the secret garden – thus finds its natural complement here in the re-establishment of Mary's authority as voiceover narrator *of The Secret Garden*. Her restoration to that role brings with it another significant realignment of Burnett's ending, as the latter's emphasis on the father and son's reunion is replaced by a foregrounding of the harmonious situations of uncle and niece, the juxtaposition of the two clauses in that second sentence even going so far as to equate the resolution of the female child's emotional journey with that of the adult, aristocratic male.

Mary's attempt to sum up the story's happy ending in such a fairytale, clear-cut fashion is complicated, however, by the enigmatic, incomplete nature of the image itself, while her subsequent assertion that 'The secret garden is always *open* now. *Open* – and awake – and alive' (my emphasis) isn't entirely reflected in the camera's tight framing of our view in such a way as to deny a fuller, more revealing sight of the person relaxing by the pond. From Mary's point of view, this statement of hers seems clearly intended as a joyful affirmation of her uncle's fidelity to his promise (given to her during their reconciliation in the previous scene) that he 'won't shut it up again' and the continued flourishing of that special place as a result. But her assertion, while perfectly in tune with the story's happy ending, nevertheless raises the crucial question of how the more secret aspects of the garden will survive given its greater susceptibility now to intrusion from the outside world. And it is this that Holland seems intent on responding to through her composition of this image in a way that suggests the garden's resistance to yielding up its innermost mysteries. In giving us an only partial yet privileged glimpse into its private world, though, the director at the same time registers the film's receptiveness – its own *openness*, if you like, as a text – to the continued existence therein of other realms of female experience that lie outside conventional frameworks of perception.

This meditation on the garden's newfound state of openness is greatly extended and enriched in the second part of the epilogue when, as Mary utters the words 'Open – and awake – and alive', the camera begins, very gradually, to lift and tilt upwards until it takes in a view of the first stone step leading from the pond. It is at this point that Mary begins her last line of narration. 'If you look the right way you can see that the *whole world* is a garden,' she says emphatically, while the camera continues to rise until the rest of the steps and the path beyond come into sight. It is only on Mary's completion of this sentence that the camera (still rising) manages to catch a fleeting glimpse of a young woman in a white dress (reminiscent of Colin's mother during Lord Craven's dream) as she retreats along the path. Lasting only a moment, this view of her becomes increasingly obscured by a canopy of leaves that appears in the foreground just before she finally disappears altogether

behind a bush in the far right-hand corner of the frame. With this canopy of leaves now even more prominent, and with a combination of bird-song and female choral singing emerging on the soundtrack, the film dissolves to a high-level view of Dickon (Andrew Knott) riding on his white horse across the moors.

As the camera continues to crane upwards and away from him, Linda Ronstadt's rendition of the song 'Winter Light' begins:

> Hearts call
> Hearts fall
> Swallowed in the rain
>
> Who knows
> Life grows
> Hollow and so vain
>
> Wandering in the winter light
> The wicked and the sane
> Bear witness to salvation
> And life starts over again …

In enacting this shift from garden to moors, the epilogue takes us even further away from the upper-class, male-ordered world of Misselthwaite Manor, thereby completing its reversal of Burnett's decision to end her story by foregrounding Colin's triumphant walk back to the house with his father. But to appreciate the full significance and enriching effects of this transition we also have to consider the epilogue's roots in two earlier key incidents – namely, the moment in Mary's dream where her mother, having reached out smiling towards her, suddenly turns and walks away down a path in the secret garden, leaving her daughter distraught and all alone; and the one (prior to that) where Mary is interrupted in her search for the garden by her first encounter with Dickon. Having drawn attention to himself by his laughter, the boy on that occasion was shown running away through the winding paths of the grounds and out onto the moors via an archway in the wall before jumping onto his horse and riding off into the distance.

Creatively imagined in ways that are once again unique to this particular adaptation of Burnett's story, both of these moments deal with situations where important people in Mary's life are shown turning and hurrying away from her. But if the one involving her mother seems designed to re-enact her sense of abandonment as a young child (in not feeling loved and in being left alone following her parents' death), then the one relating to Dickon carries much more positive suggestions, associated as it is with childlike notions of play (she is now prompted to *chase after* him) and, considering the look of curiosity she gives him on arriving herself at the archway, emerging friendship and attraction between them. The precise timing of Dickon's appearance, following on directly as it does from Mary's appeal to the robin, perched on the handle of a nearby spade, to lead her to the garden ('If you know the way, show me'), is crucial in suggesting the boy's potential to act as an alternative guide for Mary. Someone who, rather than directing her to the 'womb-like' space of the garden, is capable of drawing her away from this and out towards a wilder, less protective realm redolent of freedom, independence and the discovery of romantic desire.

In invoking and reworking these two visual tropes (the mother's act of walking away down a path in the garden, Dickon's act of riding out onto the moors), the epilogue therefore brings them together in ways that now invite them to be read as two parts of one overall continuum of movement. The exact structuring of the film's last two shots – as the woman is shown exiting to the right of frame in the first, only for Dickon to pick up the trajectory of her movement through his appearance from left of frame in the next – is vital in generating such an effect and this is enhanced all the more by the use of a dissolve to hold them together. The superimposition arising from such a device in fact creates the very particular impression of Dickon *emerging from* the canopy of leaves that had first obscured our fleeting glimpse of this woman, prior to her disappearance behind a bush. The mother's act of walking away during Mary's dream is consequently transformed through this process of juxtaposition from its original negative meaning of abandonment into something signifying progression and release: the woman's retreat down the path and out of sight is now readable on this occasion as a gesture of freedom and independence for both adult female and child and one that, provoking none of Mary's earlier distress, seems to pave the way for this transition into the world outside. And if the open-ended vision of Dickon riding away across the moors seems designed to symbolise the child's journey towards independence and growing up, then the manner in which the film dissolves from the previous shot to this invites us to consider such a process as involving not a

rejection of the maternal figure but a continuation of the values and qualities she embodies.

This is accentuated by the fact that it is, appropriately, Dickon – a boy rendered Other by his working-class position and embodying 'feminine' qualities of nurturing through his caring for animals and nature – who picks up the impetus and direction of that woman's movement, and this underlying sense of him as an extension of the maternal figure finds further expression in the mirroring of the woman's *white* dress in the colour of his shirt and horse. Ronstadt's song (the darker thematics of which develop the garden's own associations with nature's cycle of life, death and rebirth) adds another dimension to Dickon's links with the feminine, while the use of an ascending chorus of female voices as an aural bridge between the two shots also helps generate a feeling of the mother's spirit being released and diffused out onto the moors.

It is not only the mother whose sensibility finds outlet in this way but Mary too, since it is her newly discovered vision of the 'whole world [as] a garden' that the film seeks to realise in this concluding shot. Its effectiveness in doing so owes much to Holland's rich orchestration of a whole range of detailed continuities between these two spaces. We have already noted one such instance of this in the aural bridge created by the rising chorus of female voices that marks the beginning of Ronstadt's song, and this is reflected in the craning of the camera itself as it rises away from the pond right up into the trees in the garden before soaring high above the heath. This camera trajectory in turn reveals another visual link, with the close-up view of the water-lily pond eventually giving way to the image of a distant tarn. The use of a dissolve also results in the garden's canopy of leaves being momentarily superimposed over the heather-clad moors and this visual overlapping is beautifully mirrored on the soundtrack through the carrying forward of the garden's glorious bird-song into the film's final stunning vista.

Awareness of such effects counters the sense of class isolation otherwise invoked by the camera's retreating aerial view of Dickon, gesturing instead towards Mary's deepening emotional affinity with this character who, having imparted his vision of nature to her, now becomes part of her own pastoral outlook. In allowing Mary to arrive at this point of insight, the film thereby completes a broader transformation of perspective that began earlier in the narrative when she was shown telling Colin a story she'd learnt back in India about a young god who was just like other people except for the fact that 'when you looked down his throat you could see the whole universe there'. This is something that Colin initially finds impossible to accept, using science and rationality to argue that 'it doesn't make sense … it's so stupid'. But his scornful rejection of the magical properties of children's fiction is completely discarded when, on entering the secret garden for the first time, he attempts to explain his feelings of fullness and wonderment by saying, 'It's like the story', and adding (as he points to his chest), 'The whole universe is in here.' In giving expression to Mary's vision of 'the whole world [as] a garden' in its final shot, the film thus extends its fascination with the imaginative flexibility of the child's perspective and in a way that now seems intent on suggesting the need to move on from that earlier process of internalising the garden's wonders to learning to project what one has discovered from it onto one's experience of the world outside.

In doing so, the film's epilogue refuses a more conventionally pessimistic reading of the story's ending, the implied question of what will happen now that the secret garden is no longer secret being met not with an admission of its vulnerability to intrusion from the outside world (something that the enigmatic image of the woman's hand trailing through the water-lily pond strenuously resists) but with an assertion, rather, of the garden's capacity to expand outwards into the child's experience of the world at large. As such, the epilogue fulfils the director's overall designs in opening up *The Secret Garden* as a text to its earlier complexities, with Holland using the distinctive properties of film to breathe new life into the story's ending. To extend the meaning of Mary's closing voiceover, one might indeed be tempted to sum up the achievements of this adaptation in the following terms: '*The Secret Garden* is always open now. Open ... and awake ... and alive.'

NOTE

1. See Shirley Foster and Judy Simons, *What Katy Read: Feminist Re-readings of 'Classic' Stories for Girls* (Basingstoke and London: Macmillan, 1995), pp. 172–91.

BIBLIOGRAPHY

Burnett, Frances Hodgson, *The Secret Garden* (London: Walker Books, 2008 [1911]).
Foster, Shirley and Simons, Judy, *What Katy Read: Feminist Re-readings of 'Classic' Stories for Girls* (Basingstoke and London: Macmillan, 1995).

A Magnified Meeting in *Written on the Wind* (1956)

STEVEN PEACOCK

The meeting – that is to say the point of first acquaintance – of central characters is an inevitable and important moment in many narrative films. Some films build dramatically to a long-awaited encounter, creating an appointment fraught with tension and anticipation. For example, *Heat* (Mann, 1995) plots a 'cat-and-mouse' course of pursuit towards the face-off of cop (Al Pacino) and robber (Robert De Niro), in doing so, infamously bringing these two actors together on screen for the very first time. Others shape the moment of meeting as apparently inconsequential or happenstance, only later revealing its significance (in films from *City Lights* [Chaplin, 1931] to *Psycho* [Hitchcock, 1960] to *Pulp Fiction* [Tarantino, 1994]). Still more simply pass over the instant, marking a necessary social contract without ceremony (getting on with business), or immediately declare their impact (as a femme fatale walks into the office of a suddenly flustered PI, or, more strangely, as the eponymous protagonist apparently comes back from the dead to meet the entranced gumshoe in *Laura* [1944]). *Written on the Wind* (Sirk, 1956) finds ways to present a first encounter that is both exaggerated and indeterminate.

We are five minutes into the film. In the hot nightspot setting of '21', oil tycoon Kyle Hadley (Robert Stack) is introduced for the first time to his future wife Lucy (Lauren Bacall) arriving with his best friend Mitch (Rock Hudson). The film moves to the meeting via two preparatory moments: Lucy and Mitch whisking to '21' in a taxi, and Kyle waiting (with two stopgap companions) for their arrival. Kyle has routinely arranged to see Mitch (and, customarily, he gets what he wants). The appearance of Lucy is a pleasant surprise.

One would tend to overlook this meeting in a film filled with more demonstrative instances of dramatic richness.[1] Elsewhere in this book, and across his work, Andrew Klevan has explored ordinary, in-between or 'apparently unrealised' moments in film.[2] In the light of Klevan's work, I am interested in looking at a moment that expresses 'apparently unrealised' feeling within an environment of dramatic amplification. The meeting in *Written on the Wind* is both passing and emphatic; diffuse impressions float

around forceful declarations. It takes its lead from Kyle Hadley: insistent arrangements of *mise en scène* convey this character's tendency for overbearing displays. At the same time, the film's compositions carry subtle appeals and drifting concerns. Showy signs of décor, gesture and colouring match aspects of Kyle's declamatory presence, but also prickle with subliminal energies.

The channelling of psychological elements into style is a noted characteristic of melodramas like *Written on the Wind*. As Thomas Elsaesser famously suggests in 'Tales of Sound and Fury', such films often present 'a sublimation of dramatic conflict into décor, colour, gesture and composition of the frame, which in the best melodramas is perfectly thematised in terms of the characters' emotional and psychological predicaments'.[3] *Written on the Wind* offers exemplary renderings and Elsaesser draws out one such instance from the film, detailing how:

> When Robert Stack ... standing by the window he has just opened to get some fresh air into an extremely heavy family atmosphere, hears of Lauren Bacall expecting a baby, the most eloquent thing about his misery is the way in which he squeezes himself into the frame of the half-open window, every word his wife says to him bringing torment to his lacerated soul and body.[4]

The moment of first meeting highlights a different handling of suggestive *mise en scène*. While it presents a 'sublimation of dramatic conflict into décor', the sequence is foremost charged with Kyle's assertiveness. It rearranges the melodramatic effect described by Elsaesser. Instead of a small gesture eloquently capturing a hidden magnitude of feeling (the totality of 'torment'), expressions of overstatement convey more mute impulses. At this point in the film, Kyle can't help showing off, and his brash displays are subtly revealing.

In the first of the two precursory instants, red colouring, while bold, expresses something more diffuse.[5] The colour's forceful presence in the frame is suggestive of undecided associations that remain, for the characters in this scene, 'apparently unrealised'. A pattern of red picks up as Mitch and Lucy take the cab to '21'. Wryly commenting on Kyle's indulgences – travelling 1,580 miles for a steak sandwich – they rest back on the deep-red leather seating. The image recalls the shape and hue of earlier instances. Red placards stand between the two when *they* first meet in Lucy's office. It also rhymes with the initial view of Lucy in the credit sequence, tumbling down on her red-backed bed. Like Kyle, red stresses the characters' arrangements by implication. The tone of a conversation can become tainted by thoughts of an illustrious figure, especially in their absence. Lucy smiles in accord with Mitch's remark that they might be 'two of a kind'. The bright red of her lipstick plays off the richer, darker shade of the leather. Although they are not yet aware of it, they will become two of a kind only in their link to Kyle. The colour is assertive and allusive, forming a backdrop to a relationship that is both overwrought and unsure. Even before these three people come together, Mitch and Lucy are indirectly associated with Kyle's brashness.

The next scene takes us to the rendezvous point, introducing how a focus on Kyle's overstatement leads to more scattered suggestions. Already holding court in '21', Kyle sits at a table with two female companions.

The brightness of the occasion threatens to peter out. As if participants in a lacklustre card game, the women stare into their drinks, down to the flat surface and red edge of the tablecloth. The camera angle places the characters in the middle of the frame: a loud but jaded centre table. More animation comes from surrounding bodies. A course of bustling customers and white-coated waiters passes in front of and behind the seated party. (Far left, Harry the barman wipes a glass clean: a sidling reminder of Kyle's craving – most of his conduct banks on drink.) A flow of agitation on the verge of the table hints at how the present company grates, while thoughts of Mitch niggle. In a roundabout way, the diverting appeal of Mitch coming is central, yet its significance remains indirectly articulated. Placing Kyle (at the) dead centre, the film asserts the position of an overassertive character. At the same time, in the surrounding bustle, it introduces the suggestion of more circuitous stimulations to come in this place.

Things on the edge make the scene's domineering personality complex. Particular decorative trappings, placed above Kyle, evoke products of a lifestyle that hang over his undertakings. Set along a horizontal arc tracing top left of the frame down to Kyle's head, a bright-red toy truck tilts towards a strung-up model biplane. These toys recall other more ostensibly adult objects that reveal Kyle as a childish hedonist. The red truck brings to mind the first sight of Kyle, racing along in his yellow roadster; the biplane is a pre-echo of his private jet, the means to take Lucy on an ill-fated trip to Miami. The models are flagrantly referential as symbols and at the same time peripheral, creating an impression of significance that is at once emphatic and adrift.

A decisive gesture encapsulates Kyle's misguided force of forward direction. His first words of the restaurant scene – 'Harry, put it on my tab' – are accompanied by a jabbing forefinger, his hand cocked gun-like towards the barman to stress the drinks order. Like Kyle, the gesture is a little too aggressive: an oddly effortful play at playfulness. (As he delivers the order, little dragon puffs of cigarette smoke issue from his mouth with each word.) Command and gesture suggest this character's belief in his belligerent control of surroundings and circumstances.

In film, a cut to a close shot often conveys a gathering of focus and determination, but in this instance it also points to more diffuse currents of feeling. The cut comes midway through Kyle's description of the anticipated guest, as 'Mitch Wayne, my sidekick'. On 'my sidekick', the camera reframes nearer to Kyle and his blonde companion (Dani Crayne). Tossing a spent match into the ashtray, Kyle casts his words as throwaway. Yet splitting the sentence in an edit faintly underscores the line, encouraging a little more attention on this particular turn of phrase. 'Sidekick' conjures jocular associations of a knockabout playmate. The dismissive edge to phrase and delivery suggests prescribed subordination. Kyle's tipsiness adds another kind of slur, with 'sidekick' muddling in his mouth to sound like 'psychic'. The precise form of this unconscious correlation hints at a more entrenched connection between the men, an unspoken depth of feeling now fuzzily floating to the surface in champagne bubbles.

Having described his 'sidekick', Kyle gazes smiling down at his drink, caught in a little reverie. His eyes dart defensively upwards when pressed on Mitch's history by the blonde girl. The spat of patter starts with her blunt question:

COMPANION (UNNAMED): Where do his millions come from?
KYLE: He's eccentric; he's poor.
COMPANION: Ha ha ha! I bet.
KYLE: Honey, you lose; Mitch is just a country boy; the kind of assets he's got you can't buy for money.

Suddenly the stale card-game gamble of cocktail-hour conversation flutters back to life. The revelation of Mitch's 'lot' is played by Kyle as an ace. Using his friend to trump the girl is rather vulgar, and frostily characteristic. The framing of the shot places the bartering couple under a brash piece of décor: an oversized gold coin on a blue placard hangs on the wall behind them. Its obtrusive appearance matches the garish tone of chatter and the crude stake of their exchange. Kyle vaunts Mitch's natural appeals ('the kind of assets he's got you can't buy for money') in a brassy boast. Forming under the sign of the coin, his words are at once caustic, clichéd and longing.

As the characters chat over their drinks, headiness mixes with flickers of conflicting energy. Having swirled her drink's olive-topped swizzle stick in champagne, the blonde girl brushes it against her lips, toying with it as she toys with Kyle about Mitch. A cruel lightness of luxuriant play is weighted down by the heavy loops of white pearls coiling around the girl's neck. Aiming for arch frivolity, she instead places a chokehold on the chatter. As Kyle puts down and praises Mitch, the girl's hand falls to the table-top, but stick and olive keep perked upright. While the words seem one-note, the cocktail stick directs a less certain refrain, suspending a morsel of interest. It is a needling show of diverse feeling, disappointment blending with intrigue. The stick's quiver adds an inflection to the moment's emphasis, pricking Kyle's inflated claims.

Rather than cut to Mitch and Lucy entering the restaurant, the film stays with Kyle: it is a final act on the periphery of a domineering dramatic centre. The accomplishment of the arrival suggests Kyle's (over)asserted authority of the instant and more drifting aspects. On 'you can't buy for money', Kyle takes a proud gulp of champagne. Tipping hand and head to glass in an oft-repeated gesture, he swivels in the direction of the door. The camera nudges left with Kyle's quaff, bringing Mitch and Lucy into view. Kyle completes a boastful spell and Mitch materialises. The coupled move of Kyle and camera underlines the tycoon's sway. (That the camera movement is the first of the scene adds a further note of emphasis.) At the same time, a waft of Kyle's cigarette smoke floats across the sight of the couple just as they enter the vestibule. At the point of his merits being voiced, his 'assets' now at the forefront of Kyle's mind, Mitch steps over the threshold, but still there is a haziness about the effect of his appearance.

Seeing Mitch instantly lifts Kyle's spirits, yet casts more ruminative musings out, along with the female companions. Kyle stands with a clipped farewell to the girls, dipping his cigarette down to fizzle in his glass of champagne. The small gesture is full of drink, snuffed desire, power and impotence. It is a transitory move on the cusp of a connection, all the more eloquent for its automatic execution. Emphatically completed, the little plunge sullies and moves into a stressed greeting.

After a passage of rich opacity, the first physical meeting between Kyle, Lucy and Mitch is dramatically decisive and uncertain. Lucy's reaction counters Kyle's pomposity, quickly thinning the moment out. Yet possibilities are in the air. As Kyle strides over to deliver his greeting, the film cuts to a medium shot of the three figures. Whereas the tycoon's outspoken manner dictated the previous encounter's surface displays, Lucy's more demure attitude flattens a showy moment into formal staidness. The three characters stand in a uniform row, colours muted to tawny browns (for Mitch) and pale blues (for Lucy and Kyle), arms outstretched, faces fixed in cautious pleasantries.

This more restrained assembly is quietly expressive of things to come. The colours of their clothing set Mitch alone in the middle, beginning a pattern of coupling and isolation that finds its fullest expression on the plane trip to Miami. In this later moment, as Kyle and Lucy stoop to enter the aircraft, the couple's matching light-grey jackets brush together. Mitch's surprise presence quickly complicates a moment of parity. His tawny brown jacket fits with the interior of the plane: he is, perhaps reluctantly, somewhat at home in this familiar place. While accustomed to these confines, he muddies the new light tone of the fledgeling relationship, standing in between Lucy and Kyle in the overcrowded cabin.

Equally, on the point of their first meeting at the restaurant, while Lucy is sceptical of Kyle's dubious charms, her top three open coat buttons may already hint at the consequent capacity to loosen her guard (and come undone). A curt handshake seals their initial encounter, their joined hands holding them together and forming a barrier across Mitch in the middle. Minor details make a simple gesture complex. Lucy takes the initiative, extending her hand first. Wariness meets resolve: her hand is gloved. (Only later, in Kyle and Lucy's doomed and quarrelsome marriage, will the gloves come off.) As her hand finds Kyle's, their eyes turn instead to Mitch. A love triangle of involved combinations is held in a stark tableau of greeting. The fledgeling firm link between Lucy and Kyle is bound across and through Mitch (he is, in many ways, the star-crossed abettor, a better man but go-between). They hold him in. Alert to the expected automatic enactment of a handshake on first meeting, the film hints at the base impulses in a basic, impulsive connection. For better or worse, Kyle and Lucy are now joined, just like that.

In a quick shift, a sober first meeting's final gesture suggests Kyle leaning towards his more usual lusty position. Grabbing at control, a presumptuous hand falls on Lucy's shoulder. Her eyes are icy, yet she yields. Keen to change the outlook of the encounter, a grip on the shoulder allows Kyle to turn Lucy away from Mitch, to guide her into the den.

The previous dull party is put out with the dunked butt, making way for freshly audacious designs. Kyle leads his new guests to a clean table. Wealth's enchantment again touches the scene, with Kyle as society's sorcerer. The film does not make the change of tables clear; there is the suggestion that the two tedious girls have simply disappeared. The sparkle of fresh champagne takes their place, magically appearing in the melt of a dissolve. As the new threesome sits, the camera tilts to loom over the tablecloth. Whereas the red cloth previously added only an edge of colour, it now fills the frame in a burst of brightness. Here is the first flush – too much. The move matches the effect of Kyle's own grandiose gestures; both overreach.

For Lucy, the day's dealings are undeniably exciting, yet Kyle's showy boasts and shallow clichés are embarrassing. Held for a beat too long, the commanding shot of the red cloth is suggestively emphatic. Pushing into an extreme position, this melodrama's poise threatens to topple over into embellishment. The camera passes over the tablecloth, the closest it will get in this film to the surface of things: the moment of greatest magnification. Just as quickly, the dissolve brings the champagne glasses into view over the dense red block. The moves are at once declamatory and mysterious. As the camera tips, colour swells and glasses gradually appear, meaning is at once suspended, opaque and dissolved. While Kyle remains steadfast in his self-belief, the looming camera fleetingly and forcefully marks a little crisis. It urges attention and yet the significance of these urges remains unspecified. As in many other films, the future of two lovers hinges on the form of their first meeting; here a first encounter balances precariously – as the couple's relationship will do – between crude declarations and more tacit disturbances.

NOTES

1. For example, Tag Gallagher writes about the plane ride to Miami, and the death-dealing dance of Kyle's sister Marylee (Dorothy Malone), as she 'writhes in sado-masochistic masturbation, craving power' ('White Melodrama: Douglas Sirk', *Senses of Cinema* vol. 5 no. 36); Fred Camper notes the scene in which Lucy is taken to an 'unimaginably opulent hotel suite' (*The Films of Douglas Sirk: The Epistemologist of Despair*, <www.fredcamper.com> (accessed 19 September 2009)); and James Harvey talks with Douglas Sirk about moments embracing the 'blatancy of symbols ... for example, the boy on the rocking horse whom Stack sees just after the doctor has told him that he can never have children ... it gets such emphasis – Stack bugs his eyes and the music swells' ('Sirkumstantial Evidence', in Lucy Fischer (ed.), *Imitation of Life* (New Brunswick, NJ: Rutgers University Press, 1991), p. 223).

2. See also Andrew Klevan, *Disclosure of the Everyday: Undramatic Achievement in Narrative Film* (Trowbridge: Flicks Books, 2000).

3. Thomas Elsaesser, 'Tales of Sound and Fury: Observations on the Family Melodrama', *Monogram* no. 4, 1972, p. 7.

4. Ibid., p. 11.

5. For a sustained appraisal of colour in *Written on the Wind*, see Steven Peacock, *Colour: Cinema Aesthetics* (Manchester: Manchester University Press, 2010).

BIBLIOGRAPHY

Camper, Fred, *The Films of Douglas Sirk: The Epistemologist of Despair*. Available at <www.fredcamper.com> (accessed 19 September 2009).

Elsaesser, Thomas, 'Tales of Sound and Fury: Observations on the Family Melodrama', *Monogram* no. 4, 1972, p. 7.

Fischer, Lucy (ed.), *Imitation of Life* (New Brunswick, NJ: Rutgers University Press, 1991).

Gallagher, Tag, 'White Melodrama: Douglas Sirk', *Senses of Cinema* vol. 5 no. 36.

Harvey, James, 'Sirkumstantial Evidence', in Lucy Fischer (ed.), *Imitation of Life* (New Brunswick, NJ: Rutgers University Press, 1991).

Klevan, Andrew, *Disclosure of the Everyday: Undramatic Achievement in Narrative Film* (Trowbridge: Flicks Books, 2000).

Peacock, Steven, *Colour: Cinema Aesthetics* (Manchester: Manchester University Press, 2010).

'Everything is connected, and everything matters': Relationships in *I ♥ Huckabees* (2004)

JOHN GIBBS

In the spirit of the line of dialogue quoted above, this chapter looks at not one moment but two from *I ♥ Huckabees* (Russell, 2004), both tracking shots involving Albert Markovski (Jason Schwartzman) and Tommy Corn (Mark Wahlberg) riding bicycles.

In late afternoon sunshine Albert and Tommy approach along the nearside of an urban, multi-lane road, the camera panning through 180 degrees with Albert as he passes. They ride across the mouth of a junction and negotiate the curb, Tommy's bicycle looping out in a wide arc. A dissolve shifts us to a residential setting, now overcast. In mobile long shot we see Tommy; Albert then swings onto the street, as though from round the corner, and the two cycle side by side, gradually nearing the camera until they are held in medium shot.

They are looking for the house where Steven Nimieri (Ger Duany), the Sudanese refugee and the subject of Albert's coincidences, lives with his adoptive family. Albert has the address on a scrap of paper, which he consults as he rides, but it is Tommy who sees Steven first, pointing off screen to where he is playing basketball on the drive: 'Hey, is that him there?' The shot ends between the first two words of Tommy's question, with a cut to a camera position at the side of the road.

The shot is twenty-five seconds long, which gives time for us to experience movement and, in combination with the framing, to achieve a good view of how each rides. They are half coasting, but Tommy manages an easy, even action while Albert pedals in faster bursts. Tommy's saddle is fixed too low, but this contributes to an open-legged stance, which evokes a relaxed but robust approach. The design of Albert's bike is toward a traditional roadster, with hub gear, three-quarter mudguards, a basket and a rack: slightly prim, perhaps, for a man in his early twenties. Tommy rides a more modern, hybrid design, with wide handlebars. Albert wears a suit and shirt and his hair shoulder length.

Tommy wears blue trousers, a collared short-sleeved shirt with the buttons done up unevenly and his firefighter's boots, folded down below the knee. Both are unshaven.

The score combines an upbeat guitar rhythm, light percussion elements evocative of bicycle bells and a cooing chorus of male voices, broadening across the mix, as the shot gets into its stride, with the gentle addition of strings.

The movie has darted off in an unforeseen direction – one not anticipated even by the existential detectives, hitherto the film's leading source of the unexpected – and the whole enterprise is rolling through space, us with it. We have been invited to join the extraordinary, preposterous investigation of Albert's coincidences, and suddenly, spontaneously, we are on the move. Immediacy and duration, music and movement catch us up in this endeavour which the characters take so seriously.

That it is a two-shot is important. We have journeyed with Albert on his own before, in the Steadicam shots which appear under the titles as he searches for the Jaffes' office in a maze of corridors, first energetically then hesitantly. Now he and Tommy ride together. The foundations for the partnership are laid in the preceding scene, in which trust rapidly develops between Albert and Tommy, despite Brad's (Jude Law) attempts to enlist Tommy in undermining Albert, and which turns on Tommy's readiness to jeopardise his standing to create a diversion for Albert. The stand-off which ensues reminds me of an exciting moment in a Western, like *Bend of the River* (Mann, 1952), where various characters throw their cards in together, based on a shared respect and a sense of uniting against a common antagonist, even though they may be on different journeys.

Bicycles have a playful aspect and provide freedoms uncommon in other forms of transport, qualities which contribute to the pleasures and character of the moment. For these particular riders, cycling corresponds to deeply held views: Tommy refuses to use petroleum on ethical grounds and Albert is the leader of a local environmental group fighting suburban sprawl. The shot forms one component in the film's commitment to dramatising abstract ideas in physical forms, particularly through movement.

Albert always wears a suit, but never a tie. He is much more concerned about image than Tommy, and the investigation has already exposed his desire for attention and acclaim, an end for which his environmental commitments partially provide a means. Nevertheless, he remains an attractive as well as a fallible protagonist. Tommy's badly buttoned shirt and stubble (his fellow firefighters are clean-shaven) imply a disregard for external things. That he is wearing his boots indicates an enduring bond with his profession; hardly ideal footwear outside work, we may also remember his argument about child labour in shoe manufacture and conclude that wearing them is a principled economy. It is because he sees the connections between his

actions and their economic, political and environmental consequences that Tommy's life is in crisis.

My response to the moment – and I suspect I'm not alone in this – is partly shaped by my liking for Tommy. Though less central to the story than Albert, he is the movie's most charismatic and compelling character. He is also the most violent, prone to expressing frustration verbally and physically, though the impact of this violence is softened by the context in which it is received, by the tolerance of his colleagues or the Jaffes (Dustin Hoffman and Lily Tomlin) and by the tone of the film.

Tommy has an intensity and directness that demands respect, even though his views are expressed with energy rather than persuasive argument, and his outbursts fail to influence those around him. Some good examples occur over dinner with Steven's family which follows:

TOMMY: If Hitler were alive he'd tell you not to worry about oil.
MRS HOOTEN (Jean Smart): You're the Hitler! We took a Sudanese refugee into our home!
TOMMY: You did. But how did Sudan happen, Mam? Could it possibly be related to dictatorships which we support for some stupid reason?

Another of Tommy's condensed arguments appears in the corresponding movement away from Steven's house that provides our second moment. Albert and Tommy emerge to find the Jaffes standing in the flowerbed, where they have been listening to the conversation. Albert and particularly Tommy are scathing about the detectives' methodology, Tommy taking on directly Bernard's conviction concerning the benefits of recognising the interrelationship of all matter and experience, which Bernard tends to consider in metaphysical rather than socio-economic terms.

The second bicycling tracking shot begins, with Tommy and Albert pushing themselves along before starting to pedal and the Jaffes accompanying them from the sidewalk.

TOMMY: Okay, how does this connect? Mr Nyere's [sic] an orphan from Sudan who was chased by soldiers and crocodiles. So how does the love glow fit into *that*, man?

As the bikes begin to move faster the Jaffes begin to jog, Bernard pointing toward Albert to emphasise his point.

BERNARD: It's connected. Albert and Mr Nimieri share a great deal. It's just that … . Oh! Oh, my God!

Matching the speed of the bicycles, in the frame-right foreground, but for most of the shot unnoticed by the characters, is the hood of a pale yellow sedan.

It becomes more prominent to us after speeding up and as a new element of the score emerges on the right-

hand speakers. When Bernard catches sight of the passenger, he breaks off, and we cut to a reverse field close-up of Caterine Vauban (Isabelle Huppert) riding on the back seat of the car, motionless, staring fixedly.

> VIVIAN: What's *she* doing here? … . Oh, this is worse than I thought!
> BERNARD: Oh, it's much worse.

The configuration of this second movement, with Tommy and Albert flanked on one side by the attentions of the Jaffes and on the other by Caterine's adversarial approach, neatly articulates the choice that confronts the cyclists on their philosophical and political journey. Tommy has already been reading the work of the steely Vauban, and against his instinct finds the idea that 'nothing is connected, it doesn't matter what you do' compelling, at least in explaining 'why people do destructive things like it doesn't matter'. After Albert has been thrown out of the environmental coalition, he too is ready to 'come over to [her] side', and the two leave the Jaffes, embarking on an encounter with the 'cruelty, manipulation, meaningless' which Caterine claims is the nature of the universe. Ultimately, Albert and Tommy will find a middle way, which holds the Jaffe and Vauban methods in dialectic, but this is not yet the case and the two are caught between competing philosophies.

It is characteristic of the film that such matters are played out in this absurd situation, and with everybody on the move, the Jaffes gamely battling with headphones and handbag as they scurry along, Vauban coolly chauffeured, looking not at Tommy and Albert but directly at her adversaries. Ridiculous and serious simultaneously, the film gives the action the same weight as the characters do.

Bernard doesn't mind standing in a flowerbed or running with headphones around his neck. His shaggy moptop and skewed suit suggest that he chooses his clothes deliberately but doesn't wear them carefully, consistent with someone whose attention lies beyond his immediate circumstances. Vivian gives more attention to self-presentation, dressing in a series of immaculate outfits, but she is equally prepared to run along a sidewalk in heels, dive into a trashcan or run through lawn sprinklers in following a case. The unself-conscious manner with which they conduct their investigations is matched by the film's presentation of these extraordinary pursuits.

Caterine's controlled entrance, in appropriate contrast, is in keeping with her hard-edged approach. Soon she has Tommy and Albert riding in her car, Albert's bicycle poking uncomfortably out of the trunk in one shot: a powerful detail, given Tommy's convictions concerning motoring and that the preference for cycling was one of the things which helped establish his friendship with Albert.

Despite the charming qualities the Jaffes bring to the picture, including their commitment to their clients, the film's journey exposes problems with the service their agency provides. Vivian draws on psychoanalysis, working through the evidence betrayed by personal behaviour. In cohort, but with a different emphasis, Bernard encourages clients to dismantle their ordinary perceptions and recognise a fundamental interconnection between the self and the rest of the universe, using a blanket as illustration: 'When you get the blanket thing, you can relax, because anything you could ever want or be, you already have and are.' However, Bernard's understanding of these connections clearly isn't working for Tommy, who comes to regard it as offering merely personal equilibrium without answering to broader social realities. Caterine's paradigm admits to the inequalities and destructive trajectories of society but delights in them, inviting her followers to embrace desire and degradation, wallow in the deep sorrow of existence and take cynical and self-serving pleasure in suffering.

The end of the film gives us Tommy and Albert sitting on the rock, Tommy still in his boots, Albert now with dishevelled clothes, reunited after the divisions which Caterine's promise of 'human drama' introduced between them. They have drawn on the personal investigation offered by Vivian and on the sense of connection which is central to Bernard's 'method', but also faced up to some of the more challenging consequences of recognising the interdependence of everything. (Also, Tommy has connected with Dawn [Naomi Watts] and Albert has worked through an understanding of his relationship with Brad, but that's another part of the story.) Friendship restored, they plan to chain themselves to the bulldozers which will arrive to develop the marsh the next day, and the rival detectives, watching from the sidelines, agree that something important has been achieved. And should this charting of the film's philosophical structures have become unduly earnest, it's worth remembering that Tommy still has time to hit himself and Albert in the face with a space hopper (or 'hoppity hop') as the final image recedes from focus.

There remains a flaw in the film's exploration of these issues, however, one that concerns Steven. The problem lies not with the dinner scene between the bike rides but later, when Caterine reveals her explanation of Albert and Steven's coincidental encounters. Her argument is that Steven, an orphan, is a displaced symbol of Albert's neglect by his indifferent parents, a conclusion which appears to speak to Albert and which the Jaffes largely go along with. The problem here – one that Tommy might appreciate – is that this reduces Steven to a mute symbol of Albert's family drama. The explanation claims a connection, but one that renders Steven's experience (or, rather, his reported experience) a simile for Albert's upbringing. This is a Caterine explanation, certainly, but not one which the film ought simply to accept. Unnoticed by the other characters, Steven gives a quizzical look as Albert and friends leave the building, but rather than leaving him a prop in Caterine's *coup de théâtre*, the film might have invited his thoughts on the subject of the comparison, and what the coincidences might mean for him; an opportunity missed, not least as Ger Duany is one of the Sudanese 'lost boys'.

Alongside its interest in finding dynamic and amusing ways of physicalising elaborate debates, the film is characterised by taking seriously the badly argued but deeply felt ways in which characters, and especially Tommy, express themselves. We know to invoke Hitler is one of the poorest forms of rhetoric and that if the ethnic conflicts of Sudan are linked to the pursuit of American interests then establishing this demands careful marshalling of evidence. The more cogent *The Root Causes of Sudan's Civil Wars* indicates that US support for Nimeiri and his successors, which included military aid, was indeed one of the major factors that contributed to the second civil war.)[1] Yet there are real pleasures offered in watching Tommy argue, partly because of his directness and disregard for niceties; and if Tommy were able to fully elaborate his arguments it would damage the film's qualities of vital comic drama, slipping damagingly toward the didactic.

Equally, though Tommy is right in seeing the relationship between shoes in a western closet and labour conditions in other parts of the world, his way of vocalising this is incendiary, and we can see why his wife has left him. The film achieves a balance here too. While emotionally and conceptually on Tommy's side in the argument with the Hootens, the dinner scene also manages to give his opponents weight, realising the members of the family in only a few minutes, and registering qualities as well as limitations. This is a tribute to dramatic construction and to performance but also to the tone of a film which won't reduce its characters to caricatures.

Relationships between people and events are among the conceits which narratives impose upon the world, and when they become too evidently a design we reach for words like contrivance and implausibility. In this film, however, seeking out connections and investigating coincidences are matters in which the characters are actively engaged, and major concerns of the film. That to an unusual degree everything is connected (and everything matters) also presents a critical challenge: rather than be content to plumb the depths of a single moment, this chapter needed to range widely across the film's length in order to put into words the ways both moment and film work. Any good film, and any sensitive analysis, obliges us to think in both dimensions: to consider the patterns and systems of the whole as well as study the interaction of different elements in the instant. Here, however, explicating the moment has demanded unusually extended recourse to structures and information deployed through time, and considerable care in fashioning an argument which respects these relationships in the form of a close reading. There may be something highly characteristic about the film in this regard, or lengthier enquiry might reveal this to be a significant feature of, say, comedic, as opposed to melodramatic, forms of popular cinema. For the time being, it can act as a reminder that if we are interested in moments, we need also be alive to connections. *I ♥ Huckabees* is strong in both.

NOTE

1. Douglas H. Johnson, *The Root Causes of Sudan's Civil Wars* (Oxford: International African Institute in association with James Currey, 2003).

BIBLIOGRAPHY

Johnson, Douglas H., *The Root Causes of Sudan's Civil Wars* (Oxford: International African Institute in association with James Currey, 2003).

The Ending of 8½ (1963)

RICHARD DYER

What happens at the end of 8½? Guido (Marcello Mastroianni) is on the set of the film he has abandoned trying to make. With him is his advisor, the critic Carini (Jean Rougeul), who is telling him that his decision not to make the film shows great intellectual rigour. They get into a car. Maurice (Ian Dallas), a master of ceremonies and old acquaintance of Guido's, appears; he makes a beckoning sign with his baton and people from Guido's life, dressed in white, are seen and begin to move forwards. Carini's discourse eventually stops, and Guido in voiceover speaks of a 'glow of happiness' that has come over him that 'makes me tremble but gives me strength and life' and of his readiness to love and be loved by everyone he knows. Maurice oversees the putting in place of lights and a makeshift circus ring, and a quintet of musicians, four dressed as clowns, the other a little boy in a schoolboy's cape, appear. Guido joins in the organising and eventually joins everyone as they dance along the circus ring. Then only the musicians are left and finally only the little boy, who marches off.

There are various ways to understand this sequence. It could be daydream, a 'wouldn't it be nice?' comparable to the earlier harem sequence. It could be a more transcendent vision of paradise on earth. Perhaps it is a kind of visual equivalent for Guido's words, a way of visualising his 'glow of happiness'. It might be an idea for a film, as earlier sequences in the film have been (for example, the Saraghina sequence, where little boys pay a hefty peasant woman [Edra Gale] to dance the rumba for them, a sequence evidently manipulated, visibly and aurally, with speeded-up motion, exaggerated close-ups and an acrid musical arrangement of a popular dance tune, 'Fiesta'; after it, the film cuts back to Carini who comments that such a sequence would be of no interest).[1] The latter possibility does not eliminate any of the former: the sequence might be an idea for a film of a daydream, vision or mental state.

The only things we can state with certainty are that it is a piece of film (part of 8½) and the end of a film (to wit, 8½). Like many sequences in 8½, it contrasts with a relatively conventionally observed overall narrative in which a

film director, Guido, tries to make a film; this narrative frames these sequences, which can be variously construed as dreams, visions, thoughts, memories. However, in so far as the sequences are – also – ideas for a film, they embody a paradox, since they are not only ideas for a film but actually bits of film themselves. They suggest the magic of art: paint on canvas, ink shapes on paper, sounds produced from wood, brass and string, or fragments of celluloid strung together, which may seem to embody a feeling, disclose a world. 8½'s framed sequences achieve this even while, indeed by, making more explicit the fact that they are – just! only! – filmic constructions.

The sequence is also not just the end of but an ending for 8½. All films come to a halt but most also have an ending that gives some kind of sense to what has gone before, tying up loose ends, explaining, ending on an emotionally satisfying note. 8½ has nowhere logical to go in this sense: Guido has abandoned the film, there is nothing to suggest his personal relationships are other than beyond repair. Yet the film wants an ending. Fellini regularly seeks out endings that affirm the fact of ending in the face of stories and possibilities petering out: Moraldo (Franco Interlenghi) in the train in I vitelloni (1953); Zampanò (Anthony Quinn) on the beach in La strada (1954); Cabiria (Giulietta Masina) walking down the road with singing youngsters in Le notti di Cabiria (1957). And what better way to round things up (literally) than the buoyant ending of a circus, the walk round of all the participants? The sequence achieves this because a film can magically reunite people (performers) who (as characters) are temporally, spatially and temperamentally drastically at odds. It also achieves it in the magic of moments that mobilise specifically cinematic and musical qualities. I turn now to look at two of these.

The first occurs as the climax of one long take, beginning with Guido entering the ring, then the musicians coming on, Guido picking up a megaphone to direct operations; they march past a bandstand and a high white curtain; the little boy marches towards the curtain which, on Guido's command, parts to reveal people from earlier in the film walking down a long flight of steps (suggesting a

variety stage finale). The camera has not been still throughout this sequence, moving to keep Guido and the musicians in the frame, including turning to the right as the boy
goes to take up his position to the right of the curtain. At
that point, however, the camera's movement ceases to be
so functional and subordinate in relation to the characters
but rather homes in, first apparently on the boy but then
curving round and tilting up so that it gets the best – full-
on, spectacular – view of the walk down.

With the camera movement, the music gets louder and
also rises through two key changes. When the curtains
part, the quintet is augmented by a full band, playing loud,
slightly dissonantly, with a certain enthusiastic abandon,
very much in the style of the circus or pit band in Fellini
and Rota's work. There is a source for this, the band on the
bandstand glimpsed behind, but the sound is far greater
than anything they could produce. At this moment in the
film, the camera movement breaks free of its motivation in
on-screen movement and the music loosens its diegetic
moorings, both instead participating in the conjuring of
this fabulous walk down. Part of the magic is the mesmeric
effect of the frame of an image shifting of its own accord
and the logistics of producing the shot (one take with such
complexity of camera and on-screen moments and so
many people involved) and also of the way mere sounds
getting louder and changing key produce a sense of excitement. Part also though is this possibility of somehow
almost entering into a fictional world, not in the illusion of
identification, but getting nearer, sharing in the enthusiastic welcome for this walk down, helping to manage to have
an ending.

The second moment occurs after Guido has asked
Maurice to accompany Carla (Guido's mistress [Sandra
Milo]) into the ring. Guido continues to shout orders, there
is a fanfare and Maurice leads everyone into the dance
round the ring. The fanfare precedes a cut to an extreme
close-up of Maurice; immediately the fanfare is finished
there is the cut, a big jump forward, cutting onto Maurice
already shouting and smiling to encourage everyone along
behind him.

Rota makes great use of fanfares throughout his film
work. Their pronounced syncopation embodies sonically
their function, in both military and theatrical (especially
circus and variety) contexts, of a call to activity, a herald of
something new. They also have that 'duh-daah!' quality
attendant on the completion of a magic trick as well as on
a performer's first appearance. Especially in Fellini, they
occur as a new release of energy in situations of stasis or
blockage,[2] something fundamental to the sense of movement in his films, movement sometimes felt as confusion
and headlong rush, but elsewhere as energising and heal-
ing, above all in the endless flow of circularity, something
promised by the very basic architecture of, and word for,
the circus.[3] The fanfare – a mere sound – as if by magic

Maestro!...
All hold hands!

provokes movement, and, what's more, circular movement. It also heralds a dramatic cut, from Maurice in long
shot to close-up and from stasis (of camera and people) to
movement, and especially to the beginning of movement.
One of Fellini's most characteristic edits is to cut to a shot
just at the point that movement is starting in it (that is, no
or only an infinitesimal pause before on-screen movement
but not coming in on movement already clearly underway).
It is an effect of editing that produces the sense of getting
going, of the release of energy and will necessary for
motion to occur. The fanfare and this editing pattern
together give a particular élan to the moment: 'Here we
go!', 'We're off!'

The circular movement and gradual crescendo and key
changes of the earlier moment usher in a splendid movement (and, in a kind of cutting, the people are already in
movement before the curtain opens), but one that is all
moving in one direction and seems to be going somewhere.
The fanfare and the spatial jump, cut on incipient movement, of the second sequence, on the other hand, in themselves jerky and disruptive, nonetheless herald circular
movement, movement that holds out the possibility of
movement that can go on forever, the glorious neverend-
ingness of circularity, going nowhere but keeping going. In
both cases, one form of filmic and musical movement conjures a different kind of on-screen movement.

Conjuring. The man who leads the dance, Maurice, has
been seen earlier in the film as part of a nightclub mind-
reading act. There Guido takes him aside and asks him
what the trick is. 'There is some trick in it,' says Maurice,
'but sometimes also something real.' Guido asks if he can

try it and Maurice's assistant, Maya (Mary Indovino), the mind-reader, correctly guesses that Guido is thinking the apparent nonsense phrase 'Asa Nisi Masa'. This introduces a sequence of children being put to bed, which explains the phrase as a childhood incantation that, as one of the boys says, will bring to life 'the woman in the picture' who will give the children treasure. The likelihood of Maya guessing correctly what is in Guido's mind is so remote as to be impossible, suggesting that she really does read it. Moreover, it is magic heralding magic: what she reads is itself a magic incantation; the phrase is made up by a standard childhood game of adding syllables to words, which, when the additional syllables are shed, spells 'Anima', that is spirit, mind, soul.

The music accompanying Maurice's act is the 'passerella' (walk past) that is played by the quintet in the final sequence. In the film, it is heard for the first time in the nightclub; it is presumably diegetic but its source is not made clear and it is a very characteristic piece of Rota–Fellini music. Often in the film, music that seems to be playing diegetically and unobtrusively crops up non-diegetically and obtrusively in the framed sequences. This could be explicable rationally: Guido unconsciously registers them as he goes about his life and brings them to the fore in his thoughts/ideas for a film. Yet this process too has something uncanny about it, another species of magic.

Fellini and Rota took the idea of magic very seriously. They consulted and took decisions on the advice of clairvoyants; Rota and his friend Vinicio Verginelli amassed one of the biggest collections of hermetic literature in the world; they were also, Rota less equivocally than Fellini, Catholics. It is not surprising that Maurice is involved in an act that has something real about it. Nor is it inconsistent that this real is there in a rather lacklustre nightclub. In *La strada* there is a conflation of circus and church music, with the same tune used by the little group of musicians (who clearly anticipate those of the ending of 8½) who appear from nowhere when Gelsomina (Giulietta Masina) has run away from Zampanò *and* for the religious procession and service in the nearby town *and*, immediately following it, for the high-wire act of Gelsomina's saviour, il Matto (Richard Basehart), who is dressed as an angel. In *Le notti di Cabiria*, Cabiria is restored to life by a current popular Neapolitan song sung by some kids as she walks back into Naples after her new bridegroom has robbed her and nearly killed her. In the least solemn, even the most tawdry or commercial art, there is always the possibility of magic.

The term magic is easy to band about. It is also highly ambivalent, since it can mean polar opposites. It first meant something amazing that was achieved by esoteric means, something fabulous that was not exactly inexplicable but rather could only be explained by recourse to notions of the supernatural. It came to mean something

amazing that could be explained in material terms, a trick, a skill, a sleight of hand. Magicians moved from being those who evoked and controlled mystic, perhaps diabolical, forces to those who, with your agreement, hoodwinked you. For some the pleasure of magic may be baffling – if it is only a trick, where's the wonderment? Yet for Fellini and Rota there remains a glimpse of something beyond the explicable, something esoteric, something transcendent, in the capacity to enthral and be enthralled. In the finale of 8½, and especially in the two moments I have highlighted, you know it is the cinema that is doing this yet it is precisely its capacity to do so that is a source of wonderment.[4]

The film ends though on the little boy. He is dressed like the boy in the Saraghina sequence; we may reasonably take him to be the child Guido. At one point he waves his hand like a conductor, which is to say also like a film director. Just as adult Guido in the sequence takes charge, so does the boy, for a moment, take over from Maurice: both become the conjuror. Then, as the lights start to go out, the other musicians march off (the boy's gesture might even indicate that they should leave), and finally so does he, in a follow spot, until it too is extinguished, leaving only the sound of his flute. The moment is past. Helen Stoddart argues that the desire for cinema – and life – to be like a circus is always limned in Fellini's work with awareness of the fact that it can't be.[5] There is sadness – the boy lost in the dark, Rota's music forever on the cusp of melancholy and effervescence – in the perception. The walk round is itself evanescent: a few fleeting shots, the whole ring never seen. But evanescence is perhaps the price we must pay for the magic of the moment. By definition a moment cannot last – and yet only in a moment can there be that conjuring of the magic promise of the circus. Or moments. It is in the intensity of the coming together of a camera movement, a couple of key changes, a crescendo, a curtain whipped back, crowds appearing from nowhere, all in a few seconds, or of a musical flourish and a spatially thrilling cut, that the magic is conjured. It can only be for a moment, but at least it is a moment.

NOTES

1. For further discussion of this sequence and its cinematic qualities, see Marilyn Fabe, *Closely Watched Films* (Berkeley: University of California Press, 2004), pp. 158–72.
2. See Sergio Miceli, *La musica nel film. Arte e artigianato* (Fiesole: Discanto, 1982), pp. 265ff.
3. See Peter Harcourt, *Six European Directors* (Harmondsworth: Penguin, 1969), pp. 183–211.
4. I should like to thank Frank Kessler and Michele Pierson for conversations about magic and film while I was thinking about this article.
5. Helen Stoddart, 'Subtle Wasted Traces: Fellini and the Circus', in Frank Burke and Margaret Waller (eds), *Federico*

Fellini: Contemporary Perspectives (Toronto: University of Toronto Press, 2002), pp. 47–64.

BIBILIOGRAPHY

Burke, Frank and Waller, Margaret (eds), *Federico Fellini: Contemporary Perspectives* (Toronto: University of Toronto Press, 2002).

Fabe, Marilyn, *Closely Watched Films* (Berkeley: University of California Press, 2004).

Harcourt, Peter, *Six European Directors* (Harmondsworth: Penguin, 1969).

Miceli, Sergio, *La musica nel film. Arte e artigianato* (Fiesole: Discanto, 1982).

Stoddart, Helen, 'Subtle Wasted Traces: Fellini and the Circus', in Frank Burke and Margaret Waller (eds), *Federico Fellini: Contemporary Perspectives* (Toronto: University of Toronto Press, 2002), pp. 47–64.

PART TWO: History

Over the last two decades of scholarship on the cinema, film history has perhaps increasingly dominated the field.[1] Of course, film history has always been a key constituent of writing on the medium, but now, the phrase 'film history' connotes a relatively discrete field of scholarship that generates its own internal debates about its primary subject (the history of the film) and its methodologies (historiography). At the same time and in increasing numbers, there are undergraduate and postgraduate film studies courses around the UK and USA that specialise in the historiography of the cinema and the disciplines of archiving and film preservation. Given the range of work being done in this field, the present collection cannot hope to be representative of 'film history', nor can it demonstrate the different ways the practice of film history has been and can be defined.[2] Indeed, the essays brought together in this section are perhaps more illustrative of approaches *not* being widely taken: that is, the combination of historical enquiry with close attention to the detail, texture and style of individual films and moments from those films. It is not uncommon now to see conferences devoted to exploring the material and methodologies of film history at which few or none of the speakers show extracts from films. Proceedings might be dominated by the demonstration and discussion of various computer databases and means for collating and examining large amounts of data on, for example, exhibition strategies and the ethnography and geography of cinema audiences. Among practitioners of film history, there is often an apparent concern at the lack of a strong empirical basis for 'textual' analysis. As discussed in the 'criticism' introduction, evaluation, interpretation and the close reading of film sequences are dependent on the 'I' of the viewer. Of course, why should scholars of the cinema have to look closely at films themselves? Robert Allen and Douglas Gomery have shown that, '[f]or certain investigations, film viewing is [even] an inappropriate research method'.[3] The fact that film historians feel increasingly confident in turning away from films as primary sources is an understandable compensation for the unreflective way in which much film history was written before the 1980s and for the ahistorical manner in which some of the influential film theory (or 'Theory') of the 1970s and 1980s was seen to have been undertaken (see the introduction to the next part for further discussion). It is not the place of this book to counter these important advances in film studies. However, one of this collection's central aims is to show what can be gained by allowing historical questions to emerge out of the discussion of an individual film moment.

If we say that the past two decades saw film history increasingly setting the agenda for film scholarship, we should remind ourselves of modern historians' wariness of fitting events into such neat divisions. Indeed, it is impossible to point to a single moment at which what was widely termed 'the new historicism' or 'the historical turn' began. The 1980s saw the emergence of a number of landmark works that have had important implications for how the film moment has been or has not been considered historically. Barry Salt's *Film Style and Technology*,[4] David Bordwell, Janet Staiger and Kristin Thompson's *The Classical Hollywood Cinema*[5] and Robert Allen and Douglas Gomery's *Film History: Theory and Practice* are key indices of this shift. These books saw film history adopt more overtly 'scientific' methodologies: Salt, for example, making extensive use of average shot length (ASL) data to survey different filmmakers and national cinemas during different periods;[6] Bordwell *et al.* compile an 'unbiased sample' of randomly selected films on which to build their analysis of a classical Hollywood style. The huge scope of these studies and the very nature of their methodologies clearly mean that the practice of close sequence analysis is of limited interest to them, with moments from films instead being called upon (if at all) in order to illustrate a 'norm' or a momentary deviation. However, another key book emerging from the new historicism of this period suggests other ways in which the film moment took on new importance for the film historian.

In *Early Cinema: Space, Frame, Narrative*, Thomas Elsaesser compiled some of the key work emerging from the new wave of scholarship on 'silent' cinema[7] that set off from the FIAF (International Federation of Film Archives) conference in Brighton in 1978.[8] Energised by the need to protect, preserve and expand the existing archives, a generation of scholars was also rethinking cinema's origins and the teleological histories that had dominated film scholarship. 'Teleological' refers to history conceived as having a specific end, a purpose, a 'telos', and in the case of the cinema, that end had often been perceived as being ever-greater 'realism' or an ever-greater 'illusionism' (like realism, illusionism seeks to hide its artifice). In reconsidering film history's ends, moments can take on a particular importance:

> Evolutionary theories of the cinema … are problematic wherever a single objective is deemed to push in one direction to the exclusion of others. Historically, the modalities of change are perhaps best understood as compromises arising out of contending options and priorities.[9]

Elsaesser contrasts teleological 'theory' with the cinema considered 'historically'. For Elsaesser, historical research is about examining 'the modalities of change' and it stands to reason that these are to be found operating within particular moments. Of course, 'moments' would refer, in this case, primarily to 'historical moments' (a way of describing particular historical time periods), but the film historian may also think of the *film moment* as a dramatisation of the 'contending options and priorities' film-makers experienced in the culture of which they were a part. This approach to historical analysis is practised by a number of the contributors to Elsaesser's volume and in the essays in this part.

Perhaps the best-known essay collected in *Early Cinema: Space, Frame, Narrative*, because it provided 'this film studies generation's … most quoted watchword',[10] is Tom Gunning's on 'the cinema of attractions'.[11] Gunning's account is precisely that of a pre-1907 cinema that is a cinema *of moments*:

> … the cinema of attractions directly solicits spectator attention, inciting visual curiosity, and supplying pleasure through an exciting spectacle – a unique event, whether fictional or documentary, that is of interest in itself. The attraction to be displayed may also be of a cinematic nature, such as the early close-ups … or trick films in which cinematic manipulation (slow motion, reverse motion, substitution, multiple exposure) provides the film's novelty … . [The cinema of attractions'] energy moves outward towards an acknowledged spectator rather than inward towards the character-based situations essential to classical narrative.[12]

The cinema of attractions is opposed to what Gunning calls 'the cinema of narrative integration' (in most respects, a term synonymous with 'classical cinema') in

that it is focused on delivering moments of sensation or spectacle that display the possibilities of the medium itself, rather than construct a self-enclosed fictional world. It is for this reason that 'the cinema of attractions' is frequently cited in work on modern, special effects-driven cinema;[13] it provides, for many writers, a short-hand way of historicising contemporary cinematic spectacle. However, its current ubiquity (to the point now, perhaps, of cliché) as a concept should not blind us to what 'the cinema of attractions' represented, alongside the other scholarship of its time, as a radical rethinking of early cinema history. Famous moments such as the close-up of the ankle in Edwin S. Porter's *The Gay Shoe Clerk* (1903) had at one time been viewed, retrospectively, as steps towards the 'natural' evolution of continuity editing. Considered alongside the films of its time, for Gunning and others, this same close-up was, rather, a marker of a different economy of audience address in early cinema. Other moments, such as film history's possibly most famous moment, when the first cinema spectators fled from the Lumières' images of a train arriving at the station (1896; if, indeed, this ever actually happened),[14] were reconsidered in the light of this new historicism. In this book, Elsaesser considers this very moment in relation to one from Lang's *Siegfried* (1924) as a means of excavating its place within the radical shifts that early film spectatorship represented for western cultures. It should be admitted, however, that this collection favours moments that *are* integrated into a wider narrative pattern, moments that, in Gunning's words, 'look … inward towards … character-based situations'. However, in this section, for example, Tom Brown (in considering a musical 'number')[15] and Helen Hanson (in examining the 'bus' in 1942's *Cat People*) consider moments that create sensations that to a large extent pull the spectator out of the narrative and demand different kinds of emotional/affective response.

Crucially, the new understandings of early cinema presented in Elsaesser's book were enabled by both more rigorous analysis of the cinema's 'secondary' materials (trade and industry journals, etc.) and by a renewed engagement with the films themselves, belying the false opposition of empirical research with critical 'interpretative' analysis. Another flourishing area of film scholarship that counters this perceived conflict is that on film sound. The period of film history's ascendancy coincided with an attempt by scholars to redress the overwhelmingly visual bias of previous film theory, history and criticism. Consequently, film-sound scholarship is often strongly historical in its focus. However, as this works alongside a reassessment of film form (reconsidering the *audio*-visual basis of the medium), film-sound scholarship is an excellent place to look for synthesis between historical analysis (examining the 'moment' or, more accurately, series of 'moments' of the transition to synchronised sound, for example) and the analysis of film moments. An excellent example of this synthesis is Charles Wolfe's essay on *The Jazz Singer* (Crosland, 1927).[16] Wolfe's investigation of the competing aesthetic possibilities operative at the time (on the one hand, the 'theatrical' presentation of a live performance, on the other, the 'cinematic' penetration of filmic space) is pursued by a strongly contextualised analysis of the style and presentation of different 'numbers' within this first of Hollywood's musicals.

In this volume, Rick Altman and Helen Hanson talk similarly of the distinction between 'recording' and 'reshaping', 'fidelity' versus 'drama' operating within and across different film moments. Charles Barr looks at a more idiosyncratic moment in the narrative of film sound's development (Chaplin's 'silent' *City Lights* of 1931) as the collision of two 'worlds' (cinema's new emphasis on words as against the previous world of images) and as a response to the more peculiar question of how to film (meaning, in this case, make auditory as well as visualise) blindness. By attending to such competing and contending options and priorities (to echo Elsaesser again), Altman and other film-sound scholars have shown us that there is nothing inevitable or natural about the development of film technique and technology. This is perhaps the most important lesson film history can teach us; this and the importance of contextualising the individual instance within the wider context.

As suggested earlier, history is of course also often broken up into 'moments'. Indeed, with the increasing distrust of 'grand narratives', the wider discipline of history has seen a focus on the complexities and contradictions operating within individual 'historical moments'. As with the analysis undertaken in all the essays here, this is not a negation of the importance of the wider 'narrative' (the bigger picture of history in this case), but a focus on the relationship of the specific, the local, to the larger context. Contextualisation is the very subject of Pam Cook's essay, below, in which she demonstrates how a moment from *Bonnie and Clyde* (Penn, 1967) 'exemplifies the process of accumulation of meaning and the interweaving of myth and documented evidence that characterise historical analysis and reconstruction'. Similarly, Ginette Vincendeau examines the same moment from a variety of different perspectives (as a moment from the work of its director, its star and in the international noir style), demonstrating that historical and textual analysis is a process of marshalling what the critic/historian presents as the most revealing context. Richard Ellis contextualises his moment by showing that what is *not* said, a gap in speech, or a gap in what is visually or verbally permissible, may suggest what is repressed within both the history of the industry (the Hollywood Production or Hays Code, for example) and within wider political, international history (the USA's traumatic interventions in wars overseas).

Unique opportunities emerge from keeping the moment central to one's analysis. For example, Mark Broughton's essay in this section suggests how the moment may reveal 'history as palimpsest'. (A palimpsest is a manuscript on which more than one text has been written, each new text involving the erasure and writing over of the previous; the different layers of text nevertheless remain partially visible beneath the surface.) The palimpsest is an apt metaphor for the layering one encounters in the rich and complex 'moments' of certain texts and, in Broughton's example, this layering is a modernist concern: in *Les Deux Anglaises et le continent* (1971), Truffaut seems to grapple with the question of how to visualise history by layering Rodin's sculpture of Balzac upon other layers, Rodin's sculptural forms being themselves a response to the question of how to visualise an individual subjectivity. (In seeking a *new* language – one that was, as Broughton discusses, ahead of its time – Rodin's sculpture represents high modernism.) The metaphor of the palimpsest has also proved attractive to theorists of the postmodern because it is suggestive of the layering of associations and 'intertextual' references characteristic of postmodern cultural products.[17] Thus, Jonathan Bignell's analysis of the opening of *Star Wars* (Lucas, 1977) looks at what might be thought of as a very different kind of palimpsest to Truffaut's. Bignell's discussion of the postmodernism of Lucas's film counters the apolitical associations that term carries for many critics; similarly, Claudia Gorbman's analysis of a moment from *The World/Shijie* (Jia, 2004), a film whose subject is the alienation of the individual in the postmodern 'any-space-whatever', shows how the meanings a given text accumulates (in this case, Beethoven's 'Ode to Joy' considered, in a broad sense, as a 'text') can be used for profoundly political ends. It is a characteristic of the 'postmodern' culture in which we live that texts come to us increasingly without a sense of a strongly moored, single meaning. (This is relative of course; few classic or modernist texts of accomplishment are singular in their meanings.) Gorbman and Broughton's essays demonstrate what can be gained by historicising the processes through which individual cultural objects (Beethoven's Ninth and certain Rodin sculptures, respectively) accrue meanings within a single moment in film history.

This brings us to the final point which is to note the peculiar status of the film moment in relation to contemporary 'digital' technologies for presenting and re-editing the key material of film history: films themselves. With the proliferation of means for displaying and sharing videos on the web, we are perhaps encountering, at this moment in the history of film, an ironic return to aspects of cinema in its first years, when it was a medium consisting entirely of moments: short sequences that provided a snapshot of a scene or event. The interesting thing here is that technical limitations dictated this moment-ness (early cameras could only shoot a very limited length of film), whereas now it is technical advancement that has seen a return to the moment. YouTube and other video-sharing websites have enabled an unprecedented ease of access to films and parts of films: the sequence Brown examines below is, for example, only readily available because of such sites, and this suggests the potential for such technologies to preserve moments from film history that might otherwise vanish from cultural memory. However, it is in the very nature of the sites themselves (breaking up, perhaps re-editing clips of an unknown provenance; compressing the files and thus greatly reducing image quality) to present *fragments* of film history rather than *moments*. In this period of digital plenty, extra effort is needed to contextualise such fragmentary texts. The previously mentioned FIAF conference of 1978 was partly motivated by the desire of film scholars to preserve the celluloid archives.[18] In a shift towards digital archives, access is much easier but contact with the literal material of film history (celluloid, for the most part) is being lost.[19] That is why, at this moment in film history, particular care should be focused on the textual and contextual meanings of film moments of the past.

NOTES

1. D. N. Rodowick, *The Virtual Life of Film* (London: Harvard University Press, 2007), p. 3.
2. For an excellent introduction to the key debates, see Robert Allen and Douglas Gomery, *Film History: Theory and Practice* (London: McGraw-Hill, 1985).
3. Ibid., p. 38.
4. Barry Salt, *Film Style and Technology: History and Analysis* (London: Starword, 1983).
5. David Bordwell, Janet Staiger and Kristin Thompson, *The Classical Hollywood Cinema: Film Style and Mode of Production to 1960* (London: Routledge and Kegan Paul, 1985).
6. In this book and in some of her other work, Ginette Vincendeau has employed ASL data. Another scholar of

1930s French cinema, Charles O'Brien, works extensively with average shot length and other statistical analyses, and there is now a website devoted to compiling this kind of data: <www.cinemetrics.lv>.
7. As is now widely acknowledged, early cinema was very rarely ever silent and 'mute cinema' might be a more accurate description. See, for example, Rick Altman, *Silent Film Sound* (Chichester, NY: Columbia University Press, 2004).
8. Thomas Elsaesser (ed.), *Early Cinema: Space, Frame, Narrative* (London: BFI, 1990), especially pp. 1–7.
9. Ibid., p. 405.
10. Altman, *Silent Film Sound*, p. 9.
11. Gunning cites André Gaudreault as a collaborator on his initial work on the cinema of attractions.
12. Tom Gunning, 'The Cinema of Attractions: Early Film, Its Spectator and the Avant-Garde', in Thomas Elsaesser, *Early Cinema*, pp. 58–9.
13. There is even a collection entitled *The Cinema of Attractions Reloaded*, edited by Wanda Strauven (Amsterdam: Amsterdam University Press, 2006).
14. See, for example, Tom Gunning, 'An Aesthetic of Astonishment: Early Film and the (In)credulous Spectator', in Leo Braudy and Marshall Cohen (eds), *Film Theory and Criticism: Introductory Readings* (5th edn) (Oxford: Oxford University Press, 1999), pp. 818–32.
15. In suggesting that the cinema of attractions doesn't entirely disappear after 1907, the musical is the narrative cinema form that Gunning offers as illustration ('The Cinema of Attractions', p. 57).
16. Charles Wolfe, 'Vitaphone Shorts and *The Jazz Singer*', *Wide Angle* vol. 12 no. 3, July 1990, pp. 58–78.
17. For an entry into these debates, see John Hill, 'Film and Postmodernism', in John Hill and Pamela Church Gibson (eds), *The Oxford Guide to Film Studies* (Oxford: Oxford University Press, 1998), pp. 97–105.
18. Elsaesser, *Early Cinema*, p. 2.
19. See Rodowick, *The Virtual Life of Film*, for a much more expansive discussion of these debates.

BIBLIOGRAPHY

Allen, Robert and Gomery, Douglas, *Film History: Theory and Practice* (London: McGraw-Hill, 1985).

Altman, Rick, *Silent Film Sound* (Chichester, NY: Columbia University Press, 2004).

Bordwell, David, Staiger, Janet and Thompson, Kristin, *The Classical Hollywood Cinema: Film Style and Mode of Production to 1960* (London: Routledge and Kegan Paul, 1985).

Braudy, Leo and Cohen, Marshall (eds), *Film Theory and Criticism: Introductory Readings* (5th edn) (Oxford: Oxford University Press, 1999).

Elsaesser, Thomas (ed.), *Early Cinema: Space, Frame, Narrative* (London: BFI, 1990).

Gunning, Tom, 'The Cinema of Attractions: Early Film, Its Spectator and the Avant-Garde', in Elsaesser, *Early Cinema*, pp. 58–9.

Gunning, Tom, 'An Aesthetic of Astonishment: Early Film and the (In)credulous Spectator', in Leo Braudy and Marshall Cohen (eds), *Film Theory and Criticism: Introductory Readings* (5th edn) (Oxford: Oxford University Press, 1999), pp. 818–32.

Hill, John and Gibson, Pamela Church (eds), *The Oxford Guide to Film Studies* (Oxford: Oxford University Press, 1998).

Hill, John, 'Film and Postmodernism', in Hill and Church Gibson, *The Oxford Guide to Film Studies*, pp. 97–105.

Rodowick, D. N., *The Virtual Life of Film* (London: Harvard University Press, 2007).

Salt, Barry, *Film Style and Technology: History and Analysis* (London: Starword, 1983).

Strauven, Wanda (ed.), *The Cinema of Attractions Reloaded* (Amsterdam: Amsterdam University Press, 2006).

Wolfe, Charles, 'Vitaphone Shorts and *The Jazz Singer*', *Wide Angle* vol. 12 no. 3, July 1990, pp. 58–78.

Haptic Vision and Consumerism: A Moment from Fritz Lang's *Siegfried* (1924)

THOMAS ELSAESSER

Fritz Lang's two-part *Die Nibelungen* is, everyone agrees, a masterpiece of Weimar cinema: a landmark in the development of cinematographic art and special effects, an extraordinary display of the use of light and shadow in the staging of mass scenes, an exquisite example of Ufa set design, which – made between 1922 and 1924 – shows Erich Pommer's famous Decla studio at one of the peaks of its creative power. So much is evident, so much has been many times repeated. Equally well known is the fact that, with a script based on the ancient twelfth-century German and Norse epic poem, *Das Nibelungenlied*, this monumental film of 288 minutes (in its most complete, restored version) has never been anything but steeped in controversy: for its slow-moving, bombastic *mise en scène*, for its pastiche iconography, borrowed mainly from Carl Otto Czeschka's Jugendstil designs,[1] and above all for its nationalist, 'revanchist' ideology. The latter, in the famous image of Siegfried, cowardly murdered by Hagen's lance and unwittingly betrayed by his own wife Kriemhild, seemed to give credence to the so-called *Dolchstoss-Legende*, the myth that the German army had been defeated in the war of 1914–18 not on the battlefield but because it was 'stabbed in the back' by 'socialist' politicians and communists on the home front, undermining the morale of the civilian population.

Like the original saga, but differing from Wagner's opera *The Ring of the Nibelungen*, Fritz Lang and Thea von Harbou here present the 'origins' of the German nation as a fratricide, a story of 'hate, murder and revenge' and as an act of ethnic cleansing that wipes out the leading elite of an entire people (the Burgundians). And like other 'myths of origin' (that of the Serbs' defeat at Kosovo in 1389, the last stand at the Alamo in 1836, the Israeli mass suicide at the Massada Fortress in 73 BC, or the Palestinians' Nakba of 1948, for instance) this national epic of Germany insists that a nation is forged from catastrophe and disaster.

For these complex historical reasons, and because of other, specifically filmic features, *Die Nibelungen* has elicited many different interpretations and critical readings. Among the more remarkable recent ones are Tom Gunning's chapter in *The Films of Fritz Lang: Allegories of Vision and Modernity*[2] and David J. Levin's *Richard Wagner, Fritz Lang, and the Nibelungen: The Dramaturgy of Disavowal*.[3] Picking up on one of Levin's suggestions, I want to focus on a particular moment from *Siegfrieds Tod*.[4] Perhaps, following a suggestion that I originally made in my book *Das Weimarer Kino: Aufgeklärt und Doppelbödig*,[5] Levin argues that, like Lang's *Metropolis* from 1927, the *Nibelungen* film can also be read as part of the competitive struggle between the German film industry and Hollywood. He amplifies this point by arguing that it should be read as an allegory of the international film industry, insinuating that it is in the hands of 'Jewish' world capital, from which Germanic 'epic' blockbusters like *Die Nibelungen* have to rescue it. Levin, in other words, sees in the film a significant anti-Semitic subtext.

I shall comment on Levin's reading later. First I want to present the moment I have selected. My theme will be that inside this magnificent and problematic film-epos there are many other films. And one of these – quite literally, a film within the film – is to be found in a brief sequence, no more than a few seconds, and is thus capable of being encapsulated in a still image. This image, depicting a moment in the encounter between Siegfried (played by Paul Richter) and Alberich (Georg John), the guardian of the Nibelungen treasure (about thirty minutes into the film), shows Siegfried, after having defeated Alberich by wresting from him his helmet of invisibility, the *Tarnkappe*, as he intently gazes at the fabled riches that he thinks are soon to be his. But rather than presenting Siegfried with the real Rheingold, Alberich has conjured it up in the form of a moving image, projected on a rock, with an army of dwarfs labouring in the depths of the scene. Stunned by its splendours, Siegfried wants to grasp the image, upon which the projection disappears like a mirage, sucking him forward and into further penetrating the magic but also menacing world of Alberich.

Levin sees the scene as an allegory of anti-Semitism, strangely conflated with anti-Americanism, and he

adduces some quite persuasive arguments. Yet it is equally plausible to read it as a homage to the American cinema, in fact as a nostalgic-ironic invocation of a filmic genre belonging to the early years of the cinematic medium, but testifying to its wit and sophistication, even during the years of its so-called 'infancy'. The genre I have in mind is that of the so-called 'Rube' film, and it emerged at the turn of the century, first in Great Britain and the USA, but similar films were also produced in other countries.[6] Rube films often presented a film within a film, that is, they showed a member of the cinema audience who does not seem to know that film images are representations to be looked at rather than objects to be touched and handled, or that the screen is not a door through which to enter a space. These 'Rubes' (a slang word for simpletons from the countryside) are spectators who climb up onto the stage and either attempt to grasp the images on the screen, or want to join the characters on the screen, or look 'behind' or 'inside' to discover what is hidden or kept out of sight. The best-known example is *Uncle Josh at the Movies*, made by Edwin S. Porter, for the Edison Company in 1902, but characteristically enough, this is itself a remake of a British prototype,

Robert Paul's *The Countryman's First Sight of the Animated Pictures* (1901).

These *Uncle Josh* films pose a twofold question. Are they intended, as is often claimed, to be didactic parables, teaching a rural or immigrant audience how not to behave in the cinema by putting up to ridicule someone like themselves?[7] Yet was there ever such an audience, or moment of naive simplicity in the history of the movies, where such an ontological confusion with regard to objects and persons might have existed? What comes to mind are the reports that, at the first Lumière showings of *L'Arrivée d'un train à La Ciotat/Arrival of a Train* (1896), viewers fled from the theatre and the oncoming train – a situation explicitly cited in Paul's and Porter's countrymen films. There is, as historians have pointed out, no documentary evidence that such panics ever occurred, other than as self-promotion on the part of movie theatres.[8] In other words, they belong to the folklore and urban mythology that early cinema generated about itself, realising that stories of the spectatorial effects of moving images make good publicity for the cinema as an 'attraction'. In relation to this first level of self-reference, the *Uncle Josh* films present a second level of self-reference, citing the first, and thus they stage a cinema of attractions by promoting a form of spectatorship where the spectator watches, reacts to and interacts with a motion picture, while remaining seated and still, retaining all affect resolutely within him or herself.

This, then, would raise the further question: do these films construct their meta-level of self-reference in order to 'discipline' their audience? Not by showing them how not to behave (i.e. by way of negative example, shaming and proscription) but, rather, by a more subtle process of internalised self-censorship? Do the Rube films not discipline their audience by allowing them to enjoy their own superior form of spectatorship, even if that superiority is achieved at the price of self-censorship and self-restraint? The audience laughs at a simpleton, who is kept at a distance and ridiculed, and thereby it can flatter itself with a self-image of urban sophistication. The punishment meted out to Uncle Josh by the projectionist is both allegorised as the reverse side of cinematic pleasure (watch out, 'behind' the screen there is the figure of the 'master') and internalised as self-control: in the cinema – as elsewhere in the new world of display and self-display – the rule is 'you may look – but don't touch'.[9] This makes possible an additional dimension of the genre, in which the cinema colludes with the civilisation process as conceived by Norbert Elias (or Pierre Bourdieu),[10] according to whom the shift of bodily orientation from the proximity sense of touch to the distance and proximity-regulating sense of sight constitutes a quantum leap in human evolution. What, however, characterises the cinema would be that it supports but also exacerbates this quantum leap by 'performing' the kind of cognitive–sensory double-binds which are usually associated with the commodity fetishism inculcated by the shop-window display that also says 'look, don't touch' in order to resolve the conflict by relieving the eye with the promise of control (the plenitude of touch) through purchase (the reality of possession). In the cinema, by contrast, the same scene of desire and discipline is staged as a form of 'trauma' of touch and sight, with both senses at once overstimulated and censored, seduced and chastised, obsessively and systematically tied to the kinds of delays and deferrals we associate with narrative.

I can now return to the moment from *Siegfrieds Tod*. Here, too, the film spectator's implicit contract with the (barred) haptic palpability of the moving image and the inherent perversity of this contract are made explicit. In Siegfried's case, the allegorical import with respect to commodity fetishism is made further explicit but rendered quite vertiginous in its unfolding implications. At one level, Siegfried, seduced by the cinematic spectacle, shows himself to be the simpleton, the *Tumbe Tor*, in the Rube tradition. Ironically inverted in the hard, impenetrable rock is the notion of the shop window as display case. At another level, Siegfried is the hero as conqueror, lording it over a subservient and servile Alberich, whose image is made the more troubling, as Levin rightly points out, by his stereotypical representation as a Jewish merchant and department-store owner. However, at the meta-meta-level of Weimar cinema's predilection for tyrants, puppetmasters and their acolytes, the unruly slave or sorcerer's apprentice, Alberich, and Siegfried are not only a Hegelian master–slave dialectical duo, they also belong in the same tradition that connects the carnival-stall owner, Caligari, to his medium Cesare, or Mephisto to Faust in F. W. Murnau's film of that title. The treasure dangling before Siegfried's eyes acts as a visualisation or allegory of the cinema itself as a machine that plants the never-to-be-satisfied desire for palpability in the viewer, and thus makes the cinema itself into an obsessional wish-generating but fulfilment-deferring machine, as if to indicate by the enthronement of the eye over hand and touch already the eye's eventual ruin, at the end of the century.

The theorist of this promise of proximity enshrined in the cinema, and also elegiac allegorist of its traumatic deferral, is of course Walter Benjamin. One recalls the famous passage from the 'Artwork' essay, in which he outlines the cultural-political significance of tactile proximity and haptic perception as it takes shape around the moving image and its contact with the masses:

> The desire of contemporary masses to bring things 'closer' spatially and humanly, which is just as ardent as their bent toward overcoming the uniqueness of everyday reality by accepting its reproduction. Every day the urge grows stronger to get hold of an object at very close range by way of its likeness, its reproduction.[11]

What here is hinted at through the act of substitution – likeness – and mechanical duplication – reproduction – is the ontological gap that opens up in the trade-off between the sense of proximity (hand) and the other of distance and proximity (eye), and also the irreversible nature of the deferral, which pushes haptic perception into the realm of the optical (unconscious) and ownership into the realm of obsessional and phantasmagoric possession. The appropriate cinematic illustration of Benjamin might be a scene from Jean-Luc Godard's *Les Carabiniers* (1963) – a film precisely about the category mistake of thinking the civilisational 'quantum leap' from hand to eye to be reversible, when the two country bumpkins go to war in order to rape, plunder and possess, and happily return with a suitcase full of postcards of the sights, monuments and women they believe they have conquered and taken possession of from the enemy. As will be recalled, *Les Carabiniers* also features a famous re-creation of the Rube film, whose own complex double frame of reference cleverly comments on the second level of self-reference of the original via the inscription of the camera.[12]

Thus, Fritz Lang – allegorist of vision and modernity (Gunning) that he is from his earliest films, such as *Die Spinnen* (1919) onwards – presents us for a few seconds in *Siegfrieds Tod* with a film within the film, which emblematises, above all, the cinematic apparatus in its political meanings and ontological ramifications. In a multiple *mise en abyme* of the action hero, the spectator, early film history, national mythology and modern consumer society, the still image becomes readable across the many discourses it evokes and, at the same time, enfolds. Its ironic-playful self-referentiality removes the film, for a few instances, from the associations of suspected nationalism, revanchism and anti-Semitism that *Die Nibelungen* carries for the modern viewer without thereby freeing it from this heavy burden. But by playing with us, across the memory of the Rube films, it makes us – who have the advantage of almost a century of wisdom by hindsight – implicit, complicit and ultimately also responsible.

NOTES

1. Czeskcha made the design for a popular picture book, Franz Keim's *Die Nibelungen: Dem Deutschen Volk* (Vienna: Gerlach und Wiedling, 1909).
2. Tom Gunning, *The Films of Fritz Lang: Allegories of Vision and Modernity* (London: BFI, 2000).
3. David J. Levin, *Richard Wagner, Fritz Lang, and the Nibelungen: The Dramaturgy of Disavowal* (Princeton, NJ: Princeton University Press, 1999).
4. *Siegfrieds Tod* ('Siegfried's death') is the original German title for part one of the two-part *Die Nibelungen*. It is more often known simply as *Siegfried*, as with, for example the two-disc Kino DVD.

5. Thomas Elsaesser, *Das Weimarer Kino: Aufgeklärt und Doppelbödig* (Berlin: Vorwerk8, 1999).

6. For an extensive discussion of Rube films in American cinema, see Miriam Hansen, *Babel and Babylon* (Cambridge, MA: Harvard University Press, 1997), pp. 25–30.

7. See Isabelle Morissette, 'Reflexivity in Spectatorship: The Didactic Nature of Early Silent Films', *Offscreen*, July 2002. Available at <www.horschamp.qc.ca/new_offscreen/reflexivity.html>. 'The spectator [in the film] is a country bumpkin and, in this case, someone that more sophisticated city people would laugh at for his display of naivety. It functions on two levels even for contemporary audiences. Initially, the countryman seems to play the role of an entertainer, providing emphasis to the action happening on the screen, by imitating the woman dancing on the movie screen that the bumpkin sees. But the countryman's happy moment is suddenly interrupted by the arrival of a train, a very popular cinematic theme at the end of the 19th century, made famous by the fact that the historically significant *L'Arrivée d'un train a La Ciotat* had a surprise effect on its audience similar to the reaction of the countryman's experiences.'

8. Steve Bottomore, 'The Coming of the Cinema', *History Today* vol. 46 no. 3, 1996, pp. 14–20.

9. For an inverse reading of the relation between looking and touching, see Wanda Strauven, 'Touch, Don't Look', in Alice Autelitano, Veronica Innocenti and Valentina Re (eds), *The Five Senses of Cinema* (Udine: Forum, 2005), pp. 283–91.

10. Norbert Elias, *The Civilising Process* (Oxford: Blackwell, 2000); Pierre Bourdieu, *Language and Symbolic Power* (Cambridge: Polity Press, 1991).

11. Walter Benjamin, 'The Work of Art in the Age of Mechanical Reproduction', *Illuminations* [trans. Harry Zohn] (London: Fontana, 1992), pp. 211–44.

12. See also Wanda Strauven, 'Re-disciplining the Audience: Godard's Rube-Carabiniers', in Marijke de Valck and Malte Hagener (eds), *Cinephilia: Movies, Love and Memory* (Amsterdam: Amsterdam University Press, 2005), pp. 125–33.

BIBLIOGRAPHY

Autelitano, Alice, Innocenti, Veronica and Re, Valentina (eds), *The Five Senses of Cinema* (Udine: Forum, 2005).

Benjamin, Walter, 'The Work of Art in the Age of Mechanical Reproduction', *Illuminations* [trans. Harry Zohn] (London: Fontana, 1992), pp. 211–44.

Bottomore, Steve, 'The Coming of the Cinema', *History Today* vol. 46 no. 3, 1996, pp. 14–20.

Bourdieu, Pierre, *Language and Symbolic Power* (Cambridge: Polity Press, 1991).

de Valck, Marijke and Hagener, Malte (eds), *Cinephilia: Movies, Love and Memory* (Amsterdam: Amsterdam University Press, 2005).

Elias, Norbert, *The Civilising Process* (Oxford: Blackwell, 2000).

Elsaesser, Thomas, *Das Weimarer Kino: Aufgeklärt und Doppelbödig* (Berlin: Vorwerk8, 1999).

Gunning, Tom, *The Films of Fritz Lang: Allegories of Vision and Modernity* (London: BFI, 2000).

Hansen, Miriam, *Babel and Babylon* (Cambridge, MA: Harvard University Press, 1997), pp. 25–30.

Keim, Franz, *Die Nibelungen: Dem Deutschen Volk* (Vienna: Gerlach und Wiedling, 1909).

Levin, David J., *Richard Wagner, Fritz Lang, and the Nibelungen: The Dramaturgy of Disavowal* (Princeton, NJ: Princeton University Press, 1999).

Morissette, Isabelle, 'Reflexivity in Spectatorship: The Didactic Nature of Early Silent Films', *Offscreen*, July 2002. Available at <www.horschamp.qc.ca/new_offscreen/reflexivity.html>.

Strauven, Wanda, 'Touch, Don't Look', in Alice Autelitano, Veronica Innocenti and Valentina Re (eds), *The Five Senses of Cinema* (Udine: Forum, 2005), pp. 283–91.

Strauven, Wanda, 'Re-disciplining the Audience: Godard's Rube-Carabiniers', in Marijke de Valck and Malte Hagener (eds), *Cinephilia: Movies, Love and Memory* (Amsterdam: Amsterdam University Press, 2005), pp. 125–33.

Visions of Sound in *City Lights* (1931)

CHARLES BARR

Around the mid-point of *City Lights*, the Tramp – I think that is the best way to name the character – goes to the home of the Girl whom he loves.[1] Worried already by her absence from the spot on the pavement to which she goes daily to sell flowers, he peers in anxiously at the window. In the next shot, we see what he sees: a table with a black bag and other items that indicate the presence of a doctor. Cut back to the Tramp, then back to the same point-of-view shot. This time the camera, following his concerned gaze,

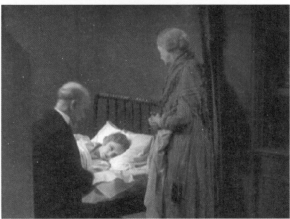

moves forward, over and beyond the table, to the Girl's bedroom, where the doctor is giving his professional verdict to her and to her grandmother: 'She has a fever and needs careful attention.' But in order to show this group of three, the camera has had not only to track forward, but to veer to the left – only a corner of the bedroom is visible from the window.

So what started as a visual point-of-view shot has become an aural one, a 'point-of-hearing' shot. Though he cannot see either doctor or patient, the Tramp clearly does hear the doctor's words: we return to the same shot of him at the window, and he reacts to the news by going to sit down pensively on the steps outside.

Ever since seeing the film for the first time, I have been fascinated by this particular moment. The transition, at some indefinable point within the tracking shot, from visual to aural point of view is intriguing in itself, creating an effect similar to one in Ingmar Bergman's early film *Fangelse* (1948, released in England as *Prison*). There, in a sequence set in a film studio, we watch actors play a scene on a boat in front of an ocean backdrop. The camera slowly tracks in, gradually excluding the studio surroundings from the frame, so that the representation of how an illusion is being created becomes, again at some indefinable point, the illusion itself, of characters on a boat at sea. In both cases the effect depends on the continuity of the shot and the steady forward camera movement – a variant of the Bazinian principle that for certain purposes 'montage is forbidden'. But the *City Lights* shot gains extra resonance from three contextual factors:

1   The character who looks, listens and loves is played by the film's writer/director, Charles Chaplin.
2   The film is silent, or, more accurately, free of dialogue; the doctor's words are given in a title card.
3   The woman herself is blind.

In the course of his book-length interview with Jon Halliday, Douglas Sirk outlined a project, never realised, for a more radical film treatment of blindness than he had been able to attempt in *Magnificent Obsession* (1954):[2]

I have always been intrigued by the problems of blindness … . And one of my dearest projects was to make a picture set in a blind people's home. There would just have been people ceaselessly tapping, trying to grasp things they could not see. What I think would be extremely interesting here would be to try and confront problems of this kind via a medium – the cinema – which itself is only concerned with things seen. It is this contrast between a world where words have only a limited importance and another world where they are nearly everything that inspires my passionate interest.[3]

City Lights is a film that demonstrates, and plays out, a concern with precisely these aesthetic issues. It was made at the time in film history when two cinematic 'worlds' were in spectacular collision: the new one, where words seemed suddenly to have become 'nearly everything', and the old one, 'concerned with things seen'. Sirk's film would presumably have had a full soundtrack, but Chaplin was, famously and with passionate tenacity, holding out against the industry-wide conversion to talking film. Initiated in 1928, completed in 1930 and shown early in 1931, *City Lights* announces itself in the credit titles as 'a comedy romance in pantomime'. And blindness was just as central to the project as the refusal of dialogue; indeed, Chaplin originally thought of playing a blind character himself.[4] This is the story that came together after a typically lengthy process of trial, error and multitudinous retakes:

> On the same day in the city, the Tramp makes two new acquaintances: a blind Flower Girl, with whom he quickly falls in love, and an eccentric Millionaire, who befriends him. The Girl imagines him to be wealthy, and he keeps up the illusion by helping her, thanks in part to the Millionaire's resources; but this man, in contrast to the Tramp, is inconstant, indulging him when drunk but forgetting and rejecting him when sober. Needing money to pay for an operation to restore her sight, the Tramp tries unsuccessfully to earn it, but is then given it by the Millionaire, who promptly sobers up and denounces him to the police as a thief; but he still manages to hand the money over to the Girl. On release from prison, he finds her, no longer blind, and with a flourishing shop of her own; and she now discovers him to be her benefactor.

The project, then, is to create an essentially visual film centred on blindness. 'Essentially', rather than 'purely': it is a truism to note that silent film from the start was seldom genuinely silent, but was accompanied by live music and sometimes by crude sound effects. Even before dialogue took over, films such as *Sunrise* (1927) were being released with integral scores and occasional effects. For *City Lights*, Chaplin put together not only a highly crafted and powerful score, but a number of prominent and precisely timed

diegetic sound effects. There was the obvious option, then, of evoking elements of the blind girl's experience via the soundtrack, which we can guess would have been part of Sirk's strategy. Remarkably, this does not happen at all. In effect, her lack of vision is evoked, in a displaced way, by the total absence of diegetic sound in her world, in contrast to the sounds that come quite frequently into the world of others.

These sounds are positive 'attractions' for an audience of 1931: a concession to the advance of sound-film technology, but also defying this advance by selectivity, exaggeration and, right from the start, parody, as in the blah-blah distortion in the opening scene of speeches by civic dignitaries. Many of the scenes from which the Girl is absent have some kind of sound effect, from the tin whistle swallowed by the Tramp at the party given to him by the Millionaire to the bell in the boxing ring, both of which generate a whole series of effective gags. Several gunshots are heard at different times, as is a police siren at the end, the eloquent herald of the Tramp's imprisonment. The non-diegetic score, moreover, morphs from time to time into diegetic music, or at least an approximation of it: at the frenetic dancing scene in the nightclub, and again at the party when the shrill burps from the swallowed whistle disrupt preparations for a musical recital. There is even a realistic musical effect in an earlier scene in the same house, when Tramp and Millionaire successively stumble forward and hit their heads discordantly on the piano.

In her much humbler home, the Girl has a wind-up gramophone which is evidently important to her: it sits near the door, and she immediately puts on a record the first time we see her enter. But neither here nor later is there any interruption to the non-diegetic musical score. In his first scene with the Millionaire, set on the bank of the river in which the man is determined to drown himself, a rock falls on the Tramp's foot, and we hear the thud. Later, on his first visit to the Girl's home, he sits outside after escorting her to the door, and a flowerpot, dislodged by a cat, falls on to his head, but this time there is no thud, even though the Girl must have heard it: we cut immediately to her inside the house, and she reacts and comes to the window. We have seen her once before at the window, when she returned home still excited by her first meeting with the man – in fact, as we know, the impecunious Tramp – whom she believes to be wealthy. In this scene, a young man from the neighbourhood stands in the courtyard below, and puts his hand to his mouth to whistle to his date that he is waiting: she comes, they go off, and the Girl at the window, responding to what she hears, 'looks' in their direction as they go, mouthing the word 'goodbye'. But we have not heard the whistle. Again, the *absence* of a key sound that, elsewhere in the film, we could expect to hear seems to stand in for her inability to *see* the couple who must be so vivid – and quietly envied – in her mind's eye.

A rigorous principle, then, underlies a system of sound effects that might at first seem simply opportunistic. Nowhere is this clearer than in the early scene in which the Tramp first meets the Girl, crucial to the setting-up of the story and the film. Probably no scene in film history, at least outside Kubrick's 1999 film *Eyes Wide Shut* (evocative title in this context), has been so long in the making, the subject of so much directorial agonising and retaking.[5]

Chaplin has to establish that she is blind, and that the Tramp falls in love with her; this was not too hard to do. He also has to establish that she from the start believes him to be rich, and that he realises this and does not want to disillusion her; this is what took so much trial and error to set up. The solution is to have her misled by a repeated sound: the slamming of a car door. Crossing a street that is temporarily jammed with traffic, the Tramp finds his way blocked and, with typical opportunism, takes a short cut through the back of a parked car, slamming it on exit. The girl, in her position on the adjacent pavement, looks up in response to the sound and offers a flower, causing him to look round at her and to turn back. As their encounter ends, and he prepares to move away from her and from the camera, a smart gentleman walks up and enters the same car, slamming the door once more, and it drives off. She again reacts, assuming that the same man who just bought the flower from her has got back into the car from which he had recently emerged.

What could be more logical, in a film with plenty of sound effects, than to give us the sound of the door slamming? But no, the fact of the sound is conveyed in purely visual terms. The Tramp's emergence from the car is contained within a simple wide shot: doing anything fancier would be premature, with the pair still to meet and her blindness not yet established. But for the second doorslam, there is camera movement. First, an unobtrusive pan left to show the smart gentleman moving purposefully from the background and into his car. Then a quicker pan back to the Girl to convey her thought process, followed by the title card, 'Wait for your change, sir.' We return to the same shot, and to an immediate repeat pan left as the car departs, followed by a pan right, back to the Girl. What *these* two pans convey are the thought processes of the Tramp, 'reading' the audiovisual data in front of him, which are presented to us solely as visual data. There is something beautifully economical about doing so much within a single shot, and about 'translating' sounds so deftly. Characteristically, Chaplin makes no use here of shot/reverse shot, but keeps us in the space opposite him, so that we go through a process of reading the full frame that is analogous to his. And at his instant of realisation, which sets up the main narrative drive of the film – it is at this same instant that the Tramp decides he must not disillusion the Girl, but must tiptoe away from her – he looks straight into the camera, as if for a moment to blur the line between character and director, and between director and audience. As if to say collusively: you are with me, aren't you, as I embark on a film that refuses the 'advances' of sound cinema, even for a story about blindness, showing that I can manage fine without them.

The scene I began with, in which the Tramp learns of the Girl's illness, is a pure crystallisation of this principle and of the film's formal strategies. The camera that moves forward and round is at once the viewpoint of the Tramp and the instrument of Chaplin the director, able magically to 'see' round corners, and to translate sound into visual terms, in daring alliance with the traditional device of the written title. It acquires extra weight from being the film's one instance of obtrusive camera movement, apart from the early panning shots just described, and from being the film's one emphatic point-of-view shot. At other moments when we might expect such a shot, it does not materialise, and Chaplin is, like Griffith, sparing altogether in his use of the shot/reverse-shot system: all his scenes, except the first and last ones, have a distinctly frontal emphasis, facing one way.[6] This might seem paradoxical. Hitchcock regretted the way that 'with the arrival of sound the motion picture, overnight, assumed a theatrical form':[7] the initial limitations of synchronised sound technology worked against the free cutting style, based on shot/reverse shot and point of view, that he had exploited brilliantly in his own late silent films, and enforced a partial return to frontality. Here Chaplin rejects synchronised sound, but without, from the Hitchcockian perspective, taking full advantage of his freedom. Nevertheless, his system, as always, renders *performance* lucidly; as always, he controls audience point of view expertly, without much need for actual camera subjectivity; and, like Griffith, he is ready at certain moments to handle space by the more modern 'cinematic' devices which are all the more striking and potent for being used sparingly. As in the scene where the Tramp leans forward to learn the doctor's verdict on the Girl.

Other contributors to this volume have no doubt experienced the same frustration: a short piece focused on a particular moment cannot do more than hint at the formal and thematic complexities of a major film, and at the way the two levels interact. But this moment, like many other moments in *City Lights*, has the potential, I think, to be convincingly related to the shape, impact and influence of the film overall, and particularly to its momentous final recognition scene. Slavoj Žižek chose to end his stimulating three-part TV programme *The Pervert's Guide to Cinema* with a commentary on that very scene, and what he said about the film applies equally to the parts I have dealt with here: 'Chaplin's *City Lights* is one of those masterpieces which are really too sophisticated for the sophisticated. It's a deceptively simple movie: when we are enraptured by it we tend to miss its complexity and extreme finesse.'[8]

NOTES

1. Familiar alternative names are 'Charlie' and 'The Little Fellow', the somewhat cloying term often used by Chaplin himself in referring to his own screen character. On the credits of this film he is simply 'A Tramp', and Virginia Cherrill plays 'A Blind Girl'.
2. *Magnificent Obsession*, directed by Sirk for Universal. Jane Wyman plays a woman who is blinded early in the film, and is cared for by the Rock Hudson character. Like the Tramp in *City Lights*, he has good reasons for being hesitant about revealing his identity.
3. Jon Halliday, *Sirk on Sirk* (London: Secker and Warburg, 1971), p. 97.
4. See for instance David Robinson, *Chaplin: His Life and Art* (London: Collins, 1985), p. 389.
5. 'He'd go on shooting the same scene over and over again until an idea came … . We did that scene 342 times. It's a record!' (from an interview with Virginia Cherrill, quoted in Miranda Seymour's biography of her: *Chaplin's Girl* (London: Simon and Schuster, 2009), p. 78).
6. Even the one unequivocal point-of-view shot, it will be noted, is not bracketed in the way that had already become common practice for Hitchcock and others, by shots of the Tramp's face as he looks.
7. François Truffaut, *Hitchcock* (New York: Simon and Schuster, 1985 [1966]), p. 61.
8. *The Pervert's Guide to Cinema*, directed by Sophie Fiennes, shown on Channel 4 in 2006, available on DVD. Two accounts of *City Lights* as a whole that I have found especially perceptive are those by John Kimber in *The Art of Charles Chaplin* (Sheffield: Sheffield Academic Press, 2000) and by William Paul in his article 'Charles Chaplin and the Annals of Anality', in Andrew Horton (ed.), *Cinema/Comedy/Theory* (Berkeley: University of California Press, 1991).

BIBLIOGRAPHY

Halliday, Jon, *Sirk on Sirk* (London: Secker and Warburg, 1971).

Horton, Andrew (ed.), *Cinema/Comedy/Theory* (Berkeley: University of California Press, 1991).

Kimber, John, *The Art of Charles Chaplin* (Sheffield: Sheffield Academic Press, 2000).

Paul, William, 'Charles Chaplin and the Annals of Anality', in Horton, *Cinema/Comedy/Theory*.

Robinson, David, *Chaplin: His Life and Art* (London: Collins, 1985).

Seymour, Miranda, *Chaplin's Girl* (London: Simon and Schuster, 2009).

Truffaut, François, *Hitchcock* (New York: Simon and Schuster, 1985 [1966]).

'Entertainment and dystopia': Maurice Chevalier Performs *Avec le sourire* (1936)

TOM BROWN

One might say that, from some perspectives, the moment examined below does not exist. Appearing on a video-sharing website (see first image), it is a fragment of a film that, outside the French national library (the BNF), is very difficult to see.[1] As a mainstream star vehicle, *Avec le sourire* (Tourneur, 1936) represents the kind of pre-war French cinema that has not fared well either in terms of film preservation or in film scholarship; the great *auteur* cinema of Jean Renoir, Marcel Carné and the generic strand (or '*optique*')[2] known as 'poetic realism' dominate our sense of the French cinema of the 1930s.[3] Moreover, as a 'musical number', Maurice Chevalier's performance of 'Le Chapeau de Zozo' stands outside prevailing understandings of the generic landscape of the French cinema.[4]

Musical numbers typically occupy a place inside *and* outside the narrative: the term 'number' implies a unit of spectacle separable from surrounding context but musical sequences that advance the narrative in some way have been favoured in accounts of the genre.[5] The narrative context of 'Le Chapeau de Zozo' is as follows: Maurice Chevalier (in his first role since his return to France from Hollywood)[6] plays Victor Larnois, a man who, after having arrived in Paris penniless, has worked his way up from doorman to a partner in a music hall; he will end up as the director of the

Paris Opera. He achieves all through the force of his personality and through manipulating people 'with a smile' (the meaning of 'avec le sourire'). The film's setting and narrative trajectory (organised around an upwardly mobile character) give it characteristics shared with 'backstage' or 'show' musicals, in which musical performance is diegetically motivated.[7] My chosen 'number' is explicitly 'backstage', occurring almost exactly halfway through the film as Victor instructs the woman who will become his wife, Gisèle (Marie Glory), on how better to perform the song, 'Le Chapeau de Zozo'. Translating as 'Zozo's hat', the lyrics, as presented by the film, appear without meaning, offering simply a platform upon which to build a performative display.[8] It should be noted that Gisèle has been elevated to star of a revue show not by any particular talent but by Victor's role as impresario and arch manipulator.

We are introduced to the scene with a side-on view of Gisèle rehearsing the number. Her voice is weak, her dancing lacks skill or even much enthusiasm, and the camera's position does nothing to flatter her fairly ragged dance movements, nor those of the chorus girls rehearsing with her. This view, combined with the contemporary spectator's knowledge of Chevalier's much greater stardom and fame as a musical performer, mean that Victor's interruption obeys an obvious logic. He comes onto stage and tells her that her performance lacks pep (*piment*). He dismisses the *girls*,[9] then sits Gisèle down in order to instruct her. She is sitting between the musical and stage directors and we watch with them as Victor/Chevalier (it is difficult during this moment to draw a line between character and actor) imparts his expertise:

> Gisèle ... when you sing to a full house ... there is every class in this group. You have polite society [*gens du monde*], average Frenchman [*Français moyens*], some *apaches*[10] and ... you have also a small minority of people ... how shall I put it ... people who are a little precious, too distinguished [*distingués*] ... . You understand what I want to say? There are all types in the house, you see? Your

A 'fragment' of film history on a video-sharing website

duty as artist, as singer, is to please all these people and to sing towards each in a way that makes them believe that you belong ... to their group. Watch me closely, I will show you.

With these last words, the film cuts to a shot further behind Gisèle. Immediately, the camera pans up to follow Chevalier's movements, and tracks forward to frame him from the waist up: for the remaining two and a half minutes of the scene, there will be only two relatively brief cutaways from this position; Chevalier's performative mastery, both displayed and deconstructed, will be the film's focus.

Victor/Chevalier now moves through the chorus of 'Le Chapeau de Zozo', performing it in four different styles, each addressed to a different group. His singing is interspersed with his spoken explanations and impersonations of its effect upon these four 'classes' of people. (When singing, Chevalier generally looks into the camera, while Victor's impressions of the different groups are delivered towards screen left and his diegetic spectators.)[11] For the *gens du monde*, he holds one hand out stiffly from his waist in a gesture, he tells his spectators, that *fait élégant*. His performance for the *Français moyens* is, in his words, more 'natural', more *bonhomie*: his movements are much freer; he also claps to emphasise the song's rhythm, his hands relaxed, not stiff. In order to 'enter into the world of the *apaches*', he performs aggressiveness, staring more intently at the camera and puffing out his chest; he exaggeratedly looks up and down to emphasise certain words, making a pig-like snort to add further rhythmic emphasis. He then performs for the 'precious' group, stressing to Gisèle not to overdo it because 'obviously they're a very small minority'. However, the vocal performance and gestures are the most exaggerated of all the segments and underline (what was hinted at in the previously quoted

Chevalier performs the *apache* direct to the camera in *Love Me Tonight* (1932)

speech) that these spectators are camp homosexuals; his movements could be described as 'mincing'. He then runs through all four versions without the spoken interruptions, seamlessly modifying his performance style each time.

The key functions of the number are (at least) double: as a performative spectacle, we appreciate Chevalier's skill (his impersonations may be distasteful but their final combination is exhilarating to watch); the number also reinforces something about the character the narrative has insisted upon (Victor is an arch manipulator). One of the most influential models for understanding both the narrative role of musical numbers, and their affective/emotional function as entertainment (or as spectacle), is Richard Dyer's 'entertainment and utopia'.[12] Considered through this lens, we can see the consonance of 'Le Chapeau de Zozo' with the conventional concerns of the Hollywood musical number, yet also its ironic take on each of them. I echo Dyer in presenting his utopian categories in table form, along with the wants they can be seen to resolve. (See the table overleaf; I have also extended Dyer's categories in order to give a wider picture of French musical production in the 1930s.)[13] It should be stressed that these categories are 'utopian' not in terms of presenting ideal worlds but as particular categories of feeling: 'It [entertainment, the musical in particular] presents head-on, as it were, what utopia would *feel* like rather than how it would be organized.'[14]

Because of its intimacy, its focus on a single performer, 'abundance' is less applicable to the presentation of this number, though it is emphasised in its narrative context: musical performance is at this moment presented as commercially driven; performance is a *job* designed for profit. The number's 'energy' is much more apparent, and indeed is presented much less equivocally than any of the other utopian values: as Victor/Chevalier's performance moves into the seamless interweaving of the different performance styles, the energy of his physical and vocal movements is spectacular; his energy is positively contrasted with Gisèle's lacklustre performance. However, 'transparency' and 'community' are the very subjects of the number and are much more ironically inflected. Clearly, Victor's speech about how there is every class in a music-hall audience imagines it as a site for the bringing together of communities. Yet, in dividing the audience into its different class constituents and by the sheer fact of its emphasis on the very existence of such differences, the number demystifies the utopianism of 'community'. It achieves this also because it combines with an inversion of standard musical 'transparency', a utopian value that is often rendered ironic in the French cinema of the 1930s.[15] Dyer defines 'transparency' as 'a quality of relationships between represented characters (e.g. true love)' and 'between performer and audience ("sincerity")'. These two sides to transparency are undermined by narrative context and by the content of the number. In terms of narrative

	Energy	Abundance	Intensity	Transparency	Community
	Capacity to act vigorously; human power, activity, potential	Conquest of scarcity; having enough to spare without sense of poverty of others; enjoyment of sensuous material reality	Experiencing of emotion, directly, fully, unambiguously, 'authentically', without holding back	A quality of relationships between represented characters (e.g. true love), between performer and audience ('sincerity')	Togetherness, sense of belonging, network of phatic relationships (communication is for its own sake rather than for its message)
Real-world problem it is response to	Exhaustion (work as a grind, alienated labour, pressures of urban life)	Scarcity (actual poverty in the society; poverty observable in the surrounding societies, e.g. developing world); unequal distribution of wealth	Dreariness (monotony, predictability, instrumentality of the daily round)	Manipulation (advertising, bourgeois democracy, sex roles)	Fragmentation (job mobility, rehousing and development, high-rise flats, legislation against collective action)
Show-biz forms (non-French)	Qualities of some chorus-line dances; can-can (performed mainly for foreigners) and tap dance – both quite rare in 30s French cinema	The Berkeleyesque; lavish sets and costumes in music-hall production numbers	'Incandescent' star performers (see Dyer) – stardom with an international flavour (i.e. Chevalier and Josephine Baker)	N/A	The music hall as modern class melting pot.
'French' cultural forms	Individual performer-centred vaudevillian/*café-concert* styles (*gambillard, épileptique, comique-troupier*); energetic styles of *chanson*	N/A	The *chanteuse réaliste*; more passionate than polished musical performers (e.g. Jean Gabin)	*Chanteuse réaliste* as 'one of us', presenting real, 'authentic' depth of emotion	*Café-concert, bals musettes* and local Parisian working-class spaces where bourgeois must accommodate working-class values
Utopian examples	Chevalier singing 'Y' a de la joie' in *L'Homme du jour* (Duvivier, 1937); energetic facial tics of Milton – his energetic performance gets him out of trouble in *Le Roi du cirage* (Colombier, 1931)	The expansive climax of *La Crise est finie* (Siodmak, 1934), a *Gold Diggers of 1933* (LeRoy) pastiche, as an end to the Depression (*la crise*) ... but utopian only by denial of commercial drive of performance; lavish earnings buy Jean's (Gabin) freedom in *Zouzou* (Allégret, 1934) but ...	Gabin and Fréhel perform sexual intensity and danger in the *bal* in *Coeur de lilas* (Litvak, 1932). (Fréhel in Duvivier's 1937 *Pépé le Moko* most 'intense' example of decade, though a largely non-'musical' film)	Josephine Baker's 'Zouzou' sings of her secret love to fellow female laundry workers Mistinguett as title character of *Rigolboche* (Christian-Jacque, 1936) sings love to her son that she can't express in words in 'Au fond de tes yeux ...'	Countless examples of *café-concert*-esque community utopias; the music hall as class melting pot in *Le Roi du cirage* and *La Crise est finie* but only by individual star disrupting the spectacle (in former) and breaking down barrier between spectacle and spectators (in latter)
Dystopian examples	End of *Zouzou*: performance is a trap, is the 'daily grind'; near the opening of *La Crise est finie*: show biz is drudgery	... wealth/material success does not bring happiness to Zouzou (Josephine Baker); it is literal fantasy in *Princesse Tam Tam* (Gréville, 1935) contrasted to orientalist ideal of Africa; the frequently money-grabbing music-hall '*miss*' (*Le Roi du cirage, Faubourg Montmartre* [Bernard, 1931])	(Intensity does not easily divide into positive and negative – see above)	... but her stage performances exploited for cons staged by impresario (Jules Berry); behind glitz, glamour of music-hall stardom, there's duplicity, money-grabbing and/or crime: *Divine* (Ophuls, 1935), *Faubourg Montmartre, Le Roi du cirage*	Musical community always positive; authentic 'French' folk culture often contrasted to music hall in terms of latter's lack of community. (Another Chevalier vehicle the exception: working-class communal solidarity presented as lie and/or mass hysteria in *L'Homme du jour*)

context, *Avec le sourire* presents a message that is almost unimaginable for a classical Hollywood musical: Victor Larnois is a cynical *arriviste* who gets to the top, less through his talent than by his willingness to manipulate people with a smile on his face; his meteoric trajectory is the inverse of that of another character, Ernest Villary (André Lefaur), whom Victor displaces as boss of the music hall and who is nearly broken by a scrupulous honesty coupled with an inability to smile. However, 'Le Chapeau de Zozo' would have provided a clear extra-diegetic, non-narrative pull for its 1936 French spectators because of its lacerating deconstruction of Maurice Chevalier's own star image.

Chevalier's reputation had been built on his ability to connect with widely divergent audiences and he himself claimed a preference for this live connection over the presence–absence of cinema: '[In 1935] Maurice Chevalier declared that performing live was the "best *métier* in the world" because it provided true contact with the public, contact he never felt before the camera.'[16] It is this sense of connection with the audience that is laid bare in close shot in 'Le Chapeau de Zozo', developing our sense that we see Chevalier *as Chevalier* rather than a self-enclosed characterisation. Moreover, between the more extreme impersonations of poshness and camp, the *Français moyens* and *apache* versions connect more directly to the 'natural Chevalier' performance style (the way of being that this film and others present as its default). His singing performance for the 'average Frenchman', in its 'natural' *bonhomie*, is closest to the register of most Chevalier musical performances in his films, while the accent and language of his *apache* audience member connect more obviously to extra-textual knowledge of the star: 'I think I know that girl [Gisèle] from *Ménilmuche*', his *apache* says, *Ménilmuche* being a slang term for Ménilmontant, the *quartier* of Paris where Chevalier was born. This would have been well known to most French spectators of the time because Chevalier had made sure it was known: during and after Chevalier's Hollywood career, his press coverage demonstrates a constant need to stress this local connection.[17]

Why would Chevalier submit to such a pointed satire of his stardom? Furthermore, how representative of wider conventions is this fragment of a film? The first question is difficult to answer directly (we cannot ask Chevalier), and, in responding to the second question, one would have to admit that the film was not a commercial success and does not therefore seem to have satisfied a French moviegoing public.[18] Judged in aesthetic terms, principally by what we expect a musical and its numbers to achieve (utopian wish-fulfilment), it is also a failure and may be seen to bear out Phil Powrie's suggestion that the French musical is rare indeed:

> My hypothesis is that the film musical is at its heart a film of community, as underlined by the work of Jane

Feuer and Richard Dyer. One of the fundamental myths of the film musical is the possibility of social integration through the utopian mode … . Its rarity in the French cinema demonstrates the difficulty of the very concept of social integration, not only in the current period, but well before, at least from the time of the Popular Front.[19]

Avec le sourire is a film of the Popular Front period, released almost exactly midway through the leftist alliance's time in power,[20] and its deconstruction of the 'myth of social integration in the utopian mould' seems to illustrate Powrie's argument precisely. However, why should one accept that this myth is what makes a musical *a musical*? To follow Powrie's line of thinking and to define a set of films by a perceived end rather than their means is to submit to a teleological view of history and to make the category mistake (in film-genre terms) of putting the cart before the horse. Why reason backwards from what a musical is presumed to be rather than reason forwards examining what musical films (films in which a major point is the on-screen performance of song and/or dance) actually *do*? As the table suggests, 'Le Chapeau de Zozo', in its negative utopianism, perhaps even *dystopianism*, is consonant with wider trends.

What is behind this French approach to musical spectacle in the 1930s? Returning to Dyer and his definition of entertainment is instructive:

> Musicals are one of a whole string of forms … that are usually summed up by the term 'show biz' … it is probably true to say that 'show biz' is the most thoroughly entertainment-oriented of all types of performance … . It is important … to stress the cultural and historical specificity of entertainment. The kinds of performance produced by professional entertainment are different in audience, performers and above all intention to the kinds of performance produced in tribal, feudal, or socialist societies … entertainment is a type of performance produced for profit, performed before a generalized audience (the 'public'), by a trained, paid group who do nothing else but produce performances which have the sole (conscious) aim of providing pleasure.[21]

Notwithstanding Dyer's emphasis on cultural and historical specificity, it is true to say that entertainment could be defined in the same way in the France of the 1930s, a western, basically capitalist society. The conscious aims of musical numbers were broadly the same in France, yet the means of offering pleasure to the audience often involved a disavowal of the commercial function of entertainment. This is in principle not so different from the Hollywood musical, which Jane Feuer (whom Powrie cites) has shown to have often emphasised 'folk' over 'mass' cultural values.[22] However, the degree of criticism of 'show *business*' is markedly different in France. This can be linked to what is suggested by the two notable gaps in the table. I suggest that 'transparency' is *not* a quality one finds in the 'show-biz' forms the French cinema presents; neither is 'abundance' a value one sees in any of its 'authentic', 'French', folk cultural forms. Martin O'Shaugnessy has noted a much wider 'reactionary' ambivalence towards the 'Parisian popular',[23] of which the un-transparent (see table) music hall is a key part. In the case of French musical production more specifically, I would suggest that this ambivalence is a means of 'product differentiation', whereby the less commercial but more intimate, more 'authentic', more 'French' musical forms are favoured over the glitz, glamour and 'abundance' of (Anglo-American flavoured) show biz. In relation to this, though highly speculative, one might wonder whether Maurice Chevalier's career as a Hollywood star was a factor in the ambivalent presentation of his characters in his French vehicles.[24] Finally, however, it should be said that the frequency with which French films of the 1930s mimic the forms of Hollywood musicals gives the lie to the rarity of this genre within the French cinema. Some may respond that a satiric approach to the musical genre means that such films are not really musicals because they lack the 'utopian sincerity' that is a supposedly defining characteristic of the genre. This response would, however, perpetuate unhelpfully narrow and Hollywood-centric definitions of the genre. As we have seen, with 'Le Chapeau de Zozo', you can still make a spectacular song and dance out of satire.

NOTES

1. 'Moment' available at <www.dailymotion.com/video/x1tewr_chevalier-avec-le-sourire-zozo_music> (accessed 10 Feburary 2010). I must thank the Arts and Humanities Research Council and the British Academy for making it possible for me to consult the film at the BNF, as well as its archives on Maurice Chevalier and the wider French film culture of the decade.

2. See Dudley Andrew, *Mists of Regret: Culture and Sensibility in Classic French Film* (Princeton, NJ: Princeton University Press, 1995).

3. Dudley Andrew provides some excellent analyses of popular French cinema of the period. However, in examining mainstream cinema, special mention must be made of Ginette Vincendeau's work, to which the research presented in this chapter is greatly indebted.

4. The notion of there being 'French musicals' (at least before Jacques Demy) barely registers in most scholarship. More broadly, the study of genre in the French cinema has, until recently, been largely neglected. Again, however, one should cite Ginette Vincendeau's work as an important exception. See especially, 'The Art of Spectacle: The Aesthetics of Classical French Cinema', in Michael Temple

and Michael Witt (eds), *The French Cinema Book* (London: BFI, 2004), pp. 137–52; and '"Avez-vous lu Freud?" Maurice Chevalier dans *Pièges* de Robert Siodmak', *Iris* no. 21, Spring 1996.

5. See Martin Rubin, *Showstoppers: Busby Berkeley and the Tradition of Spectacle* (New York: Columbia University Press, 1993), especially pp. 12–13 for a discussion of the importance of 'integration' (musical numbers being integrated into narrative) in various histories of the genre. Rubin's notion of the 'Berkeleyesque' (a style one sees referenced in numerous French films of the 1930s) is employed in the table on p. 80.

6. Chevalier was one of the world's biggest stars, particularly in the late 1920s, early 1930s. For an overview of his transatlantic career, see Martine Danan, 'The Studio, the Star and International Audiences: Paramount and Chevalier', in Alastair Phillips and Ginette Vincendeau (eds), *Journeys of Desire: European Actors in Hollywood, A Critical Companion* (London: BFI, 2006), pp. 53–60.

7. The film also contains musical numbers that are more 'integrated' into the story as expressions of character thoughts and feelings – for example, 'Y'a du bonheur' ('There is happiness') sees Victor perform on his own (to 'extra-diegetic' orchestral accompaniment) an expression of optimism for the future and his love for Paris. This is the only other clip from *Avec le sourire* with an online presence I have found: <www.dailymotion.com/video/x1texe_chevalier-avec-le-sourire-ya-du-bon_music> (accessed 10 February 2010). The number is very similar to that from the opening to one of Chevalier's earlier Hollywood films, Mamoulian's 1932 *Love Me Tonight*.

8. Lyrics available at <www.paroles-musique.com/paroles-Maurice_Chevalier-Le_Chapeau_De_Zozo-lyrics,p16662> (accessed 10 February 2010).

9. The English term 'girls' is used in a number of French musical films of the decade to refer to music-hall dancers. Gisèle also refers to her job in the chorus-line as a '*danseuse anglaise*' (meaning, literally, 'English dancer'). This and other terms (such as '*miss*') illustrate the Anglo-American flavour of the culture of the music hall, which, I would suggest, is linked to the ambivalence, if not 'dystopian' characteristics, outlined in the table on p. 80. One should stress the mythic nature of these notions of national cultural difference, as it is ironic that Paris, along with London and New York, was one of the major starting points for the international music hall's emphasis on glitz and glamour. However, France and Paris's film productions would choose to stress a mythic, nostalgic cultural past. See Chapter 6 of Dudley Andrew and Steven Ungar's *Popular Front Paris and the Poetics of Culture* (Cambridge, MA: The Belknap Press, 2005) for a discussion of the 'bad faith' of this nostalgia.

10. *Apache* is difficult to translate, as it is so located in space and time. It was the term given to a certain perceived

category of rough, white, working-class Parisian men in the 1920s and 1930s. Some accounts have suggested that a Parisian street gang particularly notorious for their violence were first called '*apaches*' as an allusion to the Native American tribe. (This would perhaps make 'hooligan' the closest translation in etymology as well as meaning – some accounts have this term as a derivation of 'Hooley's gang'.) *Apache* certainly has strongly criminal connotations, often implying, more specifically, pimps (or *maquereaux*). Indeed, there is an *apache* dance that dramatises a pimp's beating-up of a prostitute. The *apache* and associated dance occupied a fascinating position within popular culture of the 1920s and 1930s, as illustrated by the hilarious scene of the Tramp's (Charlie Chaplin) confusion of the dance's performance with 'real' violence in *City Lights* (1931). *Love Me Tonight* (see second image) provides a fascinating touchstone with Chevalier's performance direct to camera of the song, 'What's a poor *apache* to do?' ('Black her eye' being the answer to one of these refrains!)

11. I shall keep this distinction (actor/character) in operation for the moment because we should remind ourselves that fictional characters do not *usually* look at the camera. In V. F. Perkins's words, 'It is not that these characters are oblivious to the camera. There is no camera in their world' ('Where Is the World? The Horizon of Events in Movie Fiction', in John Gibbs and Douglas Pye (eds), *Style and Meaning: Studies in the Detailed Analysis of Film* (Manchester: Manchester University Press, 2005), pp. 16–41). However, the musical is a frequent exception to this norm and it is one of the genres where the division between performer and character is often indistinct.

12. The essay was first published in *Movie* in 1976. My references are to its appearance in Dyer's *Only Entertainment* (London: Routledge, 1992), pp. 17–34.

13. The first two rows (the definition of the 'utopian' characteristic and the real-world problems they are a response to) are drawn from Dyer's own tables on pages 20–1 and page 24 of his essay. The remainder of the table relates solely to French musical films and the 'show-biz' (and therefore 'foreign') forms and the indigenous cultural forms they present. I have offered some examples from a range of French films from the period, though of course no table can do justice to the range of texts in existence.

14. Dyer, *Only Entertainment*, p. 18; emphasis added.

15. The *chanteuse réaliste* (translating, roughly, as 'realist female singer') is key in understanding 'transparency' in French musical film-making of the 1930s and this requires further note. In understanding this figure's key place in the complex network of values hinted at in the table, I would draw the reader's attention to Vincendeau's 'The Mise-en-Scène of Suffering. French *Chanteuses Réalistes*', in *New Formations* no. 3, Winter 1987, pp. 107–28. See also Kelley Conway, *Chanteuse in the City: The Realist Singer in French Film* (Berkeley: University of California Press, 2004).

The *chanteuse réaliste* in film is often presented as something akin to a prostitute, but of the 'hooker-with-a-heart-of-gold' variety – she is honest, 'transparent' in her communications. I would suggest that female music-hall stardom is often presented as a different kind of 'whoring oneself', one based on deception and duplicity. There are few 'virgins' in French musical cinema; what it has instead is a (good) whore–(bad) whore dichotomy.

16. Andrew and Ungar, *Popular Front Paris*, p. 220.

17. After his return to Paris, Chevalier also staged free outdoor performances in his old neighbourhood on a number of Bastille Day celebrations (reported in *L'Intransigeant*, 17 July 1937, and *Paris Soir*, 16 July 1939). Most of the press clippings consulted for this research are held in the Rondel collection at the BNF Richelieu site. The film more broadly can be seen as a self-conscious star vehicle, '*Avec le sourire*' having been the title of one of Chevalier's own songs (recorded in 1921) as well as one of the central facets of his star image and appeal – articles on Chevalier written throughout the decade and well before the film's production often emphasise his '*sourire*'.

18. My sense of its lack of commercial success is admittedly anecdotal. For example, in Chevalier's autobiographies (which appeared in various volumes), the star himself suggested his French films from the 1930s were not very successful – *Ma route et mes chansons* (Paris: Flammarion, 1998), p. 512. Moreover, in the most rigorous survey of French box office throughout the decade, Colin Crisp does not have *Avec le sourire* appearing in the top thirty-eight most popular French films of its season: *Genre, Myth, and Convention in the French Cinema, 1929–1939* (Bloomington: Indiana University Press, 2002), p. 321.

19. Phil Powrie, 'La Communauté impossible, ou pourquoi le film musical français se fait rare', in Raphaële Moine (ed.), *Le cinéma Français face aux genres* (Paris: Association Française de Recherche sur l'Histoire du Cinéma, 2005), p. 213); my translation.

20. Date of release: <www.imdb.com/title/tt0027321/release-info> (accessed 10 February 2010). See Andrew and Ungar, *Popular Front Paris*, for an account of the cultural landscape of this period of French history.

21. Dyer, *Only Entertainment*, p. 17.

22. Jane Feuer, *The Hollywood Musical* (Bloomington: Indiana University Press, 1993).

23. Martin O'Shaughnessy, 'The Parisian Popular as Reactionary Modernization', *Studies in French Cinema* vol. 1 no. 2, 2001, pp. 80–8.

24. His next film, *L'Homme du jour* (Duvivier, 1937) is another musical with an unexpected message, in which Chevalier plays an electrician who learns that, rather than become a singing star, he should be happy with his lot. Chevalier would make only one more film in France before the war, *Pièges* (Siodmak, 1939). This film also deconstructs his star image in surprising ways – see Alastair Phillips, *City of*

Darkness, City of Light: Émigré Filmmakers in Paris 1929–1939
(Amsterdam: Amsterdam University Press, 2004), especially
pp. 152–61.

BIBLIOGRAPHY

Andrew, Dudley, *Mists of Regret: Culture and Sensibility in Classic French Film* (Princeton, NJ: Princeton University Press, 1995).

Andrew, Dudley and Ungar, Steven, *Popular Front Paris and the Poetics of Culture* (Cambridge, MA: The Belknap Press, 2005).

Brown, Tom, 'Direct Address', in John Gibbs and Douglas Pye (eds), *Close-Up 05* (London: Wallflower Press, 2011).

Chevalier, Maurice, *Ma route et mes chansons* (Paris: Flammarion, 1998).

Conway, Kelley, *Chanteuse in the City: The Realist Singer in French Film* (Berkeley: University of California Press, 2004).

Crisp, Colin, *Genre, Myth, and Convention in the French Cinema, 1929–1939* (Bloomington: Indiana University Press, 2002).

Danan, Martine, 'The Studio, the Star and International Audiences: Paramount and Chevalier', in Alastair Phillips and Ginette Vincendeau (eds), *Journeys of Desire: European Actors in Hollywood, A Critical Companion* (London: BFI, 2006), pp. 53–60.

Dyer, Richard, *Only Entertainment* (London: Routledge, 1992).

Feuer, Jane, *The Hollywood Musical* (Bloomington: Indiana University Press, 1993).

Gibbs, John and Pye, Douglas (eds), *Style and Meaning: Studies in the Detailed Analysis of Film* (Manchester: Manchester University Press, 2005).

Moine, Raphaële (ed.), *Le cinéma Français face aux genres* (Paris: Association Française de Recherche sur l'Histoire du Cinéma, 2005).

O'Shaughnessy, Martin, 'The Parisian Popular as Reactionary Modernization', *Studies in French Cinema* vol. 1 no. 2, 2001, pp. 80–8.

Perkins, V. F., 'Where Is the World? The Horizon of Events in Movie Fiction', in John Gibbs and Douglas Pye (eds), *Style and Meaning: Studies in the Detailed Analysis of Film* (Manchester: Manchester University Press, 2005), pp. 16–41.

Phillips, Alastair, *City of Darkness, City of Light: Émigré Filmmakers in Paris 1929–1939* (Amsterdam: Amsterdam University Press, 2004).

Phillips, Alastair and Vincendeau, Ginette (eds), *Journeys of Desire: European Actors in Hollywood, A Critical Companion* (London: BFI, 2006).

Powrie, Phil, 'La Communauté impossible, ou pourquoi le film musical Français se fait rare', in Raphaële Moine (ed.), *Le cinéma Français face aux genres* (Paris: Association Française de Recherche sur l'Histoire du Cinéma, 2005), pp. 213–22.

Rubin, Martin, *Showstoppers: Busby Berkeley and the Tradition of Spectacle* (New York: Columbia University Press, 1993).

Temple, Michael and Witt, Michael (eds), *The French Cinema Book* (London: BFI, 2004).

Vincendeau, Ginette, 'The Mise-en-Scène of Suffering. French Chanteuses Réalistes', *New Formations* no. 3, Winter 1987, pp. 107–28.

Vincendeau, Ginette, '"Avez-vous lu Freud?" Maurice Chevalier dans *Pièges* de Robert Siodmak', *Iris* no. 21, Spring 1996, pp. 89–98.

Vincendeau, Ginette, 'The Art of Spectacle: The Aesthetics of Classical French Cinema', in Michael Temple and Michael Witt (eds), *The French Cinema Book* (London: BFI, 2004), pp. 137–52.

Music, Crime and the Gaze: *La Bête humaine* (1938)

GINETTE VINCENDEAU

One hour and twenty-four minutes into *La Bête humaine* comes a moment which to me is an exemplary piece of 1930s French cinema. Much has been written about this film and its 'three stars',[1] the writer Émile Zola, the director Jean Renoir and the actor Jean Gabin. Much attention too has been paid to its complex relationship to the historical context. In particular the film's pessimism has been debated in terms of the demise of the Popular Front and the looming war.[2] Here I will concentrate on an apparently quiet moment (in narrative terms) to tease out its evocative density.

La Bête humaine is the story of Jacques Lantier (Gabin), a train driver with a heavy alcoholic inheritance which provokes uncontrollable murderous impulses. Lantier falls in love with Séverine (Simone Simon), the wife of the Le Havre station master, Roubaud (Fernand Ledoux). Although he rightly suspects the pair to be guilty of murder, he remains silent. The lovers plot to kill Roubaud, but instead Lantier, overtaken by one of his murderous impulses, kills Séverine and later commits suicide by jumping from his train.

The scene that interests me is wedged between the murder and the suicide. During its short span (two minutes forty-seven seconds), the camera cuts back and forth between a dance hall in which a railwaymen's ball is taking place and Séverine's apartment where Lantier, having just killed her, contemplates her dead body. The two spaces are united aurally by a song which we see being performed in the dance hall. Except in the very last take, in which Lantier walks through the night along the tracks, the scene is edited to the exact length of the song (see breakdown at the end of this chapter).

A RENOIR MOMENT: EDITING, POLITICS, ENTERTAINMENT

In his adaptation, Renoir greatly streamlined Zola's long novel, typically packed with characters, subplots and political detail; for André Bazin 'the result is better than the book'.[3] Renoir's simplified narrative contrasts the world of the railway workers with the deadly Lantier–Séverine–Roubaud triangle, an alternation mirrored in the sequence we are examining here.

The sequence both confirms and confounds traditionally held views of Renoir's *mise en scène*, situating him within a stylistic history of French cinema. The two minutes forty-seven seconds contain eight shots, averaging twenty-one seconds per shot. Even though this is greater than the French average shot length at the time, which tended towards eleven to thirteen seconds (still longer than Hollywood's seven seconds), long and mobile takes were common in 1930s French cinema; thus Renoir was in that respect following the national style. On the other hand, the sequence illustrates his exceptional use of mobile camera and staging in depth. Six of the eight shots include camera movement, Renoir's camera forever exploring: moving from spectators to singer in shot 1, creeping up the bodies of Séverine and then Lantier in shot 3, taking us round the sitting room in shot 6. Renoir's penchant for staging action in depth is also in evidence in shot 4, which shows Lantier in the bedroom at the back, through a doorway, in the position in which earlier we see him kill Séverine,[4] the framing strongly suggesting his literal and metaphorical entrapment.

While the sequence demonstrates fluid camera movement, staging in depth and long takes, the hallmarks of Bazinian realism, it also shows that, as John Anzalone argues,[5] Renoir clearly mastered fragmentation and discontinuity editing techniques. Indeed, several writers discuss how Renoir is fond of bringing together music and murder, here as well as in *La Chienne* (1931) and *Le Crime de Monsieur Lange* (1935). In an interesting reading of *La Bête humaine* Katherine Golsan sees the dance-hall sequence, where the train is reduced to a cardboard cutout, as a sad travesty of the glorious sequence at the beginning of the film when Gabin drives a real train, the film thereby expressing the failure of social progress.[6] I do not disagree with this, but *La Bête humaine* is not a political tract and it is possible to see this moment's combination of social realism and popular entertainment in a different light.

Renoir the chronicler of society: the working-class dance hall

The importance of the dance hall is signalled first of all by the fact that this sequence is absent from Zola's novel. For Renoir, popular entertainment is an opportunity to display a social group.

Shots 1 and 2 are replete with social density, both literally (sweeping across and then through the crowd) and metaphorically, for instance showing the brief reactions of the waiters behind Pecqueux (Julien Carette) and Philomène (Jenny Hélia), as the two argue about whether to wait for Lantier or not. This is Renoir the chronicler of French society. If the scene lacks the aural complexity of the murder scene in *La Chienne*, it nevertheless displays aural perspective (throughout shot 1 the song becomes increasingly audible) and careful sound embedding. The sweet, sentimental song is bracketed by Séverine's shriek as Lantier kills her in the scene immediately preceding shot 1, and by the dramatic strains of Joseph Kosma's music as Gabin walks grimly along the tracks in shot 8. Kosma's emphatic chords cut into the singer's bow to his audience, ominously replacing applause. The performance is over: now Lantier must march towards his destiny.

The song, 'Le Petit coeur de Ninon', is diegetically motivated, since we see the singer, but its lyrics also comment on the narrative. Ninon makes men suffer, just as in the film Lantier and Roubaud 'suffer' because of Séverine. Renoir meticulously matches image to words: in shot 3 Ninon's heart is 'fragile', 'a light butterfly' just as the camera briefly pauses on her (dead) face, her eyes vacant, and the lyrics proclaim 'it is not its fault, no!' at the exact moment the camera pauses on Gabin's face. Thereby Renoir signals his, and our culture's, ambivalence towards the femme fatale: is this lack of guilt addressed to her 'fatal' attractiveness or to his truly fatal murder? Probably the latter, as in shot 5 the song reiterates that men suffer from love/women at the exact moment a sombre Gabin regards himself in the mirror. The reality of the narrative is that it is she who is hurt by men: beaten by Roubaud,

abused by her godfather Grandmorin (Jacques Berlioz), killed by Lantier. Yet, judging from his words, Renoir seems to have considered Séverine's murder 'justified': 'Then, one day she went too far and Gabin killed her. I say Gabin because I'm not the man to take major decisions ...'.[7]

As is often the case in French cinema of the time, the song forms part of a self-reflexive tradition,[8] seen in the way the camera approaches the stage to foreground the singer, a crooner called Marcel Veyran. At this level too, the song cues the spectator. 'Le Petit cœur de Ninon' is not the kind of *chanson réaliste* favoured by Poetic Realist films, nor the robust comic vaudeville, but a *belle époque* romantic ballad whose feminine overtones evoke Séverine's world.[9] The décor behind Veyran is indicative of the genre's sentimentality: painted trees and flowers are echoed in the paper garlands hanging from the ceiling across the room. The precious lyrics recall Séverine's affected langage (Philomène sees her as 'above her station' and calls her 'a real princess'), while the smoothly coiffed and besuited crooner resembles Séverine's new lover Dauvergne (Gérard Landry), previously seen dancing with her. Both men's bourgeois and effete masculinity sharply contrasts with Gabin's rugged Lantier, a contrast underlined by the violent cut between the singer and Lantier walking (shots 7–8), and more generally, throughout the scene, by the extraordinary gap between the sweet melody and the darkness pervading the apartment. And yet, at the same time as he is opposed to Gabin, Veyran nevertheless belongs to the popular culture of the time, through his precisely 'dated' voice and the popularity of such songs with working-class audiences. Thus the ball scene is just as 'historical' in its depiction of the railwaymen's culture as the earlier, quasi-documentary views of Lantier and Pecqueux driving the train.

A GABIN MOMENT: STARDOM, MASCULINITY AND FRENCH FILM NOIR

La Bête humaine belongs to Gabin as much as to Renoir. The film owed its existence to his star power and interest in the project, and anecdotally his desire to drive a locomotive. Lantier's actions, while part of Zola's project, made sense in relation to his star persona. As Bazin put it, Renoir based character motivation not on psychology but on the 'metaphysics' of the actor: 'What we see on screen is not Lantier's murderous anger but Gabin's.'[10]

We have seen that the weight of the narrative, supported by the song, encourages spectator sympathy for the murderous Lantier rather than the murdered Séverine. But it is also Gabin's star persona that tips the audience in his favour. Since *La Bandera* (1935), in films such as *Les Bas-fonds* (1936), *Pépé le Moko* and *La Grande illusion* (both 1937), and later *Le Quai des brumes* (1938) and *Le Jour se lève* (1939), Gabin personified the tragic working-class hero, driven to murder and suicide by a combination of Oedipal rebellion and crushing social forces.[11] His characters were credible as much for their literary pedigree as for Gabin's charismatic projection of authenticity, in no small part through his minimalist performance style. Gabin's inscrutable expression as he watches the dead Séverine in shot 3 or looks at himself in the mirror in shot 5, the heaviness with which he carries himself when he leaves the bedroom in shot 4, all convey a powerful world-weariness through his 'proletarian body'. Within this sequence, and across the film, Gabin's dramatic persona is offset not only by Dauvergne and the singer's suave bourgeois manners but also in contrast to the comic swagger of Carette who plays his assistant Pecqueux. The two actors, also seen side by side in *La Grande illusion*, epitomise the two tendencies in French cinema highlighted by Michel Chion between extreme verbosity and extreme laconicity,[12] as well as the difference between the tragic proletarian hero and the comic working-class secondary character.

The high point of the sequence comes in shot 5. Framed by two high, fluted vases, Lantier looks at himself across the cluttered dresser, above a bottle and glasses on a tray (a possible ironic allusion to his ancestors' alcoholism, the source of his troubled personality, here in the feminised version of small, dainty glasses and liqueur bottle). He looks twice. At the first glance he immediately lowers his eyes, then he looks again, both compelled and horrified by what he sees and doesn't want to see: literally *la bête humaine*, the 'human beast', a sight which will lead to his suicide – confirming in this moment Lagny's contention that the Renoir film is structured around Gabin's flawed vision, his ability to see and yet not to see and thus that it 'both proposes and systematically denies the driver access to the gaze'.[13]

There have been many other interpretations of Lantier's gaze, notably literary (Leo Braudy)[14] and psychoanalytical (Golsan).[15] But Lantier's gaze in the mirror is

French film noir: Jean Gabin's gaze at 'the human beast'

also, and perhaps first of all, a product of Renoir's noir aesthetics. At the time, many criticised *La Bête humaine* along with other films as noir because of their excessive pessimism.[16] Many have followed suit in seeing the film as evidence of Renoir's estrangement from the left in the context of Munich and the Spanish civil war. But visually Renoir and his German émigré cinematographer Curt Courant were also experimenting with the international noir style.

The sequence brings together two distinct visual styles: the high-key lighting and expansive space of the concert hall (shots 1, 2 and 7), against the cramped and claustrophobic scenes in the flat (shots 3, 4, 5 and 6), bathed in a dark atmosphere redolent of the murder scene. In previous scenes Séverine's dresses often had white lace collars, hinting at her child-woman nature. In her death scene, her black dress has no collar, showing more of her flesh as if to highlight the space where Lantier will kill her (he tries to strangle her, then stabs her in the throat). In addition, he carries her small black muslin scarf from the bed to the dresser, like a funeral veil. The atmosphere of the scene is also distinguished by what has become a signature noir motif, that is to say strong contrasting bands of darkness and light. These are nominally produced by slats at the top of the wooden blinds, but close examination shows that these cannot realistically project light across the two rooms in such a way. In the same manner, light could not plausibly bounce off metallic surfaces and mirrors the way it does, since before the murder we saw Séverine switch off all the lights. The lighting effects are thus intended to provide a menacing, though poetic atmosphere. Yet the contrast between light and dark is not purely aesthetic, but is also relevant to Gabin, picking out his eyes as he looks at Séverine in shot 3 and especially when he looks at himself in the mirror in shot 5. The band of light that strongly isolates his eyes from the surrounding gloom gives the moment a particularly haunting quality, eerily counterpointed by the sentimental ballad. Here the stylistic effect – visual contrast within the shot and aural contrast between image and sound – echoes the inner split (worker/criminal) in Gabin's star persona and the 'fatal flaw' (*la fêlure*) in Lantier's character.

Through editing, aural and visual style and the deployment of Gabin's star image, Renoir, in this apparently 'quiet' yet pivotal moment of *La Bête humaine*, concentrates the myriad oppositions that structure the whole film, between the bright world of workers' solidarity and the loneliness of the killer, between light entertainment and crime melodrama, between French naturalist fiction and international film noir. In 1939 Pierre Bost judged the film uneven, but with 'some brilliant moments'.[17] I hope to have shown that the sequence examined here is one of them.

SCENE BREAKDOWN

Shots 1–7: song on soundtrack ('Le Petit coeur de Ninon')
Shot 8: extra-diegetic music (by Joseph Kosma)

Shot no.	Duration	Location	Description
1	51 seconds	Dance hall	MS on couple, track and pan left on stationary dancers, track forward to LS of singer on stage
2	29 seconds	Dance hall	Low-angle stationary MS of singer on stage
3	29 seconds	Séverine's flat	Tracking shot starting on CU (Séverine's) hand, travelling right to other hand, up to her face and up to CU Lantier's face looking down at her
4	16 seconds	Séverine's flat	LS of Lantier next to bed, turning towards us, track left to follow him to wardrobe
5	18 seconds	Séverine's flat	MCU Lantier putting knife down on surface, track up to MCU of his face, track left to MS of his face in mirror
6	20 seconds	Séverine's flat	LS tracking left to follow Lantier moving across room (left) towards door and leaving flat, ending on door ajar
7	11 seconds	Dance hall	Low-angle stationary MS of singer on stage (as in shot 2)
8	15 seconds	Railway tracks	Track backwards on Lantier walking towards camera on railway tracks

NOTES

1. Michèle Lagny, 'The Fleeing Gaze: Jean Renoir's *La Bête humaine* (1938)', in Susan Hayward and Ginette Vincendeau (eds), *French Film: Texts and Contexts* (London and New York: Routledge, 1990), pp. 83–101.
2. See, among the extensive literature on Renoir in English discussing *La Bête humaine*, Raymond Durgnat, *Jean Renoir* (Berkeley and Los Angeles: University of California Press, 1974); Alexander Sesonske, *Jean Renoir: The French Films, 1924–1939* (Cambridge, MA: Harvard University Press, 1980); Chris Faulkner, *The Social Cinema of Jean Renoir* (Princeton, NJ: Princeton University Press, 1986); Dudley Andrew, *Mists of Regret: Culture and Sensibility in Classic French Film* (Princeton, NJ: Princeton University Press, 1995).

3. André Bazin, *Jean Renoir* (Paris: Éditions Champ Libre, 1971), p. 64.
4. The murder scene, previously omitted from prints and VHS copies, is now visible on DVD. See François Albera, 'Restaurez, restaurez, il en restera toujours quelque chose …', 1895 no. 40, Varia, 2003. Available at <1895.revues.org/document3482.html> (accessed 20 June 2009).
5. John Anzalone, 'Sound/Tracks: Zola, Renoir and *La Bête humaine*', *The French Review* vol. 62 no. 4, March 1989, p. 587.
6. Katherine Golsan, '"Vous allez vous user les yeux": Renoir's Framing of *La Bête humaine*', *The French Review* vol. 73 no. 1, October 1999, p. 114.
7. Jean Renoir, *Écrits: 1926–1971* [Textes rassemblés par Claude Gauteur] (Paris: Belfond, 1974), p. 337.
8. See Ginette Vincendeau, 'The Art of Spectacle: The Aesthetics of Classical French Cinema', in Michael Temple and Michael Witt (eds), *The French Cinema Book* (London: BFI, 2004), pp. 137–52.
9. Lyrics by Maurice Nouhaud, aka Georges Millandy; music by E. Becucci (from an Italian waltz, 'Tesoro mio'). Written in 1900.
10. Bazin, *Jean Renoir*, p. 63.
11. See Ginette Vincendeau, 'Jean Gabin: From Working-class Hero to Godfather', in *Stars and Stardom in French Cinema* (London and New York: Continuum, 2000), pp. 59–81.
12. Michel Chion, *Le Complexe de Cyrano, La langue parlée dans les films français* (Paris: Cahiers du cinéma essais, 2008), p. 7.
13. Lagny, 'The Fleeing Gaze', p. 96.
14. Leo Braudy, 'Zola on Film: The Ambiguities of Naturalism', *Yale French Studies* no. 42, Zola (1969), p. 66–88.
15. Golsan, '"Vous allez vous user les yeux"', pp. 110–20.
16. For a discussion of the critical reception of 1930s French film noir, see Charles O'Brien, 'Film Noir in France: Before the Liberation', *Iris* no. 21, Spring 1996, pp. 7–20.
17. Pierre Bost, quoted in Lagny, 'The Fleeing Gaze', p. 89.

BIBLIOGRAPHY

Albera, François, 'Restaurez, restaurez, il en restera toujours quelque chose …', 1895 no. 40, Varia, 2003. Available at <1895.revues.org/document3482.html> (accessed 20 June 2009).

Andrew, Dudley, *Mists of Regret: Culture and Sensibility in Classic French Film* (Princeton, NJ: Princeton University Press, 1995).

Anzalone, John, 'Sound/Tracks: Zola, Renoir and *La Bête humaine*', *The French Review* vol. 62 no. 4, March 1989, pp. 583–90.

Bazin, André, *Jean Renoir* (Paris: Éditions Champ Libre, 1971).

Braudy, Leo, 'Zola on Film: The Ambiguities of Naturalism', *Yale French Studies* no. 42, Zola (1969), pp. 66–88.

Chion, Michel, *Le Complexe de Cyrano: La langue parlée dans les films français* (Paris: Cahiers du cinéma essais, 2008).

Durgnat, Raymond, *Jean Renoir* (Berkeley and Los Angeles: University of California Press, 1974).

Faulkner, Chris, *The Social Cinema of Jean Renoir* (Princeton, NJ: Princeton University Press, 1986).

Golsan, Katherine, ' "Vous allez vous user les yeux": Renoir's Framing of *La Bête humaine*', *The French Review* vol. 73 no. 1, October 1999, pp. 110–20.

Hayward, Susan and Vincendeau, Ginette (eds), *French Film, Texts and Contexts* (London and New York: Routledge, 1990), pp. 83–101.

Lagny, Michèle, 'The Fleeing Gaze: Jean Renoir's *La Bête humaine* (1938)', in Hayward and Vincendeau, *French Film: Texts and Contexts*, pp. 83–101.

O'Brien, Charles, 'Film Noir in France: Before the Liberation', *Iris* no. 21, Spring 1996, pp. 7–20.

Renoir, Jean, *Ecrits: 1926–1971* [Textes rassemblés par Claude Gauteur] (Paris: Belfond, 1974).

Sesonske, Alexander, *Jean Renoir: The French Films, 1924–1939* (Cambridge, MA: Harvard University Press, 1980).

Temple, Michael and Witt, Michael (eds), *The French Cinema Book* (London: BFI, 2004).

Vincendeau, Ginette, 'Jean Gabin: From Working-class Hero to Godfather', in *Stars and Stardom in French Cinema* (London and New York: Continuum, 2000), pp. 59–81.

Vincendeau, Ginette, 'The Art of Spectacle: The Aesthetics of Classical French Cinema', in Temple and Witt, *The French Cinema Book*, pp. 137–52.

Thunder and Lightning: *Gone with the Wind* (1939) and the Logic of Synchronisation

RICK ALTMAN

With Atlanta in flames, Rhett Butler (Clark Gable) piles Scarlett O'Hara (Vivien Leigh), Prissy (Butterfly McQueen), Melanie Hamilton Wilkes (Olivia de Havilland) and her newborn baby into a horsecart. Fighting off renegades, he skirts the conflagration and gallantly leads the ladies to safety outside the burning city. Then, unexpectedly, he abandons them to join the army, leaving Scarlett and Prissy to guide Melanie and her child to the safety of Twelve Oaks. Constantly dodging Northern troops, the women must also weather a violent storm that breaks out just as they hide beneath a bridge to avoid the passing soldiers.

Hollywood has a genius for recreating nature in its own image, bending natural phenomena to its own purposes. The storm that threatens Scarlett, Prissy and their charges offers a clear case in point. In the natural world, light travels far faster than sound, so lightning always appears well before we hear the associated thunder clap. Not so in *Gone with the Wind* (Fleming, 1939). Here the film's full-screen representation of lightning occurs simultaneously with the sound of thunder. However separate image and sound may be in nature, *Gone with the Wind* synchronises them, leaving no doubt about their connection. Why would director Victor Fleming and recording engineer Frank Maher so blithely break the rules of nature? What is

at stake in this apparent disrespect of the natural order? More broadly, why does Hollywood so often insist on close synchronisation when another approach would seem more justified?

By the time David O. Selznick produced *Gone with the Wind*, Hollywood had been grappling with sound questions for over a decade. When the industry first converted to sound, the solutions seemed obvious: all that was necessary was to place a microphone at an appropriate distance from the actors and to record their voices. Hollywood's initial approach to sound was thus fundamentally documentary in nature: the soundman's job was just to document the sound while the camera recorded the image. Yet even cursory consideration of the image portion of this formula should have warned the sound crew that things would not be so simple. During the course of the three previous decades, directors had discovered that successful film images were anything but the direct result of recording. Film actors had to be trained to appear natural, all the while posturing and acting for the camera. Lighting had to be designed with the camera in mind. Special make-up had to be invented to match the shifting needs of the period's film stock. Sets had to be constructed, not for human comfort but for maximal camera satisfaction. While early filmmakers understandably concluded that the camera's primary function was to record nature, it soon became apparent that the best film images were the result not of nature but of artifice. From scripting to acting and from set construction to lighting, it was expected that every component of the film would be specially built to match camera requirements. Instead of following the laws of nature, Hollywood created its own rules. Yet however clearly Hollywood personnel understood the artificial nature of the film image, this knowledge was not immediately extrapolated to cover sound. Even though, by 1930, the film image was clearly governed by camera-conscious conventions, early articles about the right way to handle film sound systematically stressed the natural order and the necessity for cinema sound to adhere to the laws of nature. Because they attempted to record sound rather than construct it, early sound films thus regularly frustrated audiences by offering soundtracks that were inconsistent, hard to follow, and in general incapable of taking full advantage of the new technology. Eager to follow the laws of nature, Hollywood blithely neglected the basic principle of representation: if the goal is to reshape reality rather than recreate it, it's not reality that counts, but realism.

Take the case of Fox's 1930 extravaganza, *The Big Trail*. Filmed in William Fox's proprietary 70mm Grandeur system and directed by former D. W. Griffith assistant Raoul Walsh, *The Big Trail* features a young John Wayne in his first starring role. In many ways this film aptly represents early Hollywood sound practice. Three segments of *The Big Trail* offer especially interesting points of comparison for *Gone with the Wind*'s late 1930s handling of sound. Moving back and forth between *The Big Trail* and *Gone with the Wind*, the remainder of this article will reveal the substantial differences between the handling of sound at the beginning and end of the 30s.

1. The opening scene of *The Big Trail* portrays a large wagon-train campsite. The dialogue in this scene proves rather frustrating. Even though we can see many characters, it is surprisingly difficult to tell just who is doing the talking. Why should we have so much trouble locating the sound source, and what would Hollywood do to solve this problem? The cause of the problem is very simple. Whereas the image was carefully designed to take full advantage of everything the industry had learned about visual rhetoric and realism, the soundtrack was produced in a documentary manner, simply by recording the sounds made by the people and objects in the image. For example, *The Big Trail* regularly employs extreme long shots to take advantage of the expanse afforded by Grandeur's widescreen technology. The benefits for the image are obvious: director Walsh gets to produce gorgeous wide-angle images of sweeping landscapes and expansive wagon-train camps. But the cost to the soundtrack is equally apparent: there are so many people in the image, far from the camera and spread out over a wide area, that we have a hard time locating the speaker.

In order to solve the problem of speaker location, Hollywood developed a series of cues to help audiences process the soundtrack. Instead of continuing simply to record available sound, the industry began to configure sound to satisfy spectator needs. Instead of allocating dialogue to distant or peripheral eccentric characters, Hollywood would increasingly limit dialogue to centred characters with faces large enough for audiences to recognise which one was speaking. Actors were instructed to face the camera when speaking, so that their moving lips would be visible and thus available as markers of the speech source. Directors learned that sound sources are more easily detected when dialogue passages are preceded by a cut to a medium shot or close-up. In addition, casting decisions would increasingly be influenced by the benefits of selecting actors with immediately recognisable voices. Foreign headliners with characteristic accents (Maurice Chevalier, Marlene Dietrich, Greta Garbo, Cary Grant) became especially desirable. Even supporting actors who never graduated to major roles were guaranteed regular employment by their distinctive voices (Mischa Auer, Eugene Pallette, Zasu Pitts).

From the very beginnings of Hollywood's conversion to sound, directors and soundmen had understood the value of synchronised sound as a selling point for their wares. Even before *The Jazz Singer* (Crosland, 1927), a film like Warners' *The First Auto* (Del Ruth, 1927) laboured mightily to fully exploit the synchronised sound capabilities of the new Vitaphone sound-on-disc system. With the success of *The Jazz Singer* the value of sync sound became so obvious that subsequent films would go out of their way to feature moments where the sound and the image were obviously synchronised, thereby touting the new technology. But Hollywood still had to learn that synchronisation only takes on its full value with rapid and secure sound-source location. This desire to foreground the process of synchronisation gives rise to what I have called the 'sound hermeneutic', whereby a visual source must rapidly be attributed to any sound lacking a clear image source.[1] In Hollywood's synchronisation-rich environment, sounds without a source appear anomalous. Not until the audience can match them to a visual source – i.e. not until they can be understood as synchronised with the image – do sounds take on their full meaning in the Hollywood system.

By the time of *Gone with the Wind*, Hollywood understood the importance of designing images to assure audience perception of synchronisation. The film's opening scenes offer an appropriate case in point. After an extreme long shot of Tara, the O'Hara plantation, we cut in to a medium shot of Scarlett and her suitors, then immediately track in to a close-up of Scarlett, before tracking back out to a medium three-shot clearly revealing the moving lips of all three characters. Thanks to this technique, no audience member can possibly fail to recognise who is speaking. Synchronisation is built into this editing pattern. At the end of the scene, Scarlett is called by her African-American maid, Mammy (Hattie McDaniel), who we see in medium shot leaning out of an upper window. In the next shot the sounds of Mammy's voice are accompanied by an extreme long shot of Tara, with Mammy virtually invisible in the distance. Had the extreme long shot come first, we would have suffered the same dilemma as in *The Big Trail*: we would not know where the sound was coming from. Placing the medium shot first securely identifies Mammy as the source of the sound.

The following sequences follow a similar pattern. We next dissolve to a close-up of a bell, accompanied by bell

sounds. The succeeding shot reveals the plantation slaves working the fields, accompanied by the sound of a bell that would seem sourceless and syncless had the film not preceded the shot of the fieldhands with a tight shot of the tolling bell itself. Once the sound of the bell has been located through sync, it is subsequently deemed available to accompany shots in which the bell itself is no longer visible. Even our abbreviated view of the fieldhands obeys a similar logic. At first we see them in extreme long shot, but as soon as someone speaks we immediately cut in to a medium shot to catch the dialogue (and appreciate the sync). The film's final introductory scene features extreme long shots of Scarlett's father Gerald (Thomas Mitchell) riding through Tara's fields and streams, jumping fences like a man half his age. But as soon as he prepares to speak, we cut in to a medium shot assuring easy understanding. Throughout *Gone with the Wind* we always know who is doing the talking and thus remain constantly aware of the film's commitment to tight synchronisation.

2. Just over an hour into *The Big Trail*, a substantial obstacle arises: only by lowering the wagons by rope down a steep cliff can the wagon train continue its western progress. Shot after shot shows the challenging process of lowering the wagons, first from above and then from below. In keeping with early sound cinema's documentary approach to sound, each shot is accompanied by what were at the time considered appropriate sounds, i.e. those made by everything we see in each image. But the end of this sequence suddenly and quite unexpectedly reveals aspects of then current practice that are quite unsettling for modern viewers. After many shots of the wagon-lowering process taken from the valley floor below, accompanied only by wagon-lowering sounds, we suddenly discover that a river flows through the valley and that the previous shots were taken from a location right next to the river. When the image reveals the river, we hear the river, but as long as the river is not actually in the image the soundtrack carries no sign of the river's presence.

This sequence from *The Big Trail* offers a clear example of early sound practice and points to one of the most important changes that would take place in the years to come. *The Big Trail* regularly documents the sound of all profilmic action. When we see wagon-lowering, we hear wagon-lowering. When we see a river, we hear a river. Sounds are conceived as being attached to images and not to spaces. Later practice would involve the creation of what we might term a 'sound diegesis' – a space created by sounds that have the power to bridge images. This is typically accomplished by a technique that is usefully termed 'establishing sound'. The first shot of a scene clearly synchronises a characteristic sound with an image representing the sound's source. When the scene continues, the establishing sound continues to be heard even when the screen no longer displays the sound source. In this way, the scene is held together sonically, the sound diegesis providing strong support for the image's diegetic cues. Later in the 30s, *The Big Trail*'s wagon-lowering sequence would in all probability have been handled according to this establishing-sound procedure. A shot early in the sequence would have visually and aurally established the presence of the river, with subsequent use of the river sounds – even when the river was no longer visible in the image – firmly anchoring the overall scenic space in each spectator's mind.

This is precisely the way *Gone with the Wind* treats sound and image. The first shot of a scene typically uses synchronisation to establish a new sound diegesis. Subsequent shots are then free to match the now-familiar sound with new images lacking the sound source. The film's ample diegetic music is regularly handled in this manner. While the crowd awaits the bad news about Gettysburg casualties, the band strikes up 'Dixie'. Subsequent shots tie together apparently disparate spaces by continuing the music – with the band now absent from the image. Later, as the women wait at home for some word regarding the men's raid on the shanty-town dwellers who endanger the womenfolk, we hear ticking as we see the clock on the parlour wall. In the shots that follow, the ticking continues even though the clock disappears.

3. Before *The Big Trail*'s pioneers can reach their Pacific coast Promised Land, the wagon train must cross a raging river in the middle of a storm. Repeatedly, we hear the thunder and see the lightning, but never in that order. Faithful to nature, *The Big Trail* always displays the lightning before we hear the thunder. What the film gains in terms of respect for the laws of nature, however, it loses in terms of synchronisation. *Gone with the Wind* reverses these priorities, stressing synchronisation rather than fidelity to nature. The storm that Scarlett and Prissy must dodge is just as synchronised as the sounds of the Union soldiers as they ride by over the women's heads. No longer concerned

to respect nature, film-makers were by the time of *Gone with the Wind*, on the contrary, attuned to every possible way of making nature serve cinema's needs.

Gone with the Wind is hardly the first film to stretch the natural order to the point of representing thunder and lightning simultaneously, either to celebrate a narratively important event or to heighten an especially suspenseful moment. The start of Universal's *Bride of Frankenstein* (Whale, 1935) creates an atmosphere of suspense by saturating the soundtrack with thunder while filling the image track with representations of lightning. MGM's version of Charles Dickens's *A Tale of Two Cities* (Conway, 1935) uses simultaneous thunder and lightning to prepare the famous scene in which Sydney Carton (Ronald Colman) offers to sacrifice his own life so that Charles Darnay (Donald Woods), his rival for the hand of Lucie Manette (Elizabeth Allan), might live. In Fox's *The Prisoner of Shark Island* (Ford, 1936), Samuel Mudd (Warner Baxter), the doctor condemned for treating Lincoln's assassin, John Wilkes Booth, clears his name by warding off a prison epidemic. The moment is celebrated by a series of lightning flashes, synchronised with repeated thunderclaps. Warners' *The Private Lives of Elizabeth and Essex* (Curtiz, 1939) is constructed around the confrontation of two enormous egos. When Essex (Errol Flynn) is consigned to the Tower of London by Elizabeth (Bette Davis), the woman with whom he expected to share marriage and the throne, their encounter is represented by nothing less than simultaneous thunder and lightning.

Preferring Hollywood logic over natural law, *Gone with the Wind*'s synchronised storm reminds us just how dedicated the American film industry was to synchronisation. Not only does Hollywood systematically bind image and sound together, offering spectators high levels of stability and comfort, it also develops multiple image and sound strategies to assure audience perception of sync. This commitment to synchronisation is perhaps best understood as compensation for the fundamental scandal of sound-on-film technology: for technical reasons image and sound are always separated on the filmstrip (the sound is located twenty frames ahead of the 35mm image). What technology separates, technique restores. By insisting on sync, Hollywood succeeds in erasing the image–sound separation on which its very existence depends.

NOTE

1. Rick Altman, 'Moving Lips: Cinema as Ventriloquism', *Yale French Studies* no. 60, 1980, pp. 67–79.

BIBLIOGRAPHY

Altman, Rick, 'Moving Lips: Cinema as Ventriloquism', *Yale French Studies* no. 60, 1980, pp. 67–79.

Hearing, Fearing: The Sonic Design of Suspense in *Cat People* (1942)

HELEN HANSON

To find ever-new 'busses' or horror spots is a horror expert's most difficult problem. Horror spots must be well planned and there should be no more than four or five in a picture. Most of them are caused by fundamental fears: sudden sound, wild animals, darkness. The horror addicts will populate the darkness with more horrors than all the horror writers in Hollywood can think of.

Val Lewton[1]

This is a weird drama of thrill-chill calibre, with developments of surprises confined to psychology and mental reactions, rather than transformation to grotesque and marauding characters for visual impact on the audiences.

Variety[2]

A young Serbian woman, Irena (Simone Simon), suspects, rightly, that her husband, Oliver (Kent Smith), is becoming romantically involved with a co-worker, Alice (Jane Randolph). Irena observes the pair having coffee and she follows them through the deserted night-time streets of New York. Her stalking of Alice is invested with threat because Irena is haunted by her Serbian heritage, specifically an atavistic folk legend: it is said that at times of stress or conflict her people shapeshift into an avenging 'cat people'. The action is communicated by cutting between Alice and Irena, with their proximity to each other and movement through the streets marked by the contrasting and distinct sounds of their footsteps. Alice is aware she is being followed, but part of the way down a deserted street Irena's footsteps mysteriously fall silent. Alice looks around in vain and, failing to locate her pursuer, becomes more and more frightened. At the quietest moment of the sequence a bus bursts into view. Its arrival heralds relief, but the feline growl of its brakes and hiss as its doors open momentarily shock and confuse Alice, and the audience, and evoke a strong threat of a stealthy preying presence.

Occurring roughly two-thirds of the way into *Cat People* (Tourneur, 1942), the 'bus' moment is renowned as a near-

perfect example of how to evoke fear and then surprise in an audience. The moment is constructed through a highly disciplined interplay of image and sound and is meticulous in its manipulation of character (and audience) knowledge and inference. RKO horror unit producer Val Lewton suggests the currency of 'the bus' in his use of it as 'shorthand' for a suspense/surprise construction in the opening quotation. And, as the considerable and growing body of

criticism on the film has noted, 'the bus' plays on the power of suggestion.[3] The visual and aural interaction of the sequence delicately balances its inferences, allowing the possibility that Irena's disappearance is a moment of shapeshifting, while her transformation happens off screen. But as well as being fêted for its style, 'the bus' has been celebrated as pointing back to that rare circumstance; it has been seen as the outcome of a collaborative, relatively independent team of people working within the Hollywood studio system.[4] In this essay I want to examine 'the bus' less as an exceptional moment, or the product of unusual working conditions, but more as a potent example of sound style, suggesting that it be used not, or not just, to restate the 'underground creativity' of the Lewton unit, but as a way into tracing the deeper contexts influencing sound production in the early 1940s: that is, the underlying sound technologies, practices and conventions existent at the time of its production.

While many accounts of film-sound history focus on the dramatic technological, aesthetic and industrial adjustments of the transition to sound production, followed by a restabilisation of 'classical' style, there is much to be learned by tracing the ongoing evolution of film-sound technologies and practices. Broadly speaking, by 1930, the range of technologies used in Hollywood had stabilised, with the major Hollywood studios opting to use sound-on-film 'double' systems which permitted sound and image recording to be separated, allowing greater control of sound quality.[5] But between the production of the early talkies and Cat People there were steady technological improvements in all aspects of the sound recording, editing and playback process.[6] These included refinements in the sensitivity and directionality of microphones, the advent of microphone booms, technologies which permitted increased control and manipulation of sound at the editing and mixing stage, and sensitometric improvements in the quality of film stocks and responsiveness of photographic emulsions leading to qualitative improvements in sound. Many of these technological changes were the result of research by companies associated with the motion-picture industry, such as the Radio Corporation of America (RCA) and Bell Telephone's Research Division, Electrical Research Products Incorporated (ERPI).

Accompanying the technological changes there was a growing body of specialist sound personnel who had key roles in developing, discussing and disseminating new practices in the film-sound production process. Some of these specialists migrated from the radio and telephone industries to Hollywood following the conversion to sound, where a few took on high-profile roles in the studio system. Their discussions of sound practices offer insights into the gradual formation of conventions for sound. These discussions can be found in the journals of professional bodies, such as the *Journal of the Society of Motion Picture Engineers* (JSMPE), the Academy of Motion Pictures Arts and Sciences' (AMPAS) technical bulletins and publications arising from the 'Schools of Sound'. These were training courses organised in Hollywood by the Academy's Producers and Technicians Joint Committee to assimilate new production techniques and expertise.[7]

Debates among sound personnel about post-production sound practice illustrate how new conventions developed. James Lastra traces a process in the conceptualisation of sound's relationship to narrative space in the early sound era. He argues that personnel shifted from an idea of sound recording and reproduction as governed by 'fidelity values' (the most 'realistic' reproduction possible) to a model of sound 'shot through with the hierarchies of dramatic relationships'.[8] This understanding was demonstrated by RKO's head of sound, Carl Dreher, who argued that sound engineers required an understanding of the 'story values'[9] of sound. From an early point in the sound era, sound editors were able to use new techniques, such as re-recording, to forge new conventions that fulfilled these 'story values'. Dreher recognised that 'dubbing'[10] could be used to fabricate and place sounds. He wrote that 'any desired sonic background may be supplied'[11] with 'synthetic sounds' (i.e. sound effects) co-ordinated 'at the precise intervals desired and with the exact loudness which will be most appropriate'.[12] These principles of control and precise placement are amply demonstrated by the sound editing which creates the 'bus' moment in *Cat People*.

Rick Altman has also analysed the development of sound conventions pertinent to the 'bus'. In his work on sound space, he traces debates among sound personnel on the placement of microphones to record dialogue and other sounds on the set, and their deliberations over the extent to which the scale (i.e. volume) of the sound should correspond to the scale of the image. In the early sound era this was the subject of considerable debate. The influential soundman J. P. Maxfield repeatedly argued for sound and image to match in scale. In a series of articles he provided methods for recording intelligible dialogue which preserved spatial characteristics. Altman, though, notes that, despite the widespread circulation of Maxfield's work, in practice the industry demanded (and rewarded) its sound personnel for producing clear and continuous soundtracks in auditory close-up rather than for spatial realism, most specifically in dialogue recording.[13]

However, while these practices construct distinct conventions for dialogue recording and mixing, clear in many films of the studio era, Altman suggests that sequences contain sounds with spatial characteristics, particularly where location within the diegesis is narratively important. In these situations sound frequently suggests point of audition. Altman writes:

... point-of-audition sound is identified by its volume, reverb level, and other characteristics as representing sound as it would be heard from a point within the diegesis, normally by a specific character or characters. In other words, point-of-audition sound always carries signs of its fictional audition.[14]

Films in the horror, crime and thriller genres are replete with such sequences, sequences in which specific dramatic sound elements are particularly accented. The need to evolve distinct sonic registers for different genres was explicitly acknowledged by sound specialists. In 1934 Harold Lewis – the president of the newly formed Society for Sound Engineers – distinguished between the sound recording and mixing practices appropriate for comedies, and those suitable for melodramas (the term used by the industry and reviewers for the crime and thriller film in the 1930s and 1940s).[15] Lewis writes: '... a melodrama requires strongly contrasted sound-treatment, even as it requires strongly contrasted photographic treatment. Many sequences will be recorded in a low key, suddenly punctuated by very high keyed scenes.'[16]

Lewis thus draws an explicit parallel between dramatic iconography (chiaroscuro lighting) and dramatic sonography (contrasting volume and pitch levels). This understanding of sound styles is clearly displayed in *Cat People*, particularly in the 'bus' sequence where point-of-audition sound is played with in a bravura way. Point of audition is a commonplace in the crime and detective film. Audible footsteps offer a sonic index to characters' locations within a space where darkness occludes an investigator's visual map. The soft sole of the 'gumshoe' can cloak its wearer in silence to slide unnoticed through the crime world.

Cat People extends this convention by constructing point of audition (Alice hearing Irena following her), then complicates it (as Irena's footsteps fall silent), as Alice and the film audience strain to discern where she has gone. While the sound of Irena's footsteps cue anxiety, the duration of ambient silence increases the tension and suspense of the sequence. Alice's panic is sonically marked as the rhythm of her footsteps becomes more irregular and panicked. The tension is partly dissipated by the explosive arrival of the bus, but the suggestion of Irena's transformation is further fuelled by a sequence of edits. The sequence cuts from the bus to the bushes shaking, to the zoo where the panther prowls its cage with a low throaty growl, to a flock of sheep with some injured and dead, the others bleating in distress, and finally to a trail which begins as pawprints and ends as footprints.

The 'bus' sequence is rich in its implications and potent in its associative prompts to the key theme of the film – Irena's troubled subjectivity. It is also just one element in a wider pattern of sonic motifs deployed throughout the film as a whole. Sound textures and timbres echo

and rhyme through the film, frequently mixing and blurring organic animal sounds with those that more prosaically signal urban space. The 'growl' marking the arrival of the bus is just one example suggesting how thin the division is between the world of the wild and that of mechanised modernity.

Examining the sequence as illustrative of competencies in sonic control, arrangement and design demonstrates that sound personnel created a new set of sonic conventions and a fresh stylistic repertoire that were part of a contextual expertise in the sound era.

NOTES

1. Val Lewton, 'Interview in *Liberty* Magazine', cited in Joel Siegel, *Val Lewton: The Reality of Terror* (London: Secker and Warburg/BFI, 1972), p. 32.
2. *Variety*, 'Review of *Cat People*', 18 November 1942.
3. Siegel, *Val Lewton*, p. 31; J. P. Telotte, *Dreams of Darkness: Fantasy and the Films of Val Lewton* (Champaign: University of Illinois Press, 1985), p. 39; Edmund Bansak, *Fearing the Dark: The Val Lewton Career* (Jefferson, NC: McFarland & Co., 1995), pp. 133–7.
4. Siegel, *Val Lewton*, pp. 7–107; Bansak, *Fearing the Dark*, pp. 43–140; Steve Jenkins, 'Val Lewton: Curse of the Critics?', *Monthly Film Bulletin* vol. 48, July 1981, p. 148.
5. Barry Salt, *Film Style and Technology: History and Analysis* (2nd edn) (London: Starword, 1992), pp. 179–218.
6. Edward W. Kellogg, 'History of Sound Motion Pictures: First Instalment', *Journal of the Society of Motion Picture and Television Engineers* (*JSMPTE*), June 1955; 'History of Sound Motion Pictures: Second Instalment', *JSMPTE*, July 1955; 'History of Sound Motion Pictures: Final Instalment', *JSMPTE*, August 1955. All reprinted in Raymond Fielding (ed.), *A Technological History of Motion Pictures and Television* (Berkeley and Los Angeles: University of California Press, 1967). Rick Altman, 'The Evolution of Sound Technologies', in Elisabeth Weis and John Belton (eds), *Film Sound: Theory and Practice* (New York: Columbia University Press, 1985), pp. 44–53.
7. Behind this seemingly collaborative associationism were considerable tensions. James Lastra traces the cultural clash during the transition to sound between new sound personnel and those already professionally established and embedded within the studio system, such as cinematographers. See James Lastra, *Sound Technology and the American Cinema: Perception, Representation, Modernity* (New York: Columbia University Press, 2000), pp. 167–76.
8. Ibid., p. 207.
9. Carl Dreher, 'Recording, Re-recording and Editing of Sound', *JSMPE* vol. 16 no. 6, June 1931, pp. 756–65.
10. In the early sound era, 'dubbing' was used to refer to the re-recording of all parts of the sound record, not specifically for re-recording dialogue. See Lester Cowan, 'A Glossary of Motion Picture Terms', in Lester Cowan (ed.),

Recording Sound for Motion Pictures (New York: McGraw-Hill, 1931), p. 366.

11. Dreher, 'Recording, Re-recording and Editing of Sound', p. 759.

12. Ibid.

13. Rick Altman, 'Sound Space', in Rick Altman (ed.), *Sound Theory/Sound Practice* (New York and London: Routledge, 1992), p. 54.

14. Ibid., p. 60.

15. Steve Neale, 'Melo Talk: On the Meaning and Use of the Term "Melodrama" in the American Trade Press', *Velvet Light Trap* no. 32, 1993, pp. 66–89.

16. Harold Lewis, 'Getting Good Sound Is an Art', *American Cinematographer* vol. 15 no. 2, June 1934, pp. 65, 73, 74.

BIBLIOGRAPHY

Altman, Rick, 'The Evolution of Sound Technologies', in Elisabeth Weis and John Belton (eds), *Film Sound: Theory and Practice* (New York: Columbia University Press, 1985).

Altman, Rick (ed.), *Sound Theory/Sound Practice* (New York and London: Routledge, 1992).

Altman, Rick, 'Sound Space', in Altman, *Sound Theory/Sound Practice*.

Bansak, Edmund, *Fearing the Dark: The Val Lewton Career* (Jefferson, NC: McFarland & Co., 1995).

Cowan, Lester (ed.), *Recording Sound for Motion Pictures* (New York: McGraw-Hill, 1931).

Dreher, Carl, 'Recording, Re-recording and Editing of Sound', *Journal of the Society of Motion Picture Engineers* vol. 16 no. 6, June 1931, pp. 756–65.

Fielding, Raymond (ed.), *A Technological History of Motion Pictures and Television* (Berkeley and Los Angeles: University of California Press, 1967).

Jenkins, Steve, 'Val Lewton: Curse of the Critics?', *Monthly Film Bulletin* vol. 48, July 1981, p. 148.

Kellogg, Edward W., 'History of Sound Motion Pictures: First Instalment', *Journal of the Society of Motion Picture and Television Engineers*, June 1955; 'History of Sound Motion Pictures: Second Instalment', *JSMPE*, July 1955; 'History of Sound Motion Pictures: Final Instalment', *JSMPE*, August 1955. All reprinted in Fielding, *A Technological History of Motion Pictures and Television*.

Lastra, James, *Sound Technology and the American Cinema: Perception, Representation, Modernity* (New York: Columbia University Press, 2000).

Lewis, Harold, 'Getting Good Sound Is an Art', *American Cinematographer* vol. 15 no. 2, June 1934, pp. 65, 73, 74.

Lewton, Val, 'Interview in *Liberty* Magazine', cited in Joel Siegel, *Val Lewton: The Reality of Terror* (London: Secker and Warburg/BFI, 1972), p. 32.

Morgan, Kenneth, 'Dubbing', in Cowan, *Recording Sound for Motion Pictures*.

Neale, Steve, 'Melo Talk: On the Meaning and Use of the Term "Melodrama" in the American Trade Press', *Velvet Light Trap* no. 32, 1993, pp. 66–89.

Salt, Barry, *Film Style and Technology: History and Analysis* (2nd edn) (London: Starword, 1992).

Siegel, Joel, *Val Lewton: The Reality of Terror* (London: Secker and Warburg/BFI, 1972).

Telotte, J. P., *Dreams of Darkness: Fantasy and the Films of Val Lewton* (Champaign: University of Illinois Press, 1985).

Turner, George, 'Val Lewton's Cat People', *Cinefantastique* vol. 12 no. 4, May–June 1982, pp. 23–7.

Variety, 'Review of *Cat People*', 18 November 1942.

Weis, Elisabeth and Belton, John (eds), *Film Sound: Theory and Practice* (New York: Columbia University Press, 1985).

'I've seen him take his knife …': *The Searchers* (1956)

R. J. ELLIS

Ethan Edwards (John Wayne) rides hell-for-leather out of a desert canyon to rejoin Martin Pawley and Brad Jorgenson (Jeffrey Hunter and Harry Carey Jr) on their mission to rescue Ethan's two nieces, Debbie and Lucy (Natalie Wood and Pippa Scott), from a marauding band of Nawyecka Comanches, led by Chief Scar (Henry Brandon). As he arrives, Ethan violently reins in his horse, leaps from the saddle, lurches disconcertingly, nearly falling, and hurls his rifle down. He slumps to the ground, and stabs his knife viciously into the sand several times, even though this will certainly blunt its blade. What has happened to create this fury? The viewer knows that Ethan rode into the canyon to track four Comanches who split from Scar's main band (tailed by Marty and Brad). Ethan's aim had been to find out why the band divided, but now, in answer to his companions' anxious queries, he responds with monosyllabic reluctance. He forces out the information. He found no reason why the band divided, no water in the canyon, nor any sign of Debbie or Lucy, and, in answer to Marty's question about what had happened to his 'Johnny Reb coat', he replies that he must have lost it in the canyon but will not go back for it.

Why not? Something momentous must have happened. Ethan's 'Johnny Reb' cape has already been lovingly caressed by his brother's wife, Martha (Dorothy Jordan), in a subtle intimation that, as John Ford himself explained: she 'was in love with Wayne … . You could tell from the way she picked up his cape.'[1] Martha's caress of the cape shows that it is part of Ethan's identity (his wearing of it is a sign that he never surrendered at the end of the Civil War). What has happened to cause him to leave this symbolic garment in the canyon?

The puzzle is soon apparently resolved. Ethan gets up off the ground, lurches slightly as he walks over to his horse, unsteadily remounts, and the three searchers ride off from the canyon, tracking the Comanche band. Then, Brad, scouting in advance, reports how he has spotted the blue of Lucy's dress in the Comanche camp and insists they gallop in to rescue her. Trying to prevent this, Ethan sud-denly reveals that he knows Lucy is dead: 'What you saw was a buck, wearing Lucy's dress. I found Lucy back in the canyon. Wrapped her in my [pause] coat. Buried her with my own hands.' When pressed by Brad over what he found exactly ('Did they …? Was she …?'), Ethan rounds on him and angrily shouts, 'Whaddya want me to do – draw you a picture? Spell it out? Don't ever ask me, long as you live, don't ever ask me more.' He again refuses, this time in an uncontrolled rage, to provide details. But the puzzle is apparently resolved: he found the body of Lucy in the canyon, and his eruption from the canyon to rejoin Brad and Marty can be explained by his angry grief.

Yet a sense persists that Ethan's raging at Brad and his distress at the canyon mouth together constitute an extraordinary loss of control when compared to his usual composure. For example, this episode is far more extraordinary than the occasion when he fires off round after round of rifle shots at a herd of North American bison. In this case, his apparent loss of control is a calculated replication of white Americans' slaughter of bison to drive them near to extinction, so depriving Native Americans of a staple resource. Ethan himself explains this, revealing his bison slaughter as premeditated,[2] quite unlike his rage when Brad asks what he found in the canyon.

To explicate Ethan's fury, something else needs to be adduced. His sand stabbing might simply intimate rage at what he has just discovered: it may be a displacement activity rehearsing his anger over the state of Lucy's body, with the implication that she was sexually assaulted and probably mutilated (his earlier discovery of Martha's body after Scar's raid supports this). However, it still seems reck-less.

Stabbing a knife into sand takes away its sharpness. Ethan, an experienced frontiersman, would know just how much a knife would be blunted by stabbing it into sand. Perhaps, then, his motive is different: stabbing a knife blade into sand is a means of cleaning it, albeit a very dam-aging one. The use of sand can be explained by the fact that water is precious in the desert (indeed, just before he

enters the canyon, Ethan tells Marty to go 'easy' on the water). But his knife cleaning still must lead back to the question of what happened in the canyon. What needs cleaning off Ethan's knife?

Before I answer this question, it is germane to address the mental state of Ethan. Ford himself points us in this direction when describing the film as a 'psychological epic', and many critics have followed this lead.[3] Lindsay Anderson calls Ethan an 'obsessive', 'an unmistakeable neurotic, devoured by an irrational hatred'. Andrew Sarris sees him as 'menacing', while John McBride and Michael Wilmington see him as 'nihilistic' and 'deranged'.[4] Do such depictions of Ethan as all but psychopathically monomaniacal help illuminate his actions at the mouth of the canyon?

Crucially, we have already had an intimation of Ethan's disturbed state of mind. Earlier in the film, he had desperately ridden back to his brother's farm, too late to save it from being sacked by Scar's band, entered an outhouse, discovered (off camera) Martha's body, and prevented Marty from seeing it by punching him to the ground. He then broke up his brother's and Martha's funeral prematurely so he could get on with his pursuit and then shot out both eyes of a Comanche corpse to stop it finding its way to the spirit grounds. Given the way that Ford represents Ethan at the canyon mouth as gripped by a glowering sense of rage and the first signs of loss of control, it seems plausible to suggest that the substance that needs to be cleaned off the knife at the canyon mouth is blood (there is little else it could be). Ethan could be concerned to clean all traces of blood off quickly to forestall any questions from Marty and Brad, whom he seems anxious to cut off, barely communicating with them and avoiding their gaze. But whose blood is it on the blade?

Since the Comanche braves can be ruled out (they would have carried rifles, rendering a silent daylight knife attack impossible), this leads us inevitably to the only other credible answer. We may need to be led there by Marty's increasing fears that if Ethan catches up with Debbie he

will kill her, since, as every white person in the film assumes, she will have been desecrated by Scar's band. When Marty and Ethan briefly suspend their search and return to the Jorgenson's farmhouse, Marty explains to his childhood sweetheart, Laurie Jorgenson (Vera Miles), that he knows what Ethan will do, and why this means he must travel with Ethan to stop him:

> '... I don't know what you can do about finding Debbie that he can't. He'll find her, now, Martin, I know he will.'
>
> 'That's what I'm afraid of, Laurie. Him finding her. Oh, I've seen his eyes at the very word Comanche. I've seen him take his knife ... [breaks off]. Never mind. He's a man who can go crazy wild and I intend to be there to stop him.'

The reference to Ethan's knife both recalls his sand stabbing at the canyon mouth and makes it plain that Marty recognises that Ethan's motives are deeply racist and probably murderous.

Marty's fears are well founded. Much later in the film, when Debbie runs out of Scar's desert camp to tell Ethan and Marty to leave, Ethan advances upon her, his gun levelled at her as if to kill her. This surely recalls the viewer's sense that Ethan at the canyon mouth had been in a dangerously disturbed state. Back at the canyon mouth, the low-angle shots had made him seem particularly threatening, as had the concealment of his facial expression in shadow and the stabbing movements used to clean his knife. All these point to the fact that what he told Marty and Brad was marked by suppressions. As Ethan now levels his gun at Debbie, it becomes clear that his canyon-mouth reticence may not have been solely caused by the discovery of the body of Lucy (probably raped and mutilated) in the canyon. Instead, more disturbingly, Lucy possibly survived, and Ethan was perfectly prepared to finish her off, as he apparently now wants to finish off Debbie, because he refuses to save the 'leavings of Comanche bucks', as Laurie will later put it, echoing Ethan's own sentiments ('She's been living with a buck! She's nothing but a ...').[5] Indeed, only Marty and a Comanche arrow stop him killing her.

Ethan's murderous advance upon Debbie also makes it clear why the audience could not be permitted to see what happened in the canyon. Like Martha's mutilated body, Lucy's death cannot be shown on camera – the Motion Picture Production Code in force at the time forbade such depictions. But Ethan's words to Brad, laced with ambiguity, provide an indication: 'I found Lucy back in the canyon ... . Buried her with my own hands.' This mid-point hesitation leaves open the construction: 'I found Lucy back in the canyon ... [killed and] buried her with my own hands.'

Ethan's long background in warfare (the American Civil War, the Juarez/Maximilian war and the 'Indian wars') helps explain the extraordinariness of his act, for it engages with the USA's own immediate war experiences – the most recent being the Korean War (1950–3), in which 5.7 million US troops had served. Richard Slotkin points out that *The Searchers* invites such a comparison, since the Cold War adage 'Better dead than Red' is echoed by Ethan's murderous motives.[6] *The Searchers* was made in 1955 – two years after the end of the Korean War and barely a decade after the end of World War II. Throughout the period 1945 to 1955 well over 15 million troops had returned to America. Both these bloody wars seared into many US combatants' memories scenes of violence upon the enemy, deaths of comrades and acts of revenge – even, sometimes, involving war crimes (relevant here is Ethan's early mutilation of the Comanche corpse) and mistreatment of enemy civilians (relevant in this respect are Captain Clayton (Ward Bond) and his Texas Rangers' final attack on Scar's camp and the earlier attack on another of Scar's camps by the US cavalry, both involving the killing of women and children).

The Searchers alludes to such hidden, traumatic secrets of war, so rarely revealed. Pointedly, in this respect, Ethan is depicted as a soldier who has recently participated in the particularly bloody American Civil War, with its use of modern armaments and strategies: scorched-earth campaigns, explosive shells, machine guns, rifles.[7] Not long before, in 1951, Ford made his documentary, *This Is Korea!*, a film that must also have cast his mind back to World War II. While in Colorado filming *The Searchers*, he carried a Navy officer's raincoat over his arm and when on the set itself even wore an old combat jacket.[8] Furthermore, part of John Wayne's Hollywood star persona was that of a soldier – having performed this role both during World War II propaganda film-making and after the war, most famously as Sergeant Stryker in *The Sands of Iwo Jima* (Dwan, 1949). *The Searchers* can be viewed as a provocative exploration of the state of mind of the traumatised soldier, the veteran incapable of exercising restraint beneath a veneer of control, and displacing this into hatred of the racial Other. Just as pertinent are patterns of 'Dear John' relationship breakdowns and sexual jealousy: Martha's marriage in *The Searchers* to his brother and not Ethan, despite their love, and Laurie's near-desertion of Marty while he is absent (ironically, writing letters home) all contribute to the film's engagement with the psychopathology of the traumatised veteran.

Suggesting all this may be dark enough; but things may be even more ominous. Lucy's death can be further darkened by noting the possibility of Debbie and Lucy being Ethan's children – either or both.[9] Certainly the reaction of Martha when Ethan arrives, which oscillates between almost agitated anxiety and obvious sexual attraction, suggests a past sexual liaison. The uncertainty over chronology suffusing *The Searchers* is crucial here: the length of Ethan's and Marty's search has been vari-

ously estimated at five and seven years,[10] and (more germanely) the age of Debbie estimated at fourteen or fifteen years (Natalie Wood was sixteen when she played Debbie). Given such suffusing vagueness, Ethan could have been with Martha at the correct times to father Lucy or Debbie, or both. Significant in this respect is his brother's comment that, earlier, Ethan had stayed at his ranch 'long after there was any reason'. Ethan's restrained but sexually charged embraces of Martha on his return suggest that what held him at the ranch may have been an extramarital relationship. Ethan, in the mouth of the canyon, stabbing his knife, may be expressing an impotent and misplaced desire for the daughter he has killed – in an enactment of rage over the daughter's experiencing forced sex outside of the control (dominance) of a frustrated father deeply damaged by post-traumatic stress disorder and unable to cope with his daughter's burgeoning sexuality. The sand-stabbing scene, symbolically located in a canyon mouth (like so many others in *The Searchers*), reveals the subconscious cleft in Ethan's mind. It provides an explanation as to why he must turn his back on the Jorgenson ranch at the end of the film: his traumatised psychopathology renders him inadmissible in any family home. As he finally turns away, he lurches very slightly – in a spectral reminder of his stagger at the mouth of the canyon after finishing off Lucy. The dark heart of *The Searchers* is again summoned up. It also explains why, when Ethan does catch up with Debbie near the end, he does not kill her – for his traumatic horseback pursuit of her replicates his gallop out of the canyon where he perhaps killed the despoiled Lucy. He will not kill his second and only other daughter, but he cannot exorcise the racist demons of the west and their spectres of violence. This is a startlingly prescient image to project to a country poised to enter five decades of near-continuous imperial violence – in Vietnam, Grenada, Iraq (twice), Somalia and Afghanistan. As Laurie puts it, responding to Marty's assertion that he fears Ethan will kill Debbie when he catches up with her, just before he sets out on the final pursuit (yet again delaying their wedding): 'Martha would have wanted it that way' – that is to say, Laurie is still sure that Martha would have wanted Ethan to kill Debbie and no one among the whites except the 'half-breed' Marty would consider things differently. One might say that history has, in one sense, ironically proved Laurie quite right, given the racist-laden history of the USA from its very inception.

NOTES

1. John Ford, quoted in Peter Bogdanovich, *John Ford* (London: Studio Vista, 1968), p. 93.

2. See Richard Slotkin, *Gunfighter Nation: The Myth of the Frontier in Twentieth-Century America* (Norman: University of Oklahoma Press, 1998), pp. 462–3.

3. See 'An Interview with John Ford by Jean Mirty', 1955. Reprinted in Andrew Sarris (ed.), *Interviews with Film Directors* (New York: Avon Books, 1969), p. 197.

4. Arthur M. Eckstein, 'Introduction', in Arthur M. Eckstein and Peter Lehman (eds), *The Searchers: Essays and Reflections on John Ford's Classic Western* (Detroit, MI: Wayne State University Press, 2004), p. 4; John McBride and Michael Wilmington, *John Ford* (London: Secker and Warburg, 1974), pp. 148, 153.

5. This idea was also developed by some of the students of Peter Lehman. See Peter Lehman, '"You Couldn't Hit It on the Nose": The Limits of Knowledge in and of *The Searchers*', in Eckstein and Lehman, *The Searchers*, p. 249. Lehman, however, barely endorses this reading.

6. See Slotkin, *Gunfighter Nation*, pp. 462–4.

7. Ford, while working on *The Searchers*, read numerous Civil War histories. See Andrew Sinclair, *John Ford* (London: George Allen and Unwin, 1979), p. 178.

8. See Sinclair, *John Ford*, pp. 177–8. Sinclair quotes Robert Emmet Ginna Jr.

9. Lehman's students also go down this line; see Eckstein and Lehman, *The Searchers*, p. 248. Lehman once again barely endorses their reading.

10. This uncertainty over the length of the search, despite Laurie's statement that five years have elapsed, depends on whether she refers to the whole duration of the search or only to the last five years of a seven-year search. Debbie's change of appearance supports a search of seven years. See Peter Lehman, 'Preface', in Eckstein and Lehman, *The Searchers*, pp. xv–xvi.

BIBLIOGRAPHY

Anderson, Lindsay, 'The Searchers', *Sight and Sound* vol. 26 no. 2, 1956. Reprinted in John Caughie (ed.), *Theories of Authorship* (London: Routledge, 1981), pp. 75–7.

Bogdanovich, Peter, *John Ford* (London: Studio Vista, 1968).

Caughie, John (ed.), *Theories of Authorship* (London: Routledge, 1981).

Eckstein, Arthur M. and Lehman, Peter (eds), *The Searchers: Essays and Reflections on John Ford's Classic Western* (Detroit, MI: Wayne State University Press, 2004).

Eckstein, Arthur M., 'Introduction', in Eckstein and Lehman, *The Searchers*, pp. 1–46.

Lehman, Peter, 'Preface', in Eckstein and Lehman, *The Searchers*, pp. xv–xvi.

Lehman, Peter, '"You Couldn't Hit It on the Nose": The Limits of Knowledge in and of *The Searchers*', in Eckstein and Lehman, *The Searchers*, pp. 239–64.

McBride, John and Wilmington, Michael, *John Ford* (London: Secker and Warburg, 1974).

Place, J. A., *The Western Films of John Ford* (Secaucus, NJ: Citadel Press, 1974).

Sarris, Andrew (ed.), *Interviews with Film Directors* (New York: Avon Books, 1969).

Sarris, Andrew, 'The Searchers', *Film Comment* vol. 7 no. 1. Reprinted in *Theories of Authorship*, pp. 78–82.

Sinclair, Andrew, *John Ford* (London: George Allen and Unwin, 1979).

Slotkin, Richard, *Gunfighter Nation: The Myth of the Frontier in Twentieth-Century America* (Norman: University of Oklahoma Press, 1998).

Wills, Gary, *John Wayne: The Politics of Celebrity* (London: Faber and Faber, 1997).

Another Story: Myth and History in *Bonnie and Clyde* (1967)

PAM COOK

Bonnie and Clyde (Penn, 1967) has legendary status in the history of American cinema. Controversy surrounded its making and its release, and it has since been celebrated as a landmark work that ushered in the New Hollywood and had a dramatic influence on subsequent films. It has been extensively written about in the press and in scholarly publications, and it appears on numerous internet sites. In one sense, it is an ideal subject for analysis of its relationship to the moment in which it was realised; in another, it poses the question of what more can be said about a movie that has been exhaustively discussed by successive generations. Yet precisely because of its enduring appeal, *Bonnie and Clyde* exemplifies the process of accumulation of meaning and the interweaving of myth and documented evidence that characterise historical analysis and reconstruction.

It is a truism that history is written with hindsight and tells us as much, if not more, about the public and private contexts in which it is produced as about the past with which it engages. Each new history builds on preceding layers of representation, whether they emanate from the official archive or from the imaginative reworking of popular folklore. *Bonnie and Clyde* itself is a creative reinterpretation of the contested and contentious accounts of the exploits of its young outlaws. It views the early years of the Great Depression through the filters of 1960s countercultures and the anarchic spirit of the *nouvelle vague*, paying homage to 1930s gangster movies while attempting to break new aesthetic and thematic ground. It manifests the contradictions and compromises faced by the filmmakers, whose position as independents operating at the edges of the major Hollywood studios was precarious. It is indelibly marked by its provenance, yet, like the legendary Bonnie Parker and Clyde Barrow, it reaches beyond its particular circumstances to other places and times.

As a period costume drama, *Bonnie and Clyde* is a fictional rendition of the activities of the infamous Barrow gang, outlaws who became national celebrities for a series of robberies and killings in the South-West between 1931 and 1934. Their deeds and those of the law-enforcement agencies that pursued them are documented in numerous sources, from official police records and media news reports to photographs and personal reminiscences such as Bonnie Parker's letters, Blanche Barrow's memoirs, and interviews with police officers, members of the public and gang members.[1] These accounts are often conflicting and provoke debate among historians as to their accuracy. The fruitless search over many years for the 'truth' of Bonnie and Clyde's story adds to the layers of myth surrounding them and has increased their notoriety. The couple feature in popular music, theatre and movies,[2] and there is a new film version in the pipeline.[3] The 1967 production further embellished the legend; the film-makers' disregard for historical accuracy was evident in their insouciant deviation from documented facts. This was a fable for the 1960s that translated the inchoate challenge to the American Dream motivating the 'public enemies'[4] of the 1930s into the modern epoch of anti-establishment resistance. Just as the Depression-era gangsters emerged from a period of social turmoil, *Bonnie and Clyde* appeared at a moment of transition for American society, as the 1950s consensus cracked under pressure from protest and Civil Rights movements and a youth-oriented cultural revolution in which many dissenting voices clamoured to be heard.[5]

The film's appeal has often been put down to its evocation of the subversive tremors erupting in 1960s America. Yet, like the 1930s gangster movies to which it pays homage, its attitude to its childlike, deviant desperadoes is ambivalent. Bonnie, Clyde and the Barrow gang are depicted as the aberrant underside of respectable society, a dysfunctional group that is a gross parody of 'normal' family relationships. Their crime spree brings them meagre rewards, and they seem to be driven more by desire for fame and revenge than by anti-authoritarian impulses. Unlike many urban mobsters, some of whom came from immigrant backgrounds, Bonnie and Clyde were from poor Texas families, and their criminal activities centred around the rural farming areas in the South-West, which were badly hit by the Depression. In the movie, their targets are often as disenfranchised as they are, and any affinity they have with the deprived victims of political corruption and corporate greed is tenuous. They operate against a backdrop of social meltdown, in which moral direction and community ties are absent and they become increasingly isolated. The film provides no political context for their actions, nor does it portray them as casualties of an uncaring system. Their delinquent lifestyle is shown to be motivated by self-interest and contempt for the ineffectual law-enforcement organisations that pursue them. The betrayal that brings about their shockingly violent deaths is the inevitable consequence of their chosen trajectory, something they only half understand.

Although *Bonnie and Clyde* has been seen as capturing the 1960s insurgent ethos, it could equally be interpreted as a critique of an infantilised America on the brink of anarchy. This ambivalence could have something to do with its conditions of production, which gave rise to both constraints and possibilities. The stories surrounding the making of the film have endowed the film-makers with heroic status.[6] Cinephile scriptwriters David Newman and Robert Benton produced a treatment inspired by the freewheeling styles of Jean-Luc Godard and François Truffaut, both of whom were approached to direct *Bonnie and Clyde*. When these plans did not work out, Warren Beatty picked up the project and took it to Arthur Penn, a director heavily influenced by art cinema who was responsible for innovative work in television, theatre and film.[7] The two had formed an independent company, Tatira Productions, and Beatty planned to produce as well as star in *Bonnie and Clyde*. His tenacity in negotiations with major studio Warner Bros., which was reluctant to back the film, and his supervision of every aspect of the production, led some to credit him with authorship of the movie.[8] Beatty and Penn set out to make a taboo-breaking work that would be very different from the worthy liberal output of the major studios directed at middle-aged, lower-middle-class Americans. Audience demographics were changing, and *Bonnie and Clyde* was deliberately aimed at younger, educated, cine-literate cinemagoers.

Despite the film-makers' rule-breaking aspirations, compromises were necessary. Indications of Clyde's homosexuality in the Benton–Newman script were replaced by the character's impotence, one of several changes made by 'script doctor' Robert Towne, credited on the film as script consultant. Bonnie's semi-graphic nudity in the opening sequence, an allusion to Brigitte Bardot's teasing display in *Et Dieu créa … la femme* (Vadim, 1956), alarmed the Catholic Legion of Decency,[9] and while the troubled sexual relationship between Bonnie and Clyde was relatively frankly portrayed, the *ménage à trois* between them and C. W. Moss (Michael J. Pollard) was excised.[10] Jarring slapstick humour, accompanied by incongruously jaunty bluegrass-style music, depicted the Barrow gang's criminal exploits, and the narrative consisted of disjointed episodes loosely strung together.

Nevertheless, the structure of the script, with its progressively darker tone and impetus towards bloody retribution, owed as much to classic gangster movies as to *nouvelle vague* vagaries. *Bonnie and Clyde's* innovations were in tension with its reliance on elements of classic cinema, creating a friction that intensified its disturbing aura of unfulfilled desire. Perhaps the most challenging move was to explore links between thwarted libido and violence, with Clyde's impotence and Bonnie's frustration depicted as motivating factors in their crimewave. The explicit portrayal of sexual dysfunction and its displacement onto the instruments of bloodshed and death is humorous, poignant and harrowing by turns, in keeping with the jolting rhythm that lurches unexpectedly between comedy and tragedy. The climactic death sequence, shocking in its explosive suddenness and relentless brutality, comes almost as an orgasmic release.

The blood-soaked conclusion, in which Bonnie and Clyde are ambushed and killed in a hail of bullets by a police posse, was daring in its full-frontal approach to cinematic violence, which influenced later movies and paved the way for changes in censorship regulations.[11] When the film was first released, the sensational finale provoked negative responses from some critics.[12] Forty or so years later it remains emotive, partly because of its position in the narrative as the culmination of the pair's death drive, overriding the key scene in which they successfully make love for the first time. The circumstances of Bonnie and Clyde's gory demise and the photographs of the massacre are well known; the film itself is replete with harbingers of death that leave viewers in no doubt as to the outcome of their story. There is a fragile inkling of hope in their sexual union and their flirtation with the idea of marriage. But they are still like wayward children playing at being 'normal' adults, and it is their naive trust in C. W. Moss's father (Dub Taylor), who gives them shelter and then betrays them to the police, that seals their fate.

The death sequence lasts less than a minute; the build-up takes up the final ten minutes of the movie. It begins with the couple's lovemaking in a field to the sound of bird-song and romantic music, initiated by Clyde's arousal at the newspaper publication of Bonnie's poem, 'The Story of Bonnie and Clyde', which seals his celebrity status. The pastoral imagery here, intimating the recovery of lost innocence, is picked up subsequently when Bonnie and Clyde go shopping in town with C. W. as the set-up planned by Texas Ranger Frank Hamer (Denver Pyle) and Moss Sr unfolds, with Bonnie in a simple, country-style white dress and Clyde driving a white car. Bonnie's sentimental attachment to a miniature shepherdess figurine evokes her fleeting hopes of redemption. In case it should appear that their escape is on the cards, Clyde loses one of the lenses of his sunglasses in a reference to the fate of Michel Poiccard (Jean-Pierre Belmondo), doomed anti-hero of Godard's *À bout de souffle* (1960).

Death drive: Bonnie (Faye Dunaway) and Clyde (Warren Beatty) approach the ambush

The build-up is slow-paced and calm, with none of the hysteria typical of the rest of the movie. The couple appear relaxed and happy in the brightly lit surroundings, even though they are forced to leave C. W. behind in town when they see the police arrive. In a callous touch, as they drive unsuspectingly towards the ambush, they share an over-ripe pear bursting with juice.

At this point, viewers know very well what is about to happen. Yet Bonnie and Clyde's evident *joie de vivre* causes a momentary suspension of disbelief that disrupts the narrative logic. The realisation that they are trapped, orchestrated by the amplified sound of birds taking flight and the sudden fusillade of bullets from the bushes, comes as a shock to both audience and protagonists. In the forty or so shots that make up the elaborately choreographed dance of death, a combination of slow-motion photography and rapid jump cuts emulates the relentless machine-gun fire on the soundtrack. Empathy with Bonnie and Clyde is reinforced by their exchange of glances of love

Shooting gallery: *Bonnie and Clyde*'s death sequence

and recognition as their writhing bodies are torn apart by the devastating impact of the gun shots, which leaves them and their car riddled with bullet holes.

Throughout this complex sequence, spectator point of view oscillates between the couple's perspective, that of the agitated Moss and camera positions independent of the characters. Quick-fire editing alternates between close-ups, medium and long shots of the carnage, placing the viewer both in the scene and at a distance from it, blurring the boundary between past and present. The fusion of 'then' and 'now' and the tension between absence and presence in the process of historical reconstruction are underlined in the closing moments. In the silence following the attack, the camera, positioned outside but very close to the ravaged vehicle, pans across Bonnie and Clyde's car until it looks through the shattered rear window at the ambushers and Moss as they gather to look at the dead bodies, before the screen fades to black and the end titles roll. In this shot, the camera is an onlooker, but in a different space from the eyewitnesses, who are obscured by reflections in the front windscreen and the fractured glass of the rear window. Rather than offering unmediated access to the past, this image presents screens within screens, evoking the accumulated layers of representation through which history is retrieved.

Overloaded with irony, playing fast and loose with audience sympathies and eerily prescient of the 1970 Kent State University shootings, the conclusion of *Bonnie and Clyde* revealed a lack of moral centre that was far removed from 1930s social-problem crime movies and the earnest offerings of the contemporary Hollywood establishment.[13] Warner Bros., convinced that it would flop, buried it in a limited release. US critics were polarised.[14] But young filmgoers responded with gusto. Before long, several critics retracted their negative reviews, and the film became a cultural phenomenon. Its edgy, visceral style, allusive texture, intellectual leanings and bravura approach to sexuality and violence were at the forefront of a new wave of independent productions that transformed American cinema in the 1970s and secured *Bonnie and Clyde*'s mythic status in history.

NOTES

1. The 'Bonnie and Clyde' page in *Wikipedia, The Free Encyclopedia* provides a useful starting point for thinking about history and myth, and includes a bibliography and list of references. Available at <en.wikipedia.org/w/index.php?title=Bonnie_and_Clyde&oldid=301077659> (accessed 9 July 2009).

2. 'Bonnie and Clyde in media' on the 'Bonnie and Clyde' page in *Wikipedia, The Free Encyclopedia* provides evidence of the couple's profile in popular culture.

3. See 'The Story of Bonnie and Clyde' entry on IMDb. Available at <www.imdb.com/title/tt1355646> (accessed 9 July 2009).

4. This was the term used by J. Edgar Hoover to describe out-laws such as John Dillinger, Baby Face Nelson, Bonnie Parker and Clyde Barrow wanted by the Bureau of Investigation in the early 1930s. See Bryan Burrough, *Public Enemies: America's Greatest Crime Wave and the Birth of the FBI, 1933–34* (New York: Penguin, 2004).

5. See Steven Alan Carr, 'From "Fucking Cops!" to "Fucking Media!"': *Bonnie and Clyde* for a Sixties America', in Lester D. Friedman (ed.), *Arthur Penn's 'Bonnie and Clyde'* (Cambridge: Cambridge University Press, 2000). See also Lester D. Friedman, *Bonnie and Clyde* (London: BFI, 2000).

6. See Peter Biskind, *Easy Riders, Raging Bulls: How the Sex-Drugs-and-Rock-'n'-Roll Generation Saved Hollywood* (New York: Simon and Schuster, 1998); Elaine Lennon, 'Riding the New Wave: The Case of *Bonnie and Clyde*', *Senses of Cinema* no. 38, January–March 2006. Available at <archive.sensesofcinema.com/contents/06/38/bonnie_and_clyde.html#b8> (accessed 10 July 2009); Alan Vanneman, 'Bonnie and Clyde: Together Again', *Bright Lights Film Journal* no. 43, February 2004. Available at <www.brightlightsfilm.com/43/bonnie.htm> (accessed 10 July 2009); Patrick Goldstein, 'Blasts from the Past', *Los Angeles Times Calendar*, 24 August 1997. Available at <articles.latimes.com/1997/aug/24/entertainment/ca-25274> (accessed 10 July 2009). See also BBC television documentary *American Desperadoes: The Story of 'Bonnie and Clyde'* (d. Russell Leven, 1999), tx. 3 April 1999, BBC2.

7. See Sara Fishko, '*Bonnie and Clyde*: Still Bold 40 Years Later', *NPR*, 13 August 2007. Available at <www.npr.org/templates/story/story.php?storyId=12753252> (accessed 10 July 2009).

8. See Lennon, *Riding the New Wave*.

9. See Vanneman, 'Bonnie and Clyde'; Goldstein, 'Blasts from the Past'.

10. See Lennon, *Riding the New Wave*.

11. Ibid.

12. For example, Bosley Crowther, '*Bonnie and Clyde* Review', *New York Times*, 14 April 1967. Available at <movies.nytimes.com/movie/review?res=EE05E7DF173CE361BC4C52DFB266838C679EDE> (accessed 12 July 2009).

13. See A. O. Scott, 'Two Outlaws, Blasting Holes in the Screen', *New York Times*, 12 August 2007. Available at <www.nytimes.com/2007/08/12/movies/12scot.html> (accessed 12 July 2009).

14. The extremes of critical reaction were represented by Bosley Crowther's *New York Times* hatchet job and Pauline Kael's passionate defence in the *New Yorker*, 21 October 1967, reprinted in Friedman, *Arthur Penn's 'Bonnie and Clyde'*.

BIBLIOGRAPHY

Biskind, Peter, *Easy Riders, Raging Bulls: How the Sex-Drugs-and-Rock-'n'-Roll Generation Saved Hollywood* (New York: Simon and Schuster, 1998).

Burrough, Bryan, *Public Enemies: America's Greatest Crime Wave and the Birth of the FBI, 1933–34* (New York: Penguin, 2004).

Carr, Steven Alan, 'From "Fucking Cops!" to "Fucking Media!"': *Bonnie and Clyde* for a Sixties America', in Lester D. Friedman (ed.), *Arthur Penn's 'Bonnie and Clyde'* (Cambridge: Cambridge University Press, 2000).

Cawelti, John G. (ed.), *Focus on 'Bonnie and Clyde'* (Englewood Cliffs, NJ: Prentice-Hall, 1973).

Cohan, Steven and Hark, Ina Rae (eds), *The Road Movie Book* (London: Routledge, 2001).

Cook, David A., *A History of Narrative Film* (New York: W. W. Norton and Co., 2004).

Crowther, Bosley, '*Bonnie and Clyde* Review', *New York Times*, 14 April 1967. Available at <movies.nytimes.com/movie/review?res=EE05E7DF173CE361BC4C52DFB266838C679EDE> (accessed 12 July 2009).

Fishko, Sara, '*Bonnie and Clyde*: Still Bold 40 Years Later', *NPR*, 13 August 2007. Available at <www.npr.org/templates/story/story.php?storyId=12753252> (accessed 10 July 2009).

Friedman, Lester D. (ed.), *Arthur Penn's 'Bonnie and Clyde'* (Cambridge: Cambridge University Press, 2000).

Friedman, Lester D., *Bonnie and Clyde* (London: BFI, 2000).

Goldstein, Patrick, 'Blasts from the Past', *Los Angeles Times Calendar*, 24 August 1997. Available at <articles.latimes.com/1997/aug/24/entertainment/ca-25274> (accessed 10 July 2009).

Hoberman, J., *The Dream Life: Movies, Media and the Mythology of the Sixties* (New York: The New Press, 2005).

IMDb, 'The Story of Bonnie and Clyde'. Available at <www.imdb.com/title/tt1355646> (accessed 9 July 2009).

King, Geoff, *New Hollywood Cinema: An Introduction* (London: I. B. Tauris, 2002).

Lennon, Elaine, 'Riding the New Wave: The Case of *Bonnie and Clyde*', *Senses of Cinema* no. 38, January–March 2006. Available at <archive.sensesofcinema.com/contents/06/38/bonnie_and_clyde.html#b8> (accessed 10 July 2009).

Monaco, Paul, *The Sixties, 1960–69* (Berkeley: University of California Press, 2003).

Scott, A. O., 'Two Outlaws, Blasting Holes in the Screen', *New York Times*, 12 August 2007. Available at <www.nytimes.com/2007/08/12/movies/12scot.html> (accessed 12 July 2009).

Tzioumakis, Yannis, *American Independent Cinema* (Edinburgh: Edinburgh University Press, 2006).

Vanneman, Alan, 'Bonnie and Clyde: Together Again', *Bright Lights Film Journal* no. 43, February 2004. Available at <www.brightlightsfilm.com/43/bonnie.htm> (accessed 10 July 2009).

Wikipedia, The Free Encyclopedia: 'Bonnie and Clyde' page. Available at <en.wikipedia.org/w/index.php?title=Bonnie_and_Clyde&oldid=301077659> (accessed 9 July 2009).

A Sculptural Moment: The Epilogue to *Les Deux Anglaises et le Continent* (1971)[1]

MARK BROUGHTON

> For the same reasons that impel us to make people we care for meet each other, I think there exists between books the possibilities of fascinating rapprochements.
>
> François Truffaut[2]

In *Les Deux Anglaises et le continent* (Truffaut, 1971), a film about love between two English sisters and a Frenchman, characters' relationships are paralleled with couplings of texts and/or art. Letters and a diary are exchanged; art is bought and sold; the sisters, Anne (Kika Markham) and Muriel (Stacey Tendeter), resemble the Brontës, and the Frenchman, Claude (Jean-Pierre Léaud), resembles Proust.[3] Truffaut's own dialogue with Henri-Pierre Roché, whose novel he adapted into the film, is represented in the opening credits by shots of Roché's book, annotated by Truffaut. On the pages of this 1956 novel, we thus see handwriting from over a decade later, like a palimpsest. This layering of temporality characterises other textual couplings in the film, such as the Brontë/Proust encounter. However, few artworks are on screen long enough for us to contemplate their provenance. The period references which abound in Roché's novel are stripped away for most of the film.[4] The dialogue between art, time and characters only predominates in the film's epilogue. By shooting the epilogue on location at the Musée Rodin, Truffaut created a network of intertextual allusions, via Rodin's work, to other narratives and historical events. Rodin sculptures are seen briefly in two earlier scenes, but the epilogue's emphasis on them is much more pronounced. Each sculpture is given its own, single shot. The lack of editing preserves the continuity of the sculptures' forms. As the camera tracks around the sculptures, zooming in, action is excluded from the frame and the sculptures' forms and historical themes are foregrounded. Nonetheless, their relevance to the film's narrative ensures that they never completely displace the plot, even when the voiceover narration pauses.

On one level, the epilogue's narrative space is restricted, its boundaries demarcated. The epilogue is concerned mainly with Claude's visit to the museum. It ends after he has passed through the gates; we do not see what lies beyond. On another level, the epilogue opens out the film, creating an essayistic space: a wider frame of reference. By locating the scene in a well-known museum, Truffaut enables audiences to trace the epilogue's allusions; a glance through the museum's guidebook equips the viewer with any knowledge necessary to 'read' the epilogue's textual layers. However, the location makes the scene stand out from Truffaut's oeuvre, since he generally avoided tourist sites.[5]

The intertitle, 'EPILOGUE', read out by Truffaut as voiceover narrator, marks off the scene from the main narrative.[6] The voiceover then tells us that 'fifteen years have passed like a breath'. Thus, after the intertitle, Truffaut's voiceover suddenly shifts from recounting moments in the characters' lives to surveying an era. Time is no longer linear; it has become parallel and relativist. He says 'fifteen years' three times. In each case the era measured is of a different nature: fifteen years in Muriel's life; World War I; and a period of changes in the reception of Rodin's 'Monument to Balzac'. Juxtaposed in this way, personal, sociopolitical and cultural histories are presented as alternative ways to remember time.

The voiceover combines the terseness of a newsreel with conscientious objection: 'Fifteen years! … . The earth of France is full of corpses and shrapnel. Many millions of men have died in a war whose causes have already been forgotten.' It then goes on to state that Rodin's 'Balzac', once rejected, is now universally admired.[7] The relationship between these observations is ambiguous. There is an anti-war sentiment, here, which suggests that measuring time by art is more productive than measuring it by military history. However, there could also be a causal connection: war alters the world's aesthetic perception; Rodin's externalisation of Balzac's mind now seems appropriate to a nation whose physical surfaces have been burnt away by war. Truffaut's elliptical voiceover does not provide the connection for us. It leaves gaps, spaces for the audience to form inferences.

The announcement about World War I is spoken over a shot of 'The Burghers of Calais'. This statue portrays an event in the Hundred Years War, when Calais was besieged by the British. Edward III promised to spare Calais in exchange for hostages, who would be hanged. The hostages were later shown mercy, but Rodin's sculpture captures them at the moment when death seems imminent; rather than heroic, they are emaciated. The epilogue takes place in the 1920s, while the voiceover refers to World War I and the statue to 1347. This layering of time is again elliptical and ambiguous. The reference to two wars suggests a continuity of futile conflict across history. There is a hint, too, of revisionist historiography. History tells us that, in 1347, Britain was France's enemy, but not in 1914–18. Is there an unorthodox implication, here, about Britain's alliance with France in World War I? The question has to be asked of a film whose title creates a binary between England's women and 'the continent' (Claude), symbolising a relationship between England and the rest of Europe.

The appearance of 'The Burghers of Calais' also recalls a scene in Calais, when Muriel loses her virginity.[8] This is a double sacrifice: Muriel momentarily gives up her puritanism to bring closure to her relationship with Claude. He sacrifices his relationship with her to 'arm her as a woman', having sex with her so that she can leave him for good. Claude's humiliation when Muriel departs, a consequence of his and Anne's betrayal of Muriel, is echoed in the burghers' humiliation.

The following shot, of 'Ugolino and His Children', forms a hinge between the shot of 'The Burghers of Calais' and Claude's first appearance in the epilogue. In Dante's *Inferno*, Ugolino tells how he was imprisoned with his sons and ate their corpses.[9] The sculpture is situated on an island in an ornamental lake. English schoolgirls run around the lake's edge. The sculpture has a closed form, showing Ugolino bent over, his children climbing under and over him. The closed form – humans turned in on themselves – anticipates cannibalism. On one level, this shot, following the voiceover's comment about the war, implies that masculinity has consumed itself in the futile conflict. Men have died, leaving women behind. English schoolgirls – seen throughout the epilogue, always running – are presented as Europe's future: a future without men. On another level, the sculpture is pertinent to the film's narrative. The insularity connoted in the film's title – Englishwomen versus the continent – is inverted here. The male characters, Ugolino and his sons, are isolated on the island, immobile, as the English girls run on the mainland. Claude, who earlier chose to become a writer rather than to have children, has, in a sense, allowed this choice to consume his potential fatherhood.

The contrast between the stillness of the sculptures and the dynamism of the running girls does not necessarily mean that art freezes time.[10] Truffaut emphasises that art exists in time and is transformed by history. The voiceover points to the changing reception of Rodin's 'Balzac'; the social meaning of the sculpture has metamorphosed over time. Other shifts in attitudes to Rodin's work occurred after the 1920s. The reputation of his work decreased dramatically in the 1930s. A revival began in the 1950s, which gathered pace in the 1960s.[11] Truffaut's deployment of Rodin's sculptures in the epilogue is a late example of this revival; the voiceover's comment brings to mind this second wave of Rodin appreciation.[12]

Rodin's 'Balzac' itself embodies a turning point. Its referent, a canonical novelist, points back to nineteenth-century realism. However, the form of the sculpture, which externalises Balzac's mind (as interpreted by Rodin), can be seen as modernist. When 'Balzac' first appears, halfway through the film, it is the sculpture's groundbreaking form that reflects Claude's and Anne's experiments in love. The shot of 'Balzac' in this earlier scene shows only the statue. The camera tracks around the sculpture, embodying an abstract aesthetic perspective, rather than an optical point of view. However, by the end of the film, when a war-torn earth full of shrapnel has habituated the continent to such physical forms – structures turned inside out – the sculpture is admired by all.[13] In the epilogue, we see Claude standing by the monument. It is the sculpture's referent that now seems to dominate, as Balzac-the-canonical-novelist towers over Claude, who has become an aesthete in decline. Claude is trapped in a transient existence which seems issueless; there is no mention of his writing at the end of the film.

The camera's zoom into 'Balzac' reveals the signs of weathering on the sculpture. Like these marks, changing social responses to the sculpture form a palimpsest: layers of meaning accumulate over the artwork. Another image of history-as-palimpsest follows soon after. Claude hears English schoolgirls' voices and hopes that Muriel's daughter is among them. At this point the narration shifts towards subjectivity. We see a shot representing Claude's memory of a photograph of Muriel, aged ten. The shot is a reproduction of a close-up from the start of the film, showing the photograph in Claude's hands. However, the monochrome of the photograph now covers the framing image of his hands, too. Another layer of pastness has accumulated.

The voiceover then abandons its characteristic distance and adopts free indirect discourse to present Claude's thoughts: 'And if one of them were Muriel's daughter, on holiday in Paris? This one, that one, or the small redhead?' The camera alternates between Claude's optical point of view and a reverse shot of his searching eyes. His gaze fails, as the girls, who play hide and seek, all elude it, running in and out of shot. Instead, his eyes fall on Rodin's 'The Kiss'.

Truffaut points us towards this sculpture's historical source: as the camera tracks around it, a girl shouts 'Francesca', which is also the name of the woman represented by 'The Kiss'. The sculpture depicts a moment from another story recounted in *Inferno*: that of Francesca's affair with her husband's brother, Paolo.[14] Francesca and Paolo were killed by her husband. Another reminder that 'The Kiss' is from *Inferno* is provided by the earlier appearance of its pendant sculpture, 'Ugolino and His Children': both were planned for Rodin's Dantean 'The Gates of Hell'. Love triangles proliferate; the sculpture echoes Rodin's concurrent relationships with Marie-Rose Beuret and Camille Claudel. In the film it also recalls the kiss between Muriel and Claude, in Anne's studio, where Muriel seizes him in the same way that Francesca grasps Paolo.[15]

At the start of the shot (see first image), two English girls walk between a man and a woman on the left and the sculpture on the right. The shot suggests three potential couples: a bourgeois husband and wife; siblings; and adulterous lovers. It thus presents the film's trilemma: three options, all unfavourable because they exclude a third person. These can only be held together for a moment

because of the tensions between them. As the camera tracks around, the girls run off, the man and woman disappear, and Francesca and Paolo vanish behind a tree: in time, everything fades from view. Everything is ephemeral. Claude's gaze fails to transfix even a sculpture.

Claude tries to hire a taxi, but it has already been booked. He pauses to look at his reflection in the car's window. Again, Claude's arc is placed in a wider historical context: his ghostly reflection is framed by the car, an icon of modernity. His glasses – which also signify his age – emphasise the framing, as he adjusts their frames. Suddenly his deeds seem all the more evanescent. He walks through the museum's gate, surrounded by young English girls (see second image). They offer hope for the future, but not to Claude, who is carried along in a flood of youth, out of the film's story world. The characters leave the museum like actors exiting a stage.

Except for its first shot, of the Browns' cottage, the epilogue is set entirely in the museum garden; the museum's walls seem to delimit its story world. Even the taxi is *inside* the garden. The epilogue contains reverberations from earlier parts of the film; the film's plot has become another relic in the museum. The museum becomes a microcosm, a synecdoche for this and other stories' worlds. In this space, histories rub shoulders with one another.

The gate is a self-conscious marker post for the end of the plot time. The epilogue closes on a freeze frame of the museum gateway. It is as if this image of a gateway has been caught in the camera's gate.[16] Cinema's illusion of moving images is arrested and made evident.[17] Like Rodin's 'The Kiss', in which the lovers seem to sit on the rest of the marble from which they have been carved, the film reveals its material basis in still images. After this emphasis on the materiality of the film, the end credits appear with vignettes of the characters in motion, taken from earlier scenes. It seems that the film has been stopped and reversed. Time can only be regained through cinema, which is revealed to be an illusion.

The epilogue's tragic tone balances pathos (Claude's failure to regain time) with poetic justice (Claude and Anne's betrayal of Muriel leads them to premature ageing and death, respectively). In this respect, the epilogue's role is similar to that of mainstream epilogues. Edward Branigan argues: 'The *epilogue* is the moral lesson implicit in a film's plot.'[18] However, the epilogue of *Les Deux Anglaises et le continent* is more ambiguous than a simple moral lesson. The film celebrates the characters' search for new experiences, in spite of the flux of time. The epilogue does not only reflect on these experiences; it opens the film out. The Musée Rodin becomes a stage for Claude's remembrances, but its sculptures and their narratives also perform. An essayistic space is created through which the epilogue reflects on time, history, memory, art and the materiality of film itself.

David Bordwell avers that classical epilogues reaffirm 'the stability of the state arrived at through the preceding causal chain', but can also 'afford ... self-conscious play with expectations; overtness is permitted at the end'.[19] For Bordwell, the classical epilogue can at once reassert narrative closure and open up the film as text, breaking its realism in a controlled way. Similarly, Garrett Stewart writes about the combination of freeze frames with a character's death at the end of a film as a 'controlled rupture' of the still photograph into the illusionism of film.[20] The epilogue of *Les Deux Anglaises et le continent* provides no closure as definite as a death and its contrasts between movement and stillness suggest a pervasive instability. Claude's wanderings have become aimless amid broader histories. In the essayistic space of the museum, the film plays a hide-and-seek game with history and finds itself: that is, its materiality. An unstable tissue of temporal layers is unearthed, at the heart of which is the film strip.

Sculpture is the main device with which this temporal opening out is achieved. The epilogue is best understood, therefore, in the context of sculptural moments in 1950s and 1960s European cinema.[21] The sculptural exploration of history in Truffaut's epilogue resembles the use of statuary in Roberto Rossellini's *Viaggio in Italia/Journey to Italy* (1953) and Luchino Visconti's *Il gattopardo/The Leopard* (1963).[22] When historical sculpture is used (as opposed to fictive sculpture made specially for a film), sculptural moments have a particular effect. A short shot or scene becomes weighted with historical resonances. Statues do not move, but narratives can be embedded in them, which, in turn, cinema can create the illusion of reanimating.

In Truffaut's film these are forking narratives. 'The Burghers of Calais', 'Ugolino and His Children' and 'The Kiss' all capture history *in medias res*. We know what happens next: the burghers will be released, Ugolino will eat his children and Francesca and Paolo will be killed by the cuckold. However, Rodin has sculpted each moment in such a way that a different finale seems more likely. The burghers look like they will die. The children look like they will eat Ugolino. Francesca and Paolo are locked in a kiss that does not seem fatal. In the film, then, the sculptures become emblems for the type of moment in which they feature: an epilogue in which narratives have multiplied. It becomes clear that history can be told in many different ways: in the gaps between these narratives, metahistoriography and materiality rear their heads.

NOTES

1. The film is known as *Anne and Muriel* in the UK and *Two English Girls* in the USA. This essay refers to the 1984 restored cut of the film, the editing of which Truffaut supervised. It is this cut of the film which is widely available on DVD. On the editing history of the film, see Antoine de Baecque and Serge Toubiana, *Truffaut* [trans. Catherine Temerson] (New York: Alfred Knopf, 1999), pp. 288, 385–6.

2. François Truffaut, 'Pourquoi *Les Deux Anglaises*?', reproduced in Dominique Rabourdin (ed.), *Truffaut on Truffaut* [trans. Robert Erich Wolf] (New York: Harry N. Abrams, 1987), p. 126.

3. On references to the Brontës in the film, see Joseph Kestner, 'Truffaut: Tale of Two Brontës?', *Village Voice*, 14 December 1972. On the resemblance between Truffaut's style and that of Proust, see Jean Collet, *François Truffaut* (Paris: Lherminier, 1985), p. 86.

4. See Don Allen, *Finally Truffaut* (London: Secker and Warburg, 1985), p. 150; de Baecque and Toubiana, *Truffaut*, p. 284.

5. On Truffaut's dislike of tourism, see ibid., p. 260.

6. Such chapter titles, which make the formal structure of a film obvious, are much rarer in mainstream feature films than they are in books. However, the intertitle need not be seen as 'literary'. Like Truffaut's vignette end credits, it can be seen as a throwback to the silent era. Epilogues marked off by intertitles were common in the 1910s, but disappeared as film-makers sought to conceal such 'seams'. See David Bordwell, Janet Staiger and Kristin Thompson, *The Classical Hollywood Cinema* (London: Routledge, 2008), p. 36.

7. Truffaut is accurate here. 'Balzac' was initially rejected, because it bore no physical resemblance to Honoré de Balzac: Rodin used the statue's physiognomy to represent the novelist's mental state. See Ruth Butler, 'Introduction', in Ruth Butler (ed.), *Rodin in Perspective* (Englewood Cliffs, NJ: Prentice-Hall, 1980), p. 12.

8. Barbara Coffey, 'Art and Film in François Truffaut's *Jules et Jim* and *Two English Girls*', *Film Heritage* vol. 9 no. 3, 1 April 1974, p. 10.

9. Dante Alighieri, *The Divine Comedy* [trans. C. H. Sisson] (Oxford: Oxford University Press, 1998), p. 187.

10. Annette Insdorf and Jean Collet both argue that the statuary in the film defies the passage of time. Annette Insdorf, *François Truffaut* (rev. edn) (Cambridge: Cambridge University Press, 1994), p. 124; Jean Collet, *Le Cinéma de François Truffaut: l'écriture et le feu* (Paris: Lherminier, 1977), p. 264.

11. Butler, *Rodin in Perspective*, pp. 28–9.

12. The first film to participate in this revival was probably the second version of *Shadows* (John Cassavetes, 1959), which features Rodin's 'Balzac'. See Suzanne Liandrat-Guigues, *Cinéma et sculpture: un aspect de la modernité des années soixante* (Paris: L'Harmattan, 2002), pp. 63–74.

13. As Michael Klein points out, it is, in a sense, a tragedy for Claude that what once seemed a symbol of the avant-garde has become 'accepted by the establishment'. Michael Klein, 'The Twilight of Romanticism: *Adèle H.*', in Karyn Kay and Gerald Peary (eds), *Women and the*

Cinema: A Critical Anthology (New York: E. P. Dutton, 1977), p. 54.

14. Dante, The Divine Comedy, pp. 67–8.

15. Ian MacKillop argues that the kiss between Muriel and Claude in Roché's novel mirrors Rodin's 'The Kiss', which Roché's Muriel visits. Ian MacKillop, Free Spirits: Henri-Pierre Roché, François Truffaut and the Two English Girls (London: Bloomsbury, 2001), p. 100.

16. The film gate, where each frame is held for exposure, is called couloir in French, literally a 'narrow passage'; the characters file through the narrow opening of the gateway, like a film strip through the gate/couloir.

17. On freeze-frame endings that reveal the materiality of film, see Laura Mulvey, Death 24x a Second: Stillness and the Moving Image (London: Reaktion, 2006), p. 81.

18. Edward Branigan, Narrative Comprehension and Film (London and New York: Routledge, 1992), p. 18.

19. David Bordwell, Narration in the Fiction Film (London and New York: Routledge, 2008), pp. 202–3.

20. Garrett Stewart, Between Film and Screen: Modernism's Photo Synthesis (Chicago, IL: University of Chicago Press, 1999), p. 39; see also Mulvey, Death 24x a Second, pp. 80–1.

21. Annette Insdorf argues that the film's statue motifs resemble those of Cocteau: Insdorf, François Truffaut, p. 195. However, the descendants of Cocteau's statuary are more likely to be found in films like L'Année dernière à Marienbad (Alain Resnais, 1961) and Le Mépris (Jean-Luc Godard, 1963), which both feature pastiche classical statues. See Liandrat-Guignes, Cinéma et sculpture, pp. 41–9, 59–62. In different ways, Cocteau, Resnais and Godard use statuary to explore mythologies. As Liandrat-Guignes points out, Truffaut's earlier Roché adaptation, Jules et Jim (1962), features fictive sculpture that fits into the same group as Resnais's and Godard's. In Les Deux Anglaises et le continent, however, Truffaut's deployment of Rodin's works is focused on specific levels of history.

22. On the statues in Viaggio in Italia, see Liandrat-Guignes, Cinéma et sculpture, pp. 33–40; Laura Mulvey, Death 24x a Second, pp. 116–17.

BIBLIOGRAPHY

Allen, Don, Finally Truffaut (London: Secker and Warburg, 1985).

Bordwell, David, Narration in the Fiction Film (London and New York: Routledge, 2008).

Bordwell, David, Staiger, Janet and Thompson, Kristin, The Classical Hollywood Cinema (London: Routledge, 2008).

Branigan, Edward, Narrative Comprehension and Film (London and New York: Routledge, 1992).

Butler, Ruth (ed.), Rodin in Perspective (Englewood Cliffs, NJ: Prentice-Hall, 1980).

Coffey, Barbara, 'Art and Film in François Truffaut's Jules et Jim and Two English Girls', Film Heritage vol. 9 no. 3, 1 April 1974, pp. 1–11.

Collet, Jean, Le Cinéma de François Truffaut: l'écriture et le feu (Paris: Lherminier, 1977)

Collet, Jean, François Truffaut (Paris: Lherminier, 1985).

Dante (Alighieri), The Divine Comedy [trans. C. H. Sisson] (Oxford: Oxford University Press, 1998).

De Baecque, Antoine and Toubiana, Serge, Truffaut [trans. Catherine Temerson] (New York: Alfred Knopf, 1999).

Insdorf, Annette, François Truffaut (rev. edn) (Cambridge: Cambridge University Press, 1994).

Kay, Karyn and Peary, Gerald (eds), Women and the Cinema: A Critical Anthology (New York: E. P. Dutton, 1977).

Kestner, Joseph, 'Truffaut: Tale of Two Brontës?', Village Voice, 14 December 1972.

Klein, Michael, 'The Twilight of Romanticism: Adèle H.', in Karyn Kay and Gerald Peary (eds), Women and the Cinema: A Critical Anthology (New York: E. P. Dutton, 1977), pp. 50–5.

Liandrat-Guignes, Suzanne, Cinéma et sculpture: un aspect de la modernité des années soixante (Paris: L'Harmattan, 2002).

MacKillop, Ian, Free Spirits: Henri-Pierre Roché, François Truffaut and the Two English Girls (London: Bloomsbury, 2001).

Mulvey, Laura, Death 24x a Second: Stillness and the Moving Image (London: Reaktion, 2006).

Rabourdin, Dominique (ed.), Truffaut on Truffaut [trans. Robert Erich Wolf] (New York: Harry N. Abrams, 1987).

Stewart, Garrett, Between Film and Screen: Modernism's Photo Synthesis (Chicago, IL: University of Chicago Press, 1999).

Truffaut, François, 'Pourquoi Les Deux Anglaises?', reproduced in Dominique Rabourdin (ed.), Truffaut on Truffaut [trans. Robert Erich Wolf] (New York: Harry N. Abrams, 1987), p. 126.

Star Wars (1977): Back and Forth in Time and Space

JONATHAN BIGNELL

In the opening moments of the 'original' *Star Wars* (Lucas, 1977),[1] time and space are being moulded flexibly, and in ways that point both back and forward in film history. By studying the spatial and temporal shifting within the first few shots in detail, this chapter shows how the film-makers' choices open up questions about what kind of film this is. Not all of those questions have straightforward answers because the film offers overlapping and sometimes divergent ways of understanding its fictional world.

WHERE ARE WE, AND WHEN?

The film begins with the Twentieth Century-Fox studio logo, accompanied by a fanfare first used in the 1930s. The fanfare is in the same musical key as the loud orchestral burst which begins John Williams's musical score for the film, and the fortuitous aural match between them is the first of a series of links and distinctions between past, present and future at a visual and musical level. The opening caption against a black background, 'A long time ago, in a galaxy far, far away ...', sets the film in a distant place and a distant time. At once, the phrase signals fairytale story-telling about the past (like 'Once upon a time') and futuristic science fiction ('galaxy'), and its dotted ellipsis tells the audience that a story will follow. The black background matches the mainly black star field that subsequently appears, on which the film's title logo briefly occupies the centre of the frame before rapidly shrinking into the distance. Yellow text in upper- and lower-case lettering begins to scroll upwards into the frame, moving back and diminishing into an infinite distance. Since the text refers to previous events it is clearly one among many chapters of the story, and introduces the idea that just one part of a huge saga about the past is being told.[2] The slow movement and left- and right-justification of the text connote the orderliness of this fictional world, like the conventional narrative patterning of a fairytale, despite the violent conflict between Rebels and Empire that the text describes. The musical score uses the full resources of a classical orchestra and its theme is played primarily by brass instruments.

Like the language of the captions, it refers backwards in time. Its classical symphonic music follows the conventions of an opera overture in introducing motifs and musical themes that will structure the film and identify characters. The now-famous sequence of brass notes, rising, falling back and then rising again in a triumphant major key, will be used later whenever Luke Skywalker (Mark Hamill) is on screen (and each major character has a theme particular to him or her). The upward reaching of the brass notes matches the hope for freedom that the crawl text outlines, yet its falling back also conveys the reversals of fortune and the struggle that the Rebels undergo. The main musical motif resolves, to arrive at a confident restatement of its opening note, one octave higher than when it began. While the crawl text announces the prospect of restoring 'freedom to the galaxy' but leaves the rest of the film to show whether that can be achieved, the musical opening's brass fanfare, major key and rising sequence of notes promise heroic resolution.

In these first moments, placement in space and time is being subverted. A legendary or mythical story about the past is set in a science-fictional futuristic world, and this first *Star Wars* film appears surprisingly to begin in the middle of that story. Spatially, the first brief caption seems superimposed on a two-dimensional background, while the title logo and crawling text introduce a new dimension of depth. Because the crawl text is in the present tense, it seems to be generated within the present of the story, within the three-dimensional blackness of outer space through which it moves, and thus exists in a different time from 'A long time ago'. The crawl text makes a link between *Star Wars* and the science-fiction film serials of the 1930s such as *Flash Gordon* and *Buck Rogers* that were structured as episodic narratives in weekly instalments, and here too the text's function is ambivalent. It announces that the film has begun and provides information that sets what follows in a definite context. But its allusions to other films from the past and to traditions of science-fiction storytelling draw attention to the knowledge that the audience brings into

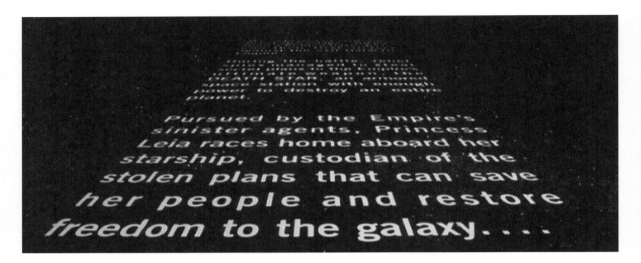

the cinema from outside. In the same way, the orchestral score draws on the familiar instrumentation and structure of classical music, and the ways it was adapted for film music in the heyday of Hollywood cinema. The music belongs to the past, but matches the tropes of heroic adventure with which the crawl text has shaped this futuristic story. Standing at the border of the film, the text and the opening music are both inside and outside the film, just as the story is ambivalently historical and futuristic.[3]

The spatial scale of the opening moments of *Star Wars* announces a new epoch in cinema technology. The crawl text does not fill the sides of the frame, which makes the sheer horizontal extent of the widescreen frame clear by leaving some of it empty. Shot in a 70mm format (one among many kinds of film stock that sought to express cinema's visual superiority over television), the film is designed to be seen in the cinema on a large screen. In this sense, *Star Wars* advertises cinema itself as a visual experience, supported by extensive orchestral music that can dominate the auditorium. Following the crawl text, a marked camera movement opens up the fictional space by panning downwards to show two moons and the edge of a planet. The main musical theme dies away, replaced by a quiet and hesitant tinkling that suggests the emptiness of space. Although in itself the camera movement might be somewhat disorienting because it suddenly changes the orientation of point of view, its purpose is to make location more specific in contrast to the generality of distant stars, since the distant moons provide a sense of scale to the space. Once the camera movement is completed, the frame is stabilised again for a spectacular use of new effects techniques when two spaceships fly over the camera. By having the first ship fly into a stable frame, the viewer is able to contemplate the details of its shape as they are gradually revealed, and to understand its motion. This sequence is clearly part of the story, rather than an interruption like

the 'beauty shots' of the USS *Enterprise* that lovingly circle the spacecraft early in the first *Star Trek* (Wise, 1979) film, for instance. *Star Wars* can have it both ways, introducing the narrative trope of pursuit and also showing off the detailed miniature. As laser beams confirm the spatial alignment of the scene, a second, much larger spacecraft flies over the camera. It gradually fills the screen's upper sector, coming much closer to the camera and offering further fascination with the detail and scale of the image. *Star Wars*' special effects are important to the film's revival of science fiction as a film genre because of its huge audiences and profitability. The director George Lucas founded the special-effects company Industrial Light and Magic (ILM) as part of the *Star Wars* project, and it pioneered the use of 'motion control' (cameras controlled by computers) for shooting complex models in apparent movement. Sequels have used increasing amounts of computer effects and animation, but some of the 1977 film's pleasure is based on the knowledge that miniatures were fabricated for it, and several international touring exhibitions have been mounted to showcase the models and the techniques used to film them. While the film uses state-of-the-art techniques to engender belief in its fictional world, it capitalises on the knowledge that its world is artificial and painstakingly constructed.

The film continues a tradition of making science-fictional worlds plausible by following the physical conventions that audiences expect.[4] The stability of the frame while the spacecraft fly into it more easily respects conventions of perspective and composition than a moving shot. The visual field is harmoniously composed, with the trajectories of the laser beams and spaceships running along the centre and diagonals of the frame according to classical conventions of painting, and later of cinema. Pointing towards the planet's rim, the two spacecraft and the laser blasts' trajectories are roughly parallel, providing

a virtual vanishing point in the centre of the frame that supports the perspectival coherence of a three-dimensional space rendered on a two-dimensional screen. Strategies to make the action comprehensible according to established expectations continue within the shot, since the hulls of the two spacecraft appear to be made of metal plates, with rivet joints visible, and each has protruding turrets, ductwork and ancillary machinery breaking their smooth surfaces. Both the spacecrafts' engines and weapons make loud sounds even though soundwaves cannot travel in the vacuum of space, and the huge exhaust cones of the Empire's ship are blackened. Lucas commented: 'What is required for true credibility is a used future.'[5] Audiences were already familiar with space travel from television coverage of the Apollo missions, in which space capsules accumulated detritus such as used food containers and were discoloured by rocket exhaust. Lucas continued:

> Although *Star Wars* has no points of reference to Earth time or space, with which we are familiar, and it is not about the future but some galactic past or some extra-temporal present, it is a decidedly inhabited and used place where the hardware is taken for granted.

His comments show how spatial perspective, point of view and the verisimilitude of the models joined together elements from diverse genres, times and fictional spaces: 'We were trying to get a cohesive reality. But since the film is a fairytale, I still wanted it to have an ethereal quality, yet be well composed and, also, have an alien look.'

This technique of assemblage or *bricolage* is potentially confusing, so patterned motifs of big and small, powerful and powerless, black and white, mechanical and mystical, are used to give order and structure to the narrative. The crawl text has already informed the audience that a Rebel ship is fleeing from the oppressive Empire, and the opening spacecraft sequence maps this positive connotation of smallness and relative powerlessness onto the smaller spacecraft attacked by a much larger one. Music is also used to map the significance of the sequence, for, as the first ship appears, the score introduces a musical motif for the Rebels. But it is gradually overridden by rhythmic bass pulses and the start of a military motif played on horns and strings, representing the Empire, as the gigantic Imperial cruiser dominates the visual field. The next scene cuts from space to inside the Rebel ship, where two robots move along a corridor towards the camera. Familiar conventions again enfold alien subjects to make them comprehensible, since, despite being in space, gravity holds the robots in place and distinctions between walls, floor and ceiling match those of Earth-bound buildings. At this point, with the appearance of the humanlike figure of C3PO, the narrative begins to link the grand scale of epic political and military conflict with the actions and emotions of particular characters who are caught up in it.

YOU HAVE SEEN THIS BEFORE

An analysis of the film's opening moments can show how *Star Wars* offers its audiences ways to make sense of its narrative. These include the opening captions' references to fairytales, to epic conflicts between an evil Empire and freedom-loving Rebels, and to the cinema serials of the 1930s. Visually, the film makes its spaceships look functional and subject to the wear and tear of everyday use. Basic conventions like perspective, gravity and a sense of up and down make outer space comprehensible, and the film introduces characters who speak English. The music of the opening moments uses a full orchestra and adopts the conventions of Hollywood film music based on late-nineteenth-century forms such as those of Richard Wagner, mixed with more recent musical styles, especially that of Aaron Copland who reworked a European tradition for nationalistic American ends.[6] The emotional tone of the musical motifs and their connection with specific characters and narrative tropes guide the spectator's relationship to the action. These interlocking, overlapping patterns and systems continue as the film proceeds, and are further developed and built upon. Fredric Jameson called *Star Wars* a 'nostalgia film' because it deploys conventions, motifs and clichés deriving from different historical periods and media, but displaces them from their contexts and collapses them together.[7] *Star Wars'* references to popular culture beyond the opening moments include the Western, especially *The Searchers* (1956) where the hero must leave his home to rescue a woman captured by the Indians,[8] and sea adventure where outlaw pirates use trickery and courage to defeat naval authority. *Star Wars* is also a medieval quest, with the Jedi Knights defending a legacy of mystical and chivalric values against its perversion in the service of the Empire,[9] and a comedy film centring on the adventures of a duo of 'little guys', C3PO and R2D2, who wrangle at the edges of the epic story. It is a coming-of-age story where Luke Skywalker leaves his rural home to grow up and realise his true identity, a Cold War thriller dramatising the struggle of the Rebel Alliance against the evil Empire, and a World War II film with aerial dogfighting and a commando raid against the Death Star.

There are some ideological notions that most of these sources share, such as the conventionally male hero and a woman in need of rescue, the valuing of youth over age, and a moral structure that leads to the expectation of a happy ending that brings order to a society and confirms the ennoblement of the protagonist. But they are also ambivalent about the home to which the hero cannot return, his implication in violence and his close association with the antagonist. *Star Wars* is not simply an affirmation of the myths it reworks but also offers a reconsideration of them. The film offers competing interpretations that can co-exist, and thus addresses diverse audiences. The opening crawl text presents it as a conservative story about gung-ho American individuals combating oppressive colonial and militaristic imperialists, and thus draws on the positive connotations of rebellion that have been used to underpin myths about the founding of the USA and the USA's support for other freedom-fighters around the world. But it is also a postmodern story about the creative and liberating possibilities for open-minded alliances that look to the future, bringing different races and cultures together.[10] This reading of the film was reinforced by Lucas's addition of the title 'Episode IV: A New Hope' to some cinema versions of the film in 1981, subsequently retained in later versions. The presence of Chewbacca, a non-human character, and two robots among the hero team seems calculated to demonstrate the inclusion of difference. The film is both a modern 'grand

narrative' that believes in progress, freedom and heroism, and a postmodern *bricolage* that celebrates diversity, critiques mythical archetypes and is one episode in a story that cannot arrive at a satisfactory closure.

Star Wars has been called the first blockbuster film, and the opening moments discussed here have been cited as the announcement of a new kind of gigantism and spectacle in US cinema.[11] Its visual scale is matched by the film's sound. The film was designed for multitrack stereo loudspeakers, so that the roar of the Imperial spacecraft in the opening scene would match the visual impact of the widescreen image. The notion of the blockbuster is not concerned exclusively with the film itself, however, since much of *Star Wars'* cultural impact and financial profit came from associated products. Its props, characters and narrative forms are 'toyetic' (a good basis for toys) in that there are visually and narratively distinctive characters who can become action figures, a range of spacecraft that can become toys, and a strong, simple narrative that can mutate into games, comics and further film and television products. Toy licensing from the 1977 film was worth $500 million for the Hasbro and Galoob companies who manufactured the toys, and franchises to associate products (such as T-shirts, lunchboxes and pyjamas) with its characters were worth $1.5 billion per year.[12] *Star Wars* entered popular culture not only because many people saw the film, but also because its imagery and themes spread more widely. For example, President Ronald Reagan's missile-defence initiative to combat nuclear attack from 'the evil empire' of the Soviet Union was nicknamed 'Star Wars' by opponents who regarded it as a fantasy that would never work, and key lines like 'May the Force be with you' became staples of everyday speech.

For these reasons, it is almost impossible to regard the opening moments of *Star Wars* as a sequence that can be freshly interpreted in its own terms. Rather, it becomes necessary to make a special effort to stop the flow of these few shots and examine them in detail, to see how they open up some of the many strands of meaning and reference that are built upon them later in the film, and that have been extended and changed by the related texts that appeared subsequently. Seeing the film now, after it has been bracketed by prequels, sequels, merchandise and computer games, further destabilises its meanings. One of these problems concerns which version of the film might be the 'original' *Star Wars*. Only some US cinemas were equipped to screen the film in 70mm using its full Dolby stereo sound in 1977, so some audiences saw a 35mm version or a 70mm version with different sound. Subsequently, video, laserdisc and DVD versions of the film were released for home viewing and television broadcast, again with differences between them. George Lucas digitally remastered the film, adding new CGI effects in 1997, claiming that this was the version he would have made originally if technology had allowed. A close analysis of the film's opening moments begins to ask the question, what is *Star Wars*? Further consideration of the rest of the film and its cultural history makes that question more insistent and harder to answer.

NOTES

1. This chapter discusses the original theatrical release of 1977, but questions about the status of this version of the film as the 'original' are debated later in the chapter.
2. Sean Cubitt, 'Preliminaries for a Taxonomy and Rhetoric of On-Screen Writing', in Jonathan Bignell (ed.), *Writing and Cinema* (Harlow: Longman, 1999), pp. 63–5.
3. Tom Conley, *Film Hieroglyphs: Ruptures in Classical Cinema* (Minneapolis: University of Minnesota Press, 1991).
4. Piers D. Britton, 'Design for Screen SF', in Mark Bould, Andrew M. Butler, Adam Roberts and Sherryl Vint (eds), *The Routledge Companion to Science Fiction* (London and New York: Routledge, 2009), p. 343.
5. Anon., 'Introduction to "Behind the Scenes of *Star Wars*"', *American Cinematographer*, July 1977. Available at <www.theasc.com/magazine/starwars/index.html> (accessed June 2009).
6. Ken McLeod, 'Music', in Bould *et al.*, *The Routledge Companion to Science Fiction* (London and New York: Routledge, 2009), p. 396.
7. Fredric Jameson, 'Postmodernism, or the Cultural Logic of Late Capitalism', *New Left Review* no. 146, 1984, pp. 53–92.
8. John Ford's *The Searchers* was a reference point for many young directors and screenwriters of the 1970s, and its motifs were reworked in films including *Mean Streets* (Scorsese, 1973), *Taxi Driver* (Scorsese, 1976) and *The Deerhunter* (Cimino, 1978). See Douglas Pye, 'Writing and Reputation: *The Searchers*, 1956–1976', in Jonathan Bignell (ed.), *Writing and Cinema* (Harlow: Longman, 1999), p. 206.
9. David Williams, 'Medieval Movies', *Yearbook of English Studies* vol. 20, 1990, pp. 1–32.
10. Will Brooker, 'New Hope: The Postmodern Project of *Star Wars*', in Peter Brooker and Will Brooker (eds), *Postmodern After-Images: A Reader in Film, Television and Video* (London: Arnold, 1997), pp. 101–12.
11. Scott Bukatman, 'Zooming Out: The End of Offscreen Space', in J. Lewis (ed.), *The New American Cinema* (Durham, NC: Duke University Press, 1998), pp. 248–72.
12. Graham Dawson, 'War Toys', in Gary Day (ed.), *Readings in Popular Culture: Trivial Pursuits?* (Basingstoke: Macmillan, 1989), pp. 104–5.

BIBLIOGRAPHY

Anon., 'Introduction to "Behind the Scenes of *Star Wars*"', *American Cinematographer*, July 1977. Available at <www.theasc.com/magazine/starwars/index.html> (accessed June 2009).

Bignell, Jonathan (ed.), *Writing and Cinema* (Harlow: Longman, 1999).

Bould, Mark, Butler, Andrew M., Roberts, Adam and Vint, Sherryl (eds), *The Routledge Companion to Science Fiction* (London and New York: Routledge, 2009).

Britton, Piers D., 'Design for Screen SF', in Bould *et al.*, *The Routledge Companion to Science Fiction*, p. 343–9.

Brooker, Peter and Brooker, Will (eds), *Postmodern After-Images: A Reader in Film, Television and Video* (London: Arnold, 1997).

Brooker, Will, 'New Hope: The Postmodern Project of *Star Wars*', in Brooker and Brooker, *Postmodern After-Images*, pp. 101–12.

Bukatman, Scott, 'Zooming Out: The End of Offscreen Space', in J. Lewis (ed.), *The New American Cinema* (Durham, NC: Duke University Press, 1998), pp. 248–72.

Conley, Tom, *Film Hieroglyphs: Ruptures in Classical Cinema* (Minneapolis: University of Minnesota Press, 1991).

Cubitt, Sean, 'Preliminaries for a Taxonomy and Rhetoric of On-Screen Writing', in Bignell, *Writing and Cinema*, pp. 59–73.

Dawson, Graham, 'War Toys', in Gary Day (ed.), *Readings in Popular Culture: Trivial Pursuits?* (Basingstoke: Macmillan, 1989), pp. 98–111.

Day, Gary (ed.), *Readings in Popular Culture: Trivial Pursuits?* (Basingstoke: Macmillan, 1989).

Jameson, Fredric, 'Postmodernism, or the Cultural Logic of Late Capitalism', *New Left Review* no. 146, 1984, pp. 53–92.

Lewis, J. (ed.), *The New American Cinema* (Durham, NC: Duke University Press, 1998).

McLeod, Ken, 'Music', in Bould *et al.*, *The Routledge Companion to Science Fiction*, pp. 393–402.

Pye, Douglas, 'Writing and Reputation: *The Searchers*, 1956–1976', in Bignell, *Writing and Cinema*, pp. 195–209.

Williams, David, 'Medieval Movies', *Yearbook of English Studies* vol. 20, 1990, pp. 1–32.

Between Freedom and Confinement: Music in *The World* (2004)

CLAUDIA GORBMAN

Jia Zhangke's *The World/Shijie* (2004) is set in Beijing's surreal 'World' theme park, 100 acres filled with small-scale replicas of the world's tourist monuments – the Giza pyramids, London Bridge, the Vatican, even the Manhattan skyline complete with the Twin Towers: 'We still have them,' says one worker proudly.[1] The young workers who are the film's main characters, migrants from China's hinterlands, present one face of contemporary China's warp-speed urbanisation. Having followed their dreams to the capital, they nevertheless remain powerless and alienated, surrounded by the simulacra of 'global' spaces and deprived of the freedom or means to travel the real world. As Yomi Braester writes, the World park 'reduces to the absurd (miniaturises to the absurd, as it were) transnational spaces, which privilege international corporations and the globetrotting class, ignoring local economies and encouraging low-wage global outsourcing'.[2]

Even with the modern trappings of twenty-first century technology, the characters' mobile phones and text messaging don't result in authentic or improved communication. When protagonist Tao (Zhao Tao), riding the monorail that rings the park, tells her security-guard boyfriend Taisheng (Chen Taisheng) on the phone that she's 'going to India', she means she's going over to the park's mini-Taj Mahal as part of her job, to do some stereotypical 'Indian' dance moves in costume before a small crowd of tourists with cameras. The film gives the lie to globalisation via the often sordid realities it produces for its characters: illegal trade in passports and human beings, sweatshops that feed first-world fashion, poverty and stunted horizons.

MOMENT 1: A BUS RIDE

A few scenes into the film, having walked away from a soured date with her boyfriend in a cheap hotel, Tao rides a city bus at night in order to make it back to her performing shift at the World park. It's a scene of transit, of no dramatic significance, an ordinary bus ride. The scene occurs all in one pan, a shot that lasts about forty-five seconds.

Above the bus's rear exit, a video monitor plays a commercial. Brightly coloured shots of world monuments include those of the Sydney Opera House and the Eiffel Tower. The tinny music that blares unattractively along with the commercial is none other than the 'Ode to Joy' from the final movement of Beethoven's Ninth Symphony, pompously pimping the grandeur of the World park. The camera pans left and down from the TV monitor, past a woman passenger, until it rests on Tao in the seat behind. Tao dons her denim jacket, then stares out the window at the wide dark avenue; the bus passes the Tiananmen Gate. Her mobile rings and she takes it out to read the message she has received.[3]

The 'Ode to Joy' chorus commences, dominating the soundtrack, just as the bus shot begins. As the camera moves away from the TV monitor, the music fades quickly, though it remains audible for the duration of the shot. By the time the camera rests on Tao, we hear the bus motor, traffic and the dying strains of the music, which is no longer present when the bus passes by Tiananmen.

The World often shows Tao and her boyfriend in transit. What is striking about most of these small travel interludes is their banality, and the no-man's-lands they traverse. Empty space generally does not signal freedom in *The World*; it's more like the prison-yard of the characters' existence, offering no stimulus or interest, one more lifeless territory to cross.

The poignant irony of the bus scene derives from the commercial's use of the 'Ode to Joy'. Even to the filmgoer who only vaguely recognises the piece, the music's grandeur is comically at odds with the bus and its oblivious passengers. The lo-fi sound reproduction makes it into yet another media intrusion, a loud cliché, to pollute auditory space.

The precision with which the scene begins on the first note of the famous chorus helps to foreground the music. Beethoven wrote the Ninth Symphony, his last, in 1824. The fourth movement of this towering work is a cantata in a symphony, which includes a quartet of vocal soloists and a large chorus as well as the symphony orchestra. For the sung text, Beethoven adapted Friedrich von Schiller's 1785 poem 'An die Freude' ('On Happiness' or 'Ode to Joy'), whose Enlightenment values resonated deeply with the composer. The poem expresses a vision of the brotherhood of man through overcoming divisions. Beethoven's exquisite musical setting yields what has stood, through the twentieth century, as a jubilant musical representation of mankind's potential for universal harmony.

O friends, not these tones,
But rather, let us strike up more pleasant
And more joyful sounds.
Joy! Joy!
...
Joy, beautiful divine spark,
Daughter of Elysium,
We enter, drunk with fire,
O heavenly one, your holy shrine;
Your music once again bonds together
What custom strictly divided,
All mankind become brothers,
Where your gentle wings hold sway.

Beethoven's 'Ode to Joy' has both gained and suffered from its 180-year history. Musicologist Richard Taruskin argues that its message might be difficult to take seriously any more: 'We have our problems with demagogues who preach to us about the brotherhood of man. We have been too badly burned by those who have promised Elysium and given us gulags and gas chambers.'[4] Even in the history of cinema, 'Ode to Joy' has appeared numerous times in both sincere and satirical guises. Think of Alex (Malcolm McDowell) in Kubrick's *A Clockwork Orange* (1971), conditioned to kill when he hears Beethoven's Ninth. In *Raising Arizona* (Coen, 1987) and *Bowling for Columbine* (Moore, 2002) the music is laced with irony. *Dead Poets Society* (Weir, 1989) and *Shine* (Hicks, 1996) call on the Ninth to reach towards the sublime. Then there are entirely comical uses, such as in *A Dennis the Menace Christmas* (Oliver, 2007). In *The World*, Jia might have a nostalgic desire for the work's message as Beethoven conceived it, but he also trivialises its musical-poetic-historical grandeur by positioning it in a commercial which itself advertises a commodified space of simulacra. It is ironic enough to juxtapose the grand (Beethoven) with the oppressively prosaic (the bus ride). It is more ironic still that the grand is rendered oppressively prosaic, used for a commercial and reproduced as noise that bothers rather than enraptures the captive audience of commuters. But consider the scene further in the combination of its historical allusions and its immediate textuality.

History has written that Schiller originally intended to write an ode to freedom (*Freiheit*) rather than joy (*Freude*), but the political regime of his time and place made such

an idea unwise. In any case, when the Berlin Wall fell two centuries later, Leonard Bernstein conducted a multinational orchestra in a performance of Beethoven's Ninth there on Christmas Day 1989 and had the singers replace the word '*Freude*' with '*Freiheit*', thereby explicitly celebrating the liberation of Eastern Europe from decades of socialist oppression.

The 'Ode to Joy' was adopted as the official anthem of the Council of Europe in 1972 and as the anthem of the European Community in 1985 (Herbert von Karajan wrote three separate arrangements of it for official use). It has also opened a number of Olympic Games. Those who bemoan its overexposure as the ultimate feelgood work would do well not to throw the baby out with the bathwater: the Ninth has occupied a primary place in twentieth-century history, and while western intellectuals might regret its trivialisation, 'the piece you love to hate' continues to hold tremendous power. 'Why?' asks Taruskin. 'Because it is at once incomprehensible and irresistible, and because it is at once awesome and naive.'[5]

Earlier in the momentous year that the communist governments fell in Eastern Europe, the Tiananmen events unfolded in Beijing. What began as mourning for a popular pro-democracy and anti-corruption official (Hu Yaobang) mushroomed into a vast movement of students, intellectuals and other citizens. Daily demonstrations exceeding 100,000 people continued until the government cracked down by killing hundreds of protesters and closing the Square on 4 June 1989. Despite international reaction, the Chinese government managed to reinstate the repressive regime and almost completely erase the protests from the historical record within China's boundaries. What had been a brief flowering of idealism and democracy was terminated by brutal repression.

Through Beethoven and the bus route, the moment in *The World* subtly brings together, fifteen years later, the peaceful unification of Germany and the brutal events in China. When the camera rests on Tao in the bus, outside her window in the night is the Tiananmen Gate, bedecked with a banner with Mao's face and the inscriptions 'Long Live the People's Republic of China' and – echoes of Schiller – 'Long Live the Great Unity of the World's Peoples'. The co-presence of Beethoven's Ninth with Tiananmen is hardly coincidental in Jia's film. A perfect ambiguity results

between its short-hand of freedom and brotherhood (and its power and beauty) and the oppressiveness of the summer night and the ubiquitous state. *The World*, the first feature film that Jia was permitted to make with state approval, is shrouded in such productive ambiguities. If protest is intended, note its subtlety, even feebleness: Tao doesn't listen, no one does, as with no fanfare the bus passes by an illuminated but empty Tiananmen.

RHYMING MOMENT: 'ULAN BATOR'

The bus scene finds echoes throughout *The World*. Other brief scenes of trajectories in vehicles, other scenes with brief strains of diegetic music, other scenes where text messages on characters' mobiles segue into brief moments of Flash-animation escape. Jia's film has a rather loose narrative line, but it is also unified like a spider web, a matrix of themes, images and motifs. Here I examine another of the moments when a video monitor is present alongside music.

Anna (Alla Shcherbakova) is a Russian brought to work at the park. Though neither speaks the other's language, Tao and Anna become friends, communicating through pantomime, family photos and small kindnesses. In a working-class restaurant, Tao and Anna share a drink. Each speaks her own language and her own thoughts: in Mandarin, Tao mistakenly admires Anna's freedom and ability to travel (Anna is actually indentured to a man who takes her passport and she will later work as a prostitute in an attempt to buy her freedom). Anna states in Russian that she is leaving the park for another job. Although the scene is as understated as all others in *The World*, Tao miraculously seems to understand, saying she'll take photos for Anna of the Christmas fireworks at the park. A television, off screen right, issues weather reports for China and surrounding areas. Hearing Ulan Bator, Anna walks over to the TV and back to the table. Anna's dream is to go to visit her sister who has married and moved to Ulan Bator. She teaches Tao a folk-song in Russian about Ulan Bator, which – as in musicals – Tao is able to sing back almost without effort.[6] The restaurant scene takes place all in one two-and-a-half-minute shot (which starts at the restaurant table, pans right to the TV and back).

Immediately after the sequence shot in the restaurant, in a tracking shot that lasts almost a minute, Tao and Anna ride wordlessly back towards the park in an open pedicab. They smile to each other, and each becomes lost in her own thoughts. A beautiful instrumental and partly electronic rendition of their 'Ulan Bator' tune, the melody now played on what sounds like a Chinese woodwind instrument, floods over the soundtrack. It is a transcendent moment of happiness and reflection.

What parallels can we draw between these two moments? In each case, the mode of musical address and the female protagonist's involvement with the music differs. In the first, Tao is alone; in the second, she is with the sympathetic and generous Anna. On the bus, the music comes from the TV monitor – great, 'sublime', western music treated as Muzak, which Tao ignores. In the scene with Anna, there is no direct relationship between the video monitor and music – only that the television weather broadcast inspires Anna to recall the song about Ulan Bator, evoking her long-lost sister. She engages Tao in the tune, teaching it to her. In becoming the recipient of the transfer of the tune, Tao becomes the sister. In a world where migration to the urban centre has severed family relations for all the main characters, this movement comes as a moment of grace. On this unique occasion, characters make music themselves. Jia cuts from the restaurant to the women's ride in the breeze along the water, the closest *The World* will come to fresh air, freedom, nature, unfettered serenity. The score turns the women's shared Mongolian tune into a beautiful theme, this time non-diegetic, endowed with full audio definition.

Contrast the 'Ode to Joy' in the bus with the 'Ulan Bator' tune on the pedicab. Both pieces play with a scene of transport back to the park. The 'Ode to Joy' is 'filtered', played through a small speaker in the image and therefore thin and tinny. Beethoven's opulent choral symphony has turned into an annoyance, as the scowling Tao rides past the very emblem of historical government repression. On the other hand, 'Ulan Bator' enjoys a textured and sensuous arrangement, its rich tonal range enhanced by reverb that gives it a spatial dimension; the tune is played on a double-reed instrument (perhaps a traditional *guanzi*). With this transfer of their moment of song to the non-diegetic soundtrack, the film consummates the two women's musical communication. We see them bathed in light (an illumination whose source never appears in frame), the wind through their hair, and the orchestral arrangement plays as if for a moment it's the soundtrack of their lives. This audiovisual segment of the film transcends the unremitting dreariness of the rest; it represents a momentary pause in the film's hurtling progression toward stasis and confinement.

Why a song about Mongolia? As with the complex and ambiguous relationship between 'Ode to Joy' (or freedom) and the Tiananmen Gate outside the bus window, Mongolia can suggest both harmony and its opposite. Identified with China for centuries, Mongolia was subsequently taken over

by the Russian empire and existed in various states of sub-
jection and dependency in relation to both China and
Russia for much of the twentieth century. After the breakdown of communist regimes in Europe in 1989, however,
Mongolia had its own democratic revolution in 1990, and,
as an independent though very poor nation, it has transi-
tioned to a market economy under a multiparty system.
More simply in the film, Mongolia lies between Anna's land
and Tao's, and the song unites the two women.

The transfer of a diegetic song to the non-diegetic
soundtrack occurs frequently in conventional narrative
cinema, but in *The World* it happens only this once. This
passage strikes me as a rare romantic gesture on Jia's part.
However fleetingly, the film here approaches freedom,
brotherhood, *jouissance*.

The moments discussed here reveal dialectical tensions between freedom and confinement, between communication and misunderstanding, and between art and
consumption. Examining the treatment of their musics
reveals a film that is structured as a matrix of combinations and recombinations more than by cause and effect.
The study further underlines the position of music as a
master communicator when the characters themselves are
inarticulate, and when Jia's film-making politically walks a
fine line between state approval and poetic subversion.

NOTES

1. Jia shot in two 'World' theme parks: the World park in
    Beijing and the Window on the World park in Shenzhen.
2. Yomi Braester, Chapter 7, in *Painting the City Red: Chinese
    Cinema and the Urban Contract* (Durham, NC: Duke
    University Press, forthcoming, 2010).
3. Immediately afterwards, the film momentarily shifts to
    Flash animation, as it frequently does in connection to
    mobile phones: we see Taisheng's text message, then the
    night sky with highway light poles passing by on both
    sides in symmetry. Braester, Chapter 7, *Painting the City Red*:
    'The Flash sequences in *The World* associate the protago-
    nist's need to escape beyond the materiality of the city in
    new, postcinematic modes of visualization. Jia films, so to
    speak, in virtual space.'
4. Richard Taruskin, 'Resisting the Ninth', in *Text and Act:
    Essays in Music and Performance* (New York: Oxford
    University Press, 1995), p. 249.
5. Taruskin, 'Resisting the Ninth', p. 245.
6. Jia has said: 'I think that the film has some of the ele-
    ments of a musical. But it's not a musical in the true sense
    of the word ... . But the musical scenes that are included
    are very important, because they are tied up with changes
    in the characters' states of mind, with the things they go
    through.' Valerie Jaffee, 'An Interview with Jia Zhangke',
    Senses of Cinema, 2004. Available at <archive.sensesof
    cinema.com/contents/04/32/jia_zhangke.html>.

BIBLIOGRAPHY

Braester, Yomi, 'Chapter 7', *Painting the City Red: Chinese Cinema
    and the Urban Contract* (Durham, NC: Duke University Press,
    forthcoming, 2010).
Jaffee, Valerie, 'An Interview with Jia Zhangke', *Senses of
    Cinema*, 2004. Available at <archive.sensesofcinema.com/
    contents/04/32/jia_zhangke.html>.
Taruskin, Richard, 'Resisting the Ninth', *Text and Act: Essays in
    Music and Performance* (New York: Oxford University Press,
    1995).

PART THREE: Theory

A man with one theory is lost. He needs several of them, or lots! He should stuff them in his pockets like newspapers.

Bertolt Brecht[1]

No film theory is worth anything which does not stay close to the concrete and which does not strive continually to check its own assumptions and procedures in relation to producible texts.

Andrew Britton[2]

By way of introducing this final part of the book, it is worth reflecting again on the issues associated with dividing the contributions according to the broad categories of criticism, theory and history. We suggested in our initial definition of these distinctions that film criticism could be said to ask, 'What is this film or these films?' and film history, 'What has "film" been?', while film theory asks a broader question: 'What is "film"?' In practice, of course, it is neither possible nor desirable to separate these questions in such definitive terms. Certain of the essays in the 'criticism' section can be seen to value a particular definition of what film is over others.[3] Similarly, without 'theory', history risks becoming merely an 'account of some things that happened'. Of course, while remaining aware of the problems of 'teleologies', we still need hypotheses or theories to make sense of historical development: 'In historical explanation, which is a retrospective process, the object of analysis only emerges as a construction of a theoretical discourse.'[4] In more simple terms, we can only ask, 'What has film been?' after asking first 'What is "film"?'

It is a sign of the vigour film studies enjoys that scholars and students of the discipline are able to define what they do in very distinct ways. However, the downside of the professionalisation of an academic discipline is that the distinctions may become territorial, represented most crudely in the statement: 'I am a film theorist. I do not *do* film criticism', for example (or vice versa). This situation is markedly different from the discipline's roots, and the writing of one of the most famous film critics/theorists/historians (depending on where one wishes to place the emphasis), André Bazin, illustrates this. Bazin's most famous collection of essays, the multi-volume *What Is Cinema?*, announces its theoretical project but is preceded by the following statement:

> The title ... is not so much the promise of an answer as the announcement of a question that the author asks himself throughout these pages. These books do not therefore pretend to offer a geology or an exhaustive geography of the cinema, but only lead the reader through a series of soundings-out [*coups de sonde*], of explorations, of overviews [*survols*] that emerged as a response to viewing films in the day to day practice of being a critic.[5]

Thus, Bazin's value judgments (which define him most clearly as a critic) become theoretical processes, a working through of the question 'What is cinema?' (In many of his essays, this question might therefore be better posed as 'What does the cinema do *best*?') For Bazin, the innovations of great film-makers, such as the 'neorealist fact images' of Rossellini[6] or the sculptural unity of time and space in Gregg Toland's photography/Orson Welles's direction,[7] made him ask fundamental questions about the 'realism' of the cinema and its material basis in photography.[8] In Laleen Jayamanne's words:

> For Bazin, theorizing and criticism were not separate activities, as they were to become, to a large extent, in the 1970s and '80s academic film studies. The overvaluation of theory over criticism has, I believe, impoverished the field. Bazin's film criticism is still rewarding to read because of the way in which theoretical ideas and criticism work together.[9]

We do not want to risk nostalgia for some 'golden age' of film scholarship where, functioning more like a cottage industry, it allowed its pioneers much freer exploration. Film studies should not regret the greater rigour and variety of its more recent developments. However, we should be alive, as Jayamanne is, to how encounters with individual films and their moments (to echo the sense of encounter Bazin conjures *as a critic*) can help advance profound *theoretical* questions about film.[10]

Jayamanne's comment about the overvaluation of theory over criticism perhaps neglects the extent of the backlash *against* theory – or, rather, 'Theory' – that has occurred over the more recent years of film scholarship. The capital 'T' of 'Theory' designated a field of scholarship that was seen to pursue a single grand theory of the cinema, seeking a definitive answer to the question 'What is film?' While not wishing to resuscitate anything as grandiose or hubristic as this caricature of 'Theory', D. N. Rodowick, writing in 2007, expresses his concerns at the effects of this backlash on the field (and its effect on contemporary understandings of the digital developments of film). He notes:

> Film theory has fallen on hard times, even within the field of cinema studies itself. In the 1970s and early 1980s, many identified the field entirely with film theory, especially its Franco-British incarnation represented by the journal *Screen* and its importation from France of the work of Christian Metz, Roland Barthes, and others.[11]

The considerable impact of Metz, Barthes and 1970s '*Screen* Theory' (named after the journal Rodowick cites) on the field of film scholarship has been discussed in a number of places,[12] but it is worth saying here a little about the 'apparatus theory' that was central to this period, because of the problems it may pose for examining the film moment on its own terms:

> As Metz explained, 'the cinematic institution is not just the cinema industry ... it is also the mental machinery – another industry – which spectators "accustomed to the cinema" have internalized historically and which has adapted them to the consumption of films' ... . Thus the term 'cinematic apparatus' refers to both an industrial machine as well as a mental or psychic apparatus.[13]

It is important to stress the politicised nature of the film theory represented by the above definition of cinema as an 'ideological' apparatus. In France especially (Metz was French), leading up to and after the near revolution of May 1968,[14] film writing became increasingly politicised during the 1970s. For Metz and others the cinema represented 'mental machinery' that locked the spectator into a passive, rapt state whereby they did not question the 'reality' or the 'message' of what mainstream cinema presented to them; cinema, seen in this way, was an apparatus of tremendous ideological control. In this context, psychoanalytical theory was often called upon as a means of explaining these processes of psychic control. By definition, a concern for the apparatus over the individual film

text would have difficulty in seeing the film moment (at least of films from inside 'dominant ideology') as anything more than *symptomatic* of the cinematic apparatus their Theory outlined. The work emerging from the period of film theory that Rodowick cites would indeed be accused by many scholars of being ahistorical and insensitive to the complexities of individual texts.[15] In the current period, this backlash has arguably seen the valuation of the seemingly theory-less database by film historians (collections of 'unbiased', 'purely factual' data) and the routine denial of 'Theory' by practitioners of 'close analysis'.

Ultimately, citing the eddies and flows of film scholarship over the last forty or so years is less useful here than considering the particular value of the film moment for the student or scholar seeking to ask broadly 'theoretical' questions of film(s) and film studies. As a number of voices have suggested, and to echo the Brecht quotation at the start of this introduction, what we need is more *theorising* and less Theory.[16] Similar to the loss of confidence in the grand narratives of history (see the introduction to Part Two), we are increasingly wary of theories that might be construed as 'monolithic', unresponsive to the individual, local case. However, valuing the particular (the individual film, the individual moment) *at the expense of* wider frameworks risks throwing the baby out with the bathwater. It is the contention of this book that, for students and scholars of the cinema, the encounter with the moment in its detail and its potential complexity can be the ideal space in which to stage encounters with much broader questions.

In the way that the 'history' section demonstrated how the film moment may capture competing tendencies and traditions operating at a given historical moment, some of the moments examined in this section present moments that could be said to 'perform' theoretical issues. This is Alex Clayton's starting point for his consideration of how a moment from *Team America* (Parker, 2004) demands that we ask sophisticated questions of the ontology (that is, the study of being, existence and/or reality) of film performance. Clayton's essay eloquently puns on the possibility and problems of considering a 'puerile' film such as this 'performing' film theory and the question, 'Is a puppet on screen "performing"?' Similarly, Alison Butler, in examining a Jean- Luc Godard film (one of the film-makers Clayton cites as being often seen to 'perform film theory'), engages with and questions some of the fundamental oppositions operating within film theory. Butler shows how Godard's famously 'intertextual' style of film-making need not be diametrically opposed to notions of (André) 'Bazinian' realism. Other interesting parallels occur between the parts of the book. Elizabeth Cowie, for example, draws on ideas and concepts discussed historically by Thomas Elsaesser in Part Two: they consider the relationship between 'proper' and 'improper' viewing strategies and the edict 'Look, but don't touch' from two very different perspectives. Drawing on notions of voyeurism, Cowie's essay can be related to traditions and theories emerging from psychoanalysis.

A strand of film scholarship that explicitly defines itself against 1970s film Theory, particularly the psychoanalytical variety, is what is often known as 'cognitive film theory'. One of the key books to represent this body of work was named *Post-Theory*.[17] The editors are very careful to distinguish disagreement with film theory in a general sense from their argument against 'Theory', particularly of the psychoanalytic variety:

> What is coming after Theory is not another Theory but *theories* and the activity of *theorizing*. A theory of film defines a problem within the domain of cinema (defined nondogmatically) and sets out to solve it through logical reflection, empirical research or combination of both. *Theorizing* is a commitment to using the best canons of inference and evidence available to answer the question posed.[18]

Bordwell and Carroll here counter what they perceive as prescriptive Theory and suggest a range of approaches to theorising and a multiplicity of theories beyond just empirical research. However, a strand favoured in their collection, perhaps because of its empirical, scientific groundings, examines the activities of film spectatorship through the lens of cognitive psychology. 'Cognitive' is a scientific term for the processes of thought and, as Jonathan Frome's essay in this part discusses, its science is often concerned with examining mental processes that operate at an unconscious level and are thus taken for granted by most traditions of analysis in the humanities. Seen from this vantage point, the film moment can take on a special resonance and/or be discussed at a different experiential level. In considering the way the spectator tries to understand the 'chestburster' in *Alien* (Scott, 1979), Frome considers the spectator's reasoning across the whole film (in relation to 'suspense', for example) and reactions that take place in a fraction of a second (surprise, shock, for example). The advantage felt by scholars such as Frome, is that this theoretical approach does not rely on notions such as the 'ideal spectator' but bases its conclusions on things demonstrated in laboratory experiments.

Cognitive film theory's hostility to psychoanalysis is often linked to an apparent hostility towards interpretation (narrowly defined).[19] Indeed, Frome's essay explicitly elides 'deeper meanings' (he cites the chestburster being seen as a metaphor for child birth)[20] to demonstrate the value of considering the emotions and affects of the immediate experience of the film. However, there is nothing in Frome's account to suggest that cognitivism is incompatible with the kind of 'interpretative' readings offered in Part One; it provides a different means of understanding and expressing the data of spectatorial experience. Another

entry, by Lisa Purse, shows how broadly 'scientific' understandings can add another layer to the detailed engagement with the texture and style of the film moment. Purse's entry is an intervention in the expanding field of 'phenomenological film theory', offering fresh insights into the ethics of both film representation and spectatorship. (Phenomenology is the study of experience and, paralleling the developments of important strands of film theory, its presence in the humanities has moved from a basis in more interpretative-philosophical traditions to a more scientific approach.)[21]

A shift to emphasise the individual experience of film over monolithic accounts of the film apparatus has marked developments in film theory much more widely. Just as cognitive film theory is motivated partly by dissatisfaction with the seemingly passive, undifferentiated spectator that some 1970s film Theory set up, psychoanalytic theory was countered along other lines by developments of different theories of spectatorship, particularly those emerging out of feminist film theory (which grew out of the 1970s high point of Theory)[22] and later by 'queer film theory'.[23] The issues of 'identity' and 'identification' (the process by which spectators link their own identities to that of on-screen characters)[24] shifted the emphasis further towards considering the different meanings of individual films for different viewing publics. In line with much of the film theory discussed in this section, this was also seen as countering 'interpretative' film analysis because, instead of advancing a single reading of a film, scholars and theoreticians emphasised the multiplicity of meanings different viewers could take from a film. An extreme caricature of this relativist position would deny there was any hierarchy of interpretations – i.e. that no single reading could claim primacy over another. In reality, few scholars would deny the extent to which meanings are moored in the texts themselves, and this collection provides a good opportunity to connect theoretical and thematic interests in spectatorship and audience studies with the aesthetics of the film text. For example, Michele Aaron discusses the politics of audience involvement with *Hotel Rwanda* (George, 2004), understanding this through Emmanuel Levinas's concept of 'respons-ibility' as relayed through a particularly charged moment of looking *within* the film. Similarly, Barbara Klinger returns to a film of considerable importance to studies of female audiences.[25] Here, Klinger examines the contested ending(s) of *The Piano* (Campion, 1993) and engages with both the detail of the film moments themselves and with the detail of a number of conflicting readings of those endings, offering 'evidence of how indeterminate endings can animate the interpretive enterprise'.

One further fascinating development in the progression of film theory is the burgeoning impact of philosophical approaches on understandings of the medium. Perhaps the central figure in this movement has been American philosopher Stanley Cavell (mentioned briefly in the introduction to the criticism section of this book). Cavell has, in the past, acknowledged that certain suspicions are held about someone who writes about philosophy and about movies:

> The question has, I think without fail, come my way with philosophy put first: How is it that a professor of philosophy gets to thinking about Hollywood films? – as though becoming a professor of philosophy were easier to accept than thinking and writing about movies. So defensive have I grown that it took me a while to recognize that for most of my life the opposite direction of the question would have been more natural: How is it that someone whose education was as formed by going to the movies as by reading books, gets to thinking about philosophy professionally?[26]

William Rothman's chapter exemplifies this convergence between film and philosophy by framing questions of human thought and intention fluently within a close appreciation of Alfred Hitchcock's directorial style.[27] In a chapter that might be said to offer a complementary approach to these concerns, George Wilson's careful analysis of narration strategies in *Scarlet Street* (Lang, 1945) is guided by his equivalent commitment to the fields of philosophy and film. In the cases of Rothman and Wilson, therefore, the distinctions of philosopher/film theorist remain unfixed and, instead, the two are taken in combination.

By way of a contrast, Kristin Thompson's chapter on *The Lord of the Rings: The Return of the King* (Jackson, 2003) is significant not only for its detailed assessment of a moment from the film, but also for integrating underlying theoretical approaches with alternative methods of research and evaluation. Her analysis rests on an understanding of the distinction between Hollywood blockbusters and experimental cinema based upon certain formal characteristics. Furthermore, her attention to a series of cues, rules and prompts within the sequence she describes connects, at least partially, with certain principles of cognitive theory (as detailed above). However, Thompson introduces a further layer of understanding by turning first to questions of adaptation and then to audience reception. This dexterity results in a diverse exploration which underlines the extent to which a number of theoretical approaches and disciplines are available in the analysis of film. Indeed, there is evidence in Thompson's work that these may be profitably used *in combination*.

This book seeks to demonstrate *some* of the range of theoretical approaches to film available within the field but it is certainly more (though very partially) representative of current trends than the whole terrain of film theory. For example, one can imagine that there might be a productive return to some of the theory or theories that most of the entries in this section are 'post'; within 'classic film theory', there are some potentially very valuable alternative ways of examining the 'moment-ness' of the film moment. For example, disparate approaches sometimes brought under the umbrella of semiotics, post-structuralism and, more vaguely, 'deconstruction'[28] might value the moment, not for its unity with the wider meaning of the text and/or its consonance with wider frameworks, but for its disunity. Semiotics in the 1960s and 1970s was greatly interested in breaking texts up into smaller units, into 'signs'. For example, Roland Barthes moves through a Balzac novella bit by bit in his famous (and famously challenging) S/Z.[29] Moreover, one can imagine there being 'surrealist' or 'hysterical' readings of film moments that revel in unmooring it from context, something in line with Salvador Dali's wild, associative reading of a painting as discussed by Naomi Schor.[30] By and large the contributions contained in this section do not explore these possibilities. They retain the shape and form of the moment in order to reach their conclusions. While not representative of all positions and directions, the essays suggest the diversity of perspectives and approaches at work in film theory today. To this end, a series of chapters that place detail and precision at their core illustrates the breadth and vitality of the field.

NOTES

1. Quoted in Irene Makaryk, *Encyclopedia of Contemporary Literary Theory: Approaches, Scholars, Terms* (Toronto: University of Toronto, 1993), p. vii.
2. Quoted in John Gibbs and Douglas Pye (eds), *Style and Meaning: Studies in the Detailed Analysis of Film* (Manchester: Manchester University Press, 2005), p. 5.
3. For example, Andrew Klevan's entry could usefully be thought of as both valuing a moment from a film and valuing a (Stanley) 'Cavellian' conception of such moments. (Also see Klevan's forthcoming essay, 'Notes on Stanley Cavell and Philosophical Criticism', in Havi Carel and Greg Tuck (eds), *Film and Philosophy* (London: Palgrave Macmillan). Cavell's importance as a theorist is related to one who is mentioned at numerous points of this introduction in William Rothman's essay, 'Bazin as a Cavellian Realist', *Film Int.* vol. 5 no. 6, 2007, pp. 54–61. Importantly, however, in thinking about the relationship between criticism and theory, Klevan's analysis makes a series of moves (particularly over its later passages) that hold back from stressing external, theoretical frameworks to insist upon the *internal* frameworks that the film itself creates. This emphasis itself could be seen as an almost 'theoretical' stance on the cinema, but here we find ourselves going in circles and to insist too much on shifts from one approach to another is to perpetuate the unfortunate separation of criticism from theory that is regretted at various points of this introduction.

4. Thomas Elsaesser (ed.), *Early Cinema: Space, Frame, Narrative* (London: BFI, 1990), p. 411.

5. André Bazin, *Qu'est-ce que le cinéma?* (11th edn) (Paris: Les Éditions du Cerf, 1999), p. 7; my translation. I quote from a 1999 French edition of the book because the English-language versions of Bazin (widely available) have not translated this original Foreword, which was written in 1958, the year of his death.

6. See André Bazin, 'An Aesthetic of Reality: Cinematic Realism and the Italian School of the Liberation', in Hugh Gray [ed. and trans.], *What Is Cinema? Volume II* (Berkeley: University of California Press, 1971), pp. 16–40. Alison Butler discusses this concept in her entry.

7. See André Bazin, 'The Evolution of the Language of Cinema', in Hugh Gray [ed. and trans.], *What Is Cinema? Volume I* (Berkeley: University of California Press, 1967), pp. 23–40.

8. See particularly André Bazin, 'The Ontology of the Photographic Image', in Gray, *What Is Cinema? Volume I*, pp. 9–16.

9. Laleen Jayamanne, *Toward Cinema and Its Double: Cross-Cultural Mimesis* (Bloomington: Indiana University Press, 2001), p. 135.

10. A sense of the film 'moment' not examined in this book is suggested by Jayamanne (ibid.) in her re-reading of *Paisà* (Rossellini, 1946) through Gilles Deleuze's re-reading of Bazin. The title of this chapter of her book, 'Deleuzian Redemption of Bazin: Notes on the Neorealist Moment', suggests this and the ways the film moment takes on new significance (for Bazin and for Deleuze) with the development of neorealism.

11. D. N. Rodowick, *The Virtual Life of Film* (London: Harvard University Press, 2007), p. 3.

12. A useful overview is offered by Anthony Easthope, 'Classic Film Theory and Semiotics', in John Hill and Pamela Church Gibson (eds), *The Oxford Guide to Film Studies* (Oxford: Oxford University Press, 1998), pp. 51–7.

13. Barbara Creed, 'Film and Psychoanalysis', in Hill and Church Gibson, *The Oxford Guide to Film Studies*, p. 79.

14. For an entertaining reflection on this historical and cultural moment, see Bernardo Bertolucci's *The Dreamers* (2003), which is about the important links between cinephilia and the political unrest of this time.

15. See, for example, Creed, 'Film and Psychoanalysis', p. 82. For a critique of some of 1970s Theory's problems in dealing with the complexities of certain texts, see especially the first half of Andrew Britton's essay 'Metaphor and Mimesis: *Madame De …*', *Movie* nos 29–30, 1982, pp. 91–107.

16. Speaking at the 2009 *Screen* Studies Conference, marking the fiftieth anniversary of the journal, one of its editors, Annette Kuhn, looked back at the period of '1970s *Screen* Theory' (the italicisation and capitalisation were consciously highlighted in her speech) and noted the recent backlash against this critical moment. She did, however, stress the continued importance of 'theorising' to the discipline of film studies.

17. The full title further underlines its polemic intent: David Bordwell and Noël Carroll, *Post-Theory: Reconstructing Film Studies* (Madison: University of Wisconsin Press, 1996).

18. Ibid., p. xiv; italics in original.

19. One of the scholars most associated with cognitive film theory, David Bordwell, has written against 'interpretation' defined as a process of 'translating' latent (e.g. beneath the surface) meaning: *Making Meaning: Inference and Rhetoric in the Interpretation of Cinema* (London: Harvard University Press, 1989). For a passionate defence of interpretation, see V. F. Perkins, 'Must We Say What They Mean? Film Criticism and Interpretation', *Movie* nos 34–5, 1990, pp. 1–6.

20. Barbara Creed has considered this level of metaphor in *Alien* from a psychoanalytic perspective in *The Monstrous Feminine: Film, Feminism, Psychoanalysis* (London: Routledge, 1993), pp. 16–30.

21. For example, Bazin drew upon the philosophy of phenomenology in his writing on the cinema. See Lisa Purse's entry in this part for references to key work in more recent phenomenological film theory. In suggesting a distinction between philosophy and science, one has to admit to a potentially false opposition. One of the key distinctions *within* western philosophy (that between 'Anglo-American' or 'analytic' philosophy and its 'continental' counterpart) is often related to the use of scientific concepts such as those derived from cognitivism. See, for example, Richard Allen and Murray Smith (eds), *Film Theory and Philosophy* (Oxford: Clarendon, 1997), which presents primarily 'Anglo-American' and/or cognitive work.

22. See especially Laura Mulvey, *Visual and Other Pleasures* (Basingstoke: Macmillan, 1989).

23. For an introduction, see Alexander Doty, 'Queer Theory', in Hill and Church Gibson, *The Oxford Guide to Film Studies*, pp. 148–52.

24. Within film theory, 'identification' has been critiqued by, for example, Murray Smith, *Engaging Characters: Fiction, Emotion, and the Cinema* (Oxford: Clarendon Press, 1995).

25. See the special section on *The Piano* in *Screen* vol. 36 no. 3, Autumn 1995, pp. 257–87. Klinger has also written about the film before: 'The Art Film, Affect, and the Female Viewer: *The Piano* Reconsidered', *Screen* vol. 47 no. 1, Spring 2006, pp. 19–41.

26. Stanley Cavell, *Themes out of School: Effects and Causes* (Chicago, IL: University of Chicago Press, 1988), p. 4.

27. Rothman was a colleague of Cavell's at Harvard for a number of years.

28. See Peter Brunette, 'Post-structuralism and Deconstruction', in Hill and Church Gibson, *The Oxford Guide to Film Studies*, pp. 91–5.

29. Roland Barthes, *S/Z* [trans. Richard Miller] (Oxford: Blackwell, 2002).

30. Naomi Schor, *Reading in Detail: Aesthetics and the Feminine* (London: Routledge, 2007), pp. 121–31. Schor's celebration of Barthes's account of the 'detail' (a unit in the analysis of the art comparable in some ways to the moment for film) is also suggestive of these potential other approaches to the film moment; see especially ibid., pp. 93–117.

BIBLIOGRAPHY

Allen, Richard and Smith, Murray (eds), *Film Theory and Philosophy* (Oxford: Clarendon, 1997).

Barthes, Roland, *S/Z* [trans. Richard Miller] (Oxford: Blackwell, 2002).

Bazin, André, 'The Ontology of the Photographic Image', in Hugh Gray [ed. and trans.], *What Is Cinema? Volume I* (Berkeley: University of California Press, 1967), pp. 9–16.

Bazin, André, 'The Evolution of the Language of Cinema', in Gray, *What Is Cinema? Volume I*, pp. 23–40.

Bazin, André, 'An Aesthetic of Reality: Cinematic Realism and the Italian School of the Liberation', in Hugh Gray [ed. and trans.], *What Is Cinema? Volume II* (Berkeley: University of California Press, 1971), pp. 16–40.

Bazin, André, *Qu'est-ce que le cinéma?* (11th edn) (Paris: Les Éditions du Cerf, 1999).

Bordwell, David, *Making Meaning: Inference and Rhetoric in the Interpretation of Cinema* (London: Harvard University Press, 1989).

Bordwell, David and Carroll, Noël, *Post-Theory: Reconstructing Film Studies* (Madison: University of Wisconsin Press, 1996).

Britton, Andrew, 'Metaphor and Mimesis: *Madame De …*', *Movie* nos 29–30, 1982, pp. 91–107.

Brunette, Peter, 'Post-structuralism and Deconstruction', in John Hill and Pamela Church Gibson (eds), *The Oxford Guide to Film Studies* (Oxford: Oxford University Press, 1998), pp. 91–5.

Carel, Havi and Tuck, Greg (eds), *Film and Philosophy* (London: Palgrave Macmillan, forthcoming).

Cavell, Stanley, *Themes out of School: Effects and Causes* (Chicago, IL: University of Chicago Press, 1988).

Creed, Barbara, *The Monstrous Feminine: Film, Feminism, Psychoanalysis* (London: Routledge, 1993).

Creed, Barbara, 'Film and Psychoanalysis', in Hill and Church Gibson, *The Oxford Guide to Film Studies*, pp. 77–90.

Doty, Alexander, 'Queer Theory', in Hill and Church Gibson, *The Oxford Guide to Film Studies*, pp. 148–52.

Easthope, Anthony, 'Classic Film Theory and Semiotics', in Hill and Church Gibson, *The Oxford Guide to Film Studies*, pp. 51–7.

Elsaesser, Thomas (ed.), *Early Cinema: Space, Frame, Narrative* (London: BFI, 1990).

Gibbs, John and Pye, Douglas (eds), *Style and Meaning: Studies in the Detailed Analysis of Film* (Manchester: Manchester University Press, 2005).

Hill, John and Gibson, Pamela Church (eds), *The Oxford Guide to Film Studies* (Oxford: Oxford University Press, 1998).

Jayamanne, Laleen, *Toward Cinema and Its Double: Cross-Cultural Mimesis* (Bloomington: Indiana University Press, 2001).

Klevan, Andrew, 'Notes on Stanley Cavell and Philosophical Criticism', in Carel and Tuck, *Film and Philosophy*.

Klinger, Barbara, 'The Art Film, Affect, and the Female Viewer: *The Piano* Reconsidered', *Screen* vol. 47 no. 1, Spring 2006, pp. 19–41.

Makaryk, Irene, *Encyclopedia of Contemporary Literary Theory: Approaches, Scholars, Terms* (Toronto: University of Toronto, 1993).

Mulvey, Laura, *Visual and Other Pleasures* (Basingstoke: Macmillan, 1989).

Perkins, V. F., 'Must We Say What They Mean? Film Criticism and Interpretation', *Movie* nos 34–5 (1990), pp. 1–6.

Rodowick, D. N., *The Virtual Life of Film* (London: Harvard University Press, 2007).

Rothman, William, 'Bazin as a Cavellian Realist', *Film Int.* vol. 5 no. 6, 2007, pp. 54–61.

Schor, Naomi, *Reading in Detail: Aesthetics and the Feminine* (London: Routledge, 2007).

Smith, Murray, *Engaging Characters: Fiction, Emotion, and the Cinema* (Oxford: Clarendon Press, 1995).

Performance, with Strings Attached: *Team America*'s (2004) Snub to the Actor

ALEX CLAYTON

A fruitful approach to certain moments in certain films is to consider them to be exploring the possibilities and conditions of their medium, to be playing out theoretical postulates and ideas in ways that might illuminate our understanding of cinema more widely. It has become almost customary to treat moments from, say, Hitchcock or Godard in this way, and indeed moments from many great films of the Hollywood studio era and European 'art cinema' can justifiably be seen as *performing* film theory, rather than merely providing illustration. The distinction is important because the word 'performing' grants a certain thought and agency to the film, whereas the word 'illustration' consigns it to the status of mere object. But how much thoughtful agency are we willing to grant to a film as silly and contemptuous as *Team America – World Police* (Parker, 2004)? It is my contention that this puerile puppet-based parody undertakes, non-systematically and with tongue in cheek, a playful meditation on the ontology of screen performance, feeding into a critique of our culture's insistent glorification of the celebrity actor. It asserts its own licence to do so precisely because no actors appear on the screen.

Team America is most appreciably a bare-toothed satire of dumb foreign policy, specifically the shock-and-awe machismo of the Bush-era 'war on terror', and also – less fashionably – of the smug complacency and self-promotion of the Hollywood liberal left. This is a belligerent world of puffed egos and insufficient intelligence on either side, a world in which everyone seems to act clumsily. Destruction and negligence issue from a pernicious fantasy of the virtue of acting decisively, unilaterally. This is a film about acting, in various senses of the word, and about the praise of actors. When a statuette is presented, with pomp and ceremony, to an individual for Best Actor, are we seeing more than the ritual ratification of Hollywood myth? What does it mean to single out an actor for praise? What is a performance, anyway?

An early moment crystallises *Team America*'s interest in these matters satirical and ontological. Gary Johnson, all-American top-gun actor, has just concluded a barnstorming,

tear-jerking performance of the progressive Broadway number, 'Everyone Has Aids'. As he emerges backstage, applause still shaking the rafters, he is greeted by a volley of sycophantic acclaim.

'That was the greatest acting I have ever seen,' quacks an obsequious stagehand. 'I just don't know how you do it, Gary,' chirps a second, his puppet mouth flashing open and closed. 'How do you make yourself so sombre and emotional and make everybody cry like that?' 'It's not that hard, really …' muses Gary, and the film cuts to a close-up of his shiny plastic face. 'I just think about the saddest moment in my life …'. With this, he moves ponderously away, his stiff body dragged out of frame, leaving the stagehands to dead-gaze after him: 'Hey, wow. Gary is such a great guy.'

Central to the comic effect of this scene is the relationship between the rhetoric of praise and the palpable non-agency of marionettes. A certain animal-robotic monotone of vocal delivery works, here as elsewhere in the film, to suggest words being mindlessly spouted rather than meant – shallow cheerleading, in this instance, rather than considered judgment. In relation to what we have seen of Gary's onstage posing and jiggling, the tribute of 'greatest acting ever' seems especially ludicrous. Clearly the word 'acting' still endows a sense of kudos and respectability to the form of showmanship being applauded. More specifically, the various dynamic verbs littered through the quoted dialogue ('to do', 'to make', along

with 'to act') appeal to an idea of acting as a form of originative *doing*, a creative solo triumph of internal volition.
The stagehands' valuation of the actor's capacity to 'make
[him]self … sombre and emotional' links the terms of
esteem in which actors are held to wider cultural values
attached to conspicuous emotional expression. Having
paraded their compassion by wearing ribbons of all stripes
on the red carpet, actors at award ceremonies stand a good
chance of winning a prize if they have portrayed a character with a disability or a disease – the starkest indication
that being a 'great actor' is all but equated with being a
'great guy'. Both are estimated according to the degree to
which one's behaviour manifests an emotional core. The
capacity to project one's own interiority outwards is
applauded above all.

Puppets, of course, have no interiority to project –
hence the joke in the dialogue's reference to method-
acting technique, with the punchline of cutting to magnify
the puppet's glassy-eyed stare. The ensuing sequence
pushes this a little further, aping the Hollywood convention of meditative off-screen gazing as trite registration of
an emotional inner life: Gary perches before his dressing
room and looks at an old family photograph pinned to the
mirror. The reverse-field editing between marionette and
photo, supplemented with half-explanatory sound effects
of growling creatures and distant screams, enacts a
Kuleshovian delineation of the character's trauma, even as
we are invited to understand this trauma as the reservoir
for Gary's Stanislavskian emotion-memory technique. The
parodic flavour of the moment presses forward something
about film performance more generally. Rather than the
on-screen figure projecting 'inner' thought and feeling outwards, the illusion of interior life is created by *external*
means: the slow zoom into the puppet's face as expressive
of an emerging memory, the shallow depth of field isolat-
ing the figure from the background to create a private
space of reflection, the echoes of ravenous baboons as an
aural flashback.

As with live-body performance, we are still able to
weigh the effect of particular physical movements – the
slight shift of the eyebrows, the blink, the slowly tilting
head – yet these no longer seem to originate from the

figure in front of us but appear as external forcings. In
other words, a puppet does not perform; it *is* performed.

Is this only the case with puppetry? Why do we not
tend to speak of human bodies 'being performed' – shep-
herded, like cattle perhaps, as in Hitchcock's famous put-
down of actors? Peter Lehman has gone so far as to say
that the film 'performance' does not exist. The 'performance' we perceive is constructed from camera positions
and movements, as well as cutting patterns, etc., over
which the actors and actresses generally have no knowledge or control. Thus, effects we attribute to them (for
example, a powerful look) may have nothing to do with
them. An effect may derive from the way the camera dol-
lies in on the actor, combined with the work the lighting
pattern may shadow on the face.[1]

Lehman's assertion, inhabiting a vein of tradition in
film studies following Pudovkin's contention that the effectiveness of acting is largely a product of 'cinematicisation',
clearly shares territory with the implications of the *Team
America* sequence.[2] Against what we might call the 'originative' conception of film acting, we might posit the
'extrinsic' conception. From this perspective, a 'performance' is not a solo achievement emerging from within, but
an effect resulting from the way (often multiple) bodies are
deployed (placed, arranged, situated in frame and narrative, and so on). Moreover, the extrinsic conception points
to film-making as a process in which gestures and movements have been communally or hierarchically devised,
hence externally urged – as they are, perceptibly, in puppetry. In this light, the motif of puppets being dragged,
along, with the often pronounced visibility of the puppets'
strings, throughout *Team America*, and particularly during
this sequence, can be seen as a claim towards the demys-
tification of an originative conception of performance.

Following the implications of the extrinsic conception
of performance, the distinction between *acting* – as technical practice – and *performance* – as the all-important mobil-
isation of that practice – becomes sharper. If we wanted to
praise the performance of uncertain menace in the opening sequence of Hitchcock's *Notorious* (1946), for example,
in which Cary Grant's largely stationary body inhabits the
foreground in silhouette, we would be unlikely to want to
praise the acting *first*. Accordingly, the line between performance and *mise en scène* becomes more blurry. A later
sequence in *Team America* enacts a comic demonstration of
this: we see the Gary puppet standing at the Lincoln
Memorial Building in a static pose of contemplation and
patriotic inner stirring. Here, the pan from the seated
Abraham Lincoln down to the marionette, resting dwarfed
and unattended at his feet, draws the relevant connection:
the puppet has become a statue. We are returned to the
idea that performance requires visible volition. If it seems
a stretch to call the patriotically roused puppet a performance, it is because the volitional movement that placed the

object there took place before the cameras started rolling – and we normally call this *mise en scène*.

A purely extrinsic conception of performance would have to admit to little ontological difference between actors and puppets. This is, indeed, part of what the Kuleshovian moment at the dressing-room mirror cheekily proposes: that a puppet can perform as well as most Hollywood actors. Yet the comic enactment of the proposal also suggests its limitations. The sequence draws attention to the severely restricted range of facial expressions in the on-screen figure, the ungainly effort of physical movement, the flatness of vocal delivery. This is as much a parody of masculine stiffness and mindlessness in the action genre as it is an exhibition of the film's own *refusal* of fluidity – specifically the fluidity that is the inevitable consequence of filming a thinking being. Puppets are not actors because puppets are not people: puppets are *literally* mindless. Hence, to define performance merely as the deployment of a body overlooks the fact that performing bodies must be, at the very least, *mindful of an audience* – something that a puppet can never be.

Besides puppetry, other useful test cases for assessing the parameters of performance may include documentary footage and the use of animals in fiction. Documentary footage – say, of people in the street – may 'deploy' bodies without their consent. But if we want to say that people in the footage are performing, it would presumably mean that we believe them to *know* they are performing, that we understand them to be mindful of the camera, or of a potential 'audience' of other people around them, in the sense of social performance.[3] Animals also offer a useful enigma. Monkeys and dogs are sometimes employed as 'actors' – but are they performing if we don't grant them the knowledge that they are performing? We would struggle to call a dog or monkey scratching itself a performance unless it had been trained to do so, and on cue. Carrying out simple procedures for a banana or a biscuit involves perhaps the *minimum* level of purposeful volition required for the attribution of the term, with the key distinction being that knowledge of a reward presupposes – perhaps – an awareness of being observed.

So what is a performance? The originative conception (a satirical target of the *Team America* sequence, as I hope I have shown) conflates acting and performance and fails to recognise sufficiently its collaboratively and externally constructed nature. The extrinsic conception (postulated by the *Team America* sequence, albeit with tongue in cheek) too readily dismisses the actor's craft and fails to appreciate sufficiently the necessary condition that performers must be understood to be conscious of performing (the reason why puppets are not performers). As a result, I suggest defining performance as the *deployment of a body that is mindful of an audience*. This would include the passerby who waves at the documentary camera and exclude the passerby who is lost in her own world. It would include Cary Grant's sitting in the foreground in *Notorious*, not because of what he does but because of what we can reasonably assume about his mindfulness of being filmed. The designation of 'mindful' does not mean that everything performed must be intentional. Rather, it allows for a performance to be a performance even if the *total* deployment of the body (through editing, framing, narrative placement and so on) renders it completely at variance with what was intended by any single actor.

In the case of *Team America*, there are bodies on screen but none of them are mindful. The performing bodies are those deployed beyond the edges of the frame, distinguishable as performers because they produce volitional movements that embody a mindfulness of the camera's placement. Their non-visibility places them, culturally speaking, as behind-the-scenes technicians and makes an award for Best Actor – or a personal audience with the President, for that matter – unlikely. Yet, in truth, actors are technicians among many who work to fashion a performance; they are not alone in pulling the strings. Singling out the actor for praise, whether in the form of criticism or award ceremonies, sustains a myth of acting as individual creative doing – a notion which may lead to misattribution of merit, encourage unbalanced or unsynthesised forms of performance, and perhaps even serve to ratify the mostly pernicious cult of celebrity of the kind that is satirised in *Team America*. We would be foolish to deny the actor's probable contribution to the skill and craft involved in creating an on-screen performance. But we should be clear, when we praise, what we are praising. Puppetry involves an on-screen–off-screen separation between technician and object, even in their symbiosis. In live-body performance, the distinction is less palpable, but it remains pertinent. On-screen actors are audiovisual entities as well as craftspeople, and the two facets are often conflated. We have a habit of praising the actor-as-artist when more truthfully we are admiring the actor-as-object.

NOTES

1. Peter Lehman, 'Editorial', *Wide Angle* vol. 6 no. 4, 1984, pp. 2–3. Thanks to Kathrina Glitre for bringing this passage to my attention.
2. V. I. Pudovkin, *Film Technique and Film Acting* (New York: Grove Press, 1960), p. 319.
3. See Erving Goffman, *The Presentation of Self in Everyday Life* (London and New York: Penguin, 1990).

BIBLIOGRAPHY

Goffman, Erving, *The Presentation of Self in Everyday Life* (London and New York: Penguin, 1990).
Lehman, Peter, 'Editorial', *Wide Angle* vol. 6 no. 4, 1984, pp. 2–3.
Pudovkin, V. I., *Film Technique and Film Acting* (New York: Grove Press, 1960), p. 319.

Éloge de l'Amour (2001): Moments in Time

ALISON BUTLER

> Practically, we perceive only the past.
>
> Henri Bergson[1]

The moment in time has particular significance in *Éloge de l'amour/In Praise of Love* (Jean-Luc Godard, France/ Switzerland, 2001). The film addresses a constellation of temporal themes, including the past, memory, history and, with specific reference to World War II, resistance, remembrance and reparation. When a character in the film urges another to read Bergson, Godard registers an interest in time as a philosophical concern. There is a significant and growing body of challenging and often very abstract scholarship on time in the cinema. In this essay I will explore some of the issues raised by these studies by focusing on two moments (single shots, in fact) from different sections of the film, which, through repetition and variation, set up a dialogue about time, memory and the image.

The narrative of *Éloge* is so elliptical that without the press book it might not have been grasped by critics and viewers. The project had a long and convoluted development, during which the script took a number of different forms. The finished film is littered with the debris of the abandoned schemes and organising structures: it has two parts, one in black-and-white 35mm film, the other in colour-saturated digital video; two timeframes, 'the present' and 'two years earlier'; it is structured reflexively around two film projects; one of these is about the four moments of love (meeting, passion, separation, reconciliation) and the three ages of man (childhood, adulthood and old age). For all this schematisation, *Éloge* remains obscure and uneventful. Edgar (Bruno Putzulu), the main character, is developing an artistic project of a relatively undecided nature, having apparently abandoned a previous project, a cantata for Simone Weil. He has some discussions with Berthe (Cécile Camp), a woman who works by day in a bookshop and by night as a cleaner, about her possible involvement in this project. His elderly patron, Rosenthal (Claude Baignières), is engaged in the reacquisition of artworks taken by the Nazis from a gallery owned by his father and Edgar's grandfather. Rosenthal's interest in Edgar comes from a romantic attachment to Edgar's

mother that endures despite the fact that she is long dead, having committed suicide after her husband's accidental death. Berthe's parents also committed suicide during her childhood, as a result, it is implied, of the failure of 1968. Berthe's grandparents, the Bayards (Jean Davy and Françoise Verny), are Holocaust survivors and former resistance fighters whose story may be bought by Steven Spielberg. Through a passing remark made by Bruno, Godard invokes the psychological theory that the traumatic historical legacy of Holocaust survivors bypasses their children and manifests itself in their grandchildren. At the end of the first section of the film Edgar learns that Berthe has killed herself.

Like Edgar's projects, the relationship between Edgar and Berthe is abortive, perhaps as a result of psychological blockages on both sides. The elliptical narrative strategy is followed through in the film's patterning of images with black leader and white-on-black intertitles. The presentation of images, sounds and words as fragments circumscribes their beauty – and truth – with a sense of loss. This melancholy tone is reinforced by the use, throughout the film, of the plangent neotonal music of Ketil Bjornstad and David Darling.[2] Godard breaks the music into phrases, some resolved, some unresolved. Because of their intensely melodic character, the resolved fragments convey a feeling of ending, while those that are unresolved evoke the feeling of an anticipated conclusion indefinitely suspended.

The first moment I am going to look at occurs towards the end of a sequence in which Edgar and Berthe take a late-night/early-morning walk by the Seine, during which they discuss a number of things, including the relationship between stories and history. The shot is preceded by black leader and by music that continues over it. The space of the shot, a medium close-up, is a portion of an earlier shot. Edgar appears on the left, viewed from behind and bisected by the edge of the frame. To the right, the river and derelict industrial buildings are visible. This composition is a stylisation of the conventional over-the-shoulder view, framed to exaggerate the elegant line of the head and shoulder. The viewer is distanced by the fact that it is held static for

longer than usual and is not followed by the conventional complementary reverse shot (which Godard habitually avoids when filming conversations). Edgar says:

> When I think of something, in fact, I'm thinking of something else. You can't think of something without thinking of something else. For example, you see a landscape that's new to you, but it's new to you because you compare it in your mind to a familiar landscape, one that you know.[3]

Berthe leans into the frame, removes her coat and hat, and speaks to Edgar, her mouth close to his ear and her speech inaudible to the viewer. This is the moment of greatest intimacy between the two characters, not least because it excludes us. Backlighting obscures her features (there are no full-face close-ups of Berthe in the film and in the first part she is usually seen in shadow). The song on the soundtrack comes to the fore briefly then stops abruptly, after which Edgar asks Berthe if that's Auteuil down there, and she says she thinks so.

The song comes from Maurice Jaubert's soundtrack for Jean Vigo's *L'Atalante* (1934), a film famously set on and around the Seine. *L'Atalante* is about love and work, Godard's perennial themes, but is as joyful and direct as *Éloge* is melancholy and oblique, evoking a cinematic lost innocence. The location is on the banks of the river facing Seguin Island, the famous home of Renault's flagship car factory, an icon of France's post-war industrial boom and, because of a thirty-three-day strike there in 1968, a major symbol of the workers' movement (Edgar calls it the 'empty fortress' of the CGT (Confédération générale du travail)).[4] While the historical significance of the setting of Seguin Island is clearly recognised by the characters, the reference to *L'Atalante* is not anchored in any diegetic point of view. The absence of a fully articulated system of diegetic points of view and the tendency of quoted texts to exist independently of the characters is a characteristic of

the film in general. Although the image of Edgar's head viewed from behind suggests a metonym for consciousness, which could lead us to expect the film to deploy the classic art-cinema strategy of free indirect subjective narration,[5] the fact that we don't hear the conversation emphasises our exclusion from Edgar's point of view. This in turn locates the reference to *L'Atalante* outside the characters' subjectivity, as shared cultural knowledge evoked by the Seine.

Godard's practice of quotation has often been understood in terms of intertextuality and, as such, opposed to certain realist aesthetics. However, his own statements about quotation suggest a more complex understanding of their use: 'I tried to establish a balance between literary quotations, verbal quotations and also quotations from nature. In this film there is the quotation of water, the quotation of trees.'[6] Many of the quotations in *Éloge* are concerned with cinematic realism, such as Roberto Rossellini's dictum, 'Things exist. Why make them up?', the numerous quotations from Robert Bresson's *Notes on the Cinematographer*, and the film posters for Samira Makhmalbhaf's *The Apple* and Bresson's *Pickpocket* (tendentiously placed beside a poster for *The Matrix*). Some of the non-professional actors who appear in the film are effectively citations of themselves, including the historian Jean Lacouture and the Holocaust survivor and film-maker Marceline Loridan Ivens.[7] Quotation here is not conceived primarily in terms of semiotic intertexts, but rather in terms of Bazinian image-facts: found fragments of reality supporting a fictional narrative.[8]

Edgar's speech, though not recognisably a quotation, evokes both the art criticism of André Malraux ('We are able to feel only through comparisons')[9] and the philosophical account of perception and memory given by Henri Bergson:

> [W]hile external perception provokes on our part movements which retrace its main lines, our memory directs upon the perception received the memory-images which resemble it [...]. Memory thus creates anew the present perception, or rather it doubles this perception by reflecting upon it either its own image or some other memory-image of the same kind.[10]

In an attempt to overcome the dualities between mind and matter, body and spirit that characterise the western philosophical tradition, Bergson argued that matter is an aggregate of images and that there is ontological continuity between matter, perception and memory. His enigmatic pronouncement that photography 'is already developed in the very heart of things, and at all the points in space'[11] seems congruent with André Bazin's film theory which posits ontological continuity between photographic images and their referents. Like Bergson, Bazin was interested in the temporality of images, famously calling cinema 'change mummified'.[12] Isabelle McNeill comments on the way that *Éloge* makes use of the 'nature of the cinematic medium, itself, which always conserves something of the profilmic event, while signifying the inevitable loss of that event, consigned to the past'.[13] By populating the film with relics of the past – including the derelict factory on Seguin Island and Jaubert's film music – Godard underscores the enduring connection between the past and the present. Edgar's frontal placement makes him the locus of a perception of this connection, but the withholding of his point of view also situates it beyond him, in a shared cultural landscape. Interposed between matter and memory, Godard's Bazinian cinema objectifies their interrelationship. By framing recollection as a matter of objective registration and shared cultural reference, this shot encapsulates cinema's function as a repository of past time.

The second moment I want to discuss comes from the second part of the film, which is in digital video and colour and is set in Brittany in the recent past. It is accompanied by a melodious ten-second phrase from Bjornstad and Darling's 'Epigraphs', on strings and piano, which fades away just before the anticipated resolution. The shot comprises two images, one superimposed on the other: a narrow headland with a lighthouse flashing at sunset, with sea in the foreground and a clouded sky above, and, in front of this, Edgar's head, seen from behind (leaning, as we subsequently realise, on the headrest of his train seat, in the shots that follow). The image is in vivid fauvist colour – cobalt blue sea and clouds, brilliant green, yellow and orange sky. At first the seascape is briefly stilled, then the waves begin to move and the shot gradually widens. The slight unsteadiness of the head shot creates a floating effect, while the use of the zoom to reframe the view cues us to read backward motion in the image, as if Edgar is travelling away from the land, until the movement ends with the appearance, at the bottom of the frame, of waves

breaking on another shore. On the soundtrack, Edgar repeats his earlier speech, this time speaking more softly, above the ambient sound of the waves. The repetition is not quite word for word, and one of the key changes is that the speech is now entirely in the first person and its final verb is in the past imperfect tense. As he speaks the words 'another landscape, one that I used to know', the film cuts to a blurred view of trees seen from the window of the speeding train taking Edgar from Brittany to Paris, with Edgar's reflection just glimpsed in the glass of the train window. Past time is layered into this image: the narrative locates it 'two years earlier', the dialogue is a repetition of something already heard (although in diegetic time, it comes later), the superimposed image of Edgar locates him on the train, which determines that the seascape is a memory-image, and the vivid colours suggest the enhancements of memory.[14] The image of the train window, with the 'found' superimposition of the reflection, echoes and prolongs the image that immediately precedes it, as if through retinal retention. Where the first moment leans towards objectivity and the Bazinian inscription of a shared past, the second moment leans towards subjectivity and the dynamic reworking of memory.

The technological shift between these two images, from film to digital video, has particular implications. Godard's fauvist or Impressionist colourism associates the use of digital video here with the historical moment when painting was released from its realist vocation by photography, of which Bazin said: 'Only when form ceases to have any imitative value can it be swallowed up in color.'[15] The association of digital video with painting and graphic art has also been made by new-media theorist Lev Manovich.[16] The transition from analogue to digital media has provoked renewed theoretical debate concerning the significance of indexicality in analogue media and new speculation about the possibilities created – and destroyed – by the severance of that tie to material reality. As one of those who has consistently and for some time lamented the death of cinema while also engaging with video technology, Godard stands in an interesting relationship to these debates. In the digital section of the film, Berthe recites a quotation from Maurice Blanchot: 'The image, alone capable of denying nothingness, is also the gaze of nothingness on us.' This comes from 'The Museum, Art and Time', an essay on Malraux's *The Voices of Silence*,[17] in which Blanchot argues that the museum extracts art from society and history, so that each work becomes a marker of time, a sign of its own absence from time, 'a fascinating arrow pointed in the direction of the impossible'.[18] Blanchot's conclusions are in marked contrast to those of Malraux, who famously remarked on the ability of humans to draw from themselves images powerful enough to deny their own nothingness. Blanchot's point acquires new meaning in the context of a film that enacts the passage from the cinematic image, which is automatically linked to the moment of registration, to the digital image, which has no ontological tie to the time in which the image was captured.

Towards the end of his working life, Godard has increasingly allied himself with painterly tradition, and in *Éloge* he seems to work through a technological transition that brings his work closer to painting but at the cost of the loss of what defined the cinema in the twentieth century. Digital video makes it easier for film-makers to create images like those in their heads, but only by turning away from material reality. Perhaps this is the meaning of the image of Edgar's head in the clouds – or the clouds in his head. Bergson associated memory with a diminished attention to the practicalities of life and a tendency to dream. It is also common to experience a resurgence of memories in old age. Just before the film's close, as the train arrives in Paris, Edgar, in voiceover, quotes Chateaubriand's memoirs, which he is holding in his hand:

> That is how everything in my story vanishes without trace, so that I am left with nothing but images of what has passed so quickly. I will descend to the Elysian Fields with more shades than any man has ever taken with him.[19]

Less about love than it is about loss, *Éloge de l'amour* is an elegy for a certain form of cinematic time.

NOTES

1. Henri Bergson, *Matter and Memory* (New York: Zone Books, 1991), p. 150.
2. Ketil Bjornstad and David Darling, 'Epigraphs' (ECM, 1998). Along with original compositions by Bjornstad and Darling, the album includes arrangements of Renaissance composers including Orlando Gibbons and William Byrd.
3. Quand je pense à quelque chose, en fait, je pense à autre chose. On ne peut penser à quelque chose que si on pense à autre chose. Par exemple, vous voyez un paysage nouveau pour vous, mais il est nouveau pour vous parce que vous le comparez en pensée, à une autre paysage ancien, celui-là que vous connaissez.
4. The buildings on Seguin Island were demolished three years after the release of *Éloge*, making the film itself a historical record.
5. Free indirect narration in a story is told in the second person but inflected by the protagonist's consciousness. On the free indirect subjective in cinema, see Pier Paolo Pasolini, 'The Cinema of Poetry', in Bill Nichols (ed.), *Movies and Methods: An Anthology, Volume 1* (Berkeley: University of California Press, 1976).
6. Godard in 1990, press conference for *Nouvelle vague*, cited in Harun Farocki and Kaja Silverman, *Speaking about Godard* (New York: New York University Press, 1998), p. 242.
7. Marceline Loridan Ivens appeared as herself in Jean Rouch and Edgar Morin's *Chronique d'un été* (1962) and made films with her husband Joris Ivens as well as on her own.
8. André Bazin, 'An Aesthetic of Reality: Neorealism', in Hugh Gray [ed. and trans.], *What Is Cinema? Volume II* (Berkeley and Los Angeles: University of California Press, 2004).
9. Cited by Antoine de Baecque, 'Godard in the Museum', in Michael Temple, James S. Williams and Michael Witt (eds), *For Ever Godard* (London: Black Dog Publishing, 2004), p. 120. De Baecque notes the pervasive influence of Malraux on Godard's later work. Probably not by coincidence, the historian, Jean Lacouture, who appears in *Éloge*, is also Malraux's biographer.
10. Bergson, *Matter and Memory*, p. 101.
11. Ibid., p. 38.
12. André Bazin, 'The Ontology of the Photographic Image', in Hugh Gray [ed. and trans.], *What Is Cinema? Volume I* (Berkeley and Los Angeles: University of California Press, 2004), p. 15.
13. Isabelle McNeill, 'Phrases, Monuments and Ruins: Melancholy History in *Éloge de l'amour* (2001)', *Studies in French Cinema* vol. 3 no. 2, 2002, pp. 111–12.
14. The image of the coast of Brittany is also linked to memory by Godard in interviews, where he talks about childhood holidays and trips with Anne-Marie Miéville's grandchildren there.
15. Bazin, 'The Ontology of the Photographic Image', p. 16.
16. Lev Manovich, 'What Is Cinema?', in *The Language of New Media* (Boston, MA: MIT Press, 2002).
17. The essay can be found in Maurice Blanchot, *Friendship* [trans. Elizabeth Rottenberg] (Stanford, CA: Stanford University Press, 1997). The same Blanchot essay is cited in Godard and Miéville's short film essay on art and the museum, 'The Old Place' (1998): 'Art wasn't protected from time. It was the protection of time.'
18. Ibid., p. 38.
19. François-René de Chateaubriand, *Mémoires d'outre-tombe* (Paris: LGF/Livre de Poche, 1984) [my translation from the film].

BIBLIOGRAPHY

Bazin, André, 'The Ontology of the Photographic Image', in Hugh Gray [ed. and trans.], *What Is Cinema? Volume I* (Berkeley and Los Angeles: University of California Press, 2004).

Bazin, André, 'An Aesthetic of Reality: Neorealism', in Hugh Gray [ed. and trans.], *What Is Cinema? Volume II* (Berkeley and Los Angeles: University of California Press, 2004).

Bergson, Henri, *Matter and Memory* (New York: Zone Books, 1991).

Blanchot, Maurice, *Friendship* [trans. Elizabeth Rottenberg] (Stanford, CA: Stanford University Press, 1997).

de Baecque, Antoine, 'Godard in the Museum', in Michael
    Temple, James S. Williams and Michael Witt (eds), *For Ever
    Godard* (London: Black Dog Publishing, 2004).

de Chateaubriand, François-René, *Mémoires d'outre-tombe*
    (Paris: LGF/Livre de Poche, 1984) [my translation from the
    film].

Farocki, Harun and Silverman, Kaja, *Speaking about Godard*
    (New York: New York University Press, 1998).

Manovich, Lev, *The Language of New Media* (Boston, MA: MIT
    Press, 2002).

McNeill, Isabelle, 'Phrases, Monuments and Ruins: Melancholy
    History in *Éloge de l'amour* (2001)', *Studies in French Cinema*
    vol. 3 no. 2, 2002.

Pasolini, Pier Paolo, 'The Cinema of Poetry', in Bill Nichols
    (ed.), *Movies and Methods: An Anthology, Volume 1* (Berkeley:
    University of California Press, 1976).

Temple, Michael, Williams, James S. and Witt, Michael (eds),
    For Ever Godard (London: Black Dog Publishing, 2004).

Contested Endings: Interpreting *The Piano*'s (1993) Final Scenes

BARBARA KLINGER

Towards the end of Jane Campion's *The Piano* (1993), Ada McGrath's (Holly Hunter) repressive husband, Alisdair Stewart (Sam Neill), lets her leave his remote New Zealand plantation with George Baines (Harvey Keitel), a worker on his estate with whom she has been having an unconventional affair. Stewart's acquiescent behaviour follows somewhat surprisingly from an otherwise blood-soaked, dramatic climax to the film's tensions. Upon discovering Ada's continued affections for George, Stewart had assaulted her physically, at the peak of his rage cutting off part of her index finger with an axe – an action that could have easily provoked more vengeful violence. Instead, with Maoris to man the boat, Ada, her daughter Flora (Anna Paquin) and George, as well as Ada's beloved piano, head for Nelson, a city in New Zealand far removed from the dank outpost that had defined her arranged marriage to Stewart, a prim land-owner well suited to the Victorian ethos that pervades the film's 1850s setting.

Yet there are more surprises or, in the parlance of melodrama, reversals or abrupt changes in narrative direction to come. During the voyage, Ada unexpectedly demands that the piano, her most prized possession (and, since she became inexplicably mute as a child, her major means of expression), be thrown overboard. Initially reluctant to do so because he knows how much the instrument has meant to her, George finally agrees and the rope tying the piano to the boat is undone. As the Maoris heave the instrument overboard, Ada suddenly slips her ankle into the rope's coils and follows the piano into the waters. It appears certain that she will perish. However, at the last moment, she resolves not to drown, struggles successfully to be free of the rope pulling her down to the ocean floor, and surfaces. Michael Nyman's plaintive score and the slow-motion underwater cinematography that capture Ada's near-drowning and self-rescue stress the suspense and gravity of her decision, as she says in voiceover, 'to choose life'.

Following this pivotal scene, the film appears to move towards a tranquil resolution. Now living in sunny Nelson with George and her daughter, Ada is teaching piano on a new instrument. Through a prosthesis George fashioned to replace the fingertip severed by Stewart's axe, she is able to play again. She is also slowly learning to speak again. Her newly constituted family's happiness is additionally signalled by George's embrace of her and his kiss as she practises her speaking sounds on their veranda, as well as by her daughter's cartwheels, which, shot in slow motion, suggest Flora's return to a more appropriately safe and carefree environment.

Yet Campion's protagonists are not fully engulfed by the status quo. Although Ada works to regain her speech within a renovated family and social structure, her complete enculturation is indefinitely postponed. Because of her prosthesis, she is considered the 'town freak' – a label that, her voiceover confirms, 'satisfies' her. George too is an outsider; not only is he married to someone else, but his Maori markings continue to define him as Other in a white context. Moreover, before coming to his senses and expressing his desire for Ada in more sympathetic terms, George had been guilty of sexual blackmail. After purchasing Ada's piano from Stewart, he struck a bargain with her in which he would ultimately return the piano if she

The happy formation of the couple in Nelson

allowed him to take liberties with her during their 'lessons'. Hence, via her prosthesis, appearance and complex choice of a partner, Ada maintains a variation of the fringe identity in society that she, as a mute and a single mother, had long experienced.

However, as *The Piano*'s last shot demonstrates, the narrative will not rest with this modestly qualified happy end. An image invoking the earlier overboard scene performs the film's final reversal. Through her mind's voice, expressed on the film's soundtrack as a voiceover, Ada discusses how at night she thinks about the fate she almost met. She imagines her piano in its ocean grave and sees her dead body tethered to it by the ankle once caught in the rope. This moment is presented through a single shot as the camera tracks back from the piano, gradually losing her figure in the murky sea until the screen fades to black and the credits roll. As the camera withdraws, Ada explains, 'Down there everything is so still and silent that it allows me to sleep. It is a weird lullaby and so it is – it is mine.' Quoting from English poet Thomas Hood, Ada utters the closing words of *The Piano*: 'There is a silence where hath been no sound. There is a silence where no sound hath been, in the cold grave under the deep, deep sea.'

Endings, of course, matter; they have the power to determine the overall experience, merits and/or success of a film. Because of the way a film ends, audiences may leave the movie theatre content that narrative threads have been woven together neatly to provide a satisfactory conclusion (whether happy or sad). Viewers may also depart the theatre disturbed, perplexed or excited by a surprise ending, or be displeased, even angered, by a conclusion they find inadequate or unsuitable. In these and other incarnations, then, endings can be deeply emotional in the effects they produce, while also setting the stage for lively discussions that seek to understand and evaluate the film more generally.

Film studies scholars have long recognised the significance closure has as both a formal and ideological device,

The final shot: Ada's body tethered to the piano at the bottom of the sea as the camera tracks back

capable of determining a film's systemic coherence, ultimate meaning and relationship to social norms. Formally, most film endings adhere to classical Hollywood narrative standards. As David Bordwell argues, while there are numerous variations to this formula, closure often acts as 'the crowning of the structure, the logical conclusion of the string of events, the final effect of an initial cause'.[1] As an additional sign that resolution and unity have been reached, film-makers frequently supply an epilogue that 'confirms the stability of the situation, while settling subplots and tying up motifs'.[2] Although epilogues also differ, they commonly 'reinforce the tendency toward a happy ending';[3] often, closure in classical narrative films involves the secure formation of a heterosexual couple, in which case the epilogue celebrates the union.

Some variations in film endings are guided by directorial sensibilities, generic conventions and/or narrative modes. Hence, film-makers Alfred Hitchcock and Douglas Sirk have both been associated with undermining studio-enforced happy endings by injecting excess, superficiality or disturbing elements into their films' otherwise seemingly 'normal' finales. Film genres contribute yet more possibilities of difference, as each has conventions concerning closure. Audiences expect that a romantic comedy will end happily with the formation of a couple and possibly marriage, while they understand just as well that horror films may close with the death of protagonists and/or the potential lingering of the horror that has pervaded the film's world. Whether the ending features success or failure, it still operates classically insofar as it represents 'the logical conclusion of a string of events'. Art films by directors as diverse as Alain Resnais and Abbas Kiarostami stray further from classical narrative modes. Rather than being driven by a goal-oriented protagonist in a narrative that flows through clear, linear chains of cause and effect and is resolved with some definitiveness, art cinema relies on ambiguity in characters' motivations and narrative actions. With ambiguity at their core, art films may offer 'open endings' where 'some events or effects' are left 'deliberately … unresolved'.[4]

However, although we can identify tendencies in types of films, sufficient differences within and similarities across types exist, meaning that no hard-and-fast rules necessarily apply. Examples mentioned so far simply begin to demonstrate the wide spectrum of possibilities – from decisive happy endings to openness and ambiguity – that characterise a film's finale and, at the same time, make it such a fascinating object of enquiry. No matter whether a film adheres strictly to tradition or is more open-ended, exactly how it finishes incites consideration of its response, ultimately, to the ideological issues it has raised. If, for example, questions of gender, sexuality or race are central, the film's resolution with respect to these issues clarifies its agenda.

As a hybrid of classical and art cinemas, a mixture of melodramatic genres[5] and the product of a director strongly associated with 'the art of feminine sensibility',[6] *The Piano*'s final moments invite especially scrupulous attention. The sequences following the film's violent climax and its aftermath present two possible classical conclusions: the tragic ending in which a central character dies and the happy ending in which the heterosexual couple is united and a family formed. Both can be seen as following the logic of what came before. On the one hand, Ada has demonstrated an unfathomably deep connection to her piano; it has been her mechanism of wilful expression and survival in hostile settings. Moreover, the circumstances she has found herself in with Stewart and Baines are less than ideal. Hence, becoming the tragic heroine who literally attaches her fate to that of the piano, leaving behind compromised relationships, makes a certain amount of sense. On the other hand, her voyage across the sea means a departure from Stewart's unyielding patriarchal authority and life instead with a man associated with the Maoris' less oppressive ways. By sundering her ties to the piano, an archetype of western culture, she appears to cast off the rituals that have regulated her life in patriarchal and colonialist contexts. Her rejection of the piano signifies the refusal of these contexts, as they incited her self-imposed exile into a rebellious state of muteness and retreat to an oasis of expression. Ada's decision to throw the piano overboard and her self-rescue suggest that she has elected to explore a life less stringently regulated by the Victorian era's stark gender inequities, while, importantly, not abandoning her daughter.

Although the Nelson ending is not, as I have mentioned, without its own complexities, it seems at first to provide official closure in its triumph over the destructive tenor of the suicide scene. As we have seen, however, neither of these potential endings will suffice. For the finale, director Campion returns us to the earlier overboard scene, with a twist: it depicts not Ada's resurrection, but her demise. The shot 'rhymes' with the film's opening, insofar as it reintroduces Ada's inner voice, absent through the rest of the film, and concentrates on her perceptions. It also depicts the outcome of the piano's embattled relationship with the sea, portrayed at the film's beginning by high-angle shots that emphasise the instrument's vulnerability to the elements when it must be left on the beach while Ada and Flora and their other belongings make the arduous journey to Stewart's residence. Yet the final shot's placement within the film's diegesis is otherwise curious. Though it is a subjective shot that harks back to the overboard sequence, it is not a flashback; instead, it imagines the space out of time and presents it in the conditional, 'what if', tense. That is, the scene depicts Ada's night-time thoughts about what would have happened had she not chosen life. Moreover, it is no longer tragic nor, despite its disturbing content, truly nightmarish. Through highly aestheticised visual and aural techniques, including a fluid long take, a hauntingly beautiful image and the soothing tones of Ada's inner voice, the scene is presented as part of a silent dreamscape that helps her to sleep.

Still, since Ada's dramatic self-rescue and the Nelson sequence encourage viewers to believe that the demons of her past have been exorcised and the narrative has come to a logical terminus, this epilogue comes as something of a shock, particularly since epilogues traditionally operate as textual stabilisers. *The Piano*'s finishing touch, by contrast, destabilises closure, providing an open ending that leaves the viewer with more questions than answers. Clearly, the piano is still a force with which to contend, but the viewer is not sure how to interpret its surprise return and the accompanying depiction of Ada's other possible fate – her death, which is portrayed with some longing. In fact, Campion's dangling of different possible endings for the film has provoked extensive discussion, particularly among feminist film scholars, about what the three endings individually signify and what they ultimately indicate about the film's gender politics.

Some feminist critics argue that the film should have concluded with the first overboard sequence. As Ann Hardy remarks, this scene is 'the closest the film comes to setting up an alternative, female source of authority';[7] a heroine decides to choose her own path, acknowledging the untenability of her continued existence in contexts of male domination. For many, the Nelson ending that follows is unacceptable for several reasons: it sanctions a union built on exploitation, in which Ada falls in love with her rapist, that is, with the man who blackmailed her into sexual submission; it embodies the 'domestication project' that characterises the close of many a woman's film, in which the only valid ultimate articulation of female desire lies in heterosexual romance and/or in motherhood;[8] and it represents a 'commercial cop-out',[9] a happy end, complete with a smiling couple, required to enhance the film's marketability.[10] As for the epilogue, in an otherwise positive assessment of the film's challenges to certain aspects of melodramatic closure, Neil Robinson is troubled by the manner in which the final shot situates Ada within 'ethereal forms' and an 'otherworldly realm' that literally places the female body and feminine subjectivity under erasure.[11]

Others offer completely different views. Stella Bruzzi, for example, argues of the first overboard sequence: 'to die in the mode of a tragic heroine would have been to succumb to another masculine tradition. Instead, Ada defines and communicates herself and her desires differently, unbalancing those traditions and instating female subjectivity.'[12] To kill off a 'troublesome' female character is simply another convention of closure in melodramas and other genres; this type of ending typically rids the film's moral universe of characters deemed too problematic to survive. Campion's decision to allow her protagonist to 'choose life', then, undermines one of closure's key ideological moves, while foregrounding the strength of female will. In further defence of the film's happy ending in Nelson, Sue Gillett refuses to equate this scene with 'heterosexist ideology', because this position ignores 'the possibility of positive changes within heterosexuality'. Thus, Ada's union with Baines is a 'new and transfiguring marriage' that not only betokens a significant change in male partners, but also 'transforms the isolation … of the heroine, without … effacing her subjectivity or forgetting her past'.[13] Indeed, that past is vividly remembered in the underwater epilogue that rapidly follows.

Perhaps critics who reject the either/or formulation offer the most interesting interpretations of *The Piano*'s multiple endings. They contend that the heterogeneous endings mark one of the film's most significant contributions both to melodrama and to feminist film-making more generally. For example, Rosemary Du Plessis and Geoff Fougere write: 'A single ending might suggest that there was a particular message in Ada's story.' But the film's message 'may be that it … makes available a variety of readings, about men, women, mothers and daughters'.[14] Pushing this point further, disparate endings enable multiple meanings that, rather than killing or domesticating the woman, keep her status and larger issues of female subjectivity and identity subject to ongoing discussion and debate, as they should be. Following this line of thought, we can revisit the impact of melodramatic reversal in these final scenes. Given the prominence of reversals here – sudden, dramatic shifts in narrative fortune – and, as we have seen, the inherent tensions within each possible finale, *The Piano* offers irresolution as a 'productive difficulty'[15] that emphasises the stresses and strains of concluding a woman's film without falling completely into the conventions of marriage or death.

Thus, *The Piano*'s unique manifestation of a contested ending – subject to intense feminist scrutiny – would be underserved by an 'either/or' interpretation, since its value lies in its vividly complex manipulation of cinematic conventions that typically regulate the depiction of femininity. Whirling finales past the viewer, the film instructively raises contradictions to the surface, while infusing them with mixed signals and ambiguities that further complicate a secure answer about meaning. For those interested in untangling the film's mysteries, its closing sequences furnish compelling evidence of how indeterminate endings can animate the interpretive enterprise, while also, in this case, suggesting that female-centred narratives worth their salt will refuse to settle their issues of identity in any way that could be mistaken for complacency.

NOTES

1. David Bordwell, 'Classical Hollywood Cinema: Narrational Principles and Procedures', in Philip Rosen (ed.), *Narrative, Apparatus, Ideology* (New York: Columbia University Press, 1986), p. 21. In recognition of the fact that classical closure may neither completely nor convincingly resolve a narrative's plots and subplots, Bordwell introduces the terms 'closure effect' and 'pseudo closure'; these less decisive endings are common variations to the 'airtight' classical end (p. 22).

2. David Bordwell, *The Way Hollywood Tells It: Story and Style in Modern Movies* (Berkeley: University of California Press, 2006), pp. 38, 41.

3. Bordwell, 'Classical Hollywood Cinema', p. 22.

4. David Bordwell, *Making Meaning: Inference and Rhetoric in the Interpretation of Cinema* (Cambridge, MA: Harvard University Press, 1989), p. 192.

5. For discussions of the film's generic tensions see, for example, Neil Robinson, 'With Choices Like These, Who Needs Enemies? *The Piano*, Women's Articulations, Melodrama, and the Woman's Film', in Felicity Coombs and Suzanne Gemmell (eds), *Piano Lessons: Approaches to The Piano* (Sydney: John Libbey & Company Pty Ltd, 1999), pp. 19–43; Laleen Jayamanne, 'Postcolonial Gothic: The Narcissistic Wound of Jane Campion's *The Piano*', in *Toward Cinema and Its Double: Cross-cultural Mimesis* (Bloomington: Indiana University Press, 2001), pp. 24–48; Dana Polan, *Jane Campion* (London: BFI, 2001), pp. 34–40. It must be mentioned that the film has also been the site of much discussion of its rendering of race and colonialism. See, for example, Lynda Dyson, 'The Return of the Repressed? Whiteness, Femininity, and Colonialism in *The Piano*', *Screen* vol. 36 no. 3, Autumn 1995, pp. 267–76.

6. Polan, *Jane Campion*, p. 7.

7. Ann Hardy, 'The Last Patriarch', in Harriet Margolis (ed.), *Jane Campion's* The Piano (Cambridge: Cambridge University Press, 2000), p. 83.

8. A position discussed in Polan, *Jane Campion*, p. 49.

9. A position discussed in Jayamanne, 'Postcolonial Gothic', p. 38.

10. The film did very well at the box office, earning $40 million in the USA alone, a major sum for an art-house film. In addition, Jane Campion was the first female director to win the top award, the Palme d'Or, at Cannes. At the Academy Awards, she also won an Oscar for Best Original Screenplay, while Holly Hunter and Anna Paquin won Best Actress and Best Supporting Actress, respectively.

11. Robinson, 'With Choices Like These', pp. 34–6 and 38 argues that *The Piano* sides not against, but with, the characters expelled from the film's world – an inversion of melodrama's typical practice.

12. Stella Bruzzi, 'Tempestuous Petticoats: Costume and Desire in *The Piano*', *Screen* vol. 36 no. 3, Autumn 1995,

p. 266. In 1995 and 1996, *Screen* was home to several other pieces on *The Piano* that began the debate about its status in relation to patriarchal and colonialist contexts. Years later, in the same journal, see also my 'The Art Film, Affect, and the Female Viewer: *The Piano* Revisited', vol. 47 no. 1, Spring 2006, pp. 19–41.

13. Sue Gillett, *Views from Beyond the Mirror: The Films of Jane Campion. The Moving Image 7* (St Kilda: Atom, 2004), pp. 47, 46. Of Ada's transfigured partnership with Baines, Gillett also argues that Baines 'can only become her lover when he realises that her docility and his domination is not what he wants … . His desire is for her desire' (p. 48).

14. Rosemary Du Plessis and Geoff Fougere, 'The Social World of *The Piano*', *Sites* no. 31, Spring 1995, p. 140.

15. The term is drawn from Jayamanne, 'Postcolonial Gothic', p. 38, in a passage in which she describes the result of the collision of melodramatic genres in the film's endings. For variations on how to regard the multiple endings, *see also* Gillett, *Views from Beyond the Mirror*, p. 46 and Kathleen McHugh, *Jane Campion* (Urbana and Chicago: University of Illinois Press, 2007), p. 93.

BIBLIOGRAPHY

Bordwell, David, 'Classical Hollywood Cinema: Narrational Principles and Procedures', in Philip Rosen (ed.), *Narrative, Apparatus, Ideology* (New York: Columbia University Press, 1986), pp. 17–34.

Bordwell, David, *Making Meaning: Inference and Rhetoric in the Interpretation of Cinema* (Cambridge, MA: Harvard University Press, 1989).

Bordwell, David, *The Way Hollywood Tells It: Story and Style in Modern Movies* (Berkeley: University of California Press, 2006).

Bruzzi, Stella, 'Tempestuous Petticoats: Costume and Desire in *The Piano*', *Screen* vol. 36 no. 3, Autumn 1995, pp. 257–66.

Coombs, Felicity and Gemmell, Suzanne (eds), *Piano Lessons: Approaches to The Piano* (Sydney: John Libbey & Company Pty Ltd, 1999).

Du Plessis, Rosemary and Fougere, Geoff, 'The Social World of *The Piano*', *Sites* no. 31 Spring 1995, pp. 130–41.

Dyson, Lynda, 'The Return of the Repressed? Whiteness, Femininity, and Colonialism in *The Piano*', *Screen* vol. 36 no. 3, Autumn 1995, pp. 267–76.

Gillett, Sue, *Views from Beyond the Mirror: The Films of Jane Campion. The Moving Image 7* (St Kilda: Atom, 2004).

Hardy, Ann, 'The Last Patriarch', in Harriet Margolis (ed.), *Jane Campion's The Piano* (Cambridge: Cambridge University Press, 2000), pp. 59–85.

Jayamanne, Laleen (ed.), *Toward Cinema and Its Double: Cross-cultural Mimesis* (Bloomington: Indiana University Press, 2001).

Jayamanne, Laleen, 'Postcolonial Gothic: The Narcissistic Wound of Jane Campion's *The Piano*', in Laleen Jayamanne (ed.), *Toward Cinema and Its Double: Cross-cultural Mimesis*, pp. 24–48.

Klinger, Barbara, 'The Art Film, Affect, and the Female Viewer: *The Piano* Revisited', *Screen* vol. 47 no. 1, Spring 2006, pp. 19–41.

Margolis, Harriet (ed.), *Jane Campion's The Piano* (Cambridge: Cambridge University Press, 2000).

McHugh, Kathleen, *Jane Campion* (Urbana and Chicago: University of Illinois Press, 2007).

Polan, Dana, *Jane Campion* (London: BFI, 2001).

Robinson, Neil, 'With Choices like These, Who Needs Enemies? *The Piano*, Women's Articulations, Melodrama, and the Woman's Film', in Coombs and Gemmell, *Piano Lessons*, pp. 19–43.

Rosen, Philip (ed.), *Narrative, Apparatus, Ideology* (New York: Columbia University Press, 1986).

Mourning, Loss and Trauma, and the Ambiguities of Proper and Improper Desire in *Exotica* (1994)

ELIZABETH COWIE

For director Atom Egoyan, film viewing is very much an engaged activity, but one that is not always conscious. He comments:

> To me, the highest aim of any film is to enter so completely into the subconscious of the viewer that there are moments and scenes and gestures which can be generated by the spectator's imagination. That becomes part of the film they're playing in their mind, and I hope the film has enough space to allow that type of exchange.[1]

In this essay I examine how *Exotica* (1994) may draw us to imagine through the way its moments, its scenes, are figured for us, not only by what we see and hear, but also by what we have already seen and heard in its stories of mourning, loss and trauma, and the ambiguities of proper and improper desire.

'Exotica', where much of the film takes place, is a nightclub offering entertainment for men that teases (including performances by strippers and table-dancing) with its prohibition on touching by the customers, while the deep velvet tones of Eric (Elias Koteas), the master of ceremonies, invite the listener to imagine the delights to be – voyeuristically – enjoyed.[2] Storytelling itself is a tease, arousing our hopes and expectations through the questions of what, why and how that it poses, while holding us in suspense as it unfolds some, but not all, of its narrative information. My discussion focuses on the sequence in which Francis (Bruce Greenwood), the film's protagonist, is lured by Eric to touch Christina (Mia Kirshner) as she dances for him at 'Exotica', and thus is banished from the club, brutally ending the possibility of future visits and the ritual he has enacted over so many nights with her. This ritual forms the central enigma of the film's plot, namely the nature of Francis's obsession with Christina and how this ritual satisfies it. Her dancing stages unsatisfiable desire, of the object as forbidden. Is this what is at stake for

Francis? But what is Christina's involvement? For she too appears invested in the ritual between them.

Exotica, however, presents a difficulty when approached in terms of specific moments, for its narrative is, as Jonathan Romney observes, a 'dense jungle'[3] of contingent and accidental interconnections that become implicated in the characters' desires as a result of its narrative form involving parallel editing, repetitions and re-enactments, which produces a doubling, exchange and interchange between characters and their actions. *Exotica*'s narrative is also highly elliptical, in delaying or giving only partial information about characters' backstories, and eliding knowledge of their motives. It unfolds in a present time of indeterminate duration of days or weeks, cutting between just a few locations as well as two different past places through subjective flashbacks that are ambiguously motivated. Egoyan has spoken of drawing on the notion of counterpoint in music within his narrative structures, developing 'a theme by playing with and creating tensions between two disparate tracks, which are ultimately reflecting or mirroring a common concern'.[4]

Exotica opens with such a counterpoint, its exploration of the 'Exotica' club ending with a voiceover as a sound bridge to the next scene that presents not the protagonist, Francis, but pet-shop owner Thomas (Don McKellar). Passing through airport customs, he is seen through a two-way mirror, as the customs inspector (David Hemblen), already heard in voiceover, continues to address his colleague, Ian (Calvin Green): 'You have to convince yourself that this person has something hidden that you have to find. You check his bags, but it's his face, his gestures, that you are really watching.' Here is the examining gaze of the law, but also that of the voyeur, and of narrative desire in the wish to uncover the truth of what, and why. Thomas functions to enable the narrative figures developed by the film; later he will be drawn into acting as a direct agent of the plot.

The film returns to the club where Christina's performance is being introduced by Eric, who exchanges looks with Zoe (Arsinée Khanjian), the young owner of 'Exotica'. Zoe has replaced him as Christina's lover, but is also heavily pregnant with the child she contracted Eric to father. Christina, dressed as a young schoolgirl complete with satchel, dances salaciously as she slowly strips to the ironic lyrics of Leonard Cohen's song, 'Everybody Knows', which provides another recurring counterpoint across the film.[5] Joining Francis at his table, her provocative dance for him is, we will learn, an established ritual encounter. Francis leaves while Eric – off screen, then on screen – is heard saying, as Christina looks up at him, 'What is it about a schoolgirl that gives her special innocence? Is it the way that they gaze at you?' The jump cut to a sunlit field, which fills the screen until slowly people appear over the distant hill, is not clearly marked as her subjective memory until we learn from later cutaways to this scene that it is a flashback to the search for Francis's missing daughter, Lisa. It is where Christina and Eric first met and will discover Lisa's body, as Eric reveals to Francis in the penultimate sequence. Cutting back to Francis, Christina's remembering becomes associated with Francis, now seen standing in a washroom stall, breathing heavily. His intense response is ambiguous: how should we read what we see in his face, his manner? Does his apparent anguish arise from desire repressed in response to the obvious sexual invitation of Christina's performance as seducing schoolgirl?

The second performance of this ritual increases this ambiguity when a distraught-looking Francis tells Christina he is thinking: 'What would happen if someone ever hurt you?' She replies, 'How could anyone hurt me?' He responds, 'If I'm not there to protect you', but she rejoins, 'You'll always be there to protect me.' Francis then seems to speak of a past traumatic event: 'Why would somebody want to do something like that? How could somebody even think of doing something like that?' But is he addressing himself and his own desire that is not only paedophiliac but also incestuous? For, as he enters the men's room, we are introduced to his daughter by way of a cut to his niece Tracey (Sarah Polley), house-sitting at his home and looking at the many photographs of his wife and daughter. When Tracey's look is replaced by the film's, we see videotaped footage of Lisa playing the piano, with her mother beside her, laughing and smiling. Francis now appears as a devoted father and husband but the next shot returns us to Francis, still in the washroom stall, breathing heavily.

The event that motivates Eric to lure Francis to touch Christina, thus changing the stable world of these characters, is not shown directly, but must be inferred as a response to the change in the emotional triangle in which he participates with Zoe and Christina. This involves both heterosexual and homosexual desire, but also maternal and perhaps paternal love, as we see Eric gently touch Zoe's distended belly, then Christina's caress followed by Zoe's passionate kiss. Eric has lost Christina to Zoe, and he will lose his unborn child to their relationship. He also loses Christina's respect and friendship when she discovers his paternity contract with Zoe, who may have lost Christina's love too. What then of Eric's desire? It soothed him to see Christina and Francis's ritual, Eric says after he has destroyed it. Is his revenge against Francis, or Christina? What is the relation of this ritual, with its problematic reference to paedophilia, and thus to the death of Lisa at the hands of a child molester? Opposed here is the proper parental love for a child against perverse and deadly desire. But with which do we associate Francis?

In the third and final ritual, Francis is seated at a balcony table, his gaze averted while Christina – removing her stockings and undoing her blouse – gazes at him. He declares: 'How could anyone hurt you? Take you away from me? How could anyone?' Rising to sit astride him in a palpably erotic gesture, Christina leans forward as if she might kiss him, but her lips skim past his as she drops her head to rest on his shoulder.

The reverse-field cut to a rapid panning shot reveals Francis leaving, matched in the next shot by Eric, watching at his MC station, who turns and leaves. A counterpoint is introduced by the cut to Thomas in his apartment with Ian (the customs officer), the explosive force of their burgeoning relationship figured in the thunderstorm heard in the distance. A cutback reveals Francis in the washroom stall pulling off a long strip of white toilet paper, which he wraps around his hand in a gesture that is both a bandage and a cleansing. We again hear a clap of thunder, but here it portends a quite different climax. Eric now enters the men's room, passing the urinals to halt by a washbasin in whose mirror he is seen reflected, opposite the door to Francis's stall, which he now bangs on. Using a fake accent, Eric begins his seduction of Francis, tempting him to touch Christina. What he voices may also be what we have been thinking: 'She seems to have a bit of a thing for you, doesn't she?' And he observes that Francis and

Christina's conversation is not 'what I would call usual ... . You get pretty intense, my friend.'

A drum, pounding like a heartbeat, is heard as shots of Eric alternate with close-ups of Francis, his expression suggesting that he is trying to control his emotions as he calmly replies: 'You're not supposed to touch.' 'Yes, but she is into it, believe me,' answers Eric, as he walks around – one might say strutting – brushing back a lock of hair, performing his part, *enjoying* his scenario of revenge: a Faustian devil who knows Francis's thoughts. Indeed, Eric appears to float above Francis's head in two shots, where the camera's high angle reveals him in frame, seen behind the filigree ironwork of the grille above the stall door, much like the devil in religious paintings. Francis asks, 'How do you know?' Eric's reply, 'Everybody knows', recalls the Cohen song: 'Trust me ... . Just a little touch. Nothing too drastic. Then you will get the full experience, my friend. And you will love it, you will love it.' Are not his words expressing what we might believe is Francis's true desire? 'What happens when I touch her?' Francis demands, and the film cuts to videotape footage seen earlier of his wife and daughter. But now his wife is covering the camera lens with her fingers, as we hear their joyous laughter together with the club music and a thunderclap. Francis repeats: 'What happens?'

In the next shot Christina is dancing for Francis but he is looking down, his fingers held together in a gesture of contemplation, or prayer. A brief cutaway reveals Eric standing watching them, then we see Francis as – still without looking at her – he places his palm upon Christina's belly, repeating Eric's gesture earlier when he touched Zoe's swollen belly to feel the growing child. The pace and tone now change to violence as the camera cuts and pans fast to Eric (as it earlier panned to follow Francis), running to Francis and pulling him away to the exit and throwing him down the stairs. Christina declares later to Zoe and Eric, however, that Francis didn't want to touch her.

In the film's third act, Francis commences a counteraction, having blackmailed Thomas to perform in his place while he listens via an audiowire. (Having audited Thomas's accounts, Francis offers to conceal the evidence of Thomas's illegal importing of protected birds' eggs.) Christina tells Thomas of Francis's tragedy – that Francis himself was suspected of Lisa's murder and, although cleared, remained deeply affected. She introduces a new enigma, never fully resolved, when she explains their ritual, saying, 'Well, we have always had this understanding. I mean, I need him for certain things, and he needs me for certain things ... . I was doing things for him and he's done things for me ... '.

Persuaded by Francis, Thomas returns and touches Christina in order to draw Eric outside, where Francis intends to shoot him. In the club, Zoe now introduces Christina, watching her as intently as Eric had, occupying his place in relation to Christina but without his rivalrous identification with Francis. When the now sacked Eric surprises Francis outside the club and tells him that it was he, with Christina, who found Lisa's body in the field (shown in flashback), jealousy, with its homoerotic overtones, becomes replaced by a brotherly, homocentric, embrace. Francis's ritual can be now understood not as repressed desire, but as a form of incomplete mourning by a father for his dead child; incomplete because the loss is marked by trauma, namely, his inability to protect her from a sexual desire he must repeatedly enact his indifference to. Are we now released from our implication in apprehending Christina as the woman-child offering herself sexually? Has our narrative desire been dashed, or fulfilled?

It is Christina's story we follow when, as Thomas touches her, a brief flashback to the finding of Lisa is followed by Christina gently removing Thomas's hand from her thigh and folding it closed, closely watched by Zoe – as Eric used to – from the private observatory. Her face, curious rather than anxious, is intercut with the smiling Christina. Can we understand Christina's gesture as signifying closure to the role the ritual has performed for her, in a process of repair? What is the importance here of the same-sex desire of these characters? For *Exotica*, cutting to the videotape of Francis's wife and daughter connects them to his tragedy in a flashback unmotivated by a character's look. The next shot shows Francis filming them before answering the door to a younger, plainer Christina arriving to babysit Lisa. Francis drives Christina home, talking proudly of Lisa's achievements, but says his daughter thinks that Christina is unhappy at home, and that if she would like to talk about things: 'You know that I'm here, okay?' Instead, as Francis pays her, Christina says how much she enjoys these drives home, and Francis replies, 'So do I.'

Here we may identify the kernel of their ritual: a father repeatedly enacting not *not* desiring the daughter, but his inability to protect her from another man's desire – a desire that is figured via a displacement, namely in the image of

Christina's seductiveness. What was shocking in our initial reading was not simply Francis's apparent paedophilic desire but that he submits to its prohibition, exposing us to what Slavoj Žižek, writing of courtly love, describes as the illusion that, without such a hindrance, the object of desire would be directly accessible, 'if only'.[6] To remove the hindrance of the prohibition by touching Christina, however, brings us up against what Lacan describes as the unattainability of the desired object as 'always-lost'. We usually question our first readings, Žižek suggests, believing that meaning only discloses itself in a second reading, but he argues that, on the contrary, such second readings are a defence formation against the shock of the first reading.[7] Francis's embrace of Eric may thus allow us to reassure ourselves in a second reading that Francis does, indeed, *not* desire his daughter, but its very abruptness – its under-motivation – makes questionable this resolution.

The film closes with the young Christina walking up the path to her unhappy home, turning us away from Francis and Eric's masculine traumas of loss and their redemptive embrace to the film's 'real', in the sense that Lacan proposed, in being unrepresentable in the experience of trauma of a different girl-child, Christina, and her story untold, unredeemed. Christina's performance at the 'Exotica' club realises the 'forbidden, disallowed image of the daughter'[8] as a subtext of desire that she also addresses to herself, reflexively performing the image of a seductiveness projected upon her by another, the perpetrator of the implied abuse experienced within her own family. Egoyan here draws on his understanding, arising from his involvement with a girlfriend who was being abused, of 'how somebody who is abused makes a parody of their own sexual identity as a means of trying to convince themselves that that part of themselves which has been destroyed is somehow not as vital as it is'.[9] If in touching her he seeks to know 'what happens', it is as reassurance that Christina's performance is truly a masquerade, for only in this way does she make Lisa live again as his innocent daughter. What Francis 'does' for Christina is not the repression of desire in a submission to the external prohibition that her father may have failed to observe, but a gift of love, signified in the traumatic re-enactment of his inability to protect his daughter, performed with Christina-as-Lisa. Christina's is the story the film does not show but that which we must conjure for ourselves, yet what Egoyan offers us for this act of magical thinking involves us in the very ambivalence of our desire.

NOTES

1. Atom Egoyan, *Exotica* (Toronto: Coach House Press, 1995), p. 50.
2. The club appears as a jungle, and Egoyan has commented on the influence of Henri Rousseau's paintings in the set designs. Emma Wilson explores this in *Atom Egoyan* (Urbana: University of Illinois Press, 2009), p. 73. Her subtle study has contributed to my own understanding of the film.
3. Jonathan Romney, *Atom Egoyan* (London: BFI), 2003, p. 110.
4. Atom Egoyan, *Speaking Parts* (Toronto: Coach House Press, 1993), p. 47
5. See <www.lyricsfreak.com/l/leonard+cohen/everybody+knows_20082809.html>.
6. Slavoj Žižek, *The Metastases of Enjoyment: Six Essays on Woman and Causality* (London: Verso, 1994), p. 92.
7. Slavoj Žižek, 'The Foreign Gaze Which Sees Too Much', in Atom Egoyan and Ian Balfour (eds), *Subtitles: On the Foreignness of Film* (Cambridge, MA: MIT Press, 2004), p. 286.
8. Wilson, *Atom Egoyan*, p. 83.
9. 'Interview', in Egoyan, *Exotica*, p. 48.

BIBLIOGRAPHY

Egoyan, Atom, *Speaking Parts* (Toronto: Coach House Press, 1993).

Egoyan, Atom, *Exotica* (Toronto: Coach House Press, 1995).

Egoyan, Atom and Balfour, Ian (eds), *Subtitles: On the Foreignness of Film* (Cambridge, MA: MIT Press, 2004).

Romney, Jonathan, *Atom Egoyan* (London: BFI, 2003).

Wilson, Emma, *Atom Egoyan* (Urbana: University of Illinois Press, 2009).

Žižek, Slavoj, *The Metastases of Enjoyment: Six Essays on Woman and Causality* (London: Verso, 1994), p. 92.

Žižek, Slavoj, 'The Foreign Gaze Which Sees Too Much', in Egoyan and Balfour, *Subtitles*, p. 286.

Stepping out of Blockbuster Mode: The Lighting of the Beacons in *The Lord of the Rings: The Return of the King* (2003)

KRISTIN THOMPSON

When I first saw the third part of Peter Jackson's trilogy, I was impressed by the sequence where the beacons of Gondor are lit, calling for the aid of the country's ally, Rohan. It involves soaring helicopter shots over New Zealand's pristine mountain ranges, swelling music by Howard Shore, and a narrative tension around whether Rohan will support Gondor in the coming war. Beyond these factors, though, I was impressed by the scene's formal strategies. With the graphic and spatial play of the placement of the beacons within the frame, this scene struck me as being like a little experimental film inserted into a story-driven blockbuster.

While I admire the sequence and think it one of the best in the trilogy, I was puzzled by its presence. Despite being forced to condense, trim and change J. R. R. Tolkien's novel to fit the film's timeframe, the makers included roughly one minute and seventeen seconds for a passage that simply shows a series of beacons flaring up on mountaintops – a highly expanded action whose length not only fails to contribute significantly to the plot but contradicts spatial and temporal premises set up earlier.

Given the unconventional nature of the sequence, I was surprised to see it singled out in laudatory reviews and cited by many fans as one of their favourite scenes. What makes the sequence work so well in its narrative context? Why would fans find it so appealing? Those are the questions I'll be tackling here.

PLAYING THE BEACONS GAME

Most spectators come to classical Hollywood films knowing how to watch them. A well-known repertoire of storytelling devices is drawn upon, and those devices are almost invariably designed to make following the narrative quite easy. Spatial continuity is maintained in order to keep the viewer oriented in relation to story space and time.[1]

In a traditional classical film, each new shot should ideally provide a new piece of information, thus furthering the telling of the story. In long shots, especially in widescreen films, the most important element of the shot is not likely to be centred, but it typically won't be placed at the far edges of the frame. If there are two or more major elements, they are roughly balanced against each other. Usually the diegetic sound in a scene will come from these key elements. In the beacons sequence, there is essentially no new information added in any given shot, and there could have been more or fewer shots without disturbing the basic causal action of Gandalf (Ian McKellen) sending a message calling for Rohan's aid. One could argue that the sequence even dissipates the tension over whether Rohan will respond by emphasising the grandeur of the landscapes and music. No diegetic sound accompanies the shots of the beacons.

The beacons sequence uses strategies more commonly associated with experimental films. From shot to shot, the new beacons appear at different locations on the screen, and the viewer quickly learns to scan the image for the next one. Essentially the sequence teaches its spectator a viewing tactic not familiar from classical films. Hollis Frampton comments on how experimental films must teach their viewers how to watch them:

> One of the things that goes on in *Critical Mass* [1971] (this is also true of much of the rest of my work and of the work by others I admire) is a process of training the spectator to watch the film.[2]

Often the training of the spectator comes through a sort of formal game of trying to figure out a pattern via clues provided by the film.

Unlike any other sequence in *The Lord of the Rings*, the lighting of the beacons plays such a game. Otherwise we would be likely to miss the final beacon, placed perversely in the far upper left corner of the screen, a spot where we ordinarily would not be looking unless cued to do so.

In the interests of space, I am considering the beacons sequence here to begin after Pippin (Billy Boyd) lights the initial heap of wood at Minas Tirith. During most of that action, a soft, tentative, suspenseful musical theme plays, blossoming out to begin the triumphal climb that accompanies the subsequent beacons. These shots follow:

1   Gandalf runs forward through an arched door and stops at a foreground balustrade. He stares expectantly off-front right and mutters 'Amon Dîn', as an impassive sentry stands beside him.

2   An extreme long shot in depth past the back of Gandalf's head, with the White Mountains extending diagonally into the distance. A tiny flame appears at the upper centre on one of the peaks.

3   As (1) Gandalf grins as the sentry shouts, 'The beacon! The beacon of Amon Dîn is lit!'

4   The embittered face of Denethor (John Noble) retreats behind some columns.

5   As (3) Track to tight framing of Gandalf, murmuring, 'Hope is kindled.'

6   An elaborate helicopter shot, with a flame already burning on a peak at the centre; the frame circles as two men with torches light another beacon in the foreground; one waves the torch, facing a ridge where a third flame appears.

7   Helicopter shot moving along a high ridge, where a beacon lights immediately.

8   A helicopter shot backward, with a dim flame appearing and remaining visible as it recedes and a second flares in the foreground.

9   Helicopter shot moving forward through a mountain pass toward a distant ridge where a beacon lights on the left side of the screen. Then a second becomes visible, further away and at the right.

10   Helicopter shot leftward past a single foreground peak with a huge range beyond. A flame appears on the peak, and a pan right reveals another smaller one in the background.

11   Movement diagonally forward past a huge dark mountain in a sea of clouds; a smaller peak becomes visible beyond it, and a beacon flame appears atop it.

12   Long shot, a couple of small buildings at Edoras, with massive mountains just beyond. Aragorn (Viggo Mortensen) sits on a porch at the right centre drinking from a bowl; he stands and looks up as a beacon flares at the upper left of the frame. The music ends.

Shots 2 and 12 act as book-ends for the scene. They contrast in almost every way, demonstrating the goal of the 'training' process. The first has Gandalf in the foreground left, prominent and brightly lit by the low morning sun. He looks rightward and into depth. The second beacon flares up in the upper centre of the image. In terms of the full width of the frame, it is slightly off centre to the left. But in the smaller frame formed by Gandalf's head and his staff, it is slightly off centre to the right, giving an illusion of it being dead centre. It is about a quarter of the way down from the top. There is little movement in the frame, only Gandalf's hair blowing gently and his staff shifting slightly. Thus we are cued to see any other movement, however small, and the character's eyeline direction prompts us to look into the depth of the represented space. The orange flame stands out against the dominant blues, greys and browns. The mountains form a long, horizontal triangle into depth, west toward Rohan, anticipating the trajectory of the successive beacons.

That trajectory ends in Rohan, but here the person who will spot the beacon and deliver its message sits at the

centre right, relatively small in the frame, almost unmoving, and nearly dark enough to be a silhouette. Even if we notice him, the direction of his gaze is unclear and, like the inattentive guards tending the Minas Tirith beacon, he is eating or drinking something from a bowl. There is a mountain peak, brightly lit, in almost the same spot where Gandalf had seen the Amon Dîn beacon, and we are very likely to look at it first. Yet the final beacon appears far to the upper left – distinctly further off centre, in fact, than any previous beacon had been at the point where it lit up. Moreover, there is no camera movement to cue us where to look. We are likely to notice the final beacon at about the same time as the seated figure does, and as he stands up, we are equally likely to finally become aware of his presence. His gaze is the reverse of Gandalf's, leftward into depth.

Shots 6 through 11 bounce our attention around the frame, though seldom in ways that severely violate guidelines of centring and balance. The points at which each shot's beacon(s) first becomes visible are: 6 just off-right upper centre, just off-right lower centre and centre right; 7 upper centre; 8 just off-right upper centre and centre; 9 left centre and right centre; 10 centre and right centre; and 11 just off-left upper centre. Naturally we quickly understand the 'rule' that the flame will always appear on a peak, but there is usually more than one to choose from. The inconsistency of the direction of camera movement, sometimes forward, sometimes backward, sometimes circling, violates the traditional continuity rule of maintaining screen direction.

Jackson has never suggested why he chose to play this game with the spectator in this particular sequence. As we shall see, however, the learning process worked, and the playfulness was probably one reason why the lighting of the beacons has proved so popular.

BEACONS IN NOVEL AND FILM

In Tolkien's novel, Gandalf and Pippin see the beacons burning on the third night of their four-night ride to Minas Tirith. Gandalf cries to his horse,

> On, Shadowfax! We must hasten. Time is short. See! The beacons of Gondor are alight, calling for aid. War is kindled. See, there is the fire on Amon Dîn, and flame on Eilenach; and there they go speeding west: Nardol, Erelas, Min-Rimmon, Calenhad, and the Halifirien on the borders of Rohan.

At that point, three messengers ride past them on their way to Edoras. Gandalf then tells Pippin of

> the customs of Gondor, and how the Lord of the City had beacons built on the tops of outlying hills along both borders of the great range, and maintained posts at these points where fresh horses were always in readiness to bear his errand riders to Rohan in the north, or to Belfalas in the south.[3]

The narrative situation is quite different from that in the film, since Tolkien's Denethor is still sane at this point and is preparing Minas Tirith for the assault by Sauron's troops. He has the beacons lit before Gandalf arrives in the city. Denethor gradually loses hope and eventually tells Gandalf to assume the leadership of Gondor. The film simplifies Denethor by making him sunk in grief and ineffectual from the start, with his city wholly unprepared for the onslaught. He resists the notion of lighting the beacons, and Gandalf must seize control by stealthily arranging for their lighting.

Such trimming and changing were no doubt necessary for the adaptation of such a long book. Yet Jackson expanded upon the relatively brief passage on the beacons for the film. While it has been commonplace for lovers of the book to criticise some of the choices made by the screenwriters in changing the narrative, it is less frequently acknowledged that in some cases they arguably improved upon the book. The beacons sequence would be one example, despite the fact that it contradicts the film's own premises of time and space.

The most relevant premises are set up near the end of *The Lord of the Rings: The Two Towers* (Jackson, 2002). Gandalf, Aragorn, Théoden (Bernard Hill) and the other main characters who participated in the battle of Helm's Deep ride to the top of a ridge near the fortress. Looking towards the eastern horizon, they can see the dark clouds that hover over Mordor and the red glow of Mount Doom. Minas Tirith lies between Helm's Deep and Mordor, so logically one would expect a few beacons to be sufficient to send Gandalf's appeal to Théoden.

The numerous beacons (with more implied than we actually see) instead suggest that a vast distance lies between the two capitals. It's difficult to construct the timeframe between Pippin's lighting of the Minas Tirith beacon and Aragorn's spotting of the final one. As Pippin starts his climb, there is a cut to the beginning of the battle at Osgiliath, which appears to take place at twilight or even the dead of night – but that may simply be because the ruined city lies under an unnatural dark cloud emanating from Mordor. (The retreating soldiers can be seen reaching the edge of the cloud in the sequence after the beacons.) Gandalf is clearly looking west as the second beacon flares, and the sun is behind him, hinting at an early-morning scene. Yet perhaps it is late afternoon instead, since soon the day-time shots of beacons give way to night-time ones. Aragorn apparently spots the final beacon in the morning; the shadows indicate that the Rohirrim ride from Edoras around noon.

Why should it take a night and parts of two days for a series of beacons to span a distance which seems relatively small in that *Two Towers* scene? Moreover, in terms of realism, a viewer might wonder how each successive beacon could possibly appear so quickly and how their keepers managed to live at such heights. In fact, it was pondering the latter question that apparently led Jackson to conceive the sequence. In the director's commentary on the extended version DVD, he says:

> What I love about the beacons is the concept of who actually are the guys who have to sit up there all day long with some matches or a flint, waiting to light them. I imagine that it's been hundreds of years, and these things have never been lit … . They must have a very lonely, solitary lifestyle, living up there by these beacons.[4]

Gandalf's description of the beacons in the novel, quoted above, suggests that the beacons were more practical, located on foothills rather than high peaks and maintained by garrisons that included stables.[5] But the mountaintop placement created a greater visual impact, and Jackson's rather fanciful cogitations about solitary beacon-keepers inspired a majestic enough sequence that most viewers either ignore or forgive the lack of plausibility.

PRESS AND FAN REACTIONS

The sequence impressed critics and fans alike. Elvis Mitchell's *New York Times* review commented: 'A sequence in which a number of signal fires are lighted on a stretch of mountain ranges simultaneously is a towering moment; it has the majesty that every studio's opening logo shot sprains itself striving to achieve.' In the *New Yorker*, Anthony Lane wrote, 'Jackson's roistering mix of speed and splendour allows us to vault from one mountaintop to the next until we reach the end of the line.'[6]

To coincide with the release of the extended version DVD of *Return* in late 2004, *Empire* ran a fourteen-page retrospective piece on the trilogy. It listed the top ten 'Classic Scenes'. The beacons were listed at number 8 as 'a moment that perfectly captures the sheer splendour of Peter Jackson's vision'.[7] Among devoted fans of the film trilogy, the beacons sequence is a favourite. The editors of the licensed fan magazine chose it as the theme for its fifteenth issue, reproducing a frame blow-up under the table of contents and including two interviews that mentioned the sequence.[8]

These are still fans who, more than six years after the third part's release, are starting and participating on discussion threads on websites like TheOneRing.net (TORN). There grammaboodawg, peredhil lover, OhioHobbit, simplyaven and many others display amazing expertise and familiarity with the film, going through the supplements, the pre-visualisations, the costumes, the technology and everything else in minute detail. A few threads testify to the popularity of the beacons sequence and include attempts to explain its appeal.[9] Given my interest in the fans' reaction to the sequence, I started my own thread concerning it on TORN.[10] I can't quote from the many responses at length, but the result was a series of thoughtful comments that are well worth reading. Elven even contributed a *découpage*, and hobbitlove does a longer analysis of the sequence than I have room for here. Darkstone responded to one of my questions in this way:

> *If you can remember back to when you first saw the film, did you spot that final beacon when it became visible?*
> Yep. Due to Jackson's little 'Where's Waldo?' exercise with the previous beacons I was able to spot it right off, especially since the amount of sky made it pretty obvious where it would be. The first choice was the peak to the right, which wasn't the one. By the time I moved my eyes and scanned the second peak (the one to the left) I caught it *exactly* as it was being lit. Amazing timing of the shot by Jackson!!

Several other contributors agreed that the film trains the viewer to scan in this way, confirming my hypothesis about why this sequence has the feel of an experimental film. And, as Weaver pointed out in the thread, the beacons music was the celebratory passage chosen to be played eleven times on 29 February 2004, as the film-makers went to the stage of the Kodak Theater to accept their Oscars.

Producers and directors sometimes claim that unconventional passages might alienate the audience, but sometimes, it seems, they can be welcomed – not only by critics, but also by viewers and fans. Jackson's boldness in this sequence might encourage mainstream film-makers to try at least occasionally to slow the pace and allow some cinematic lyricism to come forward.

NOTES

1. The rules of continuity are summarised in David Bordwell and Kristin Thompson, *Film Art: An Introduction* (9th edn) (New York: McGraw-Hill, 2010), pp. 236–55, and discussed at greater length in David Bordwell, Janet Staiger and Kristin Thompson, *The Classical Hollywood Cinema: Film Style and Mode of Production to 1960* (London: Routledge & Kegan Paul, 1985), primarily in Chapters 6 and 16.
2. Scott McDonald, *A Critical Cinema: Interviews with Independent Filmmakers* (Berkeley: University of California Press, 1988), p. 65.
3. J. R. R. Tolkien, *The Lord of the Rings*, 50th Anniversary Edition (London: HarperCollins, 2004), p. 747.
4. Jackson describes his inspiration for the sequence in similar terms in an interview: Dan Madsen's 'Update with Peter Jackson', *The Lord of the Rings Fan Club Official Movie Magazine* no. 15, June–July 2004, pp. 21–2.
5. In *Unfinished Tales* (London: George Allen and Unwin, 1980), Tolkien wrote, 'The Beacon-wardens were the only inhabitants of the Wood, save wild beats; they housed in lodges in the trees near the summit, but they did not stay long, unless held there by foul weather, and they came and went in turns of duty. For the most part they were glad to return home.' Despite Jackson's intentions, the film's action happens also to fit Tolkien's description.
6. Elvis Mitchell, 'Triumph Tinged with Regret in Middle Earth', *New York Times*, 16 December 2003. Available at <www.nytimes.com/2003/12/16/movies/film-review-triumph-tinged-with-regret-in-middle-earth.html>; Anthony Lane, 'Full Circle', *New Yorker*, 5 January 2004.

Available at <www.newyorker.com/archive/2004/01/05/040105crci_cinema?currentPage=5> (accessed 11 July 2009).
7. Ian Nathan, '*The Lord of the Rings*: The Untold Story', *Empire* no. 187, January 2005, p. 125.
8. See endnote 4.
9. Two examples: tennie75, 'Chills down your back moments', TheOneRing.net, 24 October 2008 onwards: <newboards.theonering.net/forum/gforum/perl/gforum.cgi?post=143450;sb=post_time;so=DESC;forum_view=forum_view_collapsed;;page=unread#unread> (accessed 28 May 2009); and DiveTwin, 'Which LOTR Movie Scene Is Most Iconic?', TheOneRing.net, 8 April 2009 onwards: <newboards.theonering.net/forum/gforum/perl/gforum.cgi?post=180933;sb=post_time;so=DESC;forum_view=forum_view_collapsed;;page=unread#unread> (accessed 28 May 2009).
10. 'Question about the Beacons Sequence', TheOneRing.net, 23 May 2009 onwards: <newboards.theonering.net/forum/gforum/perl/gforum.cgi?post=193593;sb=post_time;so=DESC;forum_view=forum_view_collapsed;;page=unread#unread> (accessed 11 July 2009).

BIBLIOGRAPHY

Bordwell, David, Staiger, Janet and Thompson, Kristin, *The Classical Hollywood Cinema: Film Style and Mode of Production to 1960* (London: Routledge & Kegan Paul, 1985).

Bordwell, David and Thompson, Kristin, *Film Art: An Introduction* (9th edn) (New York: McGraw-Hill, 2010).

Lane, Anthony, 'Full Circle', *New Yorker*, 5 January 2004. Available at <www.newyorker.com/archive/2004/01/05/040105crci_cinema?currentPage=5> (accessed 11 July 2009).

Madsen, Dan, 'Update with Peter Jackson', *The Lord of the Rings Fan Club Official Movie Magazine* no. 15, June–July 2004, pp. 21–2.

McDonald, Scott, *A Critical Cinema: Interviews with Independent Filmmakers* (Berkeley: University of California Press, 1988).

Mitchell, Elvis, 'Triumph Tinged with Regret in Middle Earth', *New York Times*, 16 December 2003. Available at <www.nytimes.com/2003/12/16/movies/film-review-triumph-tinged-with-regret-in-middle-earth.html>.

Nathan, Ian, '*The Lord of the Rings*: The Untold Story', *Empire* no. 187, January 2005, p. 125.

Tolkien, J. R. R., *Unfinished Tales* (London: George Allen and Unwin, 1980).

Tolkien, J. R. R., *The Lord of the Rings*, 50th Anniversary Edition (London: HarperCollins, 2004).

Dorothy's Dream: Mindscreen in *The Wizard of Oz* (1939)

BRUCE F. KAWIN

In L. Frank Baum's original novel, *The Wonderful Wizard of Oz* (1900), Dorothy actually travels to Oz when the cyclone picks up her house, and then back to Kansas; Aunt Em and Uncle Henry have built a new house by the time she returns. In the Oz movies made by Baum and others from 1910 to 1933, either a cyclone blows Dorothy to Oz or she is already there. MGM's *The Wizard of Oz* (Fleming, 1939) is the first movie to present the trip to Oz as a dream.

It is often said casually that the Kansas sequences are in black and white and the dream is in colour. To sort this out, it is profitable to examine the dream sequence as a mindscreen whose off-screen narrator is the dreaming mind of Dorothy (Judy Garland) and to establish just when the dream begins.

A mindscreen presents the audiovisual field of the mind's eye. I coined the term and developed the theory in 1978 and am glad to have the opportunity to provide here a further example of its application.[1] Mindscreen offers the cinema a first-person mode of discourse, presenting matters as a character or some other narrative agency (even the self-conscious narrative system itself) sees them. For example, a flashback – a switch from the narrative present to an objective view of the past – is third person, but a memory – a mindscreen of how the past is remembered, whether or not that memory is distorted – is first person. A POV or point-of-view shot is also first person; so is the voice of a film that presents itself as a film, as does the extremely reflexive *Persona* (Bergman, 1966). A mindscreen can present an honest tale or a lie, a dream or a fantasy, a memory or a subjective view of the present; it can narrate what it tells in voice-over or let the unseen, unheard narrator remain an implicit aspect of the narrated field. In *The Wizard of Oz* the mindscreen's narrator is unconscious, dreaming what we see, and her dream includes an image of herself as she moves through the dreamed world. Her dream has a point, which is that everyone already has everything that he or she needs – for example, the Scarecrow (Ray Bolger) is already smart before the Wizard (Frank Morgan) gives him a diploma, and Dorothy has always had the ruby slippers though she has not known how to use them. In effect, the dreaming Dorothy is giving herself a lecture on her decision to run away to keep Toto from Miss Gulch (Margaret Hamilton), her need to discover her own power, and her desire to find shelter from the twister at home.

The Kansas sequences at the beginning and end of the movie establish its narrative frame; they were shot in black and white and given a sepia tint and may best be described as monochrome. The opening sequence includes information that will make it clear, in retrospect, that Dorothy dreamed her trip to Oz, that the terms of her experience were the terms of a dream and followed, at least in part, a dreamlike logic as they masked the characters and events of the day. Hunk, the farmhand who will become the Scarecrow, tells Dorothy to use her head to solve her problem with Miss Gulch (he says one would think from the way she'd been acting that she hadn't 'any brains at all', and he does suggest a practical solution); he also says her head isn't 'made of straw'. Zeke (Bert Lahr), who will become the Cowardly Lion, shows fear after a brave act; Hickory (Jack Haley), who will become the Tin Woodman, jokes about a statue being erected in his honour and holds still to pose for it; and Dorothy calls Miss Gulch a 'wicked old witch'. All this becomes material for her dream, the key to who the characters really are and to the ways each of them seeks or manipulates power. It should be kept in mind, however, that Dorothy, the dreamer, is the true source of all the power. To take a Gestalt approach, one could say that she divides her power among the characters or projections she confronts as well as her 'small and meek' questing self. But the first time we see the movie, we are not meant to know until the end that the trip to Oz is a dream, for we see the house lifted up by the cyclone as if it were really being blown to Oz, where it very solidly lands. On second and later viewings, it is clear that by the time the house is swept away, Dorothy is already dreaming.

After Dorothy has run away with Toto, she runs back home to make sure Auntie Em (Clara Blandick) is all right and, as a twister approaches, to seek shelter. (This marks the beginning of the 'There's no place like home' theme that will run through and even past the end of her dream – the counter-theme to 'somewhere over the rainbow', the lure of the faraway and fantastic.) Unable to get into the storm cellar, she goes into the house. A blown-in window hits her on the head, and she falls onto a bed and passes out. The cut that joins the medium shot of her lying on the bed to the close shot of her multiplied, dreaming face marks the border between objective and subjective narration in this sequence; it is also accompanied by a change in the music, which becomes muted. That shot of her doubled face, a sixteen-second composite of superimposed moving images, the moment we are here to examine, is complex, for it appears at first to be a transition to a dream but is revealed before its end to include and perhaps constitute the start of that dream. And it is in sepia, as are all the events in the house, whether it is in Kansas or has landed in Oz. The dream sequence is not entirely in colour but begins in monochrome. That means that Oz is in colour – that colour is a property of Oz, not of the dream. That little discovery gives the colour a special resonance and makes the monochrome shot that starts the dream worth special attention.

In *Sherlock Jr.* (Keaton, 1924) and *Vampyr* (Dreyer, 1932) a double-exposed image of the dreamer separates from his body, signifying the start of the dream. In *The Wizard of Oz* the dream begins with a close shot of Dorothy's head – eyes closed, on the bed – from which a superimposed second head separates. The two faces, tilting into and away from each other, float above circling bands that represent the cyclone but can also be read as a sign of wooziness as Dorothy sinks or reels deeper into unconsciousness. Circling movements, doubtless inspired by the turning of the cyclone, appear to be the way into and out of Dorothy's dream; at the end, Glinda, the Witch of the North (Billie Burke), moves her wand in a circle behind Dorothy's head as contracting concentric circles form in the air, emerald at first but then losing their colour, preparing the end of the dream (which ends in sepia, outside Oz, when the house falls to earth once again, presumably in Kansas, giving the dream a nearly circular structure). The circling movements of the cyclone are also reminiscent of the optical effects – wavy lines and so on – sometimes used, particularly in Hollywood, to signify a transition to a memory, tale or dream. Although the separated faces and the whirling signify that Dorothy is already imagining that she is inside the cyclone, the shot also appears to show her sinking into that unconsciousness. But as the shot continues, dream dominates it and puts its stamp on everything that has come earlier in the shot, marking all of it as a dream. Within the composite, as the cyclone continues to roar and the faces to float, the dream takes shape. What comes is an event we later recognise could not have happened: the one

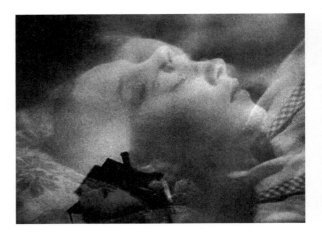

that defines this shot as part of a dream and not just – or no longer – as a transitional device into a dream. Superimposed on Dorothy's doubled face and the cyclonic bands, the turning house is drawn up into the sky.

Dorothy's face can now be recognised as that of the dreamer in the midst of her dream; the image is and has been not third but first person, the beginning of her experience inside the cyclone after she has passed out. Another way of reading this shot is to find that the dream proper begins, after a period of dizzily losing consciousness, when Dorothy's faces are at their most separate positions and the house flies up; that would mean that the composite contains the start of the dream as well as part of the objective world. (The audience understands only retrospectively that any of this may be a dream; the first time we watch the movie, we think we are watching her pass out, be swept up with the house, and come to in the middle of the cyclone.) As the composite ends, a blown tree pulls our eye to screen right, and there is a cut to a view out the frame of the busted window (it feels as if the camera had panned to follow the rushing air) as objects are whirled about in the twister, putting the dream in a frame until the audience realises (sometime during this shot, though not on a first viewing) that the dream includes the entire image, including Dorothy and Toto on the bed.

Once we leave this crucial composite shot, then, we are thoroughly in the narrative realm that we later recognise to be a dream, and Dorothy has a solid physical presence. She sits up on the bed, looks out the window frame, and sees things that are being blown around – most significantly, Miss Gulch on her bicycle, who suddenly turns into the witch Dorothy had called her earlier. But she is not just any witch; she is the Wicked Witch of the West, in costume and with her distinctive laugh. Thus the story of Oz has started, and its dream method has been made clear: Dorothy will turn the characters of her Kansas life into inhabitants of Oz. What Dorothy sees outside the window is plainly impossible and continues to be shown in monochrome. But what is inside the room is as fantastic as what is outside it. We can say that the image of Dorothy has become as much a part of the dream as what she sees outside, or that the entire world of the image, outside the window and inside the room, has taken on a unified reality. (We can also say that the established world of the inner narration includes a projection of its off-screen narrator, the dreaming Dorothy.) In that reality, impossible things happen all the time; the film later gives us the opportunity to attribute the fantastic quality of these events to their having been dreamed. What prepares us for this impossible reality is a shot that can be read as the start of a literal adventure or of a dream, a composite that appears to meld two worlds – of the dreamer and of the dream – as it prepares and yields to a coherent narrative space in which the tale of Oz can be told.

When Dorothy first lands, the house is still in sepia. When she finally opens the door to enter the colour world of Oz, the shot is necessarily on colour stock, but the interior of the house has been painted in browns to match the sepia, and Dorothy, played momentarily by a second actress, is wearing a brown and white dress until she (Garland) steps outside in a blue and white one. While she remains inside the house, she is in the equivalent of Kansas. The exterior of the house has colour, as we can see once Dorothy has stepped outside it into the colour-rich world of Oz. At the end, the monochrome of Kansas reasserts itself, together with Uncle Henry (Charley Grapewin) and Auntie Em's explanation that Dorothy, who is on the same bed with the busted window behind her (making it evident that the house never left the ground), got hit on the head and had a dream. Theirs is a realistic, down-to-earth approach and one that correctly points to mindscreen as the narrative mode that made possible the journey Dorothy insists was real. The dream begins in the mode Dorothy has always known, the monochrome of her life, before it turns to colour to present Oz. The monochrome is the known world, and colour is beyond it, transcendent.

NOTE

1. Bruce F. Kawin, *Mindscreen: Bergman, Godard, and First-Person Film* (Princeton, NJ: Princeton University Press, 1978; reprinted by Dalkey Archive Press, 2006).

BIBLIOGRAPHY

Kawin, Bruce F., *Mindscreen: Bergman, Godard, and First-Person Film* (Princeton, NJ: Princeton University Press, 1978; reprinted by Dalkey Archive Press, 2006).

Looking On and Looking the Other Way: *Hotel Rwanda* (2004) and the Racialised Ethics of Spectatorship

MICHELE AARON

In the true-story-based *Hotel Rwanda* (George, 2004), Don Cheadle plays Paul Rusesabagina, manager of the Belgian-owned Hôtel des Mille Collines in Kigali. During the period of ethnic cleansing in Rwanda in 1994, Rusesabagina turned the hotel into a haven for fleeing Tutsis and saved over 1200 lives. The sequence of shots that I'm analysing here occurs after the UN has secured the safe exit of only the western-ers trapped at the Mille Collines and Paul has told his wife the news and declared to her his own stupidity in thinking they would all be rescued. In pouring rain, the westerners leave the hotel and board the bus: white and black filter out into those saved and those who are consigned to stay and, in all likelihood, die. Where the film emphasises, often through framing and camera movement alone, the com-plicity inherent in regarding the suffering of others, these scenes tie the spectator firmly into this emphasis and do so through an ethically entangled aesthetic. While this aes-thetic might support arguments for a new and even radical personal and global consciousness in the wake of 9/11, it will be shown, ultimately, to be both troubled and troubling in its disavowal of racial consciousness.

These scenes lie at the very heart of the film. Just under halfway through they mark a pivotal point in what is unfolding in terms of both the film narrative and the wider narrative that the film represents. At the most basic level, the scenes literalise the West's abandonment of the Rwandans, which is the dramatic and moral centre of the film. Second, they evidence a crucial shift in terms of Paul's raised consciousness and his relationship to the events going on around him. Paul has stopped 'by-standing' and has become an agent of his own and, to an extent, his fellow Rwandans' volition. Third, and connected to this, Paul, here, stops being the primary coordinate in the ethi-cisation of looking on. What I mean by this is that the indi-vidual's relationship to the suffering of others, which I'm discerning as a primary conceit of *Hotel Rwanda*, shifts in these scenes to be made explicitly not just about him, or

even about the West, but about the Western spectator him or herself.

In tracing this shift in the ethics of spectatorship, we must revisit a scene that comes early on in *Hotel Rwanda* when growing tensions between Hutus and Tutsis have begun to erupt into visible hostility and violence. Paul, a man with some standing among those of authority in Kigali, is asked by his wife, Tatiana (Sophie Okonedo), to intervene as they watch from their garden gate as their neighbours are brutally arrested.

Paul replies that he can do nothing, for he is saving up the favours that he is owed for when his own family is in need. There will be further occasions shortly afterwards when Paul similarly looks the other way, but then a rever-sal happens. Paul stops turning away and starts to act, to provide a sanctuary for the Tutsis. He not only intervenes on behalf of many others, but comes to force others to do the same, summoning them into a similar state of

Looking on in *Hotel Rwanda*

Looking on, again, in *Hotel Rwanda*

response. Where once Paul resisted his responsibility – 'falsely' directing it to the welfare of hotel guests alone – he begins, in the film moments under discussion, to take on the management of the welfare of his fellow Rwandans.

In these highly emotive scenes, the horror of the 'selection lines' – of the filtering out of black and white, of those to-be-saved and those not-to-be-saved – is heightened as a group of women, nuns and children runs towards the bus. The frame becomes overcrowded: white fingers are prised from black children's arms; black and white are disentangled and pulled off in different directions. Paul moves through the Rwandans telling them: 'Go inside the hotel. We will take care of you.'

With all appropriately relocated, and the colour line fixed, the camera tracks slowly from left to right along the bus showing the white Westerners looking out. It is neither weeping nuns nor peace workers we see, nor the one black westerner among the exodus, but the nameless white characters who first left the hotel and now sit staring at the scene.

One clasps a dog, another is taking a picture. Many others have fists or fingers on their faces, as if they are putting some additional barrier between themselves and 'our' vision of them. As if the glass, the bus, their guaranteed safety and the relentless rain were not shielding enough. The westerners take their seats, in their 'darkened auditorium', like an audience, like *the* audience: the West watching such atrocities from their position both of safety and very visible disquiet. This visibility is vital here, for it marks the West as moved by what is wrong with the picture, as both self-conscious and as having a conscience, even as they are powerless to do anything about it. However, what is also being underscored of course is the West as white, a conflation-cum-elision so pervasive in Hollywood yet so sustaining of racist paradigms: what is wrong with the bigger picture very much endures.[1]

Only the picture-taker faces the camera directly. The people on the bus, the Western audience, gaze off screen back to the hotel, and to the Rwandans. Where the Westerners resist 'to-be-looked-at-ness' utterly – obscured, pensive, looking elsewhere[2] – the Rwandans, in total con-

trast, gather under the awning, the perfect spectacle. Framed by the white pillars, huddled and sheltering from the 'elements', the full force of their status as spectacle to the westerners, within and beyond the film, expands exponentially, for it is this image that becomes the movie's advertising shot: soliciting attention and patronage.

The ethics inherent in spectatorship, which is being dramatised and summoned through these scenes, are best understood via the work of Emmanuel Levinas. Establishing ethics as personal responsibility emerging in the meeting between self and other, Levinas argued that it is only through the face-to-face encounter, and through a response to the other's difference, that we gain our sense of self. This response becomes respons-ibility – both as a kind of subjectivity-in-action (a reflexive state of self-constitution) and as our obligation to the other – for it arises out of our most primary, and unavoidable, implication in the other's potential death: the murderous impulse that frames self-interest.[3] To put this most simply: *my existence necessarily compromises someone else's.* It is this ethical dynamic that is perfectly captured in the 'selection line' and 'looking on' sequences in *Hotel Rwanda*. The ethical dynamic is the unavoidable connection – implication and obligation – expressed in this staging of the individual's intersubjective encounter with the other who summons 'him' into a position of respons-ibility.

Hotel Rwanda and specifically Paul Rusesabagina provide a clear and intense version of the summoning into action and dramatisation of the response to others' suffering integral to Levinasian ethical criticism.[4] These film sequences, in staging the West's relation to the suffering of others, are central to an argument that *Hotel Rwanda* is one of a group of films that speak to the events of 9/11.[5] These films are not about the attack on the Twin Towers but represent a new take on personal and global responsibility, an emerging self-consciousness about the individual's complicity in others' despair, which has proliferated and intensified in the wake of 9/11. The group of films includes *Blood Diamond* (Zwick, 2006), *Children of Men* (Cuarón, 2006), *The Constant Gardener* (Meirelles, 2005) and *The Last King of Scotland* (MacDonald, 2006). As in *Hotel Rwanda*, each has a male protagonist who initially and explicitly resists involvement in any kind of social activism but then becomes embroiled in the events surrounding him and responds to what is demanded of him. The men's growing or eventual action provides the learning curve of the films, which stages their unavoidable obligation and sees them make the ultimate ethical decision and/or sacrifice.

While *Hotel Rwanda*, like these other films, *can* be interpreted in this way, there is a major problem with this reading. After all, where Paul is summoned to act, the West is rendered impotent. Despite the centrality of race to the on-screen events, the racist history that is being traced perpetuates more than it undoes the racist practices at its core. Rife with racial stereotypes, but more than this with a US/Eurocentric perspective, *Hotel Rwanda* naturalises white Western concerns while pretending otherwise: it uses others' stories and suffering to privilege its own. That these post-9/11 films situate white self-consciousness in Africa – or, in the case of *Children of Men*, in the dark continent of a dystopian future – means that the pretence should be all the more transparent. *Hotel Rwanda*'s ethical dynamics, then, are utterly racialised: though noteworthy in their emphasis upon implication and obligation, one must ask what this emphasis serves?

Hotel Rwanda repeats the racist clichés associated with Hollywood's depiction of Africa and Africans on film.[6] Most prominent is the savagery of the African in contrast to the European's civility and civilising affect. The Belgian-owned Mille Collines is a sanctuary of calm efficiency in contrast to the barbaric and bloody mayhem beyond its gates. However, it is more than striking how orderly, smooth and 'clean' the hotel-cum-refugee camp remains. Indeed, as Madeleine Hron suggests, such characteristics firmly align the film with the Holocaust's version of genocide – a highly Eurocentric imaginary – rather than the Rwandan experience that was markedly different in look and actualisation.[7] The 'selection line', too, recalls similar processes within Nazi concentration camps, especially as envisaged by Hollywood. That Rusesabagina was likened to Oskar Schindler and *Hotel Rwanda* to *Schindler's List* (Spielberg, 1993) confirms Terry George's aim to make the film 'comprehensible and tolerable to Western viewers' and his success in this.[8] However, the neat choreography of the unconscionable here, in contrast to the brutal tribalism outside, manages to privilege Western history and Western stereotype, while simultaneously erasing African history and black specificity.

The only specific reference in these film moments to the horror on Kigali's streets is when a Rwandan woman pleads with Jack (Joaquin Phoenix), the American photographer, not to leave her: 'They'll chop me,' she says. Emotivity, brewing through Jack's disquiet-cum-shame, is tied firmly to the prism of white experience in these sequences. Crucially, this prism keeps the postcolonial dynamic in play. The shot/reverse shot of Jack and the woman's exchange shows her upset and his flustered discomfort. He tries frantically to get money out and give it to her but she refuses. He pulls Paul over: 'If there's anything she wants … anything.' Paul simply says 'This is not necessary', as Jack, repeats 'Anything', while extricating himself.

Another key trope within Hollywood's representation of Africa is its dehistoricisation: a mythic, one-dimensional Africa provides a mere backdrop for the Western narrative.[9] *Hotel Rwanda* acknowledges this myth but it also preserves it. Paul says to his wife just prior to these scenes, 'I have no history. I have no memory.' But this sits within the confession of his flaws to Tatiana: 'They told me I was one of

them, and … I swallowed all of it.' His confession operates as a classic tale of the awakening of the house negro – one strongly associated with the USA – and leads straight on from Paul's exchange with the UN's Colonel Oliver (Nick Nolte). Oliver, telling him of the West's abandonment, states: 'You're dirt. We think you're dirt … . You're not even a nigger … you're an African.' From dirt/African to house negro to *sonderkommando* (as he smoothes the segregation of the selection line), the terms of Paul's relentless subordination change little vis-à-vis the master, that is the US/Eurocentric, narrative. While Tatiana will tell her husband, 'I know who you are', the film itself denies such surety.

Hotel Rwanda's relationship to cliché and myth is, then, more complicated than it seems. While wanting and seeming to step away from them, they remain entrenched and, as a result, viewers, as Mohamed Adhikari suggests, '[fall] back on shop-worn, racist conventions of Western attitudes toward Africa. Indeed, the film inadvertently reinforces such mystification.'[10] But does 'inadvertent' cover it? I'd like to suggest that what the film is doing is better understood as disavowal: as a wilful, though unconscious, repression of the obvious; to obscure, and hence reinforce, that which is too difficult to admit. What is disavowed, then, in *Hotel Rwanda* is the enduring racism of the white West, bolstered precisely through its supposed rejection. This double play, this balancing act, pervades these film moments.

The shot of the first flow of westerners from the hotel flanked by Belgian soldiers on either side is accompanied by a radio report from News Service Africa declaring that the 'US and British representatives on the security council will lobby for the removal of all UN peacekeepers from Rwanda.' The matter-of-fact voiceover immediately historicises the scene's events, underscoring their facticity and with it their inevitability. The camera is static and the whites walk towards it and then away towards the bus, with umbrella-toting or case-carrying hotel porters running alongside. All perform their roles unquestioningly. Objectivity and historical veracity are stressed: indeed, there is a glaring absence of point-of-view shots throughout these sequences. Instead, a combination of the unavoidable and the tragic presides through a determinedly disinterested narration. The whites can do nothing but follow instructions; the Rwandans can do nothing but smooth the whites' exodus: to serve, to save, to salve. The camera records these truisms impartially. However, this is a faux disinterest: not only does the film's affective register feed Western sentiment but the subject–object power dynamics of 'looking on' are classically, and racially, constructed. In case the bias isn't clear, when the film cuts next to the interior, the shot is of a desk just inside the hotel and a seated soldier checking the papers of the exiting westerners. The slight low angle puts the camera, and the spectator with it, at seat-, that is soldier-, level, aligning 'us' firmly with them.

Regarding the suffering of the black Other has been a long-standing preoccupation of American culture. While its revival in contemporary Hollywood aims to expose racism as 'hateful', the real goal of films as diverse as *Hotel Rwanda* and *The Green Mile* (Darabont, 1999) is to redeem and reinvent the ethically enlightened but impotent whites precisely through black suffering or 'blackpain', as Debra Walker King calls it.[11] What is more, as Heike Härting argues so well, such spectacles of black suffering 'legitimize the perceived need for economic and institutional aid while producing and reifying the inhabitants of [Africa] … as dependent nonsubjects'.[12] In other words, regarding the suffering of the black Other works to license and extol the West's ongoing intervention in the global south, and in other 'needy' nations, in terms that uphold imperialist dynamics, albeit the nature of intervention has changed. Western armies are replaced with peace forces and aid organisations – as evident in the post-9/11 white-conscience films – but the structures of power and patronage remain the same. Colonel Oliver is a focal point in these film moments. Immobile, silent, shifting uneasily, he becomes metonymic of the West's or rather the USA's paternalism-in-perpetuity.[13] Returning finally to our ethical approach, where Paul is summoned to act, the West is only summoned to feel. Its necessitated action shifts elsewhere. The swell of feeling, then, is not meant simply to absolve the audience, as Franco Moretti might have it,[14] but, as respons-ibility displaced and deferred, to foment support for Western governments' humanitarian 'interests': to summon and legitimise their acts.

NOTES

1. *Hotel Rwanda*'s whitening of the West is evidenced further by the UN troops remaining after the Belgians leave, who, as Madeleine Hron notes, 'consisted of Ghanaians, Tunisians and Bangladeshi forces, so very few Whites': Madeleine Hron, '"But I Find No Place": Representations of the Genocide in Rwanda', in Colman Hogan and Marta Marín Dòmine (eds), *The Camp: Narratives of Internment and Exclusion* (Newcastle: Cambridge Scholars Publishing, 2007), p. 215.
2. See Richard Dyer's discussion of the male pin-up: 'Don't Look Now – The Male Pin-Up', *Screen* no. 23, 1982, pp. 61–73.
3. Emmanuel Levinas, 'Ethics as First Philosophy', in S. Hand (ed.), *The Levinas Reader* (Cambridge, MA: Blackwell, 1989), p. 82. See my earlier discussion of this in Michele Aaron, *Spectatorship: The Power of Looking On* (London: Wallflower Press, 2007), pp. 111–13.
4. Levinas is at the core of an emerging body of ethical film criticism. See Sara Cooper, *Selfless Cinema? Ethics and French Documentary* (Oxford: Legenda, 2005); Aaron, *Spectatorship*;

Lisa Downing and Libby Saxton, *Film and Ethics: Foreclosed Encounters* (London: Routledge, 2009). Crucially, the issue of race is marginalised within these works. This discussion hopes to begin redressing that fact.
5. See Michele Aaron, 'From Complacency to Culpability: Conflict and Death in Post-9.11 Film', in Mei Renyi and Fu Meirong (eds), *Changes and Continuities: The United States after 9.11* (Beijing: World Affairs Press, 2009) [Chinese language]. For the 'morality' of this period's films, see Guy Westwell, *War Cinema: Hollywood on the Front Line* (London: Wallflower Press, 2006); Cynthia Weber, *Imagining America at War* (London: Routledge, 2006).
6. See, for example, Kenneth Cameron, *Africa on Film: Beyond Black and White* (New York: Continuum, 1994); Vivian Bickford-Smith and Richard Mendelsohn (eds), *Black and White in Colour: African History on Screen* (Athens: Ohio University Press, 2006).
7. Hron, '"But I Find No Place"', p. 215.
8. Ibid. The Holocaust functions more broadly as a reference point in post-9/11 cinema's visual imagining of war. *Children of Men* uses it too, underscoring the visual and ethnic links between its detention camps and those of Nazi Germany by, among other things, playing the Libertines track, 'Arbeit Macht Frei', which were the words inscribed above the entrance to Auschwitz.
9. For *Hotel Rwanda*'s historicisation see Kenneth Harrow, '"Un train peut en cacher un autre": Narrating the Rwandan Genocide and *Hotel Rwanda*', *Research in African Literatures* no. 36, 2005, pp. 223–32.
10. Mohamed Adhikari, '*Hotel Rwanda*: Too Much Heroism, Too Little History – or Horror?', in Bickford-Smith and Mendelsohn, *Black and White in Colour*, p. 281.
11. Debra Walker King, *African Americans and the Culture of Pain* (Charlottesville: University of Virginia Press, 2008), p. 63.
12. Heike Härting, 'Global Humanitarianism, Race, and the Spectacle of the African Corpse in Current Western Representations of the Rwandan Genocide', *Comparative Studies of South Asia, Africa and the Middle East* vol. 28 no. 1, 2008, pp. 16–17.
13. Nolte's presence here demands reference to his leading role in the ur-text of the white conscience film, *Under Fire* (Spottiswoode, 1983). Interestingly, the symbolic weight of the Canadian UN colonel, who Oliver is based on, has been more recently concretised in Roger Spottiswoode's own Rwandan story: *Shake Hands with the Devil* (Spottiswoode, 2007).
14. Franco Moretti, *Signs Taken for Wonders* [trans. S. Fischer, D. Forgacs and D. Miller] (London: Verso, 1983), p. 173.

BIBLIOGRAPHY

Aaron, Michele, *Spectatorship: The Power of Looking On* (London: Wallflower Press, 2007).

Aaron, Michele, 'From Complacency to Culpability: Conflict and Death in Post-9.11 Film', in Mei Renyi and Fu Meirong (eds), *Changes and Continuities: The United States after 9.11* (Beijing: World Affairs Press, 2009) [Chinese language].

Adhikari, Mohamed '*Hotel Rwanda*: Too Much Heroism, Too Little History – or Horror?', in Vivian Bickford-Smith and Richard Mendlesohn (eds), *Black and White in Colour: African History on Screen* (Athens: Ohio University Press, 2006).

Bickford-Smith, Vivian and Mendelsohn, Richard (eds), *Black and White in Colour: African History on Screen* (Athens: Ohio University Press, 2006).

Cameron, Kenneth, *Africa on Film: Beyond Black and White* (New York: Continuum, 1994).

Cooper, Sara, *Selfless Cinema? Ethics and French Documentary* (Oxford: Legenda, 2005).

Downing, Lisa and Saxton, Libby, *Film and Ethics: Foreclosed Encounters* (London: Routledge, 2009).

Dyer, Richard, 'Don't Look Now – The Male Pin-Up', *Screen* no. 23, 1982, pp. 61–73.

Hand, S. (ed.), *The Levinas Reader* (Cambridge, MA: Blackwell, 1989).

Harrow, Kenneth, '"Un train peut en cacher un autre": Narrating the Rwandan Genocide and *Hotel Rwanda*', *Research in African Literatures* no. 36, 2005, pp. 223–32.

Härting, Heike, 'Global Humanitarianism, Race, and the Spectacle of the African Corpse in Current Western Representations of the Rwandan Genocide', *Comparative Studies of South Asia, Africa and the Middle East* vol. 28 no. 1, 2008, pp. 61–77.

Hogan, Colman and Marín Dòmine, Marta (eds), *The Camp: Narratives of Internment and Exclusion* (Newcastle: Cambridge Scholars Publishing, 2007).

Hron, Madeleine, '"But I Find No Place": Representations of the Genocide in Rwanda', in Hogan and Marín Dòmine, *The Camp*.

Levinas, Emmanuel, 'Ethics as First Philosophy', in Hand, *The Levinas Reader*.

Moretti, Franco, *Signs Taken for Wonders* [trans. S. Fischer, D. Forgacs and D. Miller] (London: Verso, 1983).

Renyi, Mei and Meirong, Fu (eds), *Changes and Continuities: The United States after 9.11* (Beijing: World Affairs Press, 2009) [Chinese language].

Walker King, Debra, *African Americans and the Culture of Pain* (Charlottesville: University of Virginia Press, 2008).

Weber, Cynthia, *Imagining America at War* (London: Routledge, 2006).

Westwell, Guy, *War Cinema: Hollywood on the Front Line* (London: Wallflower Press, 2006).

Working through the Body: Textual–Corporeal Strategies in *United 93* (2006)

LISA PURSE

United 93 (Greengrass, 2006), a dramatisation of the hijacking of United Airlines flight 93 on 11 September 2001, was the first theatrical release to directly depict the events of 9/11.[1] On its arrival, debates raged in the US and British press about whether North American audiences were 'ready' for such a film, as well as about what the film should 'be' – a memorial rather than a mawkish piece of entertainment, a sober re-enactment rather than a disaster movie or political intervention, for example.[2] In interviews, the director Paul Greengrass was forceful about audiences' readiness for the film but more circumspect about the filmmakers' intentions, emphasising the dramatisation as a human story and declining to characterise the film's aims as political except in the broadest of terms:

> Collectively, we gathered together to try to make sense of this event, to try to reconstruct it, to relive it, to dramatize it ... [to] recreate a believable truth that reflects the record ... ultimately, I think, I hope what comes out is the idea of the fragility of our modernity, our democracies, our technological systems.[3]

Such rhetoric allowed the film to plot a path between the various stridently politicised discourses that had solidified around 9/11 in western societies, mobilised by politicians, the media and various special-interest groups.[4]

However, *United 93*'s restriction of the action (after the prologue) to a series of interiors directly connected to flight 93 (the plane, air-traffic and ground-control centres, and the Northeast Air Defense Command Centre), the film's lack of explicit reference to the wider contexts of and possible contributing factors to 9/11, and its omission of contextualising backstories for the main protagonists, drew criticism from some quarters. Writing in *Newsweek*, David Ansen worried that 'without context, psychology, politics or contemplative distance, you may wonder what, exactly, this re-creation illuminates'.[5] Ansen's discomfort at what

he saw as a lack of an overt political commentary in *United 93* betrays a common cultural anxiety about the drama-documentary's capacity (due to its blurred formal distinctions between fictionalised and factual aspects) to present a biased account in the guise of a factual reconstruction, and a corresponding desire for drama-documentary to be 'clear' about its position on the events it depicts. But such logic risks privileging the most obvious or most easily articulated sources of potential commentary such as dialogue and plot over other forms of meaning production that are equally communicative. This essay will suggest that *United 93* brings the human body emphatically into focus to produce a different kind of 'commentary', by harnessing a range of aesthetic strategies that evoke our physical experience of being in the world. In doing so, the film attempts rhetorical effects that move beyond the filmmakers' declared aims to directly intervene in the cultural-political debates about 9/11. The opening of the film provides a pertinent opportunity to scrutinise this aesthetic and political project.

United 93 is preceded by the animated logos of its two main production companies, Universal Studios and Working Title.[6] They unfold on the screen in complete silence. This is comparatively unusual. A brief survey of other logo sequences on films co-produced by Working Title illustrates that such logos tend to be accompanied either by a branded musical theme or by sounds (extra-diegetic or diegetic) that relate to the first images of a film or its wider subject matter.[7] Silence, then, asserts *United 93* as in some way distinct from mainstream filmed entertainment, a claim instead for its 'respectability' and also its 'respectfulness'. In the shared hush and darkness of the cinema theatre, the film's lack of sound resonates with associations of collective human contemplation, worship and sobriety, but also of the material reality of human absence (no audible breathing, voice, movement). Through a lack of conventional aural or musical accompaniment,

and the sombre connotations of the resulting silence, the logo sequences seem to acknowledge the audience's prior awareness of the fate of flight 93 and generate expectations about the seriousness of the treatment of the material that will follow. What is imposed and demanded by this silence is a correspondingly sober, contemplative viewing mode, distinct from less self-consciously reflective modes of entertainment consumption.

Following the logo sequences, the screen is black for approximately eight seconds. On the soundtrack a male voice recites a prayer softly in Arabic, a sound bridge into the first shot of the film.

Hands hold a book in extreme close-up; a medium close-up follows of a man, Ziad Jarrah (Khalid Abdalla), sitting cross-legged on a bed, gently rocking back and forth as he reads aloud from the volume, the prayer reconstituted as a diegetic sound. He is in a softly lit room, the modern convection heater and dull, pale curtains visible behind him signalling the homogenous décor of a cheap hotel. Other sounds emerge, the low hum audible under his prayer now discernible as the muffled noise of planes taking off and landing: this is an airport hotel. Another man, Ahmed Al Haznawi (Omar Berdouni), enters the shot closer to the camera and out of focus, and as he addresses Ziad a cut to a medium shot brings both men into focus simultaneously in front of the hotel window.

It is dark outside, dawn rather than morning: a period of inaction, of reflection before the day begins, forestalled as Ahmed confirms, 'It's time.' The medium shot returns, the camera tracking Ahmed as he turns away from the bed and walks into a new, connected space, the en-suite bathroom. As the bathroom door is pulled to, the sequence cuts

back to a close-up of Ziad. Despite his colleague's instruction, he has stayed in the same position on the bed, rocking back and forth, his eyes now averted in thought. The screen goes black, a low-frequency boom calling to a close this first full sequence of the film.

Greengrass has since revealed that a quite different opening was planned and shot, starting with Khalid Sheikh Mohammed (alleged mastermind of 9/11) laying out his plans at Osama Bin Laden's Afghanistan headquarters, and then 'follow[ing] characters from hotel rooms dotted around Newark Airport [one of the pilots, a stewardess, and so on]'. But this material was discarded in the edit because 'it seemed redundant'.[8] One reason for this might have been to minimise controversy: the implicit critique buried in the contrast between the grinding poverty of Taliban-controlled Afghanistan and the affluent modernity of the North American metropolis could have proved unpalatable to some viewers. Instead, according to Greengrass, the opening that made the cut sets up 'the forces in play on that day' in broader terms, contrasting western societies' 'conspicuous modernity' with 'young men in medieval religious rapture'.[9] However, Greengrass's insights also point us away from other possibilities. The film could have begun with flight 93's innocent occupants, introducing aspects of their characters and circumstances in order to underscore the sense of cruel loss as events unfold. Moreover, passengers such as Todd Beamer, who was famously overheard urging 'Let's roll' to initiate an attempt to regain control of the plane, had already been valorised as all-American heroes by the press, and so could have easily functioned as hero archetypes in a traditional 'heroic action' narrative familiar (admittedly by rather uncomfortable association) from Hollywood fiction genres and made-for-TV 'true-story' dramatisations. By beginning instead with an extended focus on the hijackers' morning routine, Greengrass rejects these other possibilities, but to what ends? Unpicking the textual detail of the opening offers the opportunity to look behind the film-makers' declared intentions (constrained as they are by competing cultural, political and media discourses about what is appropriate to show or say about 9/11, its causes and consequences), to prioritise how the film – through its execution – *actually* seeks to engage its audience.

I suggested earlier that the logo sequences' unusual silence represented a demand for a different mode of spectatorship from the audience, and I now want to develop this idea further. The absence of sound in the logo sequences has the effect of prompting the audience to strain their sense of hearing for possible sounds, to 'prick up the ears', as it were. The film's first image, a blank screen, continues this attempt, this time privileging hearing while the lack of visual stimuli prompts the eyes to become more alert. Anticipation (for the film to start) is refigured as a more explicitly sensory experience (the

It's time

spectator's awareness while in the process of waiting – of his or her own body in relation to other bodies, to the spaces and furniture of the seating, and so on – is an additional layer of sensory experience here). Thus the logos and the blank screen that follows them are an attempt to prime the senses, an ambition that depends on the conception of film viewing as an embodied experience. Vivian Sobchack, building on Maurice Merleau-Ponty's classification of the body as fundamentally central to processes of perception, experience and expression, characterises the film experience thus:

> As 'lived bodies' ... our vision is always already 'fleshed out'. Even at the movies our vision and hearing are informed and given meaning by our other modes of sensory access to the world ... . In sum, the film experience is meaningful *not to the side of our bodies but because of our bodies.* Which is to say that movies provoke in us the 'carnal thoughts' that ground and inform more conscious analysis. [italics in original].[10]

While film viewing is an inherently embodied experience, some film images have the capacity to appeal to the senses much more directly than others, as Laura U. Marks has noted. Marks calls such images 'haptic' (a word referring to the sense of touch, but transformed by Marks's emphasis on perception as involving *all* the senses), explaining that they 'do not invite identification with a figure so much as they encourage a bodily relationship between the viewer and the image'.[11] I want to suggest that the images that follow *United 93*'s initial 'priming of the senses' have similarly 'haptic' qualities.

After the silence of the logo sequences, the first sound of the film is an intimate one, a private recitation softly delivered in an aural close-up, as if the speaker is next to the ear of the listener. The rhythms and solemnity of prayer are recognisable even as the words (for non-speakers of Arabic) are not. The decision not to subtitle this prayer is significant but also ambiguous; the conventional mode of access to non-English dialogue is denied to the spectator, who must instead rely on alternatives to language-based interpretation. This linguistic disconnect – evident at several points across the narrative where the hijackers' speech is not fully subtitled – risks perpetuating a reductive, racist conception of the Muslim as unknowable 'Other', at least for some non-Muslim western spectators. But while the praying voice suggests 'difference' (in terms of linguistic access), the decision to locate the speaker 'close by' works to foreground certain commonalities of bodily experience. The aural close-up recreates physical closeness to another body; the whisper of lips quietly forming words and the click of tongue against teeth generate recognition of certain physiological mechanics of speech formation. Before an image has appeared on the

screen, then, the body of the hijacker is being spatially located 'here' rather than 'there', constructed as physically nearby and 'familiar' even while linguistically 'different'.

The aurally generated impression of physical intimacy is intensified by the first shot of the film: hands cup an open book in such an extreme close-up that the camera struggles to hold all image elements in focus at the same time, so close that the roughness of the page and the detailed textures of the thumbnail and surrounding skin are available to the spectator (see first image). Once again, in place of linguistic access (subtitles remain absent; the words on the page, when discernible, are in Arabic), a corporeal recognition is encouraged. The close-up foregrounds the creased skin of the junction between thumb and finger and the ridged surface of the fingertip, physical attributes of the cinematic body that are almost certainly shared by the spectator. These are haptic images that not only call up the memory of the sensation of touching fingertips to paper but that also foreground touch as a present possibility, showing fingers and paper that seem within touching distance.

The ensuing shots of the hijackers' hotel-room preparations continue in a similar vein. Bare-chested or dressed only in undervests, the hijackers wash, shave, trim their pubic hair, and engage in prayer and solitary reflection. This is a series of private acts that, in their framing from various close distances, their filming in a muted colour palette of flesh tones and their aural preoccupation with the familiar necessities prompted by physiological processes (rinsing sweat from skin, cutting or shaving away hair), repeatedly call attention to the hijackers as *bodies*. At the same time, incursions into the frame persistently remind the spectator of their own embodied 'presence' in relation to these figures. For example, in only the second shot of the film, as Ziad prays on the bed, the left side of the image is penetrated by an out-of-focus object located between him and the camera. Seconds later, Ahmed's blurred form also crosses the frame between the camera and Ziad, creating a more significantly obscured view (see second image). In other shots, the hijackers' ablutions are partially blocked by the blurred edges of doorways and walls that extend across substantial areas of the frame. The camera's failure to keep these intervening objects in focus is a practical difficulty defined by proximity (that is, by objects being too close to the camera lens), but the film-makers' decision not to adjust the camera lens to bring the closer objects into focus also foregrounds physical proximity-as-experience for the spectator. The effect is to create the impression that, just as the actual camera that recorded these images was 'really there' in the room, the spectator (via his or her proxy, the camera's image) is also situated within the hotel room's cramped spatial coordinates, very close to the bodies being viewed. While such shots structure the spectator's access to the room and its occupants using a voyeuristic logic that underlines the private nature of these observed rituals, they also construct the spectator as a 'presence' in the diegetic space, a body watching other bodies that appear *close enough to touch.*

In the light of the textual detail of this first scene of *United 93*, Greengrass's verbalised intention to show 'young men in medieval religious rapture' seems only a partial explanation for the choices in play.[12] The hijackers' investment in their religious pieties could have been performed and filmed in a number of alternative ways, without such attention to the intimate physicality of the hijackers and without bringing the spectator so close to their 'corporeality'. So what is at stake in this persistent appeal to the senses? It enables an emphatically proximate encounter with a body (the terrorist/hijacker) that should, for some, have remained 'always-distant', designated as 'monster' rather than 'human', 'different' not 'similar', 'there' not 'here'. Relevant here is Marks's suggestion that haptic images possess the radical potential to break down traditional, rationalist ways of seeing (and viewing film images):

> [C]inema's optical images address a viewer who is distant, distinct, and disembodied. Haptic images invite the viewer to dissolve his or her subjectivity in the close and bodily contact with the image … . In the dynamic movement between optical and haptic ways of seeing, *it is possible to compare different ways of knowing and interacting with an other.*[13]

Mobilising haptic images, the opening of *United 93* has, I suggest, a similar project: to encourage the spectator to test out different kinds of relationship to the hijackers' physical presence than are permitted within the received, pre-existing and vociferously politicised discourses on 9/11 and terrorism, and the convenient but ultimately grossly reductive figurations (heroic victim, evil terrorist, heroic terrorism-fighter) they encourage.

In these early moments, the camera's imitation of the eye's inability to keep objects of different distances in focus at the same time functions as a resonant metaphor for the human inability to achieve true objectivity, to see all sides of an issue clearly. Eschewing overt didacticism, *United 93* finds other means to confront us with the challenges involved in trying to adopt a position in relation to the complexities of 9/11. By encouraging a heightened awareness of sensory perception in the spectator, experimenting with proximity and constructing a sense of shared space, and drawing on certain commonalities of corporeal experience, *United 93* bravely attempts to open up a space for responses that move beyond the intellectual and the partisan, that test out alternatives to rigidly polarised political rhetoric. This is its political act in the most politicised and sensitive of contexts.

ACKNOWLEDGMENTS

I would like to thank the members of the Sewing Circle at the Department of Film Theatre and Television at the University of Reading for participating in an insightful discussion of the film. I am also grateful to the delegates and organisers of the Bremen International Film Conference *Word and Flesh* (Germany, 2007) and the *Body and Mind* Interdisciplinary Conference (University of Reading, 2007) for giving me the opportunity to present my early ideas on the film.

NOTES

1. Several made-for-television movies had been made, including *Let's Roll: The Story of Flight 93* (Oxley, 2002), *The Flight That Fought Back* (Goodison, 2005) and *Flight 93* (Markle, 2006), while Michael Moore's documentary *Fahrenheit 9/11* (2004) offered political commentary against the backdrop of 9/11.
2. See John W. Jordan, 'Transcending Hollywood: The Referendum on *United 93* as Cinematic Memorial', *Critical Studies in Media Communication* vol. 25 no. 2, June 2008, pp. 196–223, for an illuminating summary of the conflicting discourses in play within US media responses to the film.
3. Gavin Smith, 'Mission Statement', *Film Comment*, May–June 2006, p. 28.
4. Such comments also placed the film in the context of Greengrass's earlier 'reconstructions', television drama documentaries such as *Bloody Sunday* (2002) and *The Murder of Stephen Lawrence* (1999), which used the principles of re-enactment to try to understand politically sensitive incidents that had had a traumatic status in the public imaginary.
5. Quoted in Jordan, 'Transcending Hollywood', p. 218.
6. Studio Canal and SKE (Sidney Kimmel Entertainment) were the other two production companies involved.
7. For example, the Universal logo heralding *Smokin' Aces* (Carnahan, 2007) includes the familiar brass-heavy company theme tune, with the film's own score beginning over the Working Title logo; and the thematically significant sound of surveillance recordings accompanies both the Focus Features and Working Title logos at the beginning of the espionage-focused *Burn after Reading* (Coen, 2008). Similarly, the musical overture for *Elizabeth: The Golden Age* (Kapur, 2007) begins as the production logos play out across the screen, while a collage of 1960s radio programme snippets and the sound of tuning radios is audible over the Working Title logo before *The Boat That Rocked* (Curtis, 2009), a film about the emergence of UK pirate radio.
8. *United 93* audio commentary by Paul Greengrass, on Region 2 single-disc edition DVD release © Universal Studios, 2006.
9. This of course risks taking the hijackers' actions out of context, and we might ask what precisely the film replaces that context with.

10. Vivian Sobchack, *Carnal Thoughts: Embodiment and Moving Image Culture* (Berkeley and Los Angeles: University of California Press, 2004), p. 60. Maurice Merleau-Ponty, in *Phenomenology of Perception* [trans. Colin Smith, 1962] (London and New York: Routledge, 2006 [1945]), pp. 235, 273, writes: 'Our own body is in the world as the heart is in the organism: it keeps the visible spectacle constantly alive, it breathes life into it and sustains it inwardly ... . My body is the fabric into which all objects are woven, and it is, at least in relation to the perceived world, the general instrument of my "comprehension".' His ideas have been taken up more recently by writers such as Vivian Sobchack (*The Address of the Eye: A Phenomenology of Film Experience*, *Carnal Thoughts*), Laura U. Marks (*The Skin of the Film: Intercultural Cinema, Embodiment, and the Senses*, *Touch: Sensuous Theory and Multisensory Media*) and Jennifer Barker (*The Tactile Eye: Touch and the Cinematic Experience*) who are developing the field of phenomenological film theory (full details given in Bibliography).

11. Laura U. Marks, *Touch: Sensuous Theory and Multisensory Media* (Minneapolis and London: University of Minnesota Press, 2002), p. 3. Marks finds her examples in the experimental video and film work of artists such as Sadie Benning, Helen Lee and Michael Cho.

12. *United 93* audio commentary.

13. Marks, *Touch*, pp. 13, 18 [italics mine]. Creating such a strident opposition between European post-Enlightenment rationality and older, 'embodied' traditions of knowledge is, of course, a rhetorical move on Marks's part, but the characterisation of haptic images' power to disrupt rigid, conservative viewing practices is still suggestive and useful.

BIBLIOGRAPHY

Barker, Jennifer, *The Tactile Eye: Touch and the Cinematic Experience* (Berkeley: University of California Press, 2009).

Jordan, John W., 'Transcending Hollywood: The Referendum on *United 93* as Cinematic Memorial', *Critical Studies in Media Communication* vol. 25 no. 2, June 2008, pp. 196–223.

Kean, Thomas H., *et al.*, *The 9/11 Commission Report* (Washington, DC: National Commission on Terrorist Attacks upon the United States of America, 22 July 2004). Available at <www.9-11commission.gov/report/911Report.pdf> (accessed 1 November 2006).

Marks, Laura U., *The Skin of the Film: Intercultural Cinema, Embodiment, and the Senses* (Durham, NC and London: Duke University Press, 2000).

Marks, Laura U., *Touch: Sensuous Theory and Multisensory Media* (Minneapolis and London: University of Minnesota Press, 2002).

Merleau-Ponty, Maurice, *Phenomenology of Perception* [trans. Colin Smith, 1962] (London and New York: Routledge, 2006 [1945]).

Smith, Gavin, 'Mission Statement', *Film Comment*, May–June 2006, pp. 25–8.

Sobchack, Vivian, *The Address of the Eye: A Phenomenology of Film Experience* (Princeton, NJ: Princeton University Press, 1992).

Sobchack, Vivian, *Carnal Thoughts: Embodiment and Moving Image Culture* (Berkeley and Los Angeles: University of California Press, 2004).

United 93 Region 2 single-disc edition DVD release © Universal Studios, 2006.

Universal Pictures, *United 93 Production Notes* (Los Angeles, CA: Universal Pictures, 2006).

'I wasn't expecting that!': Cognition and Shock in *Alien*'s (1979) Chestburster Scene

JONATHAN FROME

The 'chestburster' scene from *Alien* (Scott, 1979) is one of the most iconic scenes in the history of cinematic horror. The crew of the spaceship *Nostromo* laugh together as they eat at a large circular table. One of them, Kane (John Hurt), starts to cough. His coughs grow worse and eventually develop into full body seizures. As he thrashes, his crewmates grab him and try to hold him down on the table. Suddenly, a stream of blood shoots out of Kane's chest and a small alien violently bursts through his ribcage. The alien, covered in blood, surveys the room. It emits a high-pitched squeal and runs out of the room, with its segmented tail flailing. Kane lies dead on the table as the other crew members, in shock, try to comprehend what has just occurred.

This moment is very powerful, especially for its initial audience, who had no idea how the alien reproduced and probably never considered that an alien might attack Kane from inside his own body. (Unfortunately, most modern viewers of *Alien* are fully aware of the scene before seeing the film and thus cannot fully appreciate its impact.)

There are numerous ways one might analyse this scene. Many approaches presume that there is little interest in the scene's events *per se*. For these approaches, an analysis is interesting to the degree that it can reveal apparently deeper meanings beneath these events (for example, perhaps the scene is metaphorically about the horrors of childbirth). Other approaches assume that typical audience responses are uninteresting. Their analyses might discuss unusual ways specific social groups or cultures have understood or used the film.

Cognitive film theory, by contrast, does not assume that the common responses to a film's basic story are so easily understood. How do viewers understand what is happening when the alien bursts through Kane's chest? And how is the scene able to generate such powerful emotions? We can use what cognitive psychology has learned about the human mind to help answer those questions in surprising detail.[1]

COMPREHENSION

Film viewing is often thought of as a passive experience but, in fact, watching films requires us to engage in constant mental activity. To understand a film's basic story, we must infer a great deal from the information the film provides. This process often seems passive because it is usually unconscious.

Alien never explicitly conveys how the chestburster gets inside Kane. Understanding this aspect of the story requires making inferences based on the information that is provided. Earlier in the film Kane is attacked by an alien 'facehugger' while exploring the surface of a planet. He is brought back to the ship in a coma, with the alien firmly attached to his head. After scanning Kane, the ship's captain, Dallas (Tom Skerritt), says, 'What's that down his throat?' Ash (Ian Holm), the ship's medical officer, replies, 'I would suggest it's feeding him oxygen.' This exchange most immediately functions to increase the sense of danger to Kane; as Ash later notes, if the facehugger is feeding Kane oxygen, removing it could kill him. Yet this information soon plays another role as well.

When the chestburster scene begins, we are unaware that there is an alien inside Kane and its emergence is therefore very surprising. Once our initial shock passes, we automatically try to understand what the chestburster is and how it got inside Kane. The information that the facehugger put something down Kane's throat is now crucial –

it allows us easily to infer that the facehugger implanted the chestburster in Kane. We are never explicitly told that this is the case, and other explanations are possible, but since this inference satisfactorily explains the film's events, we accept that event as part of the film's story.

Yet inference occurs at much more subtle levels as well. We are never told that Dallas is the captain of the ship, but we infer it based on his interactions with the crew, such as his telling Ripley (Sigourney Weaver): 'That's a direct order!' Inferences are usually based on our knowledge of the real world, but they can also be based on our knowledge of film conventions. For example, we first see the *Nostromo* from its exterior. The film then cuts to an interior shot of a hallway lined with pipes. It is not directly communicated that this hallway is inside the *Nostromo*, but we assume that it is, based on editing conventions. Without hundreds of inferences like these, we would never be able to understand the film.

Inferences are usually made using schemas and prototypes.[2] Schemas are clusters of features we use to organise information and form categories. Prototypes are central examples of those categories that we often use as a starting place for imagining any other member of the category. A schema of a bird, for instance, includes the characteristics 'can fly', 'has feathers' and 'whistles songs'. A prototypical bird has all of the features in the schema. When a friend tells us that they saw a bird, we generally assume that they saw a prototypical bird that can fly. Of course, there are birds that can't fly, such as penguins. Unless our friend just returned from Antarctica, however, we assume that he saw something that can fly because, in the absence of contrary information, we tend to fill missing information with prototypes and prototypical features.

Schemas (groups of features) act as baseline assumptions. Our assumptions are very often correct, so this strategy helps us successfully navigate the world with incomplete information. Schemas also allow films to convey lots of information quickly, as in the case of the ship's captain, Dallas. One characteristic of ships' captains is that they give other people orders. When we see Dallas give Ripley an order, not only do we assume that he is a captain, we also assume that he has other prototypical features of captains, such as confidence and experience, unless the film gives us reason to think otherwise.

STARTLE AND REFLEXIVE RESPONSES

We tend to think of our emotional responses to films as highly individualised because people can have very different reactions to the same film. Some people love *Alien's* suspense, while others find it unbearable. Yet it is important to remember that, although people often do have very different emotional (or *affective*) responses to films, frequently they also have similar responses, even across cultures. Emotional responses common across cultures are usually part of the low-level mental architecture shared by all human beings. Evolution developed these affective responses because they were useful for our survival when humans first evolved. They are often reflexive and require no conscious thought. One example is the startle response. Horror films exploit this reflex by having monsters suddenly pop onto the screen from some hiding place. Their sudden appearance might be accompanied by a loud sound or musical cue. The combination makes audiences jump in their seats and scream.

Although we rarely think about it, it makes little sense for us to jump or scream when the chestburster pops out of Kane's chest. We know that the monster isn't real and can't actually hurt us. So why do we jump? One common answer is that we 'suspend disbelief' when we watch films and thus act as if we believe the alien is real. But if we suspend disbelief, why don't we call the police when we see the chestburster kill Kane? We don't act as if we really believe the monster exists, which shows that we do not fully suspend disbelief.

Cognitive science provides a much more satisfying explanation of why we are startled when monsters suddenly appear in films. Our brains have evolved a mechanism that makes very quick but 'rough and dirty' evaluations of objects in our environment. You may have experienced this when walking in a forest and jumping at a stick that is shaped like a snake. Your mind first makes a 'rough and dirty' evaluation that the object is dangerous, and you jump away. This evaluation is so fast that you are not even conscious of it before you jump. Fractions of a second later, a higher-level part of your mind makes a more accurate judgment – it's just a stick. Since we are dealing with potential life-and-death issues when it comes to dangerous creatures, we have evolved a rapid response that moves us to action fractions of seconds faster than we would if we had to wait for a more accurate evaluation.[3] A similar process happens in films. You know that the chestburster on the screen cannot harm you, but before your brain even has a chance to evaluate whether it is actually dangerous, your mind makes a 'rough and dirty' judgment that you should jump away. This reflex, not 'disbelief', is at the core of the startle response.

Another low-level mental process that affects your emotional response is called 'emotional contagion'.[4] We all know that happy people can make us happier and depressed people can bring us down. Modern psychology has discovered that part of the reason is our unconscious tendency to mimic other people's facial expressions and movements. Seeing someone smile can cause us to break into a smile, but even if we don't, it makes us slightly tense the muscles that cause us to smile and the corners of our lips go up slightly. Mimicking expressions creates a feedback loop that generates the corresponding emotion, and we to some degree 'catch' another person's emotion. When

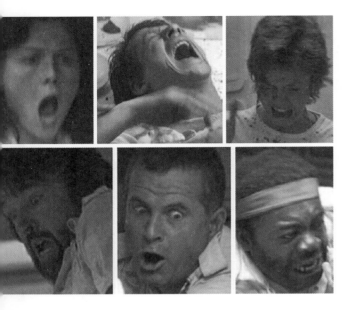

watching the chestburster scene, we see Lambert (Veronica Cartwright) scream and Dallas open his eyes wide, both of which express fear. Unconsciously, we mimic these expressions and movements, which increases the fear we feel. In contrast, if the crew members were all fairly nonchalant as the alien popped out of Kane's chest, or if they were laughing, we would still be startled, but we would probably not be as scared or shocked. Although it is not true of this scene, many times *Alien* provides close-ups of important facial expressions, such as at the end when Ripley confronts the fully grown alien in the escape shuttle. These close-ups maximise the effect of emotional contagion by giving us a very good look at a character's facial expression.[5]

A final example of the ways that films exploit our involuntary reactions to images and sounds involves music. Throughout *Alien*, we hear various mechanical sounds from the ship, such as banging, air rushing by, and humming. In the chestburster scene, starting at the first shot showing the crew at the table, there is a very faint heartbeat-like sound in the background. It is barely noticeable unless you specifically listen for it. It gets louder as the scene goes on, and is prominent when the chestburster looks around the room. Although the volume of the sound changes, its frequency stays at roughly 110 beats per minute throughout the scene – an elevated rate for most people that might occur when they are exercising or under intense stress. When the scene ends, there is a cut to an interior hallway shot. The same heartbeat sound continues across the cut, but the pace is almost exactly half as fast at fifty-five beats per minute. The sound fades fairly quickly, but acts as a cue for the audience to recover after the previous intense moment. It is almost as if the movie is telling the viewer to slow down and breathe deeply.

Although it might seem intuitive that listening to a fast or slow beat can raise or lower our heart rate, we cannot make this conclusion just by looking at our responses to the chestburster scene. After all, there are many other things going on in the scene that might cause an increased heart rate during the scene or a slower heart rate after the scene ends. However, since cognitive film theory draws from actual scientific enquiry, we can look at evidence to help evaluate our intuitions. Experiments have shown that a faster or slower musical tempo does in fact raise or lower our heart rate, as well as our breathing rate and our blood pressure.[6] Further, it has been shown that changes in our heart rate caused by factors other than our emotions, such as musical tempo, can create or intensify the emotions we feel.[7] We can conclude that the heartbeat sound during the chestburster scene contributes to our feelings of emotional intensity, and the slower rhythm in the subsequent scene helps us come down from our intense emotion.

SURPRISE AND SUSPENSE

Yet the feelings of surprise and intense emotional arousal are not the primary feelings we have when watching *Alien*. The most salient emotion we feel is suspense. And although we feel much more surprise than suspense during the chestburster scene, the scene is essential to the suspense we feel later in the film.

The chestburster scene is surprising primarily because, before the attack, we do not know that Kane has an alien inside him. However, there are other important factors that contribute to our surprise. When we watch horror movies, our expectations are shaped by the schema we associate with that genre. The prototypical horror movie attack scene shows the victim alone, perhaps recently separated from a group. Suspenseful music plays as the victim walks into a dark, shadowy area. He hears a sound and says, 'Hello? Is anybody there?' Then, out of nowhere, the monster attacks. The chestburster scene violates all of these features except the last. It opens by showing the victim as part of a large group, eating around a large table and joking around. There is no suspenseful horror music, no shadows, and no discussion of the alien. The scene is brightly lit. Our horror film schema leads us to assume that this is not a scene in which someone will be killed, which increases our surprise when the chestburster attacks.

This surprise lays the groundwork for increased suspense later in the film. Suspense is an emotion that requires feelings of fear, hope and uncertainty. In *Alien*, you fear that the alien will kill the crew, you hope they will survive, and you are uncertain which outcome will actually occur.[8] Suspense is also a prospect emotion, that is, it is an emotion related to something that might happen in the future. You can't feel suspense about something that is currently happening or has already happened. The chestburster scene doesn't generate much suspense because we are so focused on what is happening that we cannot think much about what might happen in the future.

The more uncertain you are about whether a good or bad outcome will happen, the more intense your suspense. The chestburster scene increases your uncertainty about the future in multiple ways. First, it introduces the idea that the alien brought onto the ship can violently kill the crew. Second, the scene establishes that the film is not a typical horror film. If Kane can die in a group, in a brightly lit scene, without any suspenseful music, then an attack can happen at any time. One other factor increasing uncertainty is the nature of the alien itself. The alien does not fit the prototype of a movie monster (or did not at the time of the film's release; now, the alien is one of our prototypes of a movie monster). We do not expect one alien to create another, seemingly entirely different type of alien; now, we are less certain about what will happen in the future. Will the small chestburster also reproduce? Will its offspring be another, very different type of alien? Will the other crew members discover aliens inside their own bodies? We cannot guess without more information, and our uncertainty grows substantially.

The shot right after the chestburster scene – a shot of an empty hallway with a slow heartbeat sound on the soundtrack – is a perfect complement to the previous scene. The chestburster scene shows us what horrible things can happen on the ship and makes us very uncertain about what will happen. The subsequent shot begins to calm us, which frees our minds to speculate about what might happen to the crew, trapped in a ship with a killer alien. This combination is what allows us to feel great suspense later in the film.

We are continuously processing information at many levels of awareness, mostly at a level below our level of consciousness. When we reflect on our own personal responses to films, we can only access the conscious elements of our reactions. This may explain why cognitive film theory is sometimes dismissed as dealing with obvious aspects of films and viewer responses: when you are aware only of your conscious responses to a film, those responses may erroneously seem very simple to understand. Looking more deeply into ostensibly simple reactions to film is the first step to understanding the more subtle and complex responses that everyone agrees provide intriguing challenges for film analysis.

NOTES

1. The cognitive approach was pioneered by David Bordwell in *Narration in the Fiction Film* (Madison: University of Wisconsin Press, 1985).
2. Patrick Colm Hogan, *Cognitive Science, Literature, and the Arts* (New York: Routledge, 2003).
3. Joseph LeDoux, *The Emotional Brain: The Mysterious Underpinnings of Emotional Life* (New York: Simon & Schuster, 1996).
4. Elaine Hatfield and J. T. Cacioppo et al., *Emotional Contagion* (Cambridge: Cambridge University Press, 1994).
5. Carl Plantinga, 'The Scene of Empathy and the Human Face on Film' in Carl Plantinga and Greg M. Smith (eds), *Passionate Views* (Baltimore, MD: Johns Hopkins University Press, 1999), pp. 239–55.
6. P. D. Larsen and D. C. Galletly, 'The Sound of Silence Is Music to the Heart', *Heart* no. 4, 2006.
7. Rainer Reisenzein, 'The Schachter Theory of Emotion: Two Decades Later', *Psychological Bulletin* no. 2, 2006.
8. Jonathan Frome and Aaron Smuts, 'Helpless Spectators: Generating Suspense in Videogames and Film', *TEXT Technology*, 2004.

BIBLIOGRAPHY

Bordwell, David, *Narration in the Fiction Film* (Madison: University of Wisconsin Press, 1985).

Frome, Jonathan and Smuts, Aaron, 'Helpless Spectators: Generating Suspense in Videogames and Film', *TEXT Technology*, 2004.

Hatfield, Elaine and Cacioppo, J. T. et al., *Emotional Contagion* (Cambridge: Cambridge University Press, 1994).

Hogan, Patrick Colm, *Cognitive Science, Literature, and the Arts* (New York: Routledge, 2003).

Larsen, P. D. and Galletly, D. C., 'The Sound of Silence Is Music to the Heart', *Heart* no. 4, 2006.

LeDoux, Joseph, *The Emotional Brain: The Mysterious Underpinnings of Emotional Life* (New York: Simon & Schuster, 1996).

Plantinga, Carl and Smith, Greg M. (eds), *Passionate Views* (Baltimore, MD: Johns Hopkins University Press, 1999), pp. 239–55.

Plantinga, Carl, 'The Scene of Empathy and the Human Face on Film', in Plantinga and Smith, *Passionate Views*, pp. 239–55.

Reisenzein, Rainer, 'The Schachter Theory of Emotion: Two Decades Later', *Psychological Bulletin* no. 2, 2006.

The Inflection of a Dream in *Scarlet Street* (1945)

GEORGE M. WILSON

It is a familiar fact that Fritz Lang made a pair of consecutive films, *The Woman in the Window* (1944) and *Scarlet Street* (1945), films that have similar casts and deal with notably related thematic concerns. There is also, I believe, a critical consensus that *Scarlet Street* (hereafter SS) is the more successful of the two. In this chapter, I want to discuss the way in which one early sequence in the movie sets up the basis for a distinctive solution to a fundamental expositional problem that had already arisen for Lang in making *The Woman in the Window* (hereafter WW) – a problem that is handled in WW in a much less satisfactory fashion. The sequence from SS that I will discuss is that in which the protagonist Chris Cross (Edward G. Robinson) first sees the femme fatale Kitty (Joan Bennett) in the streets of Greenwich Village. I will highlight aspects of the segment that lead up to the intersection of the two characters and aspects of the moments that more or less immediately ensue. I will sometimes refer to this as 'the sequence of the initial visual encounter'.

In both films, Lang wants to cast light for the movie's audience on the personality and character of the person played by Edward G. Robinson. (In WW the character is Professor Wanley.) To cast the intended light, Lang ultimately needs to provide the audience with rather elaborate information about the unconscious, repressed patterns that shape key features of the character's overt behaviour and thought. In WW, Lang notoriously 'solves' the problem by revealing, towards the end of the movie, that most of the ostensible dramatic action is supposed to have constituted the contents of a dream that Professor Wanley experiences when he falls asleep after dinner at his club. A key function of the extended dream sequence is to delineate the inner operations of the Professor's guilty psyche, operations that have putatively been manifested unconsciously in Wanley's conduct during the pre- and post-dream sequences. However, the value of the explanatory contribution is damaged by the awkward artificiality of the last-minute revelation that most of what has earlier been presented has been nothing more than the Professor's

nightmarish dream. SS does not resort to any such infelicitous narrational device, but it does adopt a systematic strategy that allows the audience to gain access to information about Chris Cross's unconscious dreams, feelings and desires and to a wider perspective on their relation to the intersubjective world of the story. The key to this alternative strategy is provided in the sequence of the initial visual encounter.

In an episode just prior to this sequence, Chris confides to his old friend and co-worker Charlie (Samuel S. Hinds) the content of two unfulfilled fantasies of his youth. First, he has dreamed of having the sympathetic love of a young girl, and second, he has dreamed of having a successful career as a painter. The narrative turn that ensues after this confession is rather startling. Chris almost immediately comes upon Kitty, a beautiful young woman in obvious danger, and he rescues her from an assault by her boyfriend, Johnny (Dan Duryea). Spotting the attack, Chris rushes at the couple brandishing his umbrella like a broadsword and manages, mostly by happenstance, to knock Kitty's assailant to the ground. While Chris is hitting at Johnny, he covers his own eyes with his other arm, and he gets his first close look at Kitty only when he lowers the self-protective arm to see what his flailing has achieved.

His initial vision of Kitty is given in an optical point-of-view shot. That is, as Chris lowers his arm, Kitty seems almost to materialise magically before his eyes (and ours) – a fetching, apparently vulnerable and extremely alluring young woman. This initial visual encounter seems at first to promise the prospective fulfilment of the first of the dreams that he has just confessed to Charlie – the dream of winning the affection of a pretty girl.

What is more, the conversation that Chris has with Kitty gives him the impression that he can also realise, with her imaginative support, his related fantasy of artistic fame and achievement. During their conversation after the rescue, Kitty falls under the dim but admiring illusion that Chris is a successful and wealthy painter. Given these two developments, it is as if the objective world of the fiction

has mysteriously 'summoned up a wish-fulfilling response' to Chris's acknowledgment of his youthful dreams.[1] The world *seems* finally to be making it possible for him in late middle age to become the lover of a dazzling young woman, and the situation offers him the opportunity to be seen by her as a painter who enjoys a flourishing artistic career. Of course, this sequence is *not* a dream sequence in the conventional sense. The shots in the sequence do *not* depict the dream experiences of Chris or any other character. Rather, the protagonist has recalled certain of his dreams and fantasies for his friend, and it is as if those recollections have the power in these circumstances to conjure up a state of affairs that promises to satisfy the dreams and fantasies in question. There *is* something 'dreamlike' about the narration of the sequence, but this quality derives chiefly from the fact that the meeting with Kitty is presented as if it involved the kind of mysterious wish-fulfilment that is characteristic of dreams, of primitive thought, and of other forms of unconscious association. In this respect, the film's narration mirrors Chris's own proclivities to perceive and comprehend

the world in 'magical' terms – to *project* his personal feelings onto the operations of the world.[2]

The narrative device is familiar to us from simple fairytales. A being with supernatural powers gives voice to a wish, and the wish is followed by the uncanny appearance of the item for which the character has wished. But, of course, the narrative strategy in SS does not turn upon such a straightforward and literal 'conjuring' of the relevant objects of desire. First, there is no suggestion in the film that genuine magic has been implicated in the sudden entrance of Kitty into the scene. Second, despite Chris's first reaction to the situation, it emerges pretty quickly – for the audience at least, if not for Chris – that the conjured reality answers only superficially to the objects of Chris's real fantasies and desires. Shortly I'll begin to discuss the matter of the discrepancy that emerges between Chris's wishes and their apparent fulfilment in the world. Nevertheless, the sequence gives the viewer a strong sense of the surreal but compelling impact that Kitty's first appearance has for Chris. In the course of the movie, we learn how ordinary perception and repressed fantasy are deeply but deceptively linked in Chris's obsessive experience of her, and this interpenetration of imagination and reality turns out to be emblematic of the problematic workings of his mind.

For example, as the film moves toward its conclusion, hallucination and jealous imagining play a greater and greater role in his thoughts and deeds. He is increasingly haunted by memories of a sexually charged exchange between Kitty and Johnny that he has witnessed, and his visceral impression of the physical passion that these two share comes to dominate his sensibility. In the final shot of the movie, other people in the scene simply evaporate 'by magic' from the visual world, and Chris is left alone with the yammering inner ghosts as the only beings that his perception of the world encompasses. The limited incursion of fantasy when Chris sees Kitty for the first time gradually expands until it obliterates the core of his objective experience.

As I suggested above, the extensive discrepancy between dream and reality becomes the central subject of the second half of the film. The specific link between perception and imagination when Chris meets Kitty oddly reinforces the impression of there being some kind of preordained mystery involved in their meeting. Thus, it seems more than a matter of ordinary luck that Chris's blind flailing with his umbrella dispatches Johnny so quickly from the situation. When Kitty first looms into Chris's field of vision, we barely glimpse Johnny at all. Rather, he lies motionless on the pavement beside her, and when Kitty subsequently glances over her shoulder and sees Johnny start to rise, we notice, in the very next shot, that he has vanished wordlessly from the street. Thus, when Johnny is struck down by Chris, it is as if the umbrella had the power to exorcise him from the scene. Kitty's sudden appearance and Johnny's abrupt disappearance leave an impression of a certain cinematic sleight of hand at work, but that impression is designed chiefly to mimic the logic of Chris's distinctive way of experiencing the world.

Chris is an older man, and the threat of imminent impotence has been hinted at from the very beginning of the movie. The implicit presence of the threat of age helps explain the sudden activation of fantasy and desire in Chris on this occasion. In the opening scene, Chris is being honoured at a business dinner arranged to acknowledge his twenty-five years of clerical service at the J. J. Hogarth Company. He is given an expensive pocket watch by his boss for his service. And J. J. (Russell Hicks) compares him to the solid, reliable watch which he has just awarded to him. But really time is running out for Chris. The dinner is interrupted by the arrival downstairs of a limousine that carries J. J.'s glamorous girlfriend, and her arrival attracts the leering interest of the younger guests. Chris and his friend Charlie go over to the window and survey the sexy blonde. Although they seem impressed at Holgarth's good fortune in having such a sensational mistress, they pretty clearly regard themselves as rather past the more randy enthusiasm of the younger clerks. (The blonde's attitude toward the ogling young men is expressed in the bemusement with which she watches from her car window a dancing monkey that a passing organ grinder is putting on display.)[3]

Shortly afterwards Chris and Charlie leave the party together, departing as a rainstorm suddenly engulfs the streets. The older men, while they walk together, are still ruminating on the attractions of J. J.'s girlfriend, and Chris is especially rueful on the subject. As noted above, he tells Charlie that there were two things that he had dreamed of in his youth. He says, more specifically, 'I … I … I wonder what it's like … well to be loved by a young girl like that. You know nobody ever looked at me like that, not even when I was young.' He adds, 'When I was young, I wanted to be an artist. I dreamt I was going to be a great painter some day.' Of course, neither of these fantasies had ever come close to being realised, but shortly, with the startling appearance of Kitty, it appears for a moment as if they are potentially within his grasp.

At this juncture, Chris and Charlie part ways. Charlie catches a bus and Chris continues wandering alone through the twisting streets of Greenwich Village. It is strongly suggested that Chris is disoriented by his recent reflections and 'lost' in the past dreams that he has been recalling. The rain ends after a period during which Chris fails to notice the change in weather, and he has so utterly lost track of the time that he has to ask a passing policeman to tell him. Moreover, he has also lost his way in the configuration of streets, and he comments on the confusion that the tangled geography induces. It is just

after Chris's physical and psychological disorientation has been established in these ways that he is suddenly transfixed by his view of Kitty – frozen in a kind of *tableau vivant* as a damsel in distress. It is at this moment that the dreamlike character of the segment is most sharply emphasised.

As I have stressed above, the meeting of Chris and Kitty is not a conventional dream sequence, and I've proposed that its dreamlike stylistic character chiefly serves to raise a question that is central to the movie as a whole. How is Chris's perception of the world related to his private fantasies and visions? It emerges that his perception of his environment is thoroughly infused with his inverted, idiosyncratic view of things. Not only is this psychological distortion presented as constant and thoroughgoing, but, as the movie unfolds, we gain a deepening sense of the simplifying and constricting power of his fantasies. The recurring presentation of his paintings is critical in this regard. It turns out that Chris is supposed to have considerable talent as a primitive, expressionistic painter, and we are shown an array of his formally unsophisticated and symbol-laden works. Chris, we learn, has 'no perspective' on things, but he does have the ability to render scenes and other subjects, as he registers them in his own emotional terms.

In fact, the 'dreamlike' character of his first meeting with Kitty is reinforced and elaborated in much of what we later see of these paintings. One of his works in particular is a strange, somewhat childish rendering of the Greenwich Village street where he has 'saved' her from Johnny's rough attack. Johnny appears in this painting as a phallic snake coiled around the adjacent L. In the picture, Kitty stands rigid and isolated next to the remembered streetlight. In fact, many elements from his first encounter with Kitty reappear obsessively in many of his paintings, and Kitty herself is repeatedly depicted in various ways. Most strikingly, there is a portrait of her sitting stiffly in a chair, staring out from the canvas like a vampire or a vengeful hypnotist. (For reasons I will touch on in a moment, this painting comes to be known as 'Self Portrait'.) If our initial sense is that Chris's obsessions inflect his experience in a naive and sometimes touching manner, then, in the later segments of the film, that inflection comes to be registered as compulsive, claustrophobic and threatening.

For the film's viewer, the plausibility of Chris's initial 'dream' illusion is quickly qualified. It takes only a few moments of the ensuing conversation between the pair to make it plain that Chris's wonderstruck impression of Kitty represents little more than a private projection on his part. Kitty is hardly the innocent maiden whose adoration Chris has imagined and longed for. In fact, she is almost certainly a prostitute and Johnny is her pimp. It is crucial to the development of the story that the relationship between

Chris and Kitty, founded at the dreamlike moment I have emphasised, is established on the basis of pretty extensive illusions on both sides. Kitty also has her own rather conventional and prosaic romantic dreams that motivate her. She wants to get married, and she wants to set up a respectable, bourgeois household, although, of course, it is Johnny and not Chris with whom she wants to achieve this unlikely domesticity. For that matter, Johnny has his own dreams of what a fortunate future might turn out to be. He thinks that he may be able to make big money in Hollywood by doing in movies what he already does in reality, that is, by 'acting tough and punching girls in the face'. At first the misunderstandings between the characters, based on their various illusions, seem merely pathetic and intermittently comic. However, as SS develops, the characters' obsessions deepen and darken in disturbing ways. Chris especially becomes thoroughly enmeshed in his fantasies about Kitty, and these obsessions are finally acted out in the destruction of all three of the main characters.

All of this culminates in Chris's final visual encounter with Kitty when 'Self Portrait' is carried past him on the street. This painting plainly offers a grim picture of Kitty. She looks as if she were already dead when it was painted. It is Chris himself who has dubbed it 'Self Portrait'. In the story, the choice of this title for the picture is a joke of Chris's making. The art world has come to believe that Kitty is the painter of all of Chris's canvases. So this painting is construed as a painting that she has made of herself. One might expect that Chris, the real artist, might be distressed at the overall misattribution. In fact, he makes one of the strangest comments in the movie concerning this very point. He says, referring to the confusion, 'I'm happy! It's just like a dream.' I'm not at all sure what Chris's remark here should be taken to suggest, but it frequently happens in dreams that one identity comes to be abruptly and mysteriously exchanged with another. Within the psychodrama of SS, it is completely appropriate that the artist and his obsessional subject come more and more to merge. Chris has yearned for a higher unity with the one he loves, and he seems to have achieved something like this after he murders her and she haunts him constantly thereafter in his compulsive and repetitive hallucinations.

In the moment of their initial visual encounter, as I have stressed, Chris views Kitty as a painterly subject that seems to answer to his fundamental dreams and desires. But, at the end of the movie, he encounters Kitty a final time, featured in his portrait of her and represented in that setting as an immobile and implacable spectator. In the fiction that the painting creates for him at the moment of this last encounter, she has him, as it were, under surveillance. At this juncture, he is implicitly the depicted object of her scrutiny, and the iciness with which she is depicted as watching him mocks the excessive ardour with which his original visualisation of her was conceived. From the outset to ending of SS, the dynamics of their intersecting gazes have been reversed in almost every way.

NOTES

1. Here I'm quoting John Gibbs in 'Filmmaker's Choices', *Close-Up 01* (London: Wallflower Press, 2006), p. 58. He plausibly discovers an instance in which the movie's fictional world seems mysteriously to fulfil a suppressed wish of one the characters in an important sequence of *Talk to Her* (*Hable con ella*) (Almodovar, 2002).

2. In an essay, 'Transparency and Twist in Narrative Film', in M. Smith and T. Wartenberg (eds), *Thinking through Cinema* (Oxford: Blackwell, 2006), pp. 81–96, I distinguish between various senses in which a shot or sequence may be 'subjective'. (WW is briefly discussed as a more conventional instance of 'subjective' representation. The narration of SS is systematically inflected by Chris's subjectivity in a notably different sense than any I consider there. In particular, the points I am making about SS illustrate the danger of loose talk about 'dream sequences'.)

3. For a more elaborate discussion of this opening scene (and of SS in general), see the account in Tom Gunning, *The Films of Fritz Lang* (London: BFI, 2000), pp. 307–39.

BIBLIOGRAPHY

Gibbs, John, 'Filmmaker's Choices', *Close-Up 01* (London: Wallflower Press, 2006), pp. 1–87.

Gunning, Tom, *The Films of Fritz Lang* (London: BFI, 2000), pp. 307–39.

Wilson, George M., 'Transparency and Twist in Narrative Film', in Murray Smith and Thomas E. Wartenberg (eds), *Thinking through Cinema* (Oxford: Blackwell, 2006), pp. 81–96.

Judy's Plan: A Reading of the 'Flashback' Sequence in *Vertigo* (1958)

WILLIAM ROTHMAN

Scottie (James Stewart) is an open book to Hitchcock's camera. His thoughts are legible even when we find ourselves increasingly unwilling to endorse them. The mystery at the heart of *Vertigo* (Hitchcock, 1958), the mystery that attracts Scottie himself, is not a mystery *about* him. It is a mystery *to* him. But it is a mystery the 'hard-headed Scot' does everything in his power to deny. Scottie himself is a mystery to Hitchcock only insofar as he illustrates the fact about being human that it is possible for others to know us better than we know ourselves. The camera's relationship to the woman projected on the movie screen, in her various guises, is more ambiguous, but also more intimate. She is an object of desire to Scottie, to us and to Hitchcock. Yet she and Hitchcock's camera are mysteriously attuned.

In an essay on *Vertigo* published several years after *Hitchcock – The Murderous Gaze* (1982), I drew the conclusion that, no less than the villainous Elster, this 'unknown woman' is a stand-in for Hitchcock.[1] Hence the title I gave my essay: '*Vertigo*: The Unknown Woman in Hitchcock'. And yet I had no doubt that this 'unknown woman' was known to me. Ah, the foolishness of youth!

I seem always to have known that it cannot be a simple mistake when Judy (Kim Novak) – saying 'Can't you see?' – asks Scottie to help her put on the necklace. (Freud was a genius, after all.) I said as much in my essay. The deepest interpretation of Judy's motivation for 'staying and lying', I wrote, is that

> she wishes for Scottie to bring Madeleine back (which means that it is no accident when she puts on the incriminating necklace). Judy wishes for Scottie to lead her to the point at which she can reveal that she is Madeleine – but without losing his love.

I understood that 'deep down' Judy wished for Scottie to 'change' her. But I still assumed, as has every commentator on *Vertigo*, that in the last third of the film it is Scottie who is leading Judy, not the other way around, hence that putting on the necklace is at most a slip. At least I recognised

it as a Freudian slip, one that revealed an unconscious wish for Scottie to know the truth about her. But I clung to the belief that Judy cannot be conscious of harbouring such a wish, so putting on the necklace cannot be a deliberate gesture, cannot be part of a plan calculated to make that wish come true. Nor did I ask myself why I resisted questioning the assumption – an assumption, and a resistance, common to all who have written about the film – that Judy cannot be conscious of wishing for Scottie to know the truth. Evidently, I wished to believe I knew this woman better than she knew herself. Evidently, I wished not to know this about myself. Why?

One answer is that it is vertigo-inducing to think that Judy consciously plans for Scottie to discover the necklace. One reason I find this thought so vertigo-inducing is that it calls for me to recognise that Hitchcock has deceived me. I trusted him to reveal the border separating what is real from what is not, but he betrayed my trust. Why would Hitchcock do this to me? 'Why me?' is a question Scottie poses (to Judy? to Madeleine? to whatever God there may be?) on top of the tower. 'I was the made-to-order witness, wasn't I?' is his answer to his own question. In my wish to believe I knew what I did not know, and in my wish to believe I did not know what I knew, was I Hitchcock's made-to-order witness? Was I no different from Scottie in Hitchcock's eyes? I did not wish to think that of myself – or think that of Hitchcock.

It is also vertigo-inducing to think that in *Shadow of a Doubt* (Hitchcock, 1943) Uncle Charles (Joseph Cotten) plans for young Charlie (Teresa Wright) to kill him. Or that it is Norman (Anthony Perkins), not the mother who is her son's creation, who grins at the camera at the end of *Psycho* (Hitchcock, 1960). Yet, in *The Murderous Gaze*, I found the nerve to think those thoughts, just as in *Contesting Tears* (1996), Cavell found the nerve to think the vertigo-inducing thought that Stella Dallas (Barbara Stanwyck) deliberately makes a spectacle of herself at the soda fountain, that she is already carrying out a plan to free her daughter – and herself – to accept the necessity of their separation.[2]

And yet long after I had found the nerve to think those thoughts, I continued to resist thinking that the woman in *Vertigo* knew herself better than I knew her – and better than I knew myself. Like Scottie, I loved this woman and wished to go on loving her. I did not wish to think that I was *her* made-to-order witness.

It is Judy's letter to Scottie, together with the flashback that shows us what 'really' happened, that sets us up to believe that we always know what Judy is thinking.

The passage is prefaced by the moment when Scottie, who has just walked back into Judy's life, exits her hotel room and the camera pans to Judy, framed from behind, staring at the closed door, like Stella Dallas after Stephen (John Boles) departs with their daughter Laurel (Anne Shirley).

In this framing, this woman and Hitchcock's camera are in complicity, as they are at Ernie's in presenting to Scottie – and us – the vision that makes Scottie fall in love. But this shot is so emphatic in hitting us over the head with the fact that Judy's hair is different from that of 'Madeleine' that it distracts us from registering its deeper revelation, which is that this woman is thinking her own private thoughts.

A few moments later, the flashback itself is initiated by another close-up of Judy, this time staring toward the camera, a signal that the views to follow will grant us access to what she is seeing in her mind's eye.

Scottie, in his dream, seemed unaware of the source of the images assaulting him. Judy, by contrast, seems to be marshalling the images the camera presents to us,

authorising the camera's presentation, in effect. This flashback is designed to secure our trust in Judy – and in Hitchcock's camera.

We trust that Judy's letter, which she reads in voiceover as she is writing it, proves that she loved Scottie, that she still loves him, and that if she had the nerve she would 'stay and lie' in the hope of making him 'forget the other, forget the past' and love her, as she puts it, 'as I am, for myself'. And we are moved when she admits to herself – by now, she has stopped writing; what began as a letter to Scottie has become an interior monologue – that she does not know whether she has the nerve to try.

Having confessed this self-doubt, still in close-up, Judy, expressionless, stares again in the direction of the camera, this time without meeting its gaze. Still facing the camera, her gaze still averted, she rises solemnly, her movement synchronised with the camera's as it pulls back to frame her, in eminently Hitchcockian fashion, between a lamp on the left of the screen and a mirror on the right. Steadfastly meeting the camera's gaze, acknowledging its power to bear witness, she purposefully – perhaps there is a trace of violence in her gesture – tears the letter to pieces.

She has come to a decision. Whatever the risk, she will 'stay and lie' and prove she has the nerve to make Scottie love her 'as she is, for herself'. We silently applaud her.

This passage sets us up to think that we know what Judy is thinking. We have her own words as evidence. Yet at the decisive moment she is silent, absorbed in her private thoughts. The camera, which moments before had revealed Judy's vision of the past, now refrains from revealing her vision of the future. Lacking her clairvoyance, we have no access to her thoughts at this all-important moment. And yet we *think* we know what she is thinking. We think we know what she means by 'staying and lying'; what she thinks it means for Scottie to love her 'as she is, for herself'; and what she thinks her 'self' is – what it is 'for herself'.

In '*Vertigo*: The Unknown Woman in Hitchcock' I wrote:

> When Judy writes the note she never sends to Scottie … she contemplates 'staying and lying' and making him love her 'for herself' … . She may think that the Judy persona – Judy's way of dressing, making herself up, carrying herself, speaking – is her self … . Yet … once she is transfigured into Madeleine, there is no bringing Judy back. She can act the part of Judy only by repressing the Madeleine within her, only by theatricalizing herself.[3]

I understood that 'Judy', no less than 'Madeleine', is a role she is playing (just as this woman herself, in both guises, is a role played by the actress we know as 'Kim Novak'). I also understood that the fact she has made these roles her own means that both 'Judy' and 'Madeleine' are expressions of who she is. But I assumed that these were facts I knew about her that she didn't know about herself. I continued to cling to the assumption – as all critics have done, as Hitchcock sets us up to do – that in wishing for Scottie to love her 'as she is, for herself', she was wishing for him to love 'Judy', that slightly slutty dark-haired hard-luck story who wears too much make-up and speaks not in Madeleine's near-British English but rather pronounces 'Salinas Kansas' with a whiny, exaggeratedly lower-class Midwestern twang. (In her voiceover, Kim Novak reads Judy's letter in a voice more neutral, more natural, than either of those.)

I had not yet found the nerve to think that she wishes for Scottie to love her as the actress she is, not the 'Judy' who is one of her roles – a role that so perfectly denies her 'inner Madeleine' that she must have created it for that purpose. I am not claiming that in the world of *Vertigo* the *reality* is that Judy is always acting. My claim is that Hitchcock designs the film so that every moment sustains this as a *possibility*. Again, it is Hitchcock's understanding that in the world on film there is no reality. All possibilities are equally real, all equally unreal. (I might add that we don't know that 'Judy' and 'Madeleine' are her only identities. She keeps as many suits and dresses in her closet as Marnie (Tippi Hedren). For all we know, each is a costume, a memento of one of her roles. We don't even know that 'Judy Barton' is her real name. That is what it says on her Kansas driver's licence, but she might have as many phony licences as Marnie does, or as (in *North by Northwest*, 1959) Vandamm's (James Mason) cohort Leonard (Martin Landau) assumes George Kaplan (Cary Grant) does when he contemptuously says, 'They provide you with such good ones.')

It would seem that Judy (as I will continue to call her) has set herself an impossible goal. How, by lying, can she make Scottie love her 'as she is, for herself'? Then again, if as an actress she has no identity apart from the roles she has made her own, how can she make Scottie love her 'as she is, for herself' *except* by 'lying'? Insofar as she knows that, as an actress, there is nothing she is 'for herself', she possesses the knowledge possessed by the heroines of such melodramas as *Stella Dallas* (Vidor, 1937), *Now, Voyager* (Rapper, 1942) and *Letter from an Unknown Woman* (Ophuls, 1948) (all films intimately related to *Vertigo*). It is the knowledge, the self-knowledge, that, as Cavell puts it, her identity is ironic, that her 'self' is not fixed, that everything she is, she also is not, that in the condition in which she finds herself – Emerson would call this the human condition – she stands in need of creation.

Terrified of death, longing to become someone 'for herself', she stakes her quest for selfhood on winning Scottie's love. Why Scottie? For one thing, both as 'Judy' and as 'Madeleine', she loves him. As she writes in her letter, she wants him to find 'peace of mind'. Unless she saves him, she cannot be saved. For another, Scottie loves her. If she lets him 'change' her so he can love her as 'Madeleine' again – or, for that matter, if he falls in love with 'Judy' and forgets 'Madeleine' – she would not win his forgiveness, apart from which she cannot be saved. She cannot tell him the truth without making him stop loving her, but his love cannot save her unless he knows the truth. Neither of them are saved if Scottie loves 'Madeleine' but not 'Judy', or 'Judy' but not 'Madeleine', or even if he loves both but without recognising that they are 'positively the same dame', as Muggsy (William Demarest) puts it in *The Lady Eve* (Sturges, 1941). Only if Scottie finds 'Madeleine' in 'Judy' and 'Judy' in 'Madeleine' can his love heal the rift in her soul and enable her 'unattained but attainable self' to be born. Her challenge is to make this happen.

NOTES

1. William Rothman, '*Vertigo*: The Unknown Woman in Hitchcock', *Forum for Psychiatry and the Humanities* vol. 10, 1987 (reprinted in Joseph H. Smith and William Kerrigan (eds), *Images in our Souls: Cavell, Psychoanalysis and Cinema*, Baltimore, MD: Johns Hopkins University Press, 1987, and in William Rothman, *The 'I' of the Camera: Essays in Film Criticism, History, and Aesthetics*, Cambridge: Cambridge University Press, 1988 and 2004). William Rothman, *Hitchcock – The Murderous Gaze* (Cambridge, MA: Harvard University Press, 1982).
2. Stanley Cavell, *Contesting Tears: The Hollywood Melodrama of the Unknown Woman* (Chicago, IL: University of Chicago Press, 1996), pp. 197–222
3. Rothman, *The 'I' of the Camera*, p. 229

BIBLIOGRAPHY

Cavell, Stanley, *Contesting Tears: The Hollywood Melodrama of the Unknown Woman* (Chicago, IL: University of Chicago Press, 1996).

Rothman, William, *Hitchcock – The Murderous Gaze* (Cambridge, MA: Harvard University Press, 1982).

Rothman, William, '*Vertigo*: The Unknown Woman in Hitchcock', *Forum for Psychiatry and the Humanities* vol. 10, 1987 (reprinted in Joseph H. Smith and William Kerrigan (eds), *Images in our Souls: Cavell, Psychoanalysis and Cinema*, Johns Hopkins University Press, 1987, and in Rothman, *The 'I' of the Camera*.

Rothman, William, *The 'I' of the Camera: Essays in Film Criticism, History, and Aesthetics* (Cambridge: Cambridge University Press, 2004).

Index

Page numbers in **bold** indicate a film is the main subject of an article; those in *italics* denote illustrations.
n = endnote.

LIST OF ILLUSTRATIONS

While considerable effort has been made to correctly identify the copyright holders, this has not been possible in all cases. We apologise for any apparent negligence and any omissions or corrections brought to our attention will be remedied in any future editions.

The Night of the Hunter, © Paul Gregory Productions; *Under the Skin of the City*, Omid Film; *The Band Wagon*, Loew's Incorporated; *Theorem*, Aetos Film; *Kill Bill Vol. 2*, © Supercool Manchu, Inc.; *Blood*, Tropico Filmes; *Lust for Life*, © Loew's Incorporated; *Wild Strawberries*, Svensk Filmindustri; *Jezebel*, © Warner Bros.; *Life Is Beautiful*, Melampo Cinematografica srl; *Conte d'été*, Films du Losange/Sept Cinéma; *Rear Window*, © Patron, Inc./Paramount Pictures; *The Secret Garden*, Warner Bros./American Zoetrope; *Written on the Wind*, © Universal Pictures Company; *I ♥ Huckabees*, © N1 European Film Productions GmbH/© Twentieth Century-Fox Film Corporation; *8½*, Cineriz di Angelo Rizzoli/Francinex; *Siegfried*, Decla Filmgesellschaft/Ufa; *City Lights*, Charles Chaplin Corporation/United Artists; *Avec le sourire*, Film Marquis; *La Bête humaine*, Paris Film Production; *Gone with the Wind*, © Selznick International Pictures; *Cat People*, © RKO Radio Pictures; *The Searchers*, C.V. Whitney Pictures Company; *Bonnie and Clyde*, © Warner Bros.-Seven Arts/© Tatira Productions/© Hiller Productions; *Les Deux Anglaises et le continent*, Films du Carrosse/Cinétel/Simar Films; *Star Wars*, Lucasfilm Ltd/Twentieth Century-Fox Film Corporation; *The World*, © Office Kitano/Lumen Films/Xstream Pictures Ltd; *Team America*, © MMDP Munich Movie Development & Production GmbH; *Éloge de l'amour*, Avventura Films/Périphéria/Canal +/Arte France Cinéma/Vega Film/Télévision Suisse Romande; *The Piano*, © Jan Chapman Productions/CiBy 2000; *Exotica*, Exotica, a division of Speaking Parts Limited; *The Lord of the Rings: The Return of the King*, © Lord Dritte Productions Deutschland; *The Wizard of Oz*, Loew's Incorporated; *Hotel Rwanda*, Kigali Releasing Ltd; *United 93*, © Universal Studios; *Alien*, © Twentieth Century-Fox Film Corporation; *Scarlet Street*, Universal Pictures Company Incorporated; *Vertigo*, © Alfred J. Hitchcock Productions.